Leadership for Learning

EDUCATIONAL LEADERSHIP AND LEADERS IN CONTEXTS
Volume 1

Series Editor
Tony Townsend and Ira Bogotch
Florida Atlantic University, Boca Raton, FL., USA

Scope

The series, *Educational Leadership and Leaders in Contexts,* emphasizes how historical and contextual assumptions shape the meanings and values assigned to the term leadership. The series includes books along four distinct threads:

- *Reconsidering the role of social justice within the contexts of educational leadership*
- *Promoting a community of leadership: Reaching out and involving stakeholders and the public*
- *Connecting the professional and personal dimensions of educational leadership*
- *Reconceptualizing educational leadership as a global profession*

Perhaps to a greater extent than ever before, today's educational leaders find themselves living in a world that is substantially different from what it was just a decade ago. The threads of social justice, community leadership, professional and personal dimensions, and globalism have added contextual dimensions to educational leaders that are often not reflected in their local job descriptions. This book series will focus on how these changing contexts affect the theory and practice of educational leaders.

Similarly, the professional lives of educational leaders has increasingly impinged upon their personal well-being, such that it now takes a certain type of individual to be able to put others before self for extended periods of their working life. This series will explore the dynamic relationship between the personal and the professional lives of school leaders.

With respect to communities, recent educational reforms have created a need for communities to know more about what is happening inside of classrooms and schools. While education is blamed for many of the ills identified in societies, school leaders and school communities are generally ignored or excluded from the processes related to social development. The challenge facing school leaders is to work with and build community support through the notion of community leadership. Thus, leadership itself involves working with teachers, students, parents and the wider community in order to improve schools.

As for the fourth thread, globalism, school leaders must now work with multiple languages, cultures, and perspectives reflecting the rapid shift of people from one part of the world to another. Educational leaders now need to be educated to understand global perspectives and react to a world where a single way of *thinking and doing* no longer applies.

Leadership for Learning
International Perspectives

John Macbeath, YC Cheng

*University of Cambridge,
Hong Kong Institute of Education*

SENSE PUBLISHERS
ROTTERDAM / TAIPEI

A C.I.P. record for this book is available from the Library of Congress.

ISBN 978-90-8790-388-6 (paperback)
ISBN 978-90-8790-389-3 (hardback)
ISBN 978-90-8790-390-9 (e-book)

Published by: Sense Publishers,
P.O. Box 21858, 3001 AW
Rotterdam, The Netherlands

Printed on acid-free paper

All Rights Reserved © 2008 Sense Publishers

No part of this work may be reproduced, stored in a retrieval system, or transmitted in any form or by any means, electronic, mechanical, photocopying, microfilming, recording or otherwise, without written permission from the Publisher, with the exception of any material supplied specifically for the purpose of being entered and executed on a computer system, for exclusive use by the purchaser of the work.

TABLE OF CONTENTS

	Acknowledgements	ix
	Preface by J. MacBeath and Y.C. Cheng	xi
1	Leadership for Learning: Exploring Similarity and Living with Difference John MacBeath, University of Cambridge	1-16
2	New Learning and School Leadership: Paradigm Shift Towards the Third Wave Yin Cheong Cheng, Hong Kong Institute of Education	17-40
3	Changing Teaching from Within: Teachers as Leaders Ann Lieberman and Linda Friedrich, Stanford University	41-64
4	Professional Community or Communities? School Subject Matter and the Management of Elementary School Teachers' Work Page Hayton Lee and James P. Spillane, Northwestern University	65-79
5	Leadership for Learning: Some Ethical Connections Neil Dempster, Griffith University, Australia	81-99
6	Researching LfL through an International Collaborative Project David Frost and Sue Swaffield, University of Cambridge	101-122
7	Leadership for Learning: A Canadian Perspective Larry Sackney, University of Saskatchewan Coral Mitchell, Brock University	123-136

TABLE OF CONTENTS

8	Promoting Learning in Ghanaian Primary Schools: The Context of Leadership and Gender Role Stereotypes George K. T. Oduro, University of Cape Coast, Ghana	137-152
9	Learning About School Leadership in Australia Bill Mulford, University of Tasmania	153-172
10	Leadership Strategies for Learning Improvement: Cases from Mainland China Daming Feng, East China Normal University	173-188
11	Supporting and Guiding Learning-focused Leadership in US Schools Bradley S. Portin, Michael S. Knapp, Margaret L. Plecki and Michael A. Copland, University of Washington, Seattle,	189-203
12	Problem-Based Learning: Some Insights on Pedagogical Leadership and Administrative Challenges Oon-Seng Tan. National Institute of Education, Nanyang Technological University	205-221
13	Leadership, Learning and Italy: A Tale of Atmospheres Giovanna Barzanò and Francesca Brotto, Ufficio Scolastico Regionale Lombardia, Ministero della Pubblica Istruzione	223-240
14	Living with Accountability and Mandated Change: Leadership for Learning in a Norwegian Context Jorunn Møller, University of Oslo	241-258
15	Leadership for Learning or Learning for Leadership? The Role of Teacher Induction and Early Professional Development in England and Scotland Jim O'Brien, University of Edinburgh Janet Draper, University of Exeter	259-272

TABLE OF CONTENTS

16 Leadership for Learning in Malaysia: Understanding the Problems and Possibilities
Ibrahim Ahmad Bajunid, Universiti Tun Abdul Razak
273-288

17 School Leadership for Organizational Learning and Empowerment: The Taiwan Perspective
Hui-Ling Pan, National Taiwan Normal University
289-303

18 School Leader Development in Hong Kong: Status, Challenge and Adjustment
Allan Walker and Paula Yu-Kwong Kwan, The Chinese University of Hong Kong
305-325

19 Leadership for Learning: Concluding Thoughts
John MacBeath,
University of Cambridge
327-334

Contributors 335-342

Index 343-345

Acknowledgements

As well as thanking all the contributors to this volume who 'are' the book, we would like to thank the editors Tony Townsend and Ira Bogotch, Michel Lokhorst of Springer and Katie O' Donovan of Cambridge University for the many hours spent in proof reading and indexing with tireless goodwill.

John MacBeath
Y.C. Cheng
March 2008

PREFACE

The impact of globalization is being felt in numerous spheres of educational policy and practice, in rapid growth of information and communication technologies, in economic transformation, and international market competition, all of which conspire to create new demands and place new pressures on school leadership. With greater fluidity across national borders the character of local communities is changing and traditional curricula appear less appropriate to a changing clientele. Research, in neuroscience, genetics, environmental health and other scientific fields bring new insights and challenges to conventional views of learning, effecting a paradigm shift in both the nature of leadership and its role in promoting learning – individual, professional and organisational.

Expectations of heroic leaders turning schools around are no longer tenable and distributed leadership is now a term of common usage, raising the questions of who leads, in what direction and in what way is leadership expressed?

Progress in reform is more advanced in some countries while others come new to many of these issues. Yet, within countries there are wide variations as well as a now well documented in-school variation. In some places school leaders express confusion, concern, and even frustration with a plethora of initiatives that appear differentially effective or irrelevant to the new learning for the future. Nonetheless, there are inspiring examples of school leadership playing a critical role in creating learning schools and fostering multi-level leadership.

Europe, North America, the Asia-Pacific region and other parts of the world are now closer in time and involved in a much greater information exchange, sharing experiences at classroom, school, community and system levels. They increasingly live within similar policy environments and experience similar tensions in reconciling an educational mission with politicized agendas. Leadership for learning takes differing forms and is expressed in different language but is essentially concerned with making schools learning organisations with greater outreach to the communities they serve.

In such a fast changing global environment the need for deeper understanding of emerging issues of reform, policy and practice becomes increasingly apparent. The nature of school leadership for enhancing student learning, professional learning and organizational learning assumes more of a policy imperative. The converging trend in policy environments across countries give renewed urgency to the case for better international understanding and improved access to learning-focused practice in different parts of the world.

This book aims to address the issues and needs outlined above, drawing on examples from 12 countries in different parts of the world. We have brought together 28 renowned scholars in Europe, Australia, North America, and Asia-Pacific countries to contribute to this book. The first six chapters address key themes and provide the framework for the 12 country reports which follow. With the aim of increasing international understanding and teasing out issues of transfer and application across cultural and linguistic boundaries, we have chosen national reports which cover a range of countries representing a diversity of culture and contextual backgrounds. We believe these chapters and the book as a whole, can provide important theoretical, policy and practical implications that will inform the debate about the future of education and of schooling. While each of these country narratives underscore the importance of context, at the same time there are insights and values held in common.

We hope that the international perspectives and challenging ideas presented will be of benefit to a wide readership - educators, school leaders, policy makers, educational officers and advisers, change agents, and researchers who are concerned with educational reform, school leadership and paradigm shifts in learning wherever you are in the world.

John MacBeath (University of Cambridge)
Yin Cheong Cheng (Hong Kong Institute of Education)
October 2007

JOHN MACBEATH

CHAPTER 1

*Leadership for Learning:
Exploring Similarity and Living with Difference*

We are united as much by our differences as by our similarities. In these pages we travel deep into very different cultural territories, surprising us by turns in what we encounter and by the all-too-familiar dilemmas of leading for learning. In China Feng describes leadership as more concerned with keeping order than learning. In Norway Moller describes the embrace of managerialism as squeezing the life and vitality out of learning, while in Canada Sackney and Mitchell report:

> We have found school leaders to be more concerned with accounting than with learning, with control than with teaching, with compliance than with risk-taking, and with public relations than with student experiences.

In Neil Dempster's chapter we find Australian principals struggling to tease their way through the moral maze, their counterparts in Taiwan, Malaysia, England and Italy also experiencing the weight and loneliness of individual leadership. Brotto and Barzano quote Ribolzi, a critic of the current Italian scene, who portrays the position of Italian heads as living a paradox similar to that of the "man supposed to find a black cat in a dark room on a moonless night", having to "guarantee system outcomes that have yet to be defined, in the absence of parameters to measure them and being clueless as to how to act to change them".

Cluelessness might be an apt summary for what George Oduro describes in Ghana where headteachers arrive in their job through seniority but without guidance or preparation of any kind for the complex tasks which face them in running a school. As well as teaching classes they are solely responsible for supervising cleaning and tidying of the school campus, ensuring that vendors of food on the school compound are maintaining hygienic practices as well as overseeing food preparation in the school, taking care of health and safety measures, dealing with injuries and first aid, inspecting building projects, supervising teaching while attending to office work without secretarial support.

These varying and highly contextualised accounts of heroic and lonesome leadership find an echo in the loneliness of teachers in their own classrooms, locked in both by tradition but also by their own sense of professional autonomy. While everywhere the winds of change are requiring greater transparency and accountability many teachers remain reluctant to admit external challenge or critique, content to close their doors to the world, wary of parental 'interference' and afraid to expose themselves to their colleagues as 'frauds', write Liebermann and Friedrich.

The challenge is, as Portin and colleagues write, is both complex and multi-layered:

> [The challenge is] to conceptualize how to connect leadership practice with student learning, and then mobilize others' energies and commitment accordingly. This challenge implicates not only individual leaders, operating from their respective vantage points in a complicated system, but all of them together. *How are they to bring their collective efforts to bear on the task of improving learning for all students?* And it also implicates a larger set of actors whose actions guide or support leadership practice. *How do they create conditions that prompt and enable leaders to constructively influence learning outcomes?*

To achieve this means recognising that any change to 'the way we do things round here' pushes people out of their comfort zone and inevitably creates both discomfort and resistance. Resistance is, however, reinforced rather than attenuated, argues Jorunn Møller, by ill-conceived accountability measures in which public trust has to be secured by specifying performance compliance. In this way accountability is located in hierarchical practices of bureaucracy, in place of the professional obligations teachers and school leaders have to one another, 'answering questions about what has happened within one's area of responsibility and providing a reliable story of practice - what has happened and why it has taken place'.

This is close to what Ben Jaafar (2006) describes as inquiry-based accountability in which all measures, including large-scale and classroom-based assessments, are seen as entry points into professional dialogue about learning experiences, serving to inform practice so as to achieve the greatest learning benefits for all students. This approach to accountability, write Sackney and Mitchell, is consistent with the goals of learning-centred leadership, but is not one commonly acknowledged or valued in the accountability literature.

In Lieberman and Friedrich's words this internal accountability is realised by 'helping teachers own the work, letting go so others can reshape ideas as their own, overcoming teachers' fear of exposure'. They describe a summer writing school for teachers through which participating staff began to grasp their own potential as leaders of learning, not just of their pupils but of their colleagues too. Back in their schools these teacher leaders work to develop a collegial culture where it hasn't existed previously, drawing on their writing project experience to set about changing the norms of the school from isolation to collaboration. Their roles in the summer project afforded them opportunities not only to continue honing their own teaching practice but also to strengthen their capacities for working with their peers. They learned to recognize the fear that accompanies sharing practice publicly and came to understand more acutely that what underlies the reticence to expose practice to one's peers. They developed a wide range of strategies for building community, for drawing expertise from teachers' participating in professional development, for sharing knowledge and for sharing leadership with others. It encouraged them to work collaboratively and to go public with both their successes and their questions.

As they return to their schools, their own context helps them determine their initial leadership strategy: Where should I begin? Who will I work with? What should I focus on? How public should I be? How forceful, how gentle should I be with my approach? As Liebermann and Friedrich's relate it, these teachers continue the leadership learning that began with the writing project as they address daily leadership challenges. Behind them all is *their* community, the writing project, that renewed their excitement for learning, teaching them that they are always involved in their own improvement as well as that of others, while at the same time offering a constant source of support.

There are compelling resonances with teacher activity in a cultural and political context half a planet away. In the Italian summer schools described by Brotto and Barzano something very similar took place. As they describe it, these teachers experienced a new sense of their own professional identity, determined to return to their schools with a new élan, vigour and insight. They point to an abundance of research and theoretical texts which lay emphasis on sharing experiences "in depth" with colleagues, and they provide detailed vignettes of participants in their summer retreats as discovering richness and hidden treasure (Marta, Rossella), learning how to listen (Valeria), reflecting on one's learning (Michele). The authors add: 'It is striking to think that Michele, an experienced fully qualified teacher who proves to be open to reflection, has finally met the opportunity to become aware of how his own learning works. How can he deal with children's learning every day if he himself is not aware of his own learning?'

As these two stories from two continents unravel we see through a glass less darkly the nature of the struggles which teachers experience in their journeys between the relaxed and open space of the summer school and the enclosed space of the school classroom with its impatient agendas and the weight of political pressure. As the Italians say: *una rondine non fa primavera* ("one swallow doesn't make it summer"). Individual events may be successful in themselves, but producing a real culture of learning among teachers is a different story altogether, the ordinary life of most practitioners still being far removed from the intensive and reflective opportunities to learn. In addition, lament Brotto and Barzano, several teachers appear to stay anchored to the hierarchical learning patterns they experienced as students.

What these examples underline is the need to nurture, through continuous monitoring and feeding, those broad arenas where discussions, reflections and experiences may cross each other and grow. The potential for leadership grasped by teachers opportunistically may not always sit easily within an Italian culture. Nor elsewhere. Power sharing, writes Pan, has also to be highly sensitive to cultural tradition, so deeply embedded in the Taiwanese society about which she writes, that it may take a generation or more, indeed if that is desirable or feasible within a Western mould. Pan refers to Hofstede's 1997 studies of cultural differences which depict Asian cultures as characterised by a collective rather individual ethic and by a significantly larger power distance than found in North America, Europe or Australasia. If it is desirable and feasible to shrink the power distance, leadership for learning requires a continuous process of revisiting and reinvention while alert and mindful to the cultural inhibitions and sensitivities, and careful not to fall into to what Hayton and Spillane describe as 'structural holes'.

'Structural holes', spaces or lacunae within organisations, may present both a problem and an opportunity. The opportunity they present is for them to be filled with a change-friendly catalyst. This may be as individual or groups which connect two otherwise disconnected groups and act as a potentially powerful conduit for the transfer of new knowledge about learning and leadership. These 'cutpoints', suggest Hayton and Spillane, may be crucial in cross-fertilizing different groups, injecting new ideas, encouraging colleagues to come at issues as a collective, rather than at an isolated, privatized and individual level. The potential for undermining professional community occurs, however, when people in cutpoint roles use their positions primarily in the interest of personal power, manipulating the distance between groups for individual gain or to push against the direction of change.

PROFESSIONAL LEARNING COMMUNITIES

Commenting on professional learning communities in Canadian schools, Larry Sackney and Coral Mitchell locate the problem in three separate but inter-related phenomena. One is that such professional conversations represent too marked a departure from the traditional isolationist character of teaching. Second, many of the existing models and practices have been developed outside Canada and imported into Canadian schools with uncertain results. Third, the learning community literature itself offers little to help school leaders attempting to introduce the model into their schools.

> These issues present school leaders with serious challenges as they attempt to create learning community models and practices that are informed by local contexts, realities, capacities, and values.

Page Hayton and Jim Spillane add their own cautionary tale. "Collegiality", they write, is often limited to sharing complaints and war stories and strong ties between teachers can too easily serve to justify and defend mediocre practice, rather than challenge it. This is characteristic of weak professional communities in which there is little or no professional growth. In McLaughlin & Talbert's words (2001:30) 'without opportunities to acquire new knowledge, to reflect on practice, and to share successes and failures with colleagues, teachers are not likely to develop a sense of professional control and responsibility". By contrast, professional community is optimized when teachers feel empowered and see their work as meaningful; report more of an affiliation with the school; and have higher job satisfaction than do teachers working in weak professional communities. Seashore Louis, Kruse, and Bryk, (1995) found a positive correlation between student achievement and teachers' sense of professional community which they attributed to the sharing of expertise but also to a modelling by teachers of what it means to be a learner.

The link between leadership, professional community and student achievement has been the focus of Bill Mulford's work in Australia over a decade of research. It is a complex link which demonstrates that leaders are not the architects of achievement but rather it is the product of teachers, working together in an environment which senior leaders create and nurture a learning culture. He cites the Queensland School Reform Longitudinal Study (2001) of 24 schools over a three-year period which found that enhanced classroom pedagogies were associated with the development of professional learning communities. More specifically, the data demonstrated strong links between three key variables - the degree of teachers' collective responsibility for student learning; the overall level of professional learning community operating within a school; and the strength of leadership on pedagogy. '

> Productive school leadership was also found to include a high focus on a culture of care, a strong commitment to a dispersal of leadership and involved relationships amongst the school community, and a high focus on supporting professional development and learning community.

Drawing on the Seashore Louis, Kruse, Bryk study, Hayton and Spillane outline five dimensions of professional community:

- The extent to which teachers' classroom practice is deprivatized, that is, made available for peer observation and critique;
- The extent to which dialogue between colleagues occurs and is deeply reflective on their practice;
- The degree of focus on student learning;
- The amount of collaboration that goes beyond superficial support or assistance, to facilitate improvement of teaching practice at fundamental levels; and
- The degree to which norms and values are shared.

In communities rating high on these dimensions, write Hayton and Spillane, there is a flow of knowledge. Teachers engage in conversations that target deep rather than surface level aspects of their practice. They work together to develop and refine collective norms of practice and values guiding day-to-day decisions. Having a say gives teachers a sense of efficacy and develops social trust, a belief in your colleagues as 'competent, concerned, reliable, honest, and open'.

These five statements of principle apply in equal measure at the level of senior leadership as Walker and Kwong report in a Hong Kong context. As they argue throughout their chapter, learning is more likely to result if school leaders are members of learning and support networks. They point out that most school principals belong to many different kinds of network but these may not necessarily further either the cause of their own professional learning, that of their staff or that of students. It is important, therefore, write Walker and Kwong, that their key networks are shaped or expanded to incorporate a stronger emphasis on learning and the conditions which make learning more likely to happen. As they suggest, networks can develop at different levels, from neighbourhood to international, from educative to industrial, from principal colleagues to other leaders and educators. These must, however, have organic roots rather than being tightly structured or imposed. Informal, self-driven networks within and beyond educational and hierarchical divides. This is the real key; the major adjustment needed in Hong Kong is to work with principals so that they value learning together'.

LEARNING TOGETHER

The theme of learning together, whether as senior leaders, teachers or students is one that runs as a common thread through all of these accounts. In Malaysia it was a feature of Quality Circles, a movement whose impetus was, however, lost, writes Bajunid, in new waves of legislation which failed to spot the inherent professional capital. In its rush to modernize and bureaucratize political leaders failed to build on the cultural legacy in which teachers learned 'in the Socratic tradition of asking questions, in the Prophetic tradition of emphasizing self knowledge, in the community tradition of learning by doing, and in the story telling tradition by listening'. Life long learning, writes Bajunid, had indigenous roots in Malaysian culture but was displaced by modern schooling. His account of one-off initiatives seminars and workshops which are "implementation" driven at the expense of continuing learning conversations will strike a chord with teachers in many other countries in which governments direct by mandate rather than engaging the creative potential of teachers.

> Except for the one-off professional meetings in workshops, seminars or conferences for the fortunate few nominated and sponsored to attend such meetings, there is no continuous dialogue, no protocol and procedure of examination of practice, no recording of best practices, no examination or exploration of implicit principles and theories behind effective teaching-learning practices.

Bajunid refers to a 'reclamation of the intellect', a graphic metaphor for a process in which a terrain has fallen into disuse and needs to be rebuilt from the ground up and with teachers in the forefront of change. This carries with it the implication that leaders at all levels will be more interested in learning than in measured outcomes, that they trust teachers and students to work their magic in the classrooms, that see leadership as being distributed, arising from many different sources and that they are comfortable with ambiguity and a diminution of executive power.

The failure in large school reform in Taiwan was because top down strategies bypassed teachers, writes Pan, arguing that the deep flaw lies on conceptions of power and power sharing, as if power were an individual commodity which could be delegated through trickle down structural reform. As Binney and Williams put it:

> You can disempower somebody but you cannot empower them. They will really begin to change, take initiatives, take risks, provide real feedback, learn from mistakes and accept responsibility for what they're doing when they feel sufficiently confident to do so and are provided with a clear framework... Achieving this type of relationship is not easy. It requires much effort, openness and willingness to learn - and some humility. It feels uncomfortable, particularly for leaders in organisations where this style is not the norm. It requires a high degree of self-belief and a willingness to try. (Binney & Williams, Leaning into the Future, 1997, p.69)

Willingness to learn and to learn together does not come about without structural as well as cultural change, both mutually inseparable. It requires time to meet, interdependence, trust, respect and, argue Sackney and Mitchell, a relinquishing by teachers of their sole attachments to classroom teaching. 'Many teachers come to see themselves as *school* teachers rather than as *classroom* teachers, with an attendant shift in focus from *one group* of students to *all* students'. This implies, however, a shift in identity and a broadening of commitment, creating anxiety among some teachers who fear losing the closeness of touch which they enjoy with the students in their classrooms. Successful school leaders understand that the profound changes in professional identity bring losses as well as opportunities, but they find creative ways of helping educators to acknowledge, articulate, and deal with the losses (Bridges, 1997).

Just as teachers need to move from a singular to a pluralistic view, so, suggest Sackney and Mitchell, parents and school council members need to move beyond the interests of their own children to embrace the interests of all children in the school. Most parents, they contend, become involved in school councils and school activities in order to enhance the experiences of their own children, but as part of the school council they are asked to focus on the collective good. In strong learning communities school leaders may rotate parent volunteers through a host of different school activities, classrooms, grade levels, groups, and events so that they become familiar with a range of students and gain an understanding of the array of learning opportunities and challenges which the school offers. These Canadian academics' work with schools as learning communities schools centres on the creation of cultures in which teaching and learning 'are at the centre of every discussion, every decision, every plan, and every initiative'.

This is the essence of the first three of the five Carpe Vitam principles elaborated by David Frost and Sue Swaffield. Derived from close collaborative work with teachers, principals and School Board members these three principles – a focus on learning, conditions for learning and learning dialogue – are interwoven conceptually and in practice and tested by participating teachers in the seven countries of the study.

This first principle, one which underwrites all others, rests on the idea of learning as an activity, not the purely cognitive activity of individual students but as a social and emotional activity involving all members of the school community, flowing over the boundaries of place and status. The word 'focus' in the expression of this first principle is key because regardless of the national context and policy pressures maintaining the focus on learning has to be worked at and be the paramount concern of leadership

The second principle follows naturally from the first. If there is to be a focus on learning as activity, there is a need to work on the conditions that nurture this fragile entity and provide opportunities for the learning capacity to grow. This is as much about culture building as it is about the design of the physical environment and the use of appropriate pedagogic strategies. The development of cultures of trust and tolerance of difference were what enabled participants within and between the 24 schools of the Carpe Vitam project to open up their practice to the scrutiny of others without feeling defensive or threatened. Deep learning conversations in an open, critically friendly environment was what made it possible for collaboration to grow organically and for a learning cultures to be built from the bottom up

The third principle is about dialogue. Its Greek roots (dia logos) is a reminder that dialogue in its purest sense is a particular kind of conversation – a search for shared meaning and common understanding. This is arrived at, however imperfectly, when teachers, and students, go beyond the tacit, taken-for-granted assumptions about both leadership and learning and make their perceptions and beliefs about them visible and explicit. Frost and Swaffield describe this as 'a powerful strategy [in] which staff and students raise questions about pedagogy and gather data to fuel collective reflection'.

These principles taken together describe a quality of school culture which develops and matures over time and may be challenging for teachers moving from one school to another or for newly qualified teachers emerging from college with expectations as to their role. How new teachers are inducted into the profession is an issue dealt with in a comparative Scottish and English context by O'Brien and Draper, raising questions about the nature and quality of preparation for a rapidly changing policy context. As they point out, new staff need to be socially integrated into the work of a professional community, able to adjust to their new environment and responsibilities and to 'learn the ropes'. They have professional development needs to be met including needs associated with their long term development as potential school leaders. O'Brien and Draper's description of leadership 'fast tracking' of new recruits in England brings sharply to the surface the tensions between the leading of student learners and leading the learning of one's peers and colleagues. As O'Brien and Draper found, Fast Track trainees encountered misunderstandings and, in some cases, hostility, with concerns expressed that teaching competence was being simply assumed and 'that their management and leadership skills were being seen as more important than the core teaching role, that they were destined for elite status without having proved their strengths at "the chalk face".' There is, implicit in leadership for learning, an empathic and experiential understanding of learning as individual, collective, and organisational.

STUDENTS LEARNING

Collective reflection is returned to persistently throughout this volume as at the very heart of the learning school. It is about a focus on learning, at the centre of every discussion, every decision, every plan, and every initiative. It is the centrepiece of Tan's discussion of learning in Singapore. There, for a decade and more academics and policy makers have provoked a learning conversation, challenging the performativity culture of schools. The 2007 document *Teach Less, Learn More* published by The Ministry of Education contains these words:

> Teach Less, Learn More is about teaching better, to engage our learners and prepare them for life, rather than teaching more, for tests and examinations. TLLM aims to touch the hearts and engage the minds of learners, to prepare them for life. It reaches into the core of education – why we teach, what we teach and how we teach.

It calls for "more: for the learner, to excite passion, for understanding, for the test of life" and "less: to rush through the syllabus, out of fear of failure, to dispense information only and for a life of tests; "more: the whole child, values-centric, process and searching questions" and "less: of the subject, grades-centric, product and textbook answers."; more: engaged learning, differentiated teaching, guiding, facilitating and modelling, formative and qualitative assessing, spirit of innovation and enterprise" and "less of drill and practice, one-size-fits-all instruction, telling and set formulae standard answers".

The problem-based curriculum advocated by the Ministry rests on a number of precepts about a form of learning that is lifelong and lifewide. It posits that:

- The *problem* is the starting point of learning.
- The problem is usually a *real-world* problem that appears unstructured. If it is a simulated problem, it should be as authentic as possible.

- The problem calls for *multiple perspectives*. Cross-disciplinary knowledge encourages the solution of the problem by making use of knowledge from various subjects and topics.
- The problem challenges students' current knowledge, attitudes, and competencies, calling for identification of learning needs and *new areas of learning*.
- As *self-directed learning* is primary students assume major responsibility for the acquisition of knowledge by *harnessing of a variety of knowledge sources*, in which evaluating of information resources is an integral component.
- Learning is *collaborative, communicative and cooperative*. Students work in small groups with a high level of interaction in peer learning, peer teaching, and group presentations.
- Development of inquiry and problem-solving skills is as important as content knowledge which a Tutor facilitates through questioning and cognitive coaching.
- Problem solving episodes conclude with synthesis and integration of what has been learned, an evaluation and review of the learner's experience and the learning process.

This is a bold vision and couched in high rhetoric which, as Tan argues, should not underestimate the challenge that this presents to teachers and to school leaders, faced with large classes and students schooled with the mindset of dependence on digested information and didactics. There are close parallels with Hong Kong where there is similar drive from the Education Bureau to prepare for life beyond the school walls but at the same time has to accommodate a highly competitive and short term achievement orientation. The division of ED which is inaptly titled Other Learning Experiences is aimed not only at complementing the mainstream curriculum but infiltrating it with more active and experiential learning in and out of the classroom.

YC Cheng illustrates the challenge of living in these new and different worlds as requiring 'contextualised multiple intelligences', that is, awareness and skill to move seamlessly among sites – the site of home, community and tradition, the site of the fast changing global economy, and the school site in which learning strives to reconcile its individualised nature within a social context. The site-bounded nature of the school has, he argues, to give way to a more fluid, complex and diverse conception of learning. The concurrence of localization and globalization he sees as offering multiple avenues for learning, not simply limited to a small number of teachers in their own schools but drawing on the range of sources in the local community and in the wider world, progressively opened up through technology and affordable travel.

As in Weiss and Fines' dissertation on Construction Sites (2000) which illuminates the individual construction of intelligence, the authors in this volume shed light on the intricate architecture by which values and attitudes are built, often a conflicted process in which children and young people struggle with their emerging identity as lifelong learners. Cheng's recasting of multiple intelligences portrays these as contextualised and adaptive to the various identities learners assume as a technological person, a social person, an economic person, a political person, and a cultural person.

CONTEXTS OF GROWING UP

George Oduro injects a sobering note of reality in his description of what it means to grow up and go to school (or not) in Ghana. He depicts life in congested urban slums in which due to lack of proper drainage and sanitation children are prone to multiplicity of health problems. Malnutrition is the norm. He cites a study of children living in Kenyan slums similar to those in the capital of Ghana which found that 86.2% of school children were stunted. In Ghana, like other African countries, children become orphans as a result of AIDS. A study of orphan children in the Eastern Region of Ghana, found that children orphaned by AIDS often do not get quality care from their extended family. Without this they are vulnerable to exploitation, compelled to engage in sex either for money or for emotional comfort. For example, a 2004 study of 20 primary schools and 12 junior Secondary Schools in the Bawku East District of the Upper east Region of Ghana showed that almost 30% of AIDS orphans had had sex more than once.

Oduro quotes studies by the Ghana Education Service which confirm that poverty—resulting in parental inability to support their child's education—is the single greatest cause of school drop-out, and that many parents, particularly poor parents working in subsistence agriculture in rural setting, require their children to stay home to work on the family farm. This is compounded by parents' over-protectiveness of their children, discouraging them from the kind of play that would be exploratory and adventurous and would help to broaden their understanding of the world.

There are close parallels in Feng's description of schools in rural China. He identifies access to an effective education as being inhibited by parental lack of education and aspiration, children's low self-esteem and low motivation due to repeated experiences of failure in school; and teachers' low expectations and lack of knowledge and skill in teaching. Together with leadership focused on keeping order rather than improving pedagogy, allied to inadequate resource provision, learning-centred leadership assumes a low priority in the hierarchy of needs.

These depictions of what it means to grow up in Africa and China seem at first sight far removed from the challenges facing schools in Seattle, London or Oslo, yet one doesn't have to dig too deep to recognise the essential affinity between the lives of children in rural or urban poverty wherever they are in the world and how badly served they are by schools which simply fail to touch the reality of their needs and desires.

Stevenson and Stigler's 1992 studies which compared American classrooms with their counterparts in China and Japan arrived at broad categorical differences between teacher and student attitudes in those differing cultures. However, in an increasingly globalised world it is doubtful how far or for how long these crisp cultural distinctions hold up. Young people growing up in China, Taiwan, Malaysia and Hong Kong are caught between two worlds in which the influence of Western movies, television, video games and internet sites becomes increasingly ubiquitous, powerful and seductive while the gap between those who have and those who don't grows wider, driving children and adolescents to seek social acceptance through other avenues, what Castells (1999) terms 'perverse integration'.

In their studies of seven cultures of capitalism Hampden Turner and Trompenaars (1993) refer to 'the universal product', the growing uniformity of public services, broadcasting, cult figures, drawing young people's priorities and aspirations closer and closer. The new world of growing up is symbolised by Nintendo, Levi Jeans, McDonalds, David Beckham and Conrad Hilton's dream that wherever you were in the world you could always be at home in familiar surroundings.

LEADERSHIP FOR LEARNING: QUO VADIS?

The richness of these stories which take us into different worlds of growing up and all-too-similar worlds of schooling require us to put into a new and broader frame what we understand by leadership, by learning and by their inter connections. How well do our conceptions and prescriptions travel? How well do our principles hold up in different political, social and economic circumstances?

In virtually all of the chapters in this volume there are precepts and principles of leadership which are learning-centred. A critical reading of these will raise questions as to their applicability and feasibility in the differing contexts portrayed here. For example, Mulford offers an extensive repertoire from his research, and that of others, nationally and internationally. Those to be tested in school and classroom practice in Kaula Lumpur, Taipei, Shanghai, and Accra as well as Hobart and Saskatoon include the following:

- much less emphasis on the organisational or managerial than has previously been the case;
- a rebalancing of the relationship between the political and bureaucratic and professional that gives greater weight to the professional;
- avoidance of 'the great man or woman' theory of leadership;
- ongoing, relevant supportive professional learning;
- data and other sources of information that provide schools with valid, reliable and easily administered ways of monitoring performance, diagnosing student learning difficulties, and implementing appropriate strategies.

Acknowledging the wide variety of contextual application Mulford adds:

- leadership that enhances staff and student learning takes account of a combination of contextual, individual (self and others), organisational, outcome, and evaluative/accountability factors over time.
- a great deal depends on which of these areas the leader chooses to spend time and attention. As a single input by a leader can have multiple outcomes, they need to be able to see the whole as well as the individual factors and the relationships among them over time.

For Portin and colleagues it means those who lead having an acute grasp on three environments which 'invite or command the attention of educational leaders'. They describe these as, a) the authorizing environment - generated by governance arrangements (at all levels), collective bargaining and the contractual agreements it produces, and the interaction among educational stakeholders within and around these arrangements, b) the resource environment, including the sources of funds and human resources, and also the infrastructure for gathering information on and for the schools, as well as rules governing the use of these resources, c) the reform policy environment, comprising the forces and conditions created by state and federal policies aimed at enhancing the quality of schooling, such as standards-based reform policies.

Portin and colleagues argue that while particular policies that come to the fore reflect many interests, 'a concern for the quality of learning may be infused into the debate and interplay that produces these policies. 'At a minimum, it implies taking a hard look at what these policies might mean for leaders' ability to focus their energies on learning improvement; at best, participants in policy environments can coalesce around actions that will make leaders' job easier'.

Adopting a focus on learning in a changing global environment means, argues Y.C. Cheng, taking a harder critical look at prior, and deeply embedded, models of school effectiveness which have reached the end of their shelf life. We need, he argues, a new paradigm of education which embraces, globalization, localization, and individualization and works at resolving the tension among these three often irreconcilable movements. 'Future effectiveness' is attuned to what is critical to the future development of individuals and the society in which they live, work and learn.

No matter how much has been learned about successful leadership, however well developed the programmes, however comprehensive the list of competencies, no matter how skilfully grand narratives are tailored to local contexts, decision-making is often a perilous process and cannot be prescribed, and is very often unforeseen. Putting aside the personal preference or 'first impulse', suggests Neil Dempster, is often necessary allowing all voices to be heard. How a leader is able to draw on a repertoire of strategies and tactics is a mark of the mature leader and how a decision is reached by an ethically mature leader, argues Dempster, is almost as important as the decision itself. Ethical decision-making is highly culturally sensitive and culturally dependent, but are there some universal truths as to the process by which decision-making is examined and verified? Neil Dempster suggests three:

First they need access to a mentor for conversations about personal and professional values, as it is through disclosure in the company of a respected colleague that positions are challenged, reinforced or forged anew. Without this kind of access, it is difficult for school leaders to develop the necessary understanding of their own values, the source of their 'first impulses' or their intuition about what is ethical.

Secondly, they need to have options for immediate support when urgent ethical issues arise. This leadership support does not come in a package on appointment. It has to be deliberately acquired, because without it, principals, as a group, more so than most, are susceptible to the debilitating effects of emotional stress.

Third, they need opportunities for reflection in the company of others who face similar circumstances so that experiences can be shared, insights gained and future practice enhanced - professional learning opportunities which bring ethical theory and practical resolution together. Understanding what is theoretically possible acts as a helpful predictor of future action and, concludes Dempster, providing a strong platform for the kind of informed decision-making essential to long-term leadership.

The last word, a plea for re-education of school leaders, is premised on a belief that however acute the dilemmas and however challenging the circumstances leadership is re-invigorated by learning about learning, in all its manifestations and by the essential bonds between leading to learn and learning to lead.

From our perspective, the best way to create schools with vibrant learning climates is to re-educate school leaders, to bring them to a deep engagement with and appreciation for the excitement of true learning. Professional development for leaders needs to take them into new, interesting, and challenging territory, to push them to consider the effects of their own practice on the educational experiences of others, and to engender in them a sense of excitement as they learn something of value. If leaders do not feel this excitement, if they do not personally experience the transforming power of learning, they are ill-prepared to bring forth school cultures that fully engage the learning potential of teachers and students (Sackney and Mitchell).

REFERENCES

Ben Jaafar, S. (2006). From performance-based to inquiry-based accountability. *Brock Education*, *16*(2), 62–77.
Binney, G., & Williams, C. (1997). *Leaning into the future.* London: Nicolas Brealey.
Bridges, W. (1997). *Managing transitions: Making the most of change.* London: Nicholas Brealey
Castells, M. (200). *End of Millennium.* Oxford: Blackwell.
Hampden-Turner, C., & Trompenaars, L. (1993). *The seven cultures of capitalism.* New York: Doubleday.
Hofstede, G. (1997). *Cultures and organizations: Software of the mind.* New York: McGraw-Hill.
McLaughlin, M. W., & Talbert, J. E. (2001). *Professional communities and the work of high school teaching.* Chicago: University of Chicago Press.
Seashore Louis, K., Kruse, S. D., & Bryk, A. S. (1995). Professionalism and community: What is it and why is it important to urban schools? In K. Seashore Louis & S. D. Kruse (Eds.), *Professionalism and community: Perspectives on reforming urban schools.* Thousand Oaks, CA: Corwin Press.
Stevenson, H. W., & Stigler, J. W. (1992). *The learning gap: Why our schools are failing and what we can learn from Japanese and Chinese education.* New York: Touchstone.
Weiss, M., & Fine, L. (2000). *Construction sites: excavating race, class and gender among urban youth.* New York: Teachers College Press.

AFFILIATIONS

John MacBeath
Faculty of Education, University of Cambridge
UK

YIN CHEONG CHENG

CHAPTER 2

New Learning and School Leadership: Paradigm Shift Towards the Third Wave

INTRODUCTION

In facing up to challenges of a fast changing environment, there have been numerous educational reforms and initiatives in many countries of the world. In the past decades, these reforms have experienced three waves of movements including the effective school movement, quality school movements and world-class school movements (Cheng, 2001b, 2005a).

Each wave of reforms works within its own paradigm in conceptualizing the nature of education and formulating related initiatives for improvement at system, site, and operational levels. When there is a transition from one wave to the other, there is paradigm shift in learning, teaching and schooling and the implications for school leadership may then undergo significant change. This chapter discusses how paradigm shifts in learning relate to changes in school leadership when educational reforms move from the first or second waves towards the third wave. In particular, a new paradigm of school leadership for new learning in the third wave is explored.

FIRST WAVE: KNOWLEDGE DELIVERY AND INTERNAL LEADERSHIP

Since the 1980s, there have been effective school movements in different parts of the world including the UK, US, Australia as well as in many Asian and European countries or cities (Townsend, et al., 2007). The assumption that education is knowledge delivery and that learning is mainly a process of students receiving knowledge, skills and cultural values from teachers and the curriculum, led to the first wave of educational reforms. These were aimed at enhancing the internal effectiveness of schools in achieving pre-planned educational aims and curriculum targets (see Table 1).

For example, in Hong Kong, India, South Korea, Singapore, Taiwan, Malaysia, and mainland China, numerous initiatives were targeted at improving key features of internal school processes, examples of which are changes in school management, teacher quality, curriculum design, teaching methods, approaches to evaluation, resourcing and environment for teaching and learning (Gopinathan & Ho, 2000; Kim, 2000; Cheng, 2001a; Abdullah, 2001; Rajput, 2001; Tang & Wu, 2000, MacBeath, 2007).

Table 1: Three Paradigms: Reform, Learning & Leadership

	First Wave Paradigm	Second Wave Paradigm	Third Wave Paradigm
Type of Movements and Reforms	Effective School Movements: To improve the internal process and performance of a school in order to enhance the achievements of planned goals of education and school	Quality/ Competitive School Movements: To ensure the quality and accountability of educational services provided by school meeting the multiple stakeholders' expectations and needs	World-Class School Movements: To ensure the relevance and world-class standards of education to the multiple and sustainable developments of students and the society for the future in globalization
Conception of School Education	Delivery of the planned knowledge, skills and cultural values from teachers and curriculum to students in a comparably stable society	Provision of a service to satisfy the needs and expectations of stakeholders in a competitive market	Facilitating of multiple and sustainable developments of students and the society in a context of globalization and change

Conception of Learning in School	A process of student receiving knowledge, skills and cultural values from teachers and curriculum	A process of student receiving a service provided by the school and teachers	A process of student developing contextualized multiple intelligence for multiple and sustainable developments
Conception of School Effectiveness	Internal Effectiveness: As achievement of planned goals and tasks of delivery of knowledge, skills and values in learning, teaching and schooling	Interface Effectiveness: As satisfaction of stakeholders with the educational services including education process and outcomes; and as accountability to the public	Future Effectiveness: As relevance to the multiple and sustainable developments of individuals, the community, and the society for the future
Key Role of School Leadership	Internal Leadership with focus on internal improvements for achieving planned goals	Interface Leadership with focus on satisfaction of internal and external stakeholders and accountability	Future Leadership with focus on facilitating multiple and sustainable developments of students, teachers and the school
Related Leadership Concepts	Traditional Concepts Instructional Leadership Curriculum Leadership Structural Leadership Human Leadership Micro-Political Leadership	Traditional Concepts Strategic Leadership Environmental Leadership Public Relations Leadership Brand Leadership	A New Paradigm Triplization Leadership Multi-level Learning Leadership Sustainable Development Leadership Multiple Thinking Leadership Multiple Creativity Leadership

Main Concerns in School Leadership for Learning	How can learning, teaching, and schooling be well organized to deliver knowledge, skills and values? How can the delivery of knowledge and skills from teachers and curriculum to students be ensured through the improvement of schooling, teaching, and learning? How can teachers' teaching be well improved and developed in a given time period? How can students achieve well at a given standard in the public examinations?	How can the performance of teaching and the outcomes of learning meet the stakeholders' expectations and needs well? How can the education services be ensured accountable to the public and stakeholders through various types of monitoring, reporting and benchmarking? How can the school become competitive to provide quality services in the education market?	How can learning, teaching, and schooling be well globalized, localized and individualized? How can students' learning opportunities be maximized through IT environment, networking, and paradigm shifts in teaching and schooling? How can students' self-learning be well facilitated and sustained as potentially lifelong? How can students' ability to globalize, localize and individualize their own learning be well developed? How can students' contextualized multiple intelligence be continuously well developed by themselves?

In the first wave, the role of school leadership was mainly a form of *internal leadership* with a focus on assuring internal school effectiveness. Leadership was primarily concerned with improvement, ensuring school performance in general and methods and processes of teaching and learning in particular. It aimed at achieving planned goals and standards of delivery of knowledge, skills and values to students. There was frequent reference to concepts such as instructional leadership, curriculum leadership, structural leadership, human leadership, and micro-political leadership (Cheng, 2003, 2005a).

SECOND WAVE: SERVICE TO STAKEHOLDERS AND INTERFACE LEADERSHIP

In the 1990s, in response to concerns about educational accountability to the public and the quality of education as satisfying stakeholders' expectations, the second wave of educational reforms emerged internationally. Education was seen as a provision of service to multiple stakeholders and the nature of learning cast students as recipients of a service, the quality of which should satisfy the expectations and needs of key stakeholders - parents, employers and other social constituencies as well as students themselves. This wave emphasized *interface effectiveness* between a school and the community, typically defined by educational quality, stakeholders' satisfaction, and market competition. Most reform efforts were directed at ensuring the quality and accountability of schools to the internal and external stakeholders (see, e.g., Coulson, 1999; Evans, 1999; Goertz & Duffy, 2001; Headington, 2000; Heller, 2001; Mahony & Hextall, 2000) (see Table 1).

In some areas of the world, such as Hong Kong, India, Singapore, Taiwan, UK and USA, there was a growing trend to *quality education or competitive school movements* emphasizing quality assurance, school monitoring and review, parental choice, student coupons, marketization, parental and community involvement in governance, school charter, and performance-based funding (Mukhopadhyay, 2001; Mok, et al., 2003; Cheng & Townsend, 2000; Mohandas, Meng & Keeves, 2003; Pang, et al., 2003).

School leadership in the second wave was a form of *interface leadership* with a focus on ensuring interface school effectiveness. Implicitly or explicitly the role of school leadership within this paradigm was to ensure accountability to the public, to add value to educational services, enhance the marketability of educational provision, and ensure that learning, teaching, and schooling met stakeholders' expectations. How to manage the interface between schools and the local community successfully in a competitive and fast changing environment proved to be a crucial challenge to school leaders. The commonly used concepts of school leadership were substantively different from those in the first wave, including strategic leadership, environmental leadership, public relations leadership and brand leadership (Cheng, 2003, 2005a).

THIRD WAVE: SUSTAINABLE DEVELOPMENTS & FUTURE LEADERSHIP

At the turn of new millennium, the impact of rapid globalization, far reaching influences of information technology (IT) and urgent demands for economic and social developments in international competition stimulated deep reflection on educational reform. To ensure that the younger generation could meet future challenges and needs of rapid transformations in an era of globalization and IT, researchers, policy-makers, and stakeholders in many countries argued for a paradigm shift in learning and teaching. They advocated reform of the aims, content, practice, and management of education, in order to ensure relevance of students' learning for the future (see, e.g., Ramirez & Chan-Tiberghein, 2003; Burbules & Torres, 2000; Cheng, 2000a, 2000b, 2003; Daun, 2001; Stromquist & Monkman, 2000).

In such a global context, there is an emerging third wave of educational reform, with heavy emphasis on *future effectiveness*, often defined by the relevance of education to the future developments of individuals and their society. In particular, this has been seen as meeting changed purposes and functions of education in the new Millennium. It has been viewed as a new paradigm of education embracing contextualized multiple intelligences, globalization, localization, and individualization (Maclean, 2003; Baker & Begg, 2003; Cheng, 2005a). Different from the first and second waves, the nature of learning in the third wave is to develop contextualized multiple intelligences (CMI) of learners which are relevant to multiple and sustainable developments (including technological, economic, social, political, cultural and learning developments) in both local and global contexts (Cheng, 2005c) (see Table 1).

As a consequence of globalization and international competition, this third wave of educational reforms is driven by the notion of *world-class education movements*. Effectiveness and improvement of education are thus defined by world-class standards and global comparability so as to ensure that the future of both student, and social, development is sustainable in such a challenging era.

In the third wave, school leadership assumes the character of *future leadership* with focus on the pursuit of a new vision and new aims for education. It implies a paradigm shift in learning, teaching and curriculum, lifelong learning, sustainable development, global networking, an international outlook, and integration of IT in education (Pefianco, Curtis & Keeves, 2003; Peterson, 2003; Cheng, 2001a). How to maximize learning opportunities for students through "triplization in education" (i.e. as an integrative process of globalization, localization and individualization in education) is a key challenge inviting a new paradigm of school leadership for the third wave of educational reforms (Cheng, 2005a). So, new concepts of school leadership are emerging in the third wave, including triplization leadership, multi-level learning leadership, sustainable development leadership, and multiple thinking leadership (Cheng, 2003, in press).

What is the paradigm shift in learning when school education moves from the first and second waves towards the third wave? What implications does this paradigm shift imply for school leadership for learning? This chapter addresses these two important issues.

A PARADIGM SHIFT IN LEARNING: TOWARDS THE THIRD WAVE

In an era of globalization, there are rapid and complex developments including technological, economic, social, political and cultural development in both local and international communities. These developments have a profound and lasting impact on the future life of individuals, challenging them to re-assess their abilities to adapt to the fast changing contexts for sustainable developments in the future (Ayyar, 1996; Brown & Lauder, 1996; Green, 1999).

Given the complexity of societal and global contexts, diverse, multiple, fluid, and challenging in nature, it is quite reasonable to expect that human nature should be also be contextualized so that people can assume multiple identities as a technological person, social person, economic person, political person, cultural person, and learning person. To survive with sustainable and multiple developments intelligence also needs to be contextualized. So, *Contextualized Multiple Intelligences* (CMI), include technological intelligence, economic intelligence, social intelligence, political intelligence, cultural intelligence, and learning intelligence (Cheng, 2000a). Developing CMI thus becomes the primary goal of learning in the third wave.

Rapid globalization is one of the most salient aspects of the new millennium particularly in light of the rapid development of information technology in the last two decades (Brown, 1999). Inevitably, how education responds to the trends and challenges of globalization has become a major concern in policy making during these years (Ayyar, 1996; Brown & Lauder, 1996; Green, 1999; Henry, Lingard, Rizvi, & Taylor, 1999; Jones, 1999; Pratt & Poole, 2000; Curriculum Development Council, 1999). Not only globalization but also localization and individualization assume an important place in ongoing educational reforms. All of these processes as a whole may be described as a *Triplization Process* (i.e., triple + izations), a way of seeing and analysing educational reforms, formulating new pedagogies and re-creating environment for students' learning.

With the concepts of triplization and contextualized multiple intelligences (CMI), a paradigm shift in learning takes place, away from the traditional site-bounded paradigm of the first and second waves to *the new CMI-triplization paradigm of education* of the third wave as shown in Table 2 (Cheng, 2000a).

THE TRADITIONAL PARADIGM OF SITE-BOUNDED LEARNING

In the traditional thinking of the first wave and second wave, students' learning is part of the reproduction and perpetuation process of existing knowledge and manpower structures, sustaining developments in society, particularly its social and economic aspects (Cheng, Ng & Mok, 2002; Blackledge & Hunt, 1985; Hinchliffe, 1987; McMahon, 1987). Education is perceived as a process for knowledge delivery and reproduction to meet the needs of manpower structure in the society and as satisfying the expectations of multiple stakeholders.

Reproduced Learning: In traditional education, students are the followers of their teachers. They go through standard programs of education, in which students are taught in the same way and same pace even though their ability may be different. Individualized programs appear not to be feasible. The learning process is characterized by students absorbing certain types of knowledge, skills and cultural values. Students are "students" of their teachers, and they absorb knowledge and skills from their teachers. Learning is a disciplinary, receiving and socializing process such that close supervision and control of the learning process is necessary. The focus of learning is on how to gain some professional or academic knowledge and skills and learning is perceived as hard work in order to achieve external rewards and avoid punishment.

Site-Bounded Learning: In the traditional paradigm, all learning activities in school are site-bounded and teacher-based. Students learn from a limited numbers of school teachers and from pre-prepared materials. Therefore, teachers are the major sources of knowledge and learning. Students learn the standard curriculum from their textbooks and related materials assigned by their teachers. Students are often separated and so made responsible for their individual learning outcomes. They have few opportunities for mutual support or shared learning. Their learning experiences are mainly school experiences disconnected from the fast changing local and global communities around them. Learning happens only in school within a given time frame. Graduation tends to be seen as the end of students' learning.

Table 2: Paradigm Shift in Learning

New Paradigm of CMI-Triplized Learning (Third Wave)	Traditional Paradigm of Site-Bounded Learning (First & Second Waves)
Individualized Learning:	Reproduced Learning:
Student is the centre of education	Student is the follower of teacher
Individualized Programs	Standard Programs
Self-Learning and developing CMI	Absorbing Knowledge
Self-Actualizing Process	Receiving Process
Focus on How to Learn	Focus on How to Gain good grades
Self Rewarding	External Rewarding
Localized and Globalized Learning:	School Site-Bounded Learning:
Multiple Sources of Learning	Teacher-Based Learning
Networked Learning	Separated Learning
Life-long and Everywhere	Fixed Period and Within Institution
Unlimited Opportunities	Limited Opportunities
World-Class learning	Site-Bounded Learning
Local and International Outlook	Mainly Institution-based Experiences

THE NEW PARADIGM OF CMI-TRIPLIZED LEARNING

In the new paradigm aiming at CMI development, learning should be borderless and characterized by individualization, localization, and globalization with the support of ICT and networked environment. This new learning is a CMI-triplized (i.e. globalized, localized, and individualized) learning.

Individualized Learning: The student is the centre of education. Students' learning should be to optimize contextualized multiple intelligences (CMI) through individualized and tailor-made programs (including targets, content, methods, and schedules), as learning is a self-actualizing, discovery-led reflective process. Since knowledge accumulates at an unbelievable speed but becomes outdated very quickly, sense making is nearly impossible if education is construed as 'delivery' of knowledge, particularly given that the same knowledge can be easily accessed through the use of information technology and the Internet. This places a premium, therefore, on learning how to learn, both enjoyable and self-rewarding and laying the foundation of lifelong learning (Mok & Cheng, 2001).

Localized and Globalized Learning: Together, localization and globalization offer multiple avenues for learning. In this changing world learning is seen as happening everywhere and is life-long so that the key purpose of school education is preparation for high level life-long learning and continuing discovery, in which learning opportunities are unlimited (Mok & Cheng, 2001). Students can learn from a range of sources inside and outside their schools, locally and globally, not simply limited to a small number of teachers in their own schools. Participation in local and international learning programs (for example, learning activities conducted in the local community; overseas study visits or language immersion) can help them achieve the related local and global outlook and experience beyond the school walls.

Increasingly examples of such kind of programs can be found in France, Hong Kong, Japan, Singapore and USA. Students are typically grouped and networked locally and internationally with the support of varying forms of IT networks. Tan, So, and Hung (2003) of Singapore and Yuen (2003) of Hong Kong provide two typical examples of using IT to network learners and create collaborative learning communities. Learning groups and networks will become a major driving force to sustain the learning culture and multiply learning effects through mutual sharing and inspiration. We may envisage every student as having a group of life-long partner students in different corners of the world, sharing their learning experiences (see for example, MacBeath and Sugimine, 2002).

TRIPLIZATION LEADERSHIP FOR NEW LEARNING

To facilitate paradigm shift towards the third wave in learning, school leadership needs to be seen as a form of *triplization*. In a context where learning is exploratory, global in character involving international immersion and exchange programs, the implications for leadership are to ensure global relevance in learning objectives and content. School leaders themselves need to have a global outlook, to develop international communication skills, expanding the scope of their leadership network and influence to a wide variety of stakeholders beyond their school sites and local communities.

Localization in learning may cover a wide range of activities: (1) To ensure the aims, content and process of learning relevant to the local context so that students' learning and development can benefit socially and intellectually from local application; (2) To bring in local resources including physical, financial, cultural, social and intellectual assets to support students' learning activities; (3) To increase parental involvement, community partnership, and collaboration with various social agents or business sectors in creating opportunities for students' learning and teachers' teaching; and (4) To ensure the curriculum and students' learning meeting the future needs of multiple developments of the local community.

Given the limited resources for school education and the complexity and multiplicity in human nature and educational expectations, how school leaders can lead their schools to implement these measures successfully to meet the diverse needs of so many individuals and develop their CMI is often a core issue of future leadership.

MULTI-LEVEL LEARNING LEADERSHIP/SUSTAINABLE DEVELOPMENT LEADERSHIP

In a shift towards the third wave, how can school leaders support students so that they become genuinely life-long action learners able to continuously develop their multiple thinking ability and creativity in facing future challenges? Numerous authorities advocate action learning as the medium for development of creativity and intelligence in a rapidly changing environment (Wald & Castleberry, 2000; West-Burnham & O'Sullivan, 1998; Argyris & Schön, 1978, 1996; Senge, 1990). Action learning in school is a form of learning which takes place at individual level, group level or at organizational level. At the individual level, it may take the form of student action projects or teacher's learning from professional practices (Stevenson, 2002; Argyris, Putman, & Smith, 1985). At the organizational level or group level, action learning may be a form of learning generated by daily or ad hoc activities or from short-term or long-term actions (or projects) of the school organization or group (Argyris & Schön, 1974; Senge, 1990).

In order to support students' continuous learning at the individual and group levels, it is also necessary to support teachers' professional learning at both individual and group levels, a process integral to organizational learning. This is a process of multi-level learning which not only sustains continuous student learning but benefits teacher learning, and feeds into wider school development (Cheng, 1996; Cheng & Cheung, 2003, 2004). It follows that school leadership has to operate at multiple levels. *Multi-level learning leadership* then characterises the third wave in which school heads lead the action learning of their students, teachers and all other members of the community. Within this model school leadership itself is also a process of action learning, in which a leader or a group of leaders draw on the wisdom and the knowledge-in-action of their colleagues.

MULTIPLE THINKING LEADERSHIP FOR NEW LEARNING

There is a complexity and multiplicity of contexts in which school leaders perform multiple functions, so as to create and sustain multi-level learning. This multiplicity of tasks and roles may be described in terms of a typology which includes *Technological leadership, Economic leadership, Social leadership, Political leadership, Cultural leadership,* and *Learning leadership.* Each of these forms of leadership is matched by six types of thinking which may described as *technological thinking, economic thinking, social thinking, political thinking, cultural thinking* and *learning thinking* (Table 3).

TECHNOLOGICAL LEADERSHIP AND THINKING

Given the scale of impact of technology in different aspects of the society and the global community, technological leadership is a growing priority (Gates, 1999; Education and Manpower Bureau, 1998; Holmes, 1999). It is characterised by *technological rationality* in thinking that places emphasis on the achievement of planned goals and targets through objective and scientific methodology and structure. Technological engineering, methodological effectiveness, and technical optimization are the key components of thinking in this expression of leadership. The question this raises for multi-level learning, or new learning, address the following questions:

- What methods, procedures, techniques, and structures can be used to achieve the planned goals and targets in order to facilitate multi-level learning?
- How can the aims and related tasks of student learning be achieved more effectively through changes in structure, methodology or technology of a school? And why?
- Can any technical innovations and improvements be made, or can the process of school functioning be re-engineered to ensure sustainable development and effectiveness?

In technological thinking, the basic objective of school action is to use scientific knowledge and technology to solve existing problems and achieve planned aims. Therefore, *school effectiveness* is a predictable product of applying appropriate technology and methodology. If school outcomes are unsatisfactory, it may be explained by inadequate or flawed structures, procedures, or implementation of technology.

Table 3: Multiple Thinking Leadership

Characteristics	Typology of Multiple Thinking Leadership					
	Technological Leadership	Economic Leadership	Social Leadership	Political Leadership	Cultural Leadership	Learning Leadership
Type of thinking	Technological Thinking	Economic Thinking	Social Thinking	Political Thinking	Cultural Thinking	Learning Thinking
Rationality in leadership	Technological rationality	Economic rationality	Social rationality	Political rationality	Cultural rationality	Adaptive rationality
Ideology in leadership	Methodological effectiveness; Goal achievement; Technological engineering and optimization	Efficiency; Cost-benefit; Resources and financial management; Economic optimization	Social relations; Human needs; Social satisfaction	Interest, power and conflict; Participation, negotiation, and democracy	Values, beliefs, ethics and traditions; Integration, coherence and morality	Adaptation to changes; Continuous improvement and development
Key concerns/ questions in leadership for learning	What methods and techniques can be used in facilitating multi-level learning? How can the aims of students' learning be achieved more effectively? Why? Can any technical innovation and improvement be made and the process of learning be reengineered?	What resources and costs are needed and what benefits can be generated in enhancing learning? How can the aims of students' learning be achieved with minimal cost? Why? How to innovatively maximize the marginal benefits?	What the social relationship between the involved key actors in promoting learning? How can they affect the aims, processes and outcomes of multi-level learning? How can their human needs be satisfied and the synergy be maximized? Why?	What diversities, interests, and powers are involved in multi-level learning? How can the conflicts and struggles be minimized or managed through negotiation, democracy and other? Why? How can "win-win" strategies promote learning?	What values, beliefs and ethics are crucial and shared in multi-level learning? How do they influence the aims and nature of learning and development? How can integration, coherence or morality in values and beliefs be maximized in learning? Why?	What thinking modes and knowledge can be used? What are thinking gaps in changing realities? How can the nature of multi-level learning be conceptualized more adaptive to change? How can new thinking modes and understanding be achieved?
Beliefs about school action	Use of scientific and technological knowledge to solve problems and achieve aims	To procure and use resources to implement plan and achieve outcomes	To establish social networks to support members and implement planning	To negotiate and struggle among parties to manage or solve conflicts	To clarify ambiguities and realize the vision including key values and beliefs shared	To discover new ideas and approaches to achieving aims
Beliefs about school effectiveness	A predictable product of good technology and methodology	An output from the calculated use of resources	A product of social action; Social satisfaction is also an outcome	A result of bargaining, compromise, and interplay among interest parties	A symbolic product of meaning making or cultural actualization	Discovery of new knowledge and approaches to enhance of intelligence

Adapted from Cheng (2005c, in press)

ECONOMIC LEADERSHIP AND THINKING

Economic growth is often seen as the rationale and driving force of individual and national developments and as the cutting edge in international competition, particularly in a global context (Ohame, 2000; Burton-Jones, 1999). Economic thinking infuses action at both individual and organizational levels (Cavalcanti, 2002; Fontana, 2001) while economic leadership is based on a form of *economic rationality* concerned with maximizing benefits and achieving planned aims and targets of the school through optimal use of resources. Efficiency, cost-benefits, cost-effectiveness, resources, financial management and economic optimization are key to economic thinking in pursuit of school effectiveness (Levin, 1994a, 1994b). From an economic rationality viewpoint, questions for multi-level learning are:

- What resources and costs are needed and what benefits can be generated in the multi-level learning cycles?
- How can the planned aims of student learning be achieved with minimal costs or resources in action process? Why?
- In what way the marginal benefits can be innovatively maximized from the action process of students and teachers?

The priority for school action is to procure various types of resources from internal and external sources, deploying them to achieve targeted outcomes and other benefits. Thus, *school effectiveness* results from strategic and discriminating use of resources.

SOCIAL LEADERSHIP AND THINKING

Individual action and organizational action are set in a social context, in which human factors such as human needs and development, social relations, and social expectations can deeply influence and shape the nature, aims and outcomes of action. In education, human development and social relations are often perceived as core values in considering school effectiveness and leadership (Henderson & Cunningham, 1994; Hoy, Tarter, & Kottkamp, 1991; Rosenholtz, 1991; Guskey & Huberman, 1995; Cherniss & Goleman, 2001).

Social leadership is based on *social rationality* in thinking, emphasizing the importance of social relationships and human initiative in achieving

school aims. Therefore, social interactions and relations, satisfaction of social needs, human initiative and development are key aspects of leadership thinking (Maslow, 1970; McGregor, 1960). The common questions in social leadership in pursuing new and multi-level learning are:
- What are the social relationships between the involved key actors such as students, teachers and other staff members?
- How can their relationships affect the aims, processes and outcomes of multi-level learning and the sustainability of school development?
- How can the human needs be satisfied and synergy be maximized among actors such as students and teachers to pursue sustainable and multiple learning and development? Why?

From the perspective of social thinking, the major task of school leadership is to establish social networks, to support and motivate members, promoting their initiative and synergy in order to realize the action plan and achieve the aims of the school. *School effectiveness* is then the product of successful social networking and solidarity in action. Enhanced social satisfaction, personal or staff development, working relationships and morale among school members are often perceived as key conditions for a school to remain sustainable.

POLITICAL LEADERSHIP AND THINKING

Increasing diversity in expectations and demands, competitions for resources, and struggles for power among different parties intensify the political aspects of life at the individual, organizational, community and even international levels. In such a context, political leadership and thinking are attracting more and more attention. (Pfeffer, 1992; Bolman & Deal, 1997; Ball, 1987).

Political leadership is based on the *political rationality* in thinking, emphasizing diversity of interests and expectations of the various school constituencies. Leadership involves the resolution and management of conflicts and struggles through strategies such as alliance building, negotiation, compromise, participation and other democratic process intrinsic to the achieving the aims of the school. The major themes in political leadership include competition for interest, struggles for power, conflicts among members or parties, negotiation and compromise, participation and democracy in decision-making for school improvement (Pfeffer, 1992; Kotter, 1985; Sarason, 1998; Cloke, 2000). Typical questions in pursuing multi-level learning and sustainable school development are:

- What diversities of interest, and power of various constituencies need to be addressed by leadership in order to promote multi-level learning and sustainable school effectiveness?
- How can the conflicts and struggles in a school be managed so as to sustain organizational learning and school development through alliance building, partnership, negotiation, democratic process and other strategies or tactics?
- How can "win-win" strategies, alliances, and partnerships be built to overcome political obstacles, facilitate the school action and maximize the achievement of the school aims for learning in a long run?

In the political perspective, school leadership in a complex context involving multiple and diverse constituencies inevitably induces a process of negotiation, struggle, and conflict management among various parties. To a great extent, *school effectiveness* is a result of bargaining, compromise, and interplay among interest parties during school practice.

CULTURAL LEADERSHIP AND THINKING

In facing the challenges of ambiguity and uncertainty emerging from the fast changing internal and external environments, how schools and their members are enabled to remain consistent and confident in their values and beliefs systems is an important concern of cultural leadership (Bolman & Deal, 1997; Schein, 1999; Hofstede, 1997). Cultural leadership in pursuing school development is based on the *cultural rationality* in thinking that sees the nature, aims, and effectiveness of school action as heavily determined by the values, beliefs, ethics and traditions shared among the school actors and concerned constituencies (Cheng, 2000c; Schein, 1992, 1999). Therefore, sharing of values, beliefs and ethics, integration and coherence among school members, and morality in school practice are often key aspects of cultural leadership and thinking.

In the cultural leadership for new and multi-level learning in school, some typical questions in thinking may include the following:

- What values, beliefs and ethics are crucial and shared among school members for students' continuous self-directed learning or teachers' professional development?
- How do they consistently influence the aims, nature and even effects of school action?

- How can integration, coherence or morality in values and beliefs among school members and related stakeholders be maximized in ways that sustain students' CMI development?

The objective of leadership action for school development is to clarify ambiguities and uncertainties in and realize the school vision (including the key values and beliefs) shared by members and key constituencies. In a cultural sense, *school effectiveness* is a symbolic product of meaning making or cultural actualization by school members and other constituencies in an ambiguous context (Bolman & Deal, 1997).

LEARNING LEADERSHIP AND THINKING

Given the impacts of the fast changing context on development and survival of individuals and organizations, learning and adaptation to the challenges are crucial and necessary. The pursuit of a learning society becomes more and more important (Wain, 2004; Gorard & Rees, 2002; Jarvis, 2001; Marsick, Bitterman & van der Veen, 2000; OECD, 2000).

Multi-level learning leadership is a response to this dynamic. Learning leadership for sustainable school development is based on the *adaptive rationality* in thinking that emphasizes continuous learning and successful adaptation of a school to the changes and challenges in the internal and external environment. These are seen as the key for sustainable school development and effectiveness. Therefore, continuous improvement and development of school actors' operational and cognitive styles is a key to thinking in learning leadership (Jarvis, 2001; Raven & Stephenson, 2001; OECD, 1997; Silins, Mulford & Zarins, 2002). With the adaptive rationality, some typical concerns in learning leadership (or multi-level learning leadership) are:

- What learning styles, thinking modes and knowledge can be used to sustain student learning, teacher learning, organizational learning and school development? What are gaps between the modes of organizational learning and changing realities?
- How can the aims and nature of school action for learning be re-conceptualized to be more adaptive to the changes and challenges in the context?
- How can cognitive gaps in understanding changing realities be minimized and new understandings of sustainable effectiveness be achieved?

As there is heavy emphasis on values implicit in learning, the basic objective of school action is to engage with new ideas and new approaches to achieving its aims as embedded in ongoing and subsequent action cycles of the school. Thus, *school effectiveness* includes the discovery of new knowledge and approaches to action implementation and the enhancement of school actors' intelligence, enabling them to understand and deal with challenges from the changing environment.

CONCLUSION

In the three waves of educational reforms, there is a tangible paradigm shift, from emphases in the first and second waves on 'delivery' of knowledge towards the third wave of facilitating multiple and sustainable developments of students recognising the demands of society in the future. In concert with this is a paradigm shift in leadership for learning.

In the first wave, the key concerns in school leadership for learning were typically exemplified by the following questions: (Table 1)

1. How well can school leaders manage the internal environment and processes of learning, teaching and schooling to deliver the necessary knowledge and skills to students?
2. How well can school leaders ensure the delivery of knowledge and skills to students through the improvement of schooling, teaching and learning?
3. How well do school leaders facilitate teachers to improve their teaching in a given time period?
4. How can school leaders ensure that students arriving at a given standard in the public examinations through various internal and interface measures?

Different from the first wave, the key concerns in the second wave school leadership for learning may be illustrated by the following questions:

1. How can school leaders ensure the performance of teaching and the outcomes of learning which satisfy the expectations and needs of key stakeholders?
2. How can the educational services under their leadership be made accountable to the public and stakeholders through various types of monitoring, reporting, and benchmarking?
3. How can their schools become competitive in providing quality services in a fast changing education market?

In the third wave, a new paradigm may be summarized as follows:

1. How can school leaders globalise, localise and individualise learning, teaching, and schooling for teachers and their students?
2. How can school leaders maximize students' learning opportunities through establishing the borderless IT environment, local and international networking, and various types of innovative learning programs?
3. How can school leaders facilitate and ensure that students' self-learning is sustained and potentially life long?
4. How can school leaders direct educational practices for the development of students' ability to triplize their self-learning?
5. How can school leaders ensure that the educational environment promotes students' continuous development of their contextualized multiple intelligences?

The third wave paradigm provides a new perspective for us to understand the role and effectiveness of school leadership in an era of globalization, creating new understandings and opportunities for life-long learning and CMI development. Meeting these challenges is fast becoming a global agenda embracing research, policy formulation and leadership development.

ACKNOWLEDGMENT

The author would like to acknowledge the funding support from the Competitive Earmarked Research Grant awarded by the Research Grants Council of University Grants Committee of the Hong Kong SAR Government to the author's research project (HKIEd8003/03H) that contributed to development of this paper. Part of materials in this paper was adapted from the model presented in Cheng (2005a, 2005b).

REFERENCES

Abdullah, H. M. (2001, June 12–15). *Policy dialogue on quality improvement in education: A Malaysian experience*. Paper presented at the Second International Forum on Quality Education: Policy, Research and Innovative Practices in Improving Quality of Education, Beijing, China.

Al-Hawamdeh, S., & Hart, T. L. (2002). *Information and knowledge society*. Singapore: McGraw-Hill.

Andriopoulos, C. (2001). Determinants of organizational creativity: A literature review. *Management Decision, 39*(10), 834–840.

Argyris, C., & Schön, D. A. (1974). *Theory in practice: Increasing professional effectiveness*. San Francisco: Jossey-Bass.

Argyris, C. (1982). *Reasoning, learning and action*. San Francisco, CA: Jossey-Bass.

Argyris, C., & Schön, D. A. (1978). *Organizational learning: A theory of action perspective.* Reading, MA: Addison-Wesley.
Argyris, C., & Schön, D. A. (1996). *Organizational learning II: Theory, method and practice.* Reading, MA: Addison-Wesley.
Argyris, C., Putnam, R., & Smith, D. M. (1985). *Action science.* San Francisco, CA: Jossey-Bass.
Ayyar, R. V. V. (1996). Educational policy planning and globalisation. *International Journal of Educational Development, 16*(4), 347–354.
Baker, R., & Begg, A. (2003). Change in the school curriculum: Looking to the future. In J. P. Keeves & R. Watanabe (Eds.), *International handbook of educational research in the Asia-Pacific region* (pp. 541–554). The Netherlands: Kluwer Academic Publishers.
Ball, S. J. (1987). *The micro-politics of the school: Towards a theory of school organization.* London: Routledge.
Blackledge, D., & Hunt, B. (1985). *Sociological interpretations of education.* Sydney: Croom Helm.
Bolman, L. G., & Deal, T. E. (1997). *Reframing organizations: Artistry, choice, and leadership* (2nd ed.). San Francisco: Jossey-Bass.
Brown, P., & Lauder, H. (1996). Education, globalization and economic development. *Journal of Education Policy, 11*(1), 1–25.
Brown, T. (1999). Challenging globalization as discourse and phenomenon. *International Journal of Lifelong Education, 18*(1), 3–17.
Burbules, N. C., & Torres, C. A. (Eds.). (2000). *Globalization and education: Critical perspectives.* New York: Routledge.
Burton-Jones, A. (1999). *Knowledge capitalism: Business, work and learning in the new economy.* Oxford, England: Oxford University.
Cavalcanti, C. (2002). Economic thinking, traditional ecological knowledge and ethnoeconomics. *Current Sociology,* 50(1), 39–55.
Cheng, Y. C. (1996). *School effectiveness and school-based management: A mechanism for development.* London: Falmer Press.
Cheng, Y. C. (2000a). A CMI-triplization paradigm for reforming education in the new millennium. *International Journal of Educational Management, 14*(4), 156–174.
Cheng, Y. C. (2000b). Educational change and development in Hong Kong: Effectiveness, quality, and relevance. In T. Townsend & Y. C. Cheng (Eds.), *Educational change and development in the Asia-Pacific region: Challenges for the future* (pp. 17–56). The Netherlands: Swets and Zeitlinger Publisher.
Cheng, Y. C. (2000c). Cultural factors in educational effectiveness: A framework for comparative and cross-cultural research. *School Leadership and Management, 20*(2), 207–225.
Cheng, Y. C. (2001a). *Towards the third wave of educational reforms in Hong Kong: Triplization in the new millennium.* Plenary speech presented at the International Forum on Educational reforms in the Asia-Pacific Region "Globalization, Localization, and Individualization for the Future", HKSAR, China.
Cheng, Y. C. (2001b, January 5–9). *Educational relevance, quality and effectiveness: Paradigm shifts.* Invited keynote speech presented at the International Congress for School Effectiveness and School Improvement "Equity, Globalization, and Change: Education for the 21st Century", Toronto, Canada.
Cheng, Y. C. (2003). School leadership and three waves of education reforms. *Cambridge Journal of Education, 33*(3), 417–439.
Cheng, Y. C. (2005a). *New paradigm for re-engineering education: Globalization, localization and individualization.* Dordrecht, The Netherlands: Springer.
Cheng, Y. C. (2005b). Multiple thinking and creativity in organizational learning. *International Journal of Educational Management, 19*(7), 605–622.
Cheng, Y. C. (2005c). Multiple thinking and multiple creativity in action learning. *Journal of Education Research,* 134(June), 76–105.
Cheng, Y. C. (in press). Multiple thinking and creativity in school leadership: A new paradigm for sustainable development. In S. Huber (Ed.), *Professionalization of school leadership.* Long Hanborough, UK: Peter Lang.

Cheng, Y. C., & Cheung, W. M. (2003). Profiles of multi-level self-management in schools. *International Journal of Educational Management*, 17(3), 100–115.

Cheng, Y. C., & Cheung, W. M. (2004). Four types of school environment: Multi-level self management & education quality. *Educational Research and Evaluation*, 10(1), 71–100.

Cheng, Y. C., Ng, K. H., & Mok, M. M. C. (2002). Economic Considerations in Education Policy Making: A Simplified Framework. *International Journal of Educational Management*, 16(1), 18–39.

Cheng, Y. C., & Townsend, T. (2000). Educational change and development in the Asia-Pacific region: Trends and issues. In T. Townsend & Y. C. Cheng (Eds.), *Educational change and development in the Asia-Pacific region: Challenges for the future* (pp. 317–344). Lisse, The Netherlands: Swets & Zeitlinger.

Cherniss, C., & Goleman, D. (2001). *The emotionally intelligence workplace: How to select for, measure, and improve emotional intelligence in individuals, groups, and organizations*. San Francisco: Jossey-Bass.

Cloke, K. (2000). *Resolving conflicts as work: A complete guide for everyone on the job*. San Francisco: Jossey-Bass Publishers.

Coulson, A. J. (1999). *Market education: The unknown history*. New Brunswick, NJ: Transaction Publishers.

Curriculum Development Council. (1999, October). A holistic review of the Hong Kong school curriculum proposed reforms (consultative document). Hong Kong: Government Printer.

Daun, H. (2001). *Educational restructuring in the context of globalization and national policy*. US: Routledge Falmer.

Davenport, T. H., & Prusak, L. (2000). *Working knowledge: How organizations manage what they know*. Boston, MA: Harvard Business School Press.

Dierkes, M. (2001). *Handbook of organizational learning and knowledge*. Oxford, England: Oxford University Press.

Education Commission. (2000a). *Learning for life, learning through life: Reform proposals for the education system in Hong Kong*. Hong Kong: Government Printer.

Education Commission. (2000b). *Review of education system: Reform proposals* (Consultation document). Hong Kong: Government Printer.

Education and Manpower Bureau. (1998, November). *Information technology for learning in a new era: Five-year strategy 1998/99 to 2002/03*. Hong Kong: Government Printer.

Evans, G. R. (1999). *Calling academia to account: Rights and responsibilities*. Buckingham, Great Britain: Society for Research into Higher Education & Open University Press.

Fontana, G. (2001). Keynes on the "nature of economic thinking": The principle of non-neutrality of choice and the principle of non-neutrality of money. *The American Journal of Economics and Sociology*, 60(4), 711–743.

Gates, B. (1999). *Business@ the speed of thought: Using a digital nervous system*. New York: Warner Books.

Goertz, M. E., & Duffy, M. C. (2001). *Assessment and accountability systems in the 50 States, 1999–2000*. CPRE Research Report Series.

Gopinathan, S., & Ho, W. K. (2000). Educational change and development in Singapore. In T. Townsend & Y. C. Cheng (Eds.), *Educational change and development in the Asia-Pacific region: Challenges for the future* (pp. 163–184). Lisse, The Netherlands: Swets & Zeitlinger.

Gorard, S. & Rees, G. (2002). *Creating a learning society: Learning careers and policies for lifelong learning*. Bristol, England: Policy Press.

Green, A. (1999). Education and globalization in Europe and East Asia: Convergent and divergent trends. *Journal of Education Policy*, 14(1), 55–71.

Guskey, T. R., & Huberman, M. (Eds.). (1995). *Professional development in education: new paradigms & practices* (pp. 1–6). New York: Teachers College Press.

Headington, R. (2000). *Monitoring, assessment, recording, reporting and accountability: Meeting the standards*. London: David Fulton.

Heller, D. E. (Ed.). (2001). *The states and public higher education policy: Affordable, access, and accountability.* Baltimore: John Hopkins University Press.
Henderson, R. W., & Cunningham, L. (1994). Creating interactive sociocultural environments for self-regulated learning. In D. H. Schunk & B. J. Zimmerman (Eds.), *Self-regulation of learning and performance.* Hillsdale, NJ: Lawrence Erlbaum Associates.
Henry, M., Lingard, B., Rizvi, F., & Taylor, S. (1999). Working with/against globalization in education. *Journal of Education Policy, 14*(1), 85–97.
Hinchliffe, K. (1987). Education and the labor market. In G. Psacharopoulos (Ed.), *Economics of education: Research and studies* (pp. 315–323). Kidlington, Oxford: Pergamon Press.
Hofstede, G. (1997). Cultures and organizations: Software of the mind. New York: McGraw-Hill.
Holmes, W. (1999). The transforming power of information technology. *Community College Journal, 70*(2), 10–15.
Hoy, W. K., Tarter, C. J., & Kottkamp, R. B. (1991). *Open schools/healthy schools: Measuring organizational climate.* London: Sage Publication.
Istance, D. (2003). Schooling and lifelong learning: Insights from OECD analyses. *European Journal of Education, 38*(1), 85–98.
Jarvis, P. (Ed.) (2001). *The age of learning: Education and the knowledge society.* London: Kogan Page.
Jones, P. W. (1999). Globalisation and the UNESCO mandate: Multilateral prospects for educational development. *International Journal of Educational Development, 19*(1), 17–25.
Jorgensen, B. (2004). Individual and organizational learning: A model for reform for public organizations. *Foresight: The Journal of Futures Studies, Strategic Thinking and Policy,* January, 91–103.
Kim, Y. H. (2000). Recent changes and developments in Korean school education. In T. Townsend & Y. C. Cheng (Eds.), *Educational change and development in the Asia-Pacific region: Challenges for the future* (pp. 83–106). Lisse, The Netherlands: Swets & Zeitlinger.
Kotter, J. P. (1985). *Power and influence.* New York: The Free Press.
Lee, K. T., & Mitchell, K. (Eds.). (2003). *Proceedings of the International Conference on Computers in Education (CD-ROM).* Hong Kong: International conference on Computers in Education.
Levin, H. M. (1994a). Cost-benefit analysis. In T. Husén & T. N. Postlethwaite (Eds.), *The international encyclopaedia of education* (2nd ed., Vol. 2, pp. 1127–1131). Oxford, England/New York: Pergamon/Elsevier Science.
Levin, H. M. (1994b). Cost-effectiveness analysis. In T. Husén & T. N. Postlethwaite (Eds.), *The international encyclopedia of education* (2nd ed., Vol. 2, pp. 1131–1136). Oxford, England/New York: Pergamon/Elsevier Science.
MacBeath, J. (2007). *The impact of school self evaluation and external school review.* Hong Kong: Education Development Bureau.
MacBeath, J., & Sugimine, H. (2001). *Self evaluation in the global classroom.* London: Routledge.
Maclean, R. (2003). Secondary education reform in the Asia-Pacific region. In J. P. Keeves & R. Watanabe (Eds.), *International handbook of educational research in the Asia-Pacific region* (pp. 73–92). The Netherlands: Kluwer Academic Publishers.
Mahony, P., & Hextall, I. (2000). *Reconstructing teaching: Standards, performance and accountability.* London: Routledge.
Marquardt, M. J. (1996). *Building the learning organization.* New York: McGraw-Hill.
Marsick, V. J., Bitterman, J., & van der Veen, R. (2000). *From the learning organization to learning communities towards a learning society.* Columbus, OI: ERIC Clearinghouse on Adult, Career, and Vocational Education. (Information Series; No. 382).
Maslow, A. F. (1970). *Motivation and personality* (2nd ed.). New York: Harper & Row.
McGregor, D. (1960). *The Human side of enterprise.* New York: McGraw-Hill.
McMahon, W. W. (1987). Consumption and other benefits of education. In G. Psacharopoulos (Ed.), *Economics of education: Research and studies* (pp. 129–133). Kidlington, Oxford: Pergamon Press.

Mohandas, R., Meng, H. W., & Keeves, J. P. (2003). Evaluation and accountability in Asian and Pacific countries. In J. P. Keeves & R. Watanabe (Eds.), *International handbook of educational research in the Asia-Pacific region* (pp. 107–122). The Netherlands: Kluwer Academic Publishers.

Mok, M. M. C., & Cheng, Y. C. (2001). A theory of self learning in a human and technological environment: Implications for education reforms. *International Journal of Education Management, 15*(4), 172–186.

Mok, M. M. C., Gurr, D., Izawa, E., Knipprath, H., Lee, I., Mel, M. A., et al. (2003). Quality assurance and school monitoring. In J. P. Keeves & R. Watanabe (Eds.), *International handbook of educational research in the Asia-Pacific region* (pp. 945–958). The Netherlands: Kluwer Academic Publishers.

Mukhopadhyay, M. (2001). *Total quality management in education*. New Delhi: National Institute of Educational Planning and Administration.

OECD (Organization for Economic Co-operation and Development). (1997). *Literacy skills for the knowledge society: Further results from the International Adult Literacy Survey*. Paris: OECD, Human Resources Development Canada.

OECD (Organization for Economic Co-operation and Development). (2000). *Knowledge management in the learning society*. Paris: OECD, Center for Educational Research and Innovation.

Ohmae, K. (2000). *The invisible continent: Four strategic imperatives of the new economy*. London: Nicholas Brealey.

Pang, I., Isawa, E., Kim, A., Knipprath, H., Mel, M. A., & Palmer, T. (2003). Family and community participation in education. In J. P. Keeves & R. Watanabe (Eds.), *International handbook of educational research in the Asia-Pacific region* (pp. 1063–1080). The Netherlands: Kluwer Academic Publishers.

Pefianco, E. C., Curtis, D., & Keeves, J. P. (2003). Learning across the adult lifespan. In J. P. Keeves & R. Watanabe (Eds.), *International handbook of educational research in the Asia-Pacific region* (pp. 305–320). The Netherlands: Kluwer Academic Publishers.

Peterson, C. C. (2003). Lifespan human development. In J. P. Keeves & R. Watanabe (Eds.), *International handbook of educational research in the Asia-Pacific region* (pp. 379–394). The Netherlands: Kluwer Academic Publishers.

Pfeffer, J. (1992). *Managing with power: Politics and influence in organizations*. Boston: Harvard Business School Press.

Pratt, G., & Poole, D. (2000). Global Corporations "R" us? The impacts of globalisation on Australian Universities. *Australian Universities' Review, 43*(1) & *42*(2), 16–23.

Rajput, J. S. (2001, February 14–16). *Reforms in school education in India*. Plenary speech presented at the International Forum on Educational reforms in the Asia-Pacific Region "Globalization, Localization, and Individualization for the Future", HKSAR, China.

Ramirez, F. O., & Chan-Tiberghein, J. (2003). Globalisation and education in Asia. In J. P. Keeves & R. Watanabe (Eds.), *International handbook of educational research in the Asia-Pacific region* (pp. 1095–1106). The Netherlands: Kluwer Academic Publishers.

Raven, J., & Stephenson, J. (Eds.). (2001). *Competence in the learning society*. New York: Peter Lang.

Rosenholtz, S. J. (1991). *Teachers' workplace: The social organization of schools*. New York: Teachers College.

Ryan, S., Scott, B., Freeman, H., & Patel, D. (2000). *The virtual university: The internet and resource-based learning*. London: Kogan Page.

Sarason, S. B. (1998). *Political leadership and educational failure*. San Francisco: Jossey-Bass Publishers.

Schein, E. H. (1992). *Organizational culture and leadership* (2nd ed.). San Francisco: Jossey-Bass.

Schein, E. H. (1999). *The corporate culture*. San Francisco: Jossey-Bass.

Senge, P. M. (1990). *The fifth dimension: The art and practice of the learning organization*. New York: Doubleday.

Silins, H. C., Mulford, W. R., & Zarins, S. (2002). Organizational learning and school change. *Educational Administration Quarterly, 38*(5), 613–642.

Stevenson, T. (2002). Anticipatory action learning: Conversations about the future. *Futures, 34*(5), 417–425.
Stromquist, N. P., & Monkman, K. (2000). *Globalization and education: Integration and contestation across cultures.* Lanham, MD: Rowman & Littlefield.
Sydänmaanlakka, P. (2002). *An intelligent organization: Integrating performance, competence and knowledge management.* Oxford, UK: Capstone.
Tan, S. C., So, K. L., & Hung, D. (2003). Fostering scientific inquiry in schools through science research course and computer-supported collaboration learning (CSCL). In K. T. Lee & K. Mitchell (Eds.), *Proceedings of the International Conference on Computers in Education* (CD-ROM). Hong Kong: International conference on Computers in Education.
Tang, X., & Wu X. (2000). Educational change and development in the People's Republic of China: Challenges for the future. In T. Townsend & Y. C. Cheng (Eds.), *Educational change and development in the Asia-Pacific region: Challenges for the future* (pp. 133–162). Lisse, The Netherlands: Swets & Zeitlinger.
Townsend, T., Avalos, B., Caldwell, B., Cheng, Y. C., Fleisch, B., Moos, L., et al. (Eds.). (in press). *International handbook on school effectiveness and improvement.* Dordrecht, The Netherlands: Springer.
Wain, K. (2004). *The learning society in a postmodern world: The education crisis.* New York: Peter Lang.
Wald, P. J., & Castleberry, M. S. (Eds.). (2000). *Educators as learners: Creating a professional learning community in your school.* Alexandria, VA: Association for Supervision and Curriculum Development.
West-Burnham, J., & O'Sullivan, F. (1998). *Leadership and professional development in schools: How to promote techniques for effective professional learning.* London: Financial Times Pitman Publishers.
Yuen, A. H. K. (2003). Building learning communities through knowledge forum: A case study of six primary schools. In K. T. Lee & K. Mitchell (Eds.), *Proceedings of the International Conference on Computers in Education* (CD-ROM). Hong Kong: International Conference on Computers in Education.

AFFILIATIONS

Yin Cheong Cheng
Hong Kong Institute of Education,
Hong Kong

ANN LIEBERMAN AND LINDA FRIEDRICH

CHAPTER 3

Changing Teaching from Within: Teachers as Leaders

In the last decade some researchers have begun to talk about "distributed leadership" (Spillane, Hallett & Diamond, 2003), while others have called for a redefinition of leadership for principals and teachers (Fullan, 1995; Lambert, 2003; Leithwood, 1992; Sergiovanni, 2006). These researchers have added immeasurably to our understanding of leadership development and its possibilities in this reform era. We are learning that good principals share leadership responsibilities as they build a team; that teachers increasingly take on responsibilities for instructional improvement; and that professional learning communities need to be developed and supported for continuous growth and development of the school culture.

These and other researchers call for the development and nurturing of teacher leadership (Lieberman & Miller, 2004; Smylie, 1997; Wasley, 1991) as a critical component of distributed leadership. But we still know very little about how teachers become leaders and what sustains them and even less about how teachers learn to lead, the experiences that seem seminal to their development and how they shape and transform the many leadership positions they take on.

This was precisely the set of issues we attempted to understand when we initiated the *Vignette Study* as part of a larger group of studies of teacher-consultants in the National Writing Project (NWP). We reasoned that NWP quite purposefully creates leadership opportunities for the teachers who participate in the summer institute and wondered whether their socialization into the writing project might help them better articulate how they learned to lead in a variety of contexts; in their school, district, state, or writing project site. We also wanted to know how their experience in the writing project might have been foundational in their leadership learning. Because of NWP's history of nurturing teacher-leaders and offering opportunities for leadership, as well as its engagement of teachers as writers, we saw it as an ideal setting for exploring a broader set of questions related to teacher leadership.

THE NATIONAL WRITING PROJECT

Previous work has documented the "social practices" of the writing project's intensive, month-long summer invitational institute (Lieberman & Wood, 2003). During this time, teachers, often for the first time, go public with their practice by teaching some aspect of their instruction to their peers; work in writing groups; share and critique each others' work; and learn from research and theory in the field of writing as well as from the knowledge and practice of other consultants. During the summer institute teachers participate in a learning community that is collaborative and inquiry oriented, at the same time as they are expanding their knowledge of writing and the teaching of writing.[1] Teachers become learners engaging in the various stages of writing, which deepens their understanding of their own and their students' strengths, challenges, and development as writers; they participate as colleagues in a way that is starkly different than much of their experience as teachers in their own school. Many speak of their experience in the summer institute as being "transformative" and "magical."

Wenger (1998) has written about "learning as social participation," making the claim that participation in communities of practice "shapes not only what we do, but also who we are and how we interpret what we do" (p.4). For him such communities become important arenas for professional learning because the people imbue activities with shared meanings, develop a sense of belonging, and create new identities based, in part, on their relationships with one another. In the summer institute the social practices convey norms and purposes, they create a sense of belonging in a community, and they help shape professional identities. The teachers come to realize that they are members of a community of others who share their struggles, their desire to improve the teaching of writing, and their need to continue learning (Lieberman & Wood, 2003, p. 21). Our hunch was that the summer institute, combined with the experiences gained by being a teacher-consultant (TC), would be a part of a TC's learning as they assumed different roles.[2]

At the end of the summer institute these TCs begin to share their practice and provide professional development for their colleagues, sometimes through informal sharing with teaching colleagues in their schools, often through opportunities sponsored by their writing project sites, and other times by assuming formal professional development positions within their schools and districts. As TCs leave the summer institute where all are invested in sharing and refining their practice, they typically confront the strong egalitarian norms of teacher culture e.g., What makes you think your practice is better than mine? Why do you want me to expose my practice? (Lortie, 1975). They learn that leading in their own schools has a particular set of problems for them as leaders. One teacher-leader names this challenge:

> It's one thing to stand up in front of strangers...and ask teachers to try something they may not have tried, to show them ways to teach writing, maybe even to ask them to write and share something: if they don't buy it you may never know. It's quite another thing to get up in front of your co-workers and tell them they should teach differently.

Paul Epstein (Ruffner Elementary School)

THE VIGNETTE STUDY

As we began our study, we wondered about several things. What does teacher leadership look like in practice? How does it differ from common conceptions of leadership? What problems do these leaders face and how do they negotiate their roles and responsibilities? How do teachers learn to lead? Answering these questions required us to understand how the work of teacher-leaders unfolds both day to day and over time. We also needed to get a picture of teacher-leaders' principles, interactions, and challenges. To do so, we decided to identify a sample of NWP teacher-leaders who were locally recognized as strong and effective models of teacher-leadership and engage them in a vignette study.

In many studies of leadership, one of the problems is that leadership is daily and takes place amongst a myriad of activities and actions that accrue over time. Typical data collection strategies—interviews, surveys, or even observations and focus groups—often fail to show the interconnections and variety of activities, strategies and tactics that people come to learn over time when they take on leadership responsibilities. For these reasons, the vignette was developed. Our study, which uses vignettes as its primary data source, is built upon the assumption that when a number of people write to a common set of prompts it is more likely that people's dynamic practices of work and interaction with others can be revealed because we can both see the common elements that emerge across several stories as well as the complexities and specificity of each individual story.

The vignette was first used by Miles, Lieberman and Saxl (1988) in a study of assistance personnel who were change agents in a variety of school reform efforts in New York City. After interviewing the successful leaders in this project, the research team was told by those we were studying that "you don't get it." The participants in the study taught the research team that it was hard to describe the many things that these successful leaders did every day despite our well thought out interviews and observations of them at work. The vignette helped fill the gap. The researchers wrote several prompts that would help the participants write about a set of events (less than a year) where they learned about and helped facilitate improvement with one or more teachers. In that study, the vignettes did indeed help show how those in leadership worked on a daily basis and what they were doing that appeared to teach them how to facilitate for others (Lieberman, 1987). In this current study, we changed the prompts to get at the essence of the NWP culture and what the teachers were learning in their new leadership positions (see Appendix A).

The Sample

Writing project site directors, as well as leaders from NWP's nationally sponsored programs, observe writing project teacher-leaders at work in a variety of settings.[3] Therefore, we called on them to nominate 31 teachers who have successfully taken on leadership positions in their schools, districts, states, or NWP.[4] We invited each NWP leader to nominate one individual who they knew to be: professionally active; reflective about work s/he has done to influence students, peers, and the contexts in which s/he works; and comfortable writing about his or her work. As an additional criterion, we asked half of the nominating NWP leaders to recommend someone who played leadership roles at the writing project and the other half to recommend an individual who took leadership in other educational arenas (e.g., school, district, state). We accepted all nominated individuals to participate in the vignette study.

Of the vignette authors, 88% are women and 12% are men; 79% are Caucasian, 15% are African American, 3% are Asian American, and 3% are 'Other.' They come from 21 states and 31 writing project sites. Their leadership work spans all school levels: elementary, middle, senior high, and university. They participated in the writing project's invitational summer institute between 1983 and 2004. On average, they have worked in education for 18.5 years. At the time of the study, 91% worked in education, while 9% were retired but continuing to work in education. In their last reported position, the vignette authors were:

- Teaching (15 / 38.5%);
- Working in school systems in positions such as assistant principal, curriculum specialist, or superintendent (11 / 28.2%); and

- Working in education in positions such as curriculum specialist in state departments of education or consultant for their writing project sites (13 / 33.3%).[5]

Writing the Vignettes

The vignette writers and researchers met for two writing retreats, each lasting 2 ½ days. In the first retreat, we explained to the assembled teacher-leaders that we wanted them to write about their leadership by selecting a series of activities—less than a case, but more than one event—that "showed" rather than "told" how they were learning to lead. The retreat marked the beginning of a process of co-constructing the vignettes. At this retreat, we worked with the teacher-leaders one-on-one and in writing response groups to choose one slice of their work to write about, offering guidance about which aspects of their work seemed particularly well suited for this study. In the four months between the two retreats, each person produced at least two drafts of his or her vignette and received written responses from one lead researcher.[6] In our responses, we asked them to elaborate what they did, to focus their stories, and to make explicit their leadership and the ways in which they learned to lead in the situation described. At the second writing retreat, the teacher-leaders shared their works-in-progress with us and with their colleagues. Often hearing others' stories and listening to the questions of their peers prompted them to add nuances to their stories and to clarify information about the context in which they worked. Following the second retreat, the writers received one final round of response and polished their vignettes.

Additional Data

In addition to the vignettes, we collected an array of other data related to these teachers' leadership work and conceptions of leadership. First, we collected a professional history survey from all 31 participants in order to situate these vignettes within the trajectory of their full work lives. The survey asks about each participant's full work history, their experiences within the writing project, their personal and professional publications, their participation in other professional organizations, their ratings of the writing project's influence on their career, and their perceptions of the extent to which leadership was part of each job they held.

At the second writing retreat, we held five focus groups, which included 28 of the 31 participating teacher-leaders. We wanted to make explicit what was implicit in the vignettes—how do these accomplished professionals define teacher leadership? To what extent, if at all, do they view themselves as leaders? What role, if any, has participation in the writing project and the writing of this vignette played in shaping their conceptions of teacher leadership?

Our Approach to Analysis

After all the vignettes were finally finished, we read and made notes about the roles each author played, the key content dimensions, and common themes related to leadership, the role of the writing project in shaping the work, and the process of learning to lead. We then met to discuss our understanding of each vignette and out of our initial readings we identified three broad categories of vignettes: teachers leading change inside their own schools; teachers facilitating an array of professional development opportunities outside of their own schools; and teachers moving into formal, named leadership roles in their schools, districts, states, or writing project sites. We then read each subset of vignettes to identify and categorize the strategies these teacher-leaders used to make change as well as to understand patterns in how they learned to lead.

In each group, the leadership learning initially comes from the participants' engagement with the writing project. The first group is characterized by those teachers who find a way to make change inside their own school buildings without seeming to step out of the ranks. In this group, the teacher-leaders figure out how to match some strategic moves with the exigencies of the context. In the second group of vignettes, teacher-leaders describe offering an array of professional development opportunities for teachers outside their own schools. In these vignettes, the authors show us how they continue to build their own knowledge base and refine their practice—through reflecting on and critiquing their work, through finding out what teachers say they need and then revising the professional development offerings. In the third group, teachers write about making transitions into leadership roles outside their classrooms. They explore what happens when they "cross the line" from teacher to administrator: they describe how they work to stay true to their writing project principles and values while fulfilling their responsibilities as administrators, and they show us how they continue to learn and grow in these formal leadership positions. In this paper, we focus on the 10 teachers whose vignettes describe their leadership inside their own schools (see Appendix B).

Identity: What Does It Mean to Be a Teacher-Leader?

We are doing a study of the leadership work of writing project teacher-consultants. We are looking at what TCs do, the content of their work, how TCs develop and get supported in their work...

Vignette Prompt, n.d.

When we introduced the vignette prompt, several vocal members of the group claimed that they were not leaders, reflecting the egalitarian ethos of schools. When asked about their definition of leadership, they replied, "It is when you are told what to do." While some TCs readily identified themselves as leaders from the outset, no one wanted to describe their work as authoritarian or hierarchical and many wrestled with how to portray their collaborative approach to leadership. This ambivalent relationship with leadership seems to stem from institutionalized notions of leadership as well as direct experience with "leaders" who work in a top-down way and appear more concerned with administrative matters or career advancement than with what is best for students.

In the professional history survey, the TCs reported taking a leadership role in 89% of the positions they have held since their participation in the summer institute. The focus group interviews corroborate our survey findings; all focus group participants described times when they had performed leadership roles and all but four characterized themselves as teacher-leaders. At the same time, the focus groups reveal why these TCs expressed reluctance to name themselves as leaders, although they do lead, and how they had changed the very meaning of what it means to lead. The TCs also articulated how their participation in the writing project has shaped their perception of themselves and their notions of the meaning of leadership.

From the study some common elements of what being a teacher-leader means emerged. First, and foremost, teacher-leaders exhibit a strong moral commitment to doing what is right for children. Teacher-leaders are always learning their craft and growing in their practice in order to fulfill this commitment. As one person said, "...We're really driven to do better and to be the best we can for kids" (Focus Group, June 2006).

The TCs emphasized that leadership must be earned. Being a teacher-leader means receiving (often informal) recognition from one's colleagues for commitment to children, high quality teaching, and willingness to share ideas (a rare quality among teachers working inside isolating school cultures). These teacher-leaders noted how their colleagues turned to them for advice about teaching writing. For example, Paul Epstein described what happened after he facilitated a schoolwide benchmark-setting process. Teachers from all grade levels sought him out informally for advice about how to teach writing; he was then able to share what he had learned from writing project colleagues as well as what he knew from his own classroom.

While a teacher-leader's credibility stems from the quality of his or her teaching and commitment to continuous improvement, teacher-leaders work in realms outside their own classroom walls. The TCs repeated the refrain of "stepping up to their responsibility" to share their practice with their colleagues, to contribute to the "bigger picture," to stand up for what they believe in, and to "do what needs to be done."

The TCs also emphasized that teacher-leaders work collaboratively and in an egalitarian manner. They recognize the knowledge and expertise of their peers; they reiterate that they are teachers but may have spent a little more time studying the piece of practice they are sharing; and they share knowledge with the hope that their colleagues will adapt it to meet the needs of their own classrooms. These TCs argue that true teacher-leaders "do not have all the answers." Rather they see teacher leadership as "bringing in others and getting help from others and getting contributions from others."

When the TCs redefined the term "teacher-leader" to mean these things—making a commitment to children, taking responsibility for contributing beyond one's own classroom, working collaboratively as a fellow teacher—they felt more comfortable claiming the mantle of leadership. One statement captures this alternate vision of leadership and the dynamics of this egalitarian form of leadership inside a school:

> I've found that certain people [in my school] have turned to me for things because they know that I know a little something about it. So [teacher leadership is] about relationships and who can I ask about this. ... Even though I probably would not have defined myself as a teacher-leader before being involved in this, I now see that that's exactly what I am in my building ... and there are lots of us. It's not just one person [who] holds all the knowledge (Dina DeCristofaro, Focus Group, June 2006).

The TCs also explained how participating in the writing project, both the summer institute and in leadership opportunities within their writing project sites, contributed to their adoption of a leadership identity. For many people, becoming part of the writing project represented a shift in their identities. As one TC states,

> ... I had never presented anything to other adults at all, except in church kinds of settings, but not in a school setting. But the idea that I might have some sort of professional development to share with other

teachers had never occurred to me before the writing project (Shayne Goodrum, Focus Group, June 2006).

As these TCs came to view themselves as leaders, they took on the challenge of being prophets in their own lands and worked to make their schools better places for children and adults to learn together.

LEARNING FROM VIGNETTES: LEADING IN ONE'S OWN SCHOOL

These teachers show us how they have learned to lead within the context of the strong egalitarian norms of the teacher culture. Other researchers have written convincingly about the clash between teachers who lead collaboratively and the bureaucratic norms of most schools (Little, 1995; Smylie & Denny, 1990). In light of these persistent norms, some researchers have called for thinking of schools as communities, rather than organizations. In this way, schools would be based on believing and caring, values and commitments, and professional norms and practices (Sergiovanni, 1994). In that vein, when studying Chicago school reform, Bryk and Schneider (2002) found that a broad base of trust lubricates much of a school's day-to-day functioning. For them, social trust is key to reform. Collectively, these researchers have taught us not only about the strong teacher norms of egalitarianism, but that leading collaboratively is a learned characteristic that needs nurturing, practice, and support. Our vignette study builds on this earlier work, as we see through our analysis how these teacher-leaders deal with the potential conflict between working to make change in their schools and risking rejection for stepping out of the egalitarian expectations so tightly held by many teachers in their school culture.

Given these strong egalitarian norms and an ambivalent relationship with the notion of leadership, we wondered why they took on leadership roles. All 10 teachers expressed strong *motivations* for making change within their schools. To enact their visions (often for the teaching of writing), they described a variety of *strategies* for gaining teachers' and administrators' engagement that were uniquely situated to the particulars of their teaching contexts and reflective of the writing project's social practices. Motivation and strategic thinking alone were not enough. We observed an important dynamic that facilitated these teachers' leadership work—they were *recognized by their peers* as excellent teachers who were willing to share practice and most held *ancillary roles* that gave them some time to work with peers outside their classrooms while defusing the authority-like associations with formal administrative roles. As we analyzed the vignettes alongside the focus group interviews, we also began to understand the ways in which they *learned* a new set of skills and abilities that shaped their leadership and the roles they played as they carried out their work. The support these teacher-leaders had and their foundational learning appears to be a part of their participation in the writing project through the summer institute and as TCs.

In order to illuminate the ways in which identity, leadership, and learning interconnect, we begin by sharing brief retellings of 4 of the 10 vignettes. They illustrate two broad patterns in how teachers learn to lead inside their own schools and navigate the egalitarian culture: practicing outside to lead inside and activating passion inside the classroom. We then return to our themes of motivation, strategies, peer recognition / ancillary roles, and learning in order to situate these stories in our broader analysis.

Practicing Outside to Lead Inside

Paul Epstein and Cec Carmack help us understand how their motivations helped them think strategically about what would work in their particular context and how they negotiated their own roles to gain legitimacy and trust. Each in their own way incorporates what they learned from playing leadership roles in the writing project and elsewhere as a necessary component to their own leadership within their school walls.

Paul Epstein practiced his leadership outside the building. In fact he was a co-director of the summer institute in the West Virginia Writing Project. He was uncomfortable being a "prophet in his own country" and "maintained a low profile" in his own school. Writing was also not a part of the school improvement plan of the school. So for seven years he maintained his dual life in his school and outside in the writing project.

But when he took responsibility for helping create a new writing project site, the Central West Virginia Writing Project, and started advising others to lead in their schools, he felt he had a moral obligation to do it too. As a fourth grade teacher he observed that scores in his school were very low on the state writing assessment. With this in mind, he suggested to the principal that all grade levels might set benchmarks for their students in writing. (This was the beginning of an important strategic move.) Teachers agreed that students should reach the benchmarks that they had created, but expressed anxiety about helping their students reach them. This turned out to be Epstein's opening.

He began the year as the newly appointed Title I reading teacher. He was responsible for meeting the technology content standards and offering help in reading. But he also decided to use the computers for writing and publishing a quarterly schoolwide anthology. (This strategy enabled him to add writing to his portfolio.) In his new role, teachers started asking him for advice about teaching writing; in response he encouraged teachers to help their students write stories and hold off on pointing out corrections they needed to make. He had learned these approaches from colleagues in the writing project summer institutes and was delighted when teachers began experiencing some success in their classrooms.

Next, he recruited three teachers to go to the writing project summer institute. One of the teachers, self-described as "pathologically afraid of writing," began to collaborate with Epstein. She used many of the strategies that she learned about in the summer institute and changed from being fearful of teaching writing to becoming a great enthusiast, helping others and sharing her ideas for success.

A year later, Epstein invited another teacher to attend the summer institute and persuaded her to lead a study group in the school the following year while he supported her on the side. Under their leadership, the study group, originally formed in response to a county Title I mandate, became a space where teachers wrote, read professional literature, and made mini-presentations to each other about successful literacy practices. In effect, Epstein and his colleague recreated dimensions of the summer institute inside their building. Over time, he got half the school to go to the summer institute. Scores went up, the school became recognized for writing, and many teachers gained additional capacity to mentor those with less experience. Epstein finally felt that he no longer needed to fear offering advice in his own school. He had helped grow up a genuine learning community and a number of other teachers were now assuming leadership with him.

For Cec Carmack, a fourth grade teacher four days per week and a teacher on special assignment (TOSA) one day per week, the leadership learning and development came differently. Carmack describes how her leadership journey began inside her own classroom—nine years before the episode she writes about in her vignette—when she decided to learn about her state's on-demand writing assessment by participating in scoring. Reading and scoring thousands of papers prompted her to see on-demand writing from her students' eyes and to ask questions about her own teaching of writing. She sought to bring her students to a new standard of writing proficiency—one that assumed that every child had something valuable to say. In the process, she "intentionally modeled every best practice and research-based theory gleaned from writing project summer institutes, statewide scoring trainings, and colleagues on the same mission to improve writing in their own classrooms."

Carmack's success with her students in her own classroom established her as the "go-to person" in her building when it came to teaching writing. As a TOSA, she started to think and act strategically about how to improve the culture of writing in the school. Her superintendent's support for her work was the green light she needed to work towards changing beliefs and behaviors.

Carmack asked K–4 teachers to have their students write to a schoolwide prompt. Her idea was that each grade level team would examine all their papers to find the strengths and weaknesses in their students' writing and then engage in a plan for instruction. The second grade met first. To avoid comparisons and identification, each teacher got a code name. Using both a "teacher/parent friendly" writing rubric that the staff developed and a document from the state that described writing grade level expectations, the teachers set about to read and respond. Carmack kept the meeting businesslike and on task. They defined students' writing strengths, charted the strategies they already used to help students get there, and got excited about working on their teaching. Many teachers began openly asking for help—first from Carmack and then each other. The teachers' collective efforts yielded success for students. Teachers who were at first fearful and reluctant to reveal their practice and their questions about teaching began posting their students' writing in the hall and slipping it under Carmack's door. Looking back over the year, Carmack could see that her approach of "self-discovery, not mandates" helped her colleagues change. In the process, her vision of leadership changed from "being a messenger" to "taking an active voice for teachers and students."

Activating a Passion Inside the Classroom

A few of the teachers who led in their own schools had a somewhat different pattern. They had an overriding passion for an idea and figured out ways to enact the passion in their classrooms—focusing not on influencing other teachers, but on turning their passion into powerful practices in their own classrooms. In this way, they became models for others, not by reaching out, but by reaching in.

Austen Reilley began her teaching career in a new charter school that had few structures, an inexperienced principal and little or no direction. This made the experience tough for a novice teacher. (In fact, the experience "nearly killed [her] desire to teach.") But fortunately for Reilley, on Saturdays she attended a class where women interested in writing talked and wrote. The class was called Women Writing for Change (WWC). Women from different walks of life wrote about their divorces, cancer, abuse and more. And they learned to write and share these experiences together.

For Reilley, it was learning that as a writer, teacher, and learner she needed a community. So, finding herself in a seventh grade language arts class in rural Kentucky, she decided to create a version of WWC in her school. With her principal's okay, she invited all comers in the middle school and they met every Thursday afternoon and eventually wrote and shared their stories and even named their club "The Winged Writers: Pick up a pen and fly." This club and her writing project participation encouraged her to think about gender and its relationship to writing.

As her school began analyzing data about students' learning, Reilley began to realize that boys were not doing well in the writing area in Kentucky as a whole and at her school in particular. This spurred Reilley to read more research on gender and she persuaded her principal that they should pilot single-gender classrooms at her school. Her principal went to the school board to gain support for the pilot. As luck would have it, Reilley ended up with a class full of 12-year-old boys and now she needed to figure out how to engage boys as well as girls in writing. Although challenging, she learned that there were particular themes that most interested the boys: physical activity; friendly competition; and performance. She knew that she was on to something when the boys in her class earned the only distinguished scores at her school on the Kentucky state assessment of school progress.

Reilley shared the results of her pilot with her principal, who once again was the public face of change. Reilley's study led to each teacher in the building having at least one single-gender class period in their schedule. Reilley's own passion for writing and her membership in the WWC had eventually led to shared knowledge throughout the school about writing, about gender, and about the building of community.

Elizabeth C. Davis, a 32-year teaching veteran and a 12-year teacher-consultant with the DC Area Writing Project, wove together her passion for social justice, her lifelong work as an education activist, and her teaching practice during the 50th Anniversary of the Brown v. Board of Education decision. While reading the community newspaper, Davis discovered that her school, John Phillip Sousa Middle School, and a neighborhood student in the 1950s were central actors in the Brown decision. She seized the opportunity to support her students in discovering their own capacity for making change in their community and the powerful role of writing in that process.

Davis's students quickly learned that the lead plaintiff had grown up on the streets where they now lived. This connection between past and present motivated them to conduct historical research and to argue for improving the conditions of their own school. The project came to the attention of members of Congress: Davis and her students secured an invitation to testify during the U.S. Senate's commemoration for the 50th anniversary of the Brown decision. The national news media picked up the story and publicized the poor physical condition of the school as well as its lack of up-to-date library materials. Davis and her students' actions yielded results—the conferring of historic landmark status on the school saved it from the wrecking ball and the publicity brought substantial grants and private donations for the library. This phase of Davis's leadership was firmly rooted in enacting her pedagogical principles in her classroom and bringing attention to the powerful voices of her students.

This initial project, supported in part by the DC Area Writing Project's partnership with the Holocaust Museum, set in motion a series of activities that unfolded over the next year. Davis and her students worked to create a vision for rebuilding Sousa. They also advocated for students and teachers to pursue education in a separate building while construction was taking place rather than spending day after day warehoused in the dilapidated quarters of a wing of the building unused for 15 years. This next set of events again engaged students in writing, creating a vision for the future, and advocating publicly. It also prompted Davis to seek allies outside her school building and district. Davis networked with other teachers to lobby for physical improvements in all DC schools, she built connections with parents and political action groups, she wrote eloquent op-ed pieces, and she reached out to progressive DC politicians. Once again, Davis and her students achieved victory. During the second year of Sousa's renovation, students would move to an alternate space rather than continuing to work in unsafe conditions.

Davis not only sought to "develop [her own students'] democratic capacities to enact change" and to improve conditions for children in her own school, she embraced opportunities to share her practice with other teachers in DC public schools. She regularly facilitates workshops as well as extended professional development programs, sponsored by the DC Area WP, which focus on how teaching writing can be used "as a tool for social justice and social action." She sees this as a way to give back to her writing project site, which maintains a consistent, supportive presence in the face of constant churn within the district.

Davis is no stranger to the risks of teacher leadership. Following her advocacy at Sousa, she became, in her words, a "persona non gratae" among administrators. Davis rejects formal positions and titles—too often in her experience people in formal roles are more interested in maintaining the status quo. However, Davis has worked hard over the years to become a leader both inside her own school and beyond.

Motivations: Given the Risks, Why Lead?

In their vignettes as well as in the focus groups, these TCs articulated a long list of the professional risks that teachers take to lead inside their own schools. Putting one's ideas out there runs the risk of being perceived as bragging and working against the egalitarian culture. Others, whose practice runs counter to the norm, may be perceived as the "odd duck" until their students' accomplishments reveal that the teacher is on to something. Teachers newer to the profession are typically seen as having little to offer by their more experienced peers (What do you know that I don't?). Examining what isn't working exposes teachers to the possibility that they will be seen as frauds. Teacher-leaders run up against norms that teachers simply shouldn't work too hard because they aren't getting paid adequately. Taking stands against policies that don't support children's learning also means that TCs risk losing their positions and administrative discipline.

In light of these risks, each teacher-leader names strong reasons for making changes in their schools. At the core, all of the teacher-leaders in this study are motivated by a commitment to provide the best possible education for students, especially in the teaching of writing and the use of writing to learn. Some teachers were motivated by a long-term passion. Reilley and Davis, for example, have each developed a burning passion about gender and race, respectively. And these passions led them to devise a number of strategies in their own classrooms and to build alliances that became the impetus for change within their schools. Reilley first established the girls' afterschool writing club and then worked behind the scenes to establish single-gender classrooms inside her school. Davis engaged her students in studying the history of their own school, which led to broader political activism using writing to improve the physical condition of her own school as well as that of other DC schools.

For most of the teacher-leaders in this group, the discovery of better ways to teach writing and of the power of incorporating writing into other subject areas pushed them to encourage their peers to change. Carmack draws clear parallels between the ways in which they improved their own teaching practice and their motivation to collaborate with their peers to "change the culture of writing" (Carmack, p. 41). Similarly, Christine Wegmann, a social studies teacher who had been appointed as a master teacher in her middle school, describes overcoming the resistance of her social studies colleagues to incorporating a literacy focus into the social studies curriculum. She modeled and shared particular strategies for teaching reading and writing in social studies and the teachers' excitement with their own and their students' learning. In the process, Wegmann had built a real learning community. Her colleagues were trying new strategies, sharing their successes and their problems, and becoming better teachers of writing. The district in a quick turnaround decided to switch to a focus on preparing for the statewide social studies tests – rather than incorporating literacy into other content areas. Wegmann felt so strongly that she continued her literary focus. She *stood up* for what she knew would be a more powerful way to improve students' learning with a side benefit of raising test scores. In the end, the district coordinator agreed and encouraged her to keep at it.

For other teachers it was a seminal experience that motivated them to take on more visible leadership roles inside their schools. In the focus groups, many teachers spoke of participating in the writing project summer institute as a moment when they both understood that they had something to share and that it was their professional responsibility to do so. For Epstein, visible leadership inside his own school came seven years after his initial participation in the writing project. He had worked to rebuild his own writing project site and would now be calling on others to take leadership inside their own schools. To be an authentic leader for his writing project, he decided to take on a different kind of role in his own school.

Strategies: How Did Teacher-leaders Go about Making Change in Their Schools?

Linking change to a widespread challenge A central challenge faced by all leaders, including teacher-leaders, is to motivate others to change. Part of this motivation involves identifying problems that can best be addressed through taking collective action and by involving other teachers in finding solutions. The authors of the vignettes in this set worked to make visible the learning challenges that students faced. In Epstein's school, the fourth-*graders' scores on the state writing assessment were very low; in* Carmack's school the superintendent had charged her with creating a culture of writing and she needed to help the teachers see students' strengths as well as where their writing could be encouraged and developed; in Reilley's school, boys' writing performance lagged far behind the girls'; and in Davis's school, engaging students in writing enabled them to make public the school's poor physical conditions and inadequate learning resources.

In other vignettes, authors also wrote about the need to persuade others that they faced problems or challenges that could only be addressed by working together. Wegmann, who wanted her department to integrate reading and writing into the social studies curriculum, persuaded her skeptical colleagues to consider this approach by citing statistics that demonstrated the sheer volume of reading and writing that would be required of middle school students in social studies. Lynne Dorfman, a writing resource teacher in an elementary school, demonstrated to her faculty the power of using writers' notebooks as a means for addressing the district's focus on literacy. (She had to overcome the idea that using writers' notebooks was something that *only* she could do because she was the writing teacher.) Making schoolwide problems visible opened the door to involving other teachers in collaboratively addressing these issues.

Creating collaborative forums in which teachers learn together and make their practice public In 7 of the 10 vignettes in this group, the TCs worked to figure out a strategy for bringing teachers together to do some collaborative work, thus giving their teaching colleagues some experience in learning from and with each other. In this way, they provided opportunities for teachers to collectively go public with problems of teaching writing to their students and opened up ways for teachers to ask for help. In the process, teachers began to trust each other and learn that it was okay to ask for help.

Carmack's attempts to initiate classroom change inside her building illustrate how this process can unfold. Her strategy was to use a schoolwide prompt so that the teachers could analyze their own students' writing, identify their students' strengths and challenges, and plan instruction. Even before students' work was on the table, Carmack worked hard to create ownership and reduce fear among teachers. Collaboratively, teachers created a friendlier version of the state's scoring rubric. She spent hours talking one-on-one with teachers, including "the rock of the second grade," to assure them that making their teaching public would ultimately benefit the students. With scored student papers as the basis, Carmack helped the teachers design the next five months of instruction. She learned how to bring people together to work collaboratively; to structure support for teachers; to understand the change process (from "awkward practice, to reluctance, trials and eventual mastery"); and to lead through guidance.

The teacher-leaders seized the opportunity not only to establish learning opportunities for their peers, but to share leadership with others. Once Epstein, for example, took a public leadership role in his school, he began to actively cultivate the leadership of others and he eventually persuaded a number of teachers to go to the summer institute, thereby broadening his school's leadership base. He encouraged one of these teachers to help him establish a professional study group in which teachers read professional literature and shared ideas for building their practice. This step developed her leadership capabilities and, over time, changed the school's culture to one that fostered collaboration and learning for the adults as well as the students.

In the vignettes, teacher-leaders also shared cautionary tales about what happened when they slipped into more traditional authoritarian patterns of leadership. Mimi Dyer writes of being brought into a traditional high school as the department chair to "fix" the teaching of writing. Emboldened by her passion for effective teaching and her own classroom successes, she began to make unilateral changes to the high school's curriculum. Going in, she "knew" that teachers would be thrilled with her innovative ideas. After two years, the members of her department fought to have her removed as department chair. Despite support from administrators, she left the position and started reflecting on why she had, in her words, "failed." Ultimately she realized that she had *not* built community or drawn on the strengths of her new colleagues. In a sense, she was blinded by her own pedagogical vision. After reflecting on why her efforts fell short, she had another opportunity and adopted a more collegial (and successful) approach to making change.

Publicly celebrating others' good work Recognizing the expertise of other teachers is a central tenet of these teacher-leaders' definitions of leadership. One way to move work forward and to demonstrate respect for other teachers' knowledge is to find ways to showcase the work of other teachers. Epstein, for example, worked to make students' writing visible, at the same time integrating technology and reading, by publishing a quarterly, schoolwide anthology.[7] This gave him a chance to collaborate with these students' teachers and to highlight their students' successes. Similarly, Wegmann championed her colleagues' good work to integrate literacy into social studies. When her district returned to an emphasis on rote test preparation, she invited a district administrator to visit the classrooms of her colleagues in addition to her own. In this way, she demonstrated her belief in the progress that her colleagues were making. Dorfman invited the other writing project teachers from her school to share their practice and their students' work. By featuring their work, in addition to her own, she showed that change was possible.

Building alliances with others to create change In 3 of the 10 vignettes, the strategy for making change was different. Rather than engaging their colleagues on the faculty in collaboratively making change, they found other ways to build alliances. Reilley, a relatively new teacher, shared research on single-gender classrooms with the school's counselor and principal to get permission to launch the pilot. She also collected data on the results of her students' learning during the pilot to make the case for expansion of the single-gender classrooms. While she worked behind the scenes—modeling powerful classroom practice, conducting research—she felt more comfortable with administrators playing the public leadership role. In contrast, Davis played a more public role, seeking connections outside her building and creating opportunities for her students' learning to become visible to powerful external allies. Because of her long-time activism, Davis recognized that doing the right thing is sometimes politically unpalatable for insiders who fear losing their livelihoods. By bringing students' voices and external visibility to her school's challenges, Davis was able to make much needed change.

Navigating School Culture: Peer Recognition and Ancillary Roles

In the focus groups, TCs emphasized that continuing to grow and learn as teachers, taking a stand for what they believe in, and receiving the recognition of their peers are marks of true teacher leadership. Because of her efforts to improve her own teaching and her involvement in the writing project and statewide scoring of student writing, Carmack was already known by her colleagues as the "go-to person" for writing in her building. Epstein became seen as a resource for the teaching of writing after he opened up a series of faculty-wide dialogues about writing benchmarks in his school. Reilley shared research behind the scenes with her principal in order to advocate for a pilot of single-gender classes and then stepped out of her comfort zone to teach boys. Davis combined powerful teaching with political activism to become known as a teacher who would stand up for what is right for children. These four examples reflect the type of informal recognition received by most who wrote about making change inside their schools.

Although the TCs emphasized that leadership titles do not guarantee leadership, 8 of the 10 teacher-leaders hold some sort of ancillary role that provided extra time to work with their peers. These roles include: literacy coach; teacher on special assignment; master teacher; department chair; and third grade language arts teacher. Two out of the remaining three led by example in their classroom. One, a gifted enrichment teacher, literally created a program, a position, and a team.

These ancillary roles appear to be of a different order than the classic school-based positions of principal, assistant principal, and district literacy specialist.[8] For example, Lucy Ware contrasted her experiences working in several district literacy specialist roles with her work as a third grade language arts teacher. In both positions, she sought to improve the teaching of writing and reading. However, when working as a district staff member, Ware encountered teachers' perceptions that she was not a "real" teacher, and their fears that she was a "spy" for the administration. She was frustrated by not being with teachers daily because she often was unable to follow through on ideas and engage in collegial exchanges. In contrast, when she returned to full-time teaching, she once again became one of the teachers, albeit one with additional expertise in the teaching of writing. She worked quietly as part of her grade level team. Virtually all of these teacher-leaders continued to teach students for at least part of the day. In addition, these ancillary roles came without the administrative duties of those holding traditional leadership roles (e.g., evaluating teachers, managing bus schedules). Thus these TCs could credibly maintain their equal status of being a teacher just like their colleagues.

DISCUSSION: LEARNING LEADERSHIP

In analyzing the work of these 10 teachers leading inside their schools, we learn how they overcame the entrenched bureaucratic norms of schools and institutionalized notions of leaders. Despite challenges, across the board these individuals show strong motivations to improve education for all students, not only their own. Recognizing that the trust of their peers is crucial to making change and seeing the importance of a collaborative community in their own growth as teachers and leaders, they work collaboratively and tailor their approaches to the particular contexts in which they lead. Their ability to work in this way is enhanced by the recognition of their colleagues and the ancillary roles that allow them the time to work alongside others. Given these complexities then, how do these teachers learn to lead?

Looking closely at this set of vignettes, we begin to uncover some of the learning that goes on when teachers find themselves in leadership positions or assume leadership stances in their own classrooms that are noticed by others. In particular, we see how these teacher-leaders learn to use strategies that involve teachers in improvement efforts in their school; how they develop opportunities for teachers to work together, thus minimizing competition with one another and encouraging ways of working that are more collaborative. We also see how the context helps shape the strategies used and the learning that results.

Across these vignettes a central component of teachers learning to lead is the simultaneous development of one's own teaching practice. By improving their own abilities to teach authentic writing, to better understand and address their students' strengths and needs, and to teach content in ways that engaged their students', the teacher-leaders grew in their abilities to support their colleagues. These teacher-leaders both better understand the challenges that their peers face in making change and have more experiences from which to draw. For many teacher-leaders the writing project is critical in this process—both stretching knowledge of practice and helping them to recognize what they have to offer.

These teacher-leaders seek to enact other elements of their writing project experiences inside schools. They work to develop a collegial culture where it rarely exists and to establish time for writing and professional conversation. We see here is how these TCs adapt the writing project's social practices to be effective within a group of teachers who work together daily, year after year. Many of the authors in this set played major leadership roles inside their writing project sites: co-leading the summer institute, facilitating inservice, sharing workshops, serving as members of leadership teams. These roles outside their schools afforded them opportunities not only to continue honing their own teaching practice but also to strengthen their capacities for working with their peers. They learned to recognize the fear that accompanies sharing writing or practice publicly and could understand their colleagues' reticence to share teaching practices and questions inside the four walls of the school. They developed a wide range of strategies for building community, for drawing expertise from teachers participating in professional development, for sharing knowledge in ways that can be shaped and adapted in different contexts, and for sharing leadership with others.

A more subtle form of learning also becomes visible. That is, teacher-leaders hone their leadership skills as they encounter the daily challenges of the work: helping teachers own the work, letting go so others can reshape ideas as their own, overcoming teachers' fear of exposure as "frauds," tapping into teachers' commitment to children, seeking other strategies in order to better support students' learning, and standing up against flawed policies.

These vignettes illustrate that teachers' leadership inside their own schools develops over time—sometimes over many years. To lead inside their schools and among their peers, teachers must first demonstrate that they can teach and that they continually work to improve their teaching. This quiet, ripple-effect leadership often takes years to establish as teachers gradually turn to teacher-leaders for advice. As they gain credibility, these teacher-leaders seize opportunities—a district-wide focus, low writing scores, gaps between boys and girls' achievement, a school's unknown involvement in an historical turning point—to take more public action. Public action often involves creating opportunities for teachers to learn together and to cultivate leadership in others. Leadership involves therefore not only long-term commitment but learning how to create strategies appropriate to goals and contexts.

These vignettes bring to life how participation in the writing project supports teachers in developing the knowledge of how to work with peers and the confidence to do so. It encourages them to work collaboratively and to go public with both their successes and their questions. These teacher-consultants adopt a stance as both leaders and learners. As they return to their schools, their own context helps them determine their initial leadership strategy. (Where should I begin? With whom will I work? On shat should I focus? How public should I be? How forceful or how gentle should I be with my approach?) As they identify their initial steps, they gradually seek to recreate the social organization of learning they experienced in the summer institute by establishing similar opportunities for their colleagues to learn together and take collaborative action. They continue the leadership learning that began with the writing project as they address daily leadership challenges. They have become leaders in two communities, their school and the writing project. As they led in both places, their involvement in the writing project renewed their excitement for learning, taught them the expectation that they are always involved in their own improvement as well as that of others, and offers a constant source of support.

NOTES

[1] The social practices include: honoring teacher knowledge; creating public forums for sharing, dialogue and critique; situating learning in practice and relationships; sharing leadership; guiding reflection on teaching through reflection on learning; providing multiple entry points into the learning community; turning ownership over to learners.

[2] Teacher-consultants (TCs) are offered a variety of experiences facilitating professional development in their district or surrounding districts. A number of them become quite expert in different areas and are called upon to teach others (e.g., assessment; early childhood; multicultural literature; reading strategies) Many are called upon to teach their area of expertise during a summer institute.

[3] The leaders of NWP's National Programs and Site Development unit selected a group of 35 writing project leaders who are geographically diverse, are knowledgeable about a range of program content areas, and have nurtured the development of many teacher-leaders.

[4] We originally requested nominees from 35 individuals. Of these, 33 people nominated writers. All 33 accepted our invitation. Following the first writing retreat, two people dropped out of the vignette study for personal reasons.

[5] Data about the vignette authors' demographics and employment histories were collected on the NWP Professional History Survey. All analyses from these data were prepared by Ayumi Nagase and Sela Fessehaie.

[6] Ann Lieberman, Linda Friedrich and Liza Percer served as the lead researchers during the data collection phase.

[7] During the summer institute participants create an anthology, so this was something that Epstein had experienced many times in the writing project.

[8] Two of the teacher-leaders in this group became vice principals. Each had to work very hard to negotiate their writing project learning and their authority as VPs

REFERENCES

Bryk, A., & Schneider, B. (2002). *Trust in schools: A core resource for improvement.* New York: Russell Sage Foundation.

Fullan, M. (1995). *Broadening the concept of teacher leadership.* Paper presented at the National Staff Development Council: New Directions Conference, Chicago.

Lambert, L. (2003). Shifting conceptions of leadership: Towards a redefinition of leadership for the twenty-first century. In B. Davies & J. West Burnham (Eds.), *Handbook of educational leadership and management* (pp. 5–15). London: Pearson Education.

Leithwood, K., & Poplin, M. S. (1992). The move toward transformational leadership. *Educational Leadership, 49*(5), 8–12.

Lieberman, A. (1987, April). *Documenting professional practice: The vignette as a qualitative tool.* Paper prepared for the American Educational Research Association, Washington, DC.

Lieberman, A., & Miller, L. (2004). *Teacher leadership.* San Francisco: Jossey-Bass.

Lieberman, A., & Wood, D. (2003). *Inside the National writing project.* New York City: Teachers College Press.

Little, J. W. (1995). Contested ground: The basis of teacher leadership in two restructuring high schools. *Elementary School Journal, 96*(1), 47–63.

Lortie, D. C. (1975). *Schoolteacher: A sociological study.* Chicago: University of Chicago Press.

Miles, M. B., Saxl, E., & Lieberman, A. (1988).What skills do educational "change agents" needs? An empirical view. *Curriculum Inquiry, 18*(2), 157–193.

Sergiovanni, T. (1994). Organizations or communities? Changing the metaphor changes the theory. *Educational Administration Quarterly, 30*(2), 214–226.

Sergiovanni, T. (2005). *Strengthening the heartbeat: Leading and learning together in schools.* San Francisco: Jossey-Bass.

Smylie, M. (1997). Research on teacher leadership: Assessing the state of the art. In B. J. Biddle, T. L. Good, & I. Goodson (Eds.) *International handbook of teachers and teaching* (pp. 521–592). Dordrecht, Netherlands: Kluwer Academic Publishers.

Smylie, M. A., & Denny, J. W. (1990). Teacher leadership: Tensions and ambiguities in organizational perspective. *Educational Administration Quarterly, 26*(3), 235–259.

Spillane, J. P., Hallett, T., & Diamond, J. B. (2003). Forms of capital and the construction of leadership: Instructional leadership in urban elementary schools. *Sociology of Education, 76*(1), 1–17.

Wasley, P. (1991). *Teachers who lead: The rhetoric of reform and the realities of practice.* New York: Teachers College Press.

Wenger, E. (1998). *Communities of practice: Learning, meaning, and identity.* Cambridge, UK: Cambridge University Press.

APPENDIX A. VIGNETTE PROMPT

THE VIGNETTE PROMPT

We are doing a study of the leadership work of writing project teacher-consultants. We are looking at what TCs do, the content of their work, how TCs develop and get supported in their work with colleagues, their systems, and their students.

In no more than five pages, tell us about a concrete example of your work with colleagues, your school, your writing project site, your school district, or any other context that has occurred recently or in the past year. It may be a situation that includes a set of activities that took time to unfold.

Tell us a story of this situation framing it by using the guidelines below.
DESCRIBE:

- what you were hoping would happen or be accomplished
- the context within which this work occurred
- what was involved
- the impact of the work
- why you think it happened
- the role you played
- what feels most important about this work for you and why

APPENDIX B. VIGNETTES ANALYZED

Cecilia Carmack, "Building Capacity"
Elizabeth Davis, "Teacher Leadership through Writing and Building Alliances"
Lynne R. Dorfman, "Collaboration Fosters Teacher-Leaders"
Mimi Dyer, "Lining Up the Numbers"
Paul Epstein, "The Courage to Lead: Creating a Professional Learning Community at Ruffner Elementary School"
C. Lynn Jacobs, "Leadership: Doing the Work"
Nancy King Mildrum, "Time Is on My Side"
Austen Reilley, "Ripple Effective Leadership: Transforming Passion into Plans"
Lucy Ware, "Effecting Change Teacher to Teacher"
Christine Wegmann, "Rules Worth Breaking"

AFFILIATIONS

Ann Lieberman and Linda Friedrich
Stanford University,
California
US

PAGE HAYTON LEE AND JAMES P. SPILLANE

CHAPTER 4

Professional Community or Communities?
School Subject Matter and the Management of Elementary School
Teachers' Work

INTRODUCTION

While much research on leadership and management centres on the work of those in formally designated leadership positions, there is a substantial literature on teacher leadership. Further, scholars are increasingly interested in how the school staff as a collective – as reflected in a school's professional community - contributes to the work of leading and managing instruction. Specifically, researchers have documented and described the critical role of professional community in leading and managing teachers' instructional practice. They argue that the nature and strength of a school's professional community is an important influence on teachers' efforts to reform their practice, and their sense of accountability for that practice (Seashore Louis & Kruse, 1995; McLaughlin & Talbert, 2001; Talbert & McLaughlin, 1994). Increasingly, teaching and learning are central concerns for those interested in school management and leadership.

While some researchers show how professional communities in high schools differ depending on the academic discipline (McLaughlin & Talbert, 1991); Talbert, McLaughlin, & Rowan, 1993), insufficient attention has been paid to the influence of school subjects on elementary school teachers' professional communities. Research on leading and managing instruction at the elementary level has treated instruction as a generic practice. We challenge that notion, arguing that while most elementary teachers are generalists teaching most subjects, their professional communities differ by school subject. Hence understanding the role of teachers' professional communities at the elementary level must take subject matter into account. Mathematics and literacy are the core subjects at the elementary level, consuming the bulk of the curriculum.

In this paper we analyze the structure and function of teachers' professional communities surrounding mathematics and literacy instruction in six elementary schools. After outlining our theoretical framework, we describe our methodologies in this theory-building study. We then compare and contrast the mathematics and literacy professional communities in the schools. We find that, relative to mathematics professional communities, literacy professional communities tend to be characterized by more frequent communication, more focus on pedagogical issues of learning and best practice, and arguably less vulnerability to fragmentation.

THEORETICAL BACKGROUND

Professional community

An optimal professional community is an engaging and supportive interpersonal environment in which teachers collaborate (Seashore Louis, Kruse, & Bryk, 1995; McLaughlin & Talbert, 2001). Scholars measure professional community on dimensions that include:

- The extent to which teachers' classroom practice is deprivatized, that is, made available for peer observation and critique;
- The extent to which dialogue between colleagues occurs and is deeply reflective on their practice;
- The degree of focus on student learning;
- The amount of collaboration that goes beyond superficial support or assistance, to facilitate improvement of teaching practice at fundamental levels; and
- The degree to which norms and values are shared (Seashore Louis, Kruse, & Bryk, 1995).

In communities rating high on these dimensions, teachers engage in conversations that target deep rather than surface level aspects of their practice. They work together to develop and refine collective norms of practice and values guiding day-to-day decisions. Having a say gives teachers a sense of efficacy, and in turn those norms and values serve to maintain consistency in instructional quality through guidance and accountability. A strong professional community is also marked by social trust, a confidence that colleagues are competent, concerned, reliable, honest, and open (Bryk & Schneider, 1996; Mishra, 1996; Lewicki & Bunker, 1996). By contrast, weak professional communities do not facilitate teachers' professional growth; "Without opportunities to acquire new knowledge, to reflect on practice, and to share successes and failures with colleagues, teachers are not likely to develop a sense of professional control and responsibility" (McLaughlin & Talbert, 1994). They add that support for teachers to innovate and improve their practice is more likely in schools where professional community is optimized (Furthermore, teachers in strong professional communities tend to feel more empowered and see their work as meaningful; to report more of an affiliation with the school; and to have higher job satisfaction than do teachers working in weak professional communities (Seashore Louis, Kruse, & Bryk, 1995). Working together, teachers can more effectively combat the challenges faced by schools and their communities, which may account for the positive correlation between student achievement and teachers' sense of professional community (Seashore Louis, Kruse, & Bryk, 1995). In addition, students can learn about the character of healthy interpersonal relationships when faculty members are engaged in "a cohesive, cooperative organizational climate" (Ingersoll, 2003, p.194).

A cautionary stance is healthy with respect to professional community. Some scholars argue that the sort of collegiality associated with strong professional communities can have a downside. When the culture of teaching discourages close scrutiny of practice, "collegiality" is often limited to sharing complaints and stories, and this type of interaction does nothing to foster instructional improvement (Little, 1990). When strong ties between teachers serve to justify and defend mediocre practice, rather than challenge it, collegiality can stymie rather than enable instructional improvement.

A core dimension of teachers' professional communities that can enable instructional improvement is the flow of knowledge about instruction among teachers. Specifically, whether professional communities become mechanisms for instructional innovation depends on whether they support the exchange and development of new knowledge about instruction (Coburn, 2005; Little, 1990; Seashore Louis, Kruse, & Bryk, 1995).

Individuals who connect two otherwise disconnected groups are one potentially powerful conduit for the transfer of new knowledge about instruction. These individuals fill "structural holes," or occupy "cutpoints," in a network, and they may possess power relative to their fellow teachers, because two or more groups depend on that individual for inter-group communication and negotiation (Burt, 1992). Cutpoints have the potential to facilitate communication within the network, cross-fertilizing different groups with new ideas. Looking at the issue at the collective level, then, professional community may benefit from the presence of people who fill structural holes.

Of course, pursuit of power by individuals within a social network may harm the cohesiveness of the professional community. If individuals in cutpoint roles use their positions primarily for the manipulation of personal power, the presence of cutpoints could be detrimental to the group as a whole. Thus, structural holes may be either useful or dangerous in professional communities, by either enabling communication amongst disparate groups, or manipulating factions in pursuit of individual gain.

SCHOOL SUBJECT AND PROFESSIONAL COMMUNITY

Prior research has focused on a single *community* throughout the school. However, scholarship on teachers' differing perspectives and practices in various subject areas suggests that a focus on professional *communities*, rather than community, may be warranted. Much of the research on teachers' approaches to different subject areas has looked at the high school level and has found that high school teachers differ in their conceptions of the subjects they teach. These differences have consequences for practice, the ways teachers enact their roles, and the influence of external reform on practice (Grossman & Stodolksy, 1995; Siskin, 1990, 1991, 1994).

High school teachers' views of their subjects differ on dimensions such as the scope of the subject; the degree to which the material is sequenced; whether the subject is static or dynamic; and the degree to which the subject is core or peripheral (Grossman & Stodolsky, 1995). Mathematics teachers are more likely than teachers of other subjects to see their work as routine (Rowan, Raudenbush, & Cheong, 1993). In a study of 16 high schools involving over 500 teachers, Rowan (2002) found that a large amount of the variance in teachers' perceptions of task variability and task uncertainty was within schools rather than between schools. Teachers who subscribed to behaviourist theories about instruction (more often mathematics teachers) were more likely to view teaching as a routine task, while teachers who subscribed to constructivist theories of instruction (more often English teachers) were more likely to view teaching as a non-routine task, involving more task variety and task uncertainty. High school teachers' views of teaching and learning differ by school subject.

An important next step in the professional community literature is to address the multifaceted nature of *elementary* school teachers' work and explore whether it influences their professional communities. Elementary school teachers do not simply "teach"; rather they teach spelling, reading, social studies, science, math, and so on (Stodolsky, 1988). The assumption that teaching is a unitary practice is an oversimplification (Spillane & Burch, 2004). In fact, the available evidence suggests that subject matter is an important context for elementary school teachers' work (Drake, Spillane, Hufferd-Ackles, 2001; Spillane, in progress; Spillane & Burch,

2004; Stodolsky, 1988). Elementary school teachers experience, identify with, and act on each subject matter in a unique way.

METHOD

Data

To explore elementary school teachers' subject-specific professional communities, we conducted a mixed-method study, using data collected over several years, beginning in 1999, through the Distributed Leadership Study (DLS). Thirteen K-5 and K-8 schools in Chicago participated in the study, some for one year and others for up to five consecutive years. The Distributed Leadership Study was a longitudinal study of elementary school leadership in high poverty urban schools.

The thirteen schools participating in the DLS were selected using a purposive sampling strategy, along three dimensions. First, all schools serve high poverty populations within the city; each school has a minimum of 60% students eligible for free or reduced price lunch. Second, we selected for demographic diversity. The total sample of thirteen schools includes seven predominantly African-American schools, three predominantly Latino schools, and three schools that are more racially mixed. The schools also represent a range of student population sizes, from 287 to 1,498. Third, we were interested in schools that were working to improve instruction. Therefore, using an existing longitudinal database (Consortium on Chicago School Research), we selected schools that that had shown indications of improvement on measures including "academic press," "professional community," "instructional leadership" and "academic productivity," including some schools where these measures had remained unchanged over the previous 5 to 10 years.

Early observation and interview work at these thirteen schools suggested that the people to whom teachers turned for advice differed by subject area. To explore this issue, we conducted network surveys at the six DLS schools that agreed to participate. These schools are representative of the full sample on each variable used to purposively select the original sample: student SES, student racial background, and school size. For example, the six schools that are the focus of this paper ranged in size from a few hundred students to almost fifteen hundred students; from 29 staff at one school to 81 at another. Similarly, some of these six schools had shown substantial improvements, others had made only modest improvements and one had shown no signs of improvement and was put on probation by the school district.

Five of the six schools (Bittman, Kosten, Beecher, Fieldman, and Kelly) are urban schools serving grades K-8. The sixth school, Wayne, is a K-5 school in a suburban district just outside the city limits. At both Wayne and Bittman, faculty members completed the social network questionnaire twice over the course of two years, whereas teachers at the other four schools did so once.

In addition to completing surveys, teachers from each school participated in an extensive ethnographic study. Researchers based at each school observed a variety of meetings (including faculty, grade-level, literacy committee, mathematics committee, and school improvement team meetings), informal conversations in hallways and lunchrooms, and practice in the classroom. These researchers were present at each school multiple days per week over the course of one to four academic years. During their days at the schools, the ethnographers drafted detailed field notes of their observations and videotaped some of the meetings. More comprehensively afterwards they fleshed out their field notes.

Researchers also sought out interviews with formal and informal school leaders, teachers involved with school improvement efforts, and teachers at the 2nd and 5th grade levels. The interviews focused on school leaders' goals and practices; teachers' and administrators' responsibilities in the school's efforts to improve instruction in math, literacy, and science; teachers' classroom practice; and who or what influences the way they practice. Questions that are especially pertinent to this paper include those in the Appendix. Each interview was audio taped and subsequently transcribed.

Table 1: Interview Data

School	Number of Interviews	Number of Subjects
Beecher	50	34
Bittman	26	13
Fieldman	26	13
Kelly	12	8
Kosten	33	19
Wayne	30	17
Total	177	104

We used these interview transcripts for the purposes of this paper. In the rare case that an interview transcript did not explicitly or implicitly refer to the faculty member's professional communities or views of math or literacy, we considered the interview unrelated to this particular paper. The total number of interviews we used from these six schools was 177, from

104 respondents (see Table 1), ranging from kindergarten teachers to literacy specialists, and eighth grade science teachers to administrators. Of the teachers interviewed, 35 were subject specialists, and 60 were generalists. Respondents who were not teachers filled roles such as administrator, external partner, counsellor, and computer lab manager.

Analysis

Our analysis included both the social network survey data and the ethnographic data. First, using teachers' responses to the surveys and working with the UCINET software package (Borgatti, Everett, & Freeman, 2002) we constructed diagrams of each school's social networks of advice about reading instruction and of advice about math instruction. This technique provides a visual representation of the structure of the subject-specific professional community in each school and allows for quantitative analysis of its characteristics.

For each school's math and literacy advice networks, we obtained calculations of density and centrality, and identified cutpoints. A network's density is a measure of the proportion of potential links between people that are actualized. In a network where every member has a tie to every other member, the density is 1.0. A network's density indicates the extent of connection within the professional community. Degree centrality is a measure of the number of ties an actor has. In an advice network, each actor's *indegree* centrality score indicates the number of people who approach that actor for advice, whereas the *outdegree* centrality score indicates the number of people to whom that actor goes for advice. A cutpoint is an actor in the network whose removal would divide the network into smaller components. A network with a large percentage of cutpoints is vulnerable to splitting into factions, thus blocking communication throughout the network.

Qualitative analysis of interview transcripts was conducted initially using an open coding strategy with one school's interviews. Through open coding we identified recurrent themes and issues about the teachers' instruction of, and interactions around, mathematics and literacy. After this initial round of open coding, and based on the literature reviewed above, we shifted into a phase of focused coding. In the focused coding phase, we read through the other five schools' interviews, coding for references to the subject-specific professional communities within the school. Coding categories included teachers' depictions of the math- and reading-specific communication that took place, both within their grade-level or subject team, and across such teams; when teachers indicated that their social support and interactions were ideal or problematic; whether they considered their professional community vulnerable to breakdown; administrative involvement; and why the respondent chooses certain individuals to seek out for advice related to math or reading instruction.

As we continued analyzing interviews, we modified the coding scheme in an iterative process, to adapt to the themes that seemed most salient. While open to emergent themes, we primarily relied on this coding scheme to analyze the entirety of the interview data.

After coding each school's interviews in the TAMS Analyzer software program, we used TAMS to compare and contrast responses. We grouped together comments from each school in each coding category, and did a parallel analysis for the aggregate of all schools' data. This allowed us to seek patterns, and to compare and contrast responses both within and between schools. Throughout this process we sought disconfirming evidence and entertained alternative hypotheses. To complement the interviews, we read a total of 236 field notes from four of the schools. The field notes provided information to corroborate our findings from the network and interview data.

Subject-Specific Professional Communities: Form and Function

Professional community can develop through both top-down and grassroots efforts, as teachers navigate through the formal organizational structure to build their informal social networks (Raywid, 1995; King & Weiss, 1995; Rollow & Bryk, 1995; Lonnquist & King, 1995; Weiss, Seashore Louis, & Hopkins, 1995). Considering a school's professional community as "an emergent property of ongoing action" (Barley, 1986, p. 79) taken by its faculty members, as structured by the social situation, we can analyze that community in terms of both form and function.

By form we mean what many sociologists term structure, "the enduring, orderly, and patterned relationships between elements" (Abercrombie, Hill, & Turner, 1995). A community's function is the set of purposes it serves. By function we refer to the types of communication teachers engage in within their professional communities.

Form

At all six schools, teachers' literacy-specific advice networks were denser than their math-specific advice networks. In most cases the literacy network was about one third denser than the math network, and at Kelly the literacy network is more than four times as dense as the math network. Teachers in these schools were communicating with more of their colleagues about literacy instruction than about mathematics instruction.

Teachers' comments in interviews indicate that conversations about math instruction tend to be more rare than conversations about literacy instruction. Several teachers at Wayne, for example, explicitly contrasted their conversations about literacy and mathematics. A second grade teacher distinguished reading instruction, about which her team "talks[s] about everything," from math instruction, about which she said, "I don't really go to anyone else to help me strategize or plan for my math." Similarly, a Wayne first grade teacher stated that "collaboration of the other teachers" is very important to her efforts to improve her literacy instruction. On the other hand, she said, "I don't think anybody talks about math... my [grade level] team over the last couple years has been so concerned with reading that we don't really talk about math too much... With reading we're sharing books and we're sharing ideas... [with] math we're not... Nobody talks about math."

Likewise, teachers in a range of positions at Kosten referred to collaboration among reading team members (those teachers who specialized in literacy instruction and were officially designated by the administration as a team). By contrast, collaboration among the math specialists who made up the school's math team was mentioned as an ideal, rather than as a reality. For instance, one math teacher told another on the math team, "We really need to get everyone [math team] together. The language arts teachers did that this summer, got everyone together and set a curriculum, so they were together.... We need to get together." Additionally, a 5th grade reading teacher stated that, "We [the literacy team] do a long term range plan. What we're going to teach from day one on. We're always talking – I have a great team. We're always talking to each other, the reading teachers at least, as to where – 'OK, where are you,' for example, 'what section are you doing right now and how are you doing it?'" These comments from both math and reading specialists indicate that teachers engage more frequently in discussion about literacy instruction than about math instruction, and that this discussion tends to result in cohesion, support, and the exchange of ideas.

Communication about literacy was both initiated by teachers in informal dialogue, and facilitated by the formal organization and official opportunities presented by the school. At several schools it was clear that official staff development time was dedicated predominantly to language arts, whereas very little attention was devoted to math. For instance, Kelly's assistant principal reported that "Most of the teachers, when they get up and make presentations [at staff in-service days], it's a reading... or writing... it's usually in the language arts area." Several Bittman teachers commented on the lack of professional development offered in math, particularly in comparison to the abundance offered in reading. One teacher complained, "the Board has in place the programs for reading staff development, and they haven't quite gotten there in math yet." Both Bittman's principal and a seventh grade teacher, who with 11 other Bittman teachers had recently completed her reading endorsement, independently indicated that professional development for reading instruction is offered to the entire faculty, whereas math professional development takes place mainly during meetings for math specialists.

Furthermore there are fewer math specialists across the board than there are reading specialists. Summed for all six schools, there were a total of 17 literacy and language arts specialists, compared with 5 math specialists. One Bittman teacher stated that, in order to meet the school's math goals, teachers would need more daily collaboration in addition to formal staff professional development.

The seeking of advice about reading instruction is also more widespread than is seeking advice about math, within the same faculties. We find evidence for this in the higher indegree centrality within literacy networks. Indegree centrality refers to the extent to which individuals are identified by their peers as a source of advice. In a network with higher overall indegree centrality, participants are, on average, sought out for communication by larger numbers of peers. In all six schools the mean indegree centrality score is higher in the literacy network than in the math network.

Analyzing which actors have the highest indegree centrality suggests some interesting patterns across the schools. In reading networks, formally designated reading specialists and primary grade (K-2) teachers dominated the indegree centrality rankings. In math networks, formally designated subject specialists' prominence dropped, due in some part to the lower number of math specialists, compared with reading specialists, in each school. Intermediate grade teachers (3-5) showed up more often in the math centrality rankings. This may indicate that teachers see literacy expertise concentrated more in early grade teachers and reading specialists, and math expertise concentrated in teachers of later grades.

In sum, math professional communities tend to take a distinctly different form than do literacy professional communities, even within the same school faculty. Communities centered on advice about literacy instruction are denser, and individuals within them have more ties, leading to more communication.

Function

At the six schools, the content of teachers' communication differed between math and literacy communities. In both subject areas, teachers had conversations about practical matters of immediate concern, such as the textbook and materials, lesson plans, and time shortages. Discussions about math were typically limited to these topics. By contrast, when talking about literacy instruction, teachers tended to expand their scope to include other aspects of teaching and learning.

At Kosten literacy was discussed formally in staff meetings, as well as informally in the faculty lunchroom; teachers talked about scheduling and its impact on reading instruction, curriculum, the crucial nature of reading to other school subjects, and how to encourage a love of reading in students. Each of these reading-related issues arose in both informal settings and formal settings, including staff meetings. On the other hand, faculty members rarely discussed math instruction, officially or casually. When teachers did talk about math, field notes indicate the conversation centred on the textbook. For instance, teachers informally chatted about how well they liked the book and which lessons from the book's sequence they had covered with their classes. Formally, the administration called teachers together to choose among a few options for a new math textbook. Aside from that occasion, there was no evidence of teachers discussing math in formal meetings.

Conversations around math tended to be brief and more immediately practical; teachers discussed materials and the sequencing of content covered in the curriculum. For example, in her interview a 5th-7th grade gifted program teacher at Kosten was asked whether her grade-level teammates spent a lot of time talking about their pedagogical approaches in math. She replied, "Oh gosh, no. There wasn't time. We just stood and said, 'Here's what I'm gonna do, this, this, and this, and I'm gonna get this, this, and this done.'" Similarly, when asked whether teachers had talked about their concerns about the required curriculum, a second grade bilingual teacher replied in the negative. The interviewer followed up, "Do you foresee your group getting together and talking about those things?" The teacher responded, "Not unless I pull their teeth out."

Several other Kosten teachers described the types of dialogues they tend to have with their colleagues around math. A 5th-8th grade math teacher said an example of this dialogue would be, " 'how is your 7th grade class skill-wise?'… There'll be a fast exchange on things like that. We're not on the exact same schedule – in fact he's using a different book right now 'cause we're short, but every once in a while we just touch base." In a later interview this same teacher stated, "We don't do it a whole lot, but on occasion Frank, the 8th grade teacher, and I will talk to each other – in fact he just gave me my Trivial Pursuit cards... It's a matter of no time, but when you run into each other, you'll say a few things to each other. But otherwise [there is] really not someone I routinely work with on math." Communication about math seemed to be brief, infrequent, and more focused on touching base with each other than about sharing ideas or developing instructional approaches.

Test scores were another issue on which math conversations focused. When Beecher School saw a decrease in students' math test scores, the teachers noted, "'OK, we see there's a problem. What kind of things do you think we ought to be doing to get at this level?' So that required just a huge amount of work. Just mobilizing the conversation, to get people talking together about it, you know, was pretty significant." One teacher at Wayne stated that her teammates' conversations about math tended to ask, "What lesson are you on?" or "Do your kids understand X or struggle with Y?" This brief reference to student understanding of the material is rare, and, as described above, most Wayne teachers described virtually no analysis of math teaching or learning taking place.

By contrast, in conversations about literacy instruction, teachers described more discussion about teaching philosophy and instructional approaches. For example, one Fieldman educator explained that recent meetings about literacy instruction had focused on the variety of students' learning styles and a close examination of teachers' efficacy in impacting student understanding and progress. Furthermore, a 5th-6th grade writing teacher at Kosten said of her colleagues in the language arts team, "They have different theories, and I do believe in different theories. I try to use some of their ideas." Another member of the literacy and language arts team said, "We talk about content issues and teaching approaches. 'If you've read this novel before with a class, did they understand it? Do you think, you know, do you think this will be appropriate? Or how can I go about making sure the kids know what a verb is or how to use commas?'... They have little techniques that I find helpful." These teachers shared ideas, compared theories, and discussed student understanding.

At Beecher School, teachers also mobilized to learn more about literacy instruction. A reading resource teacher there reported, "When I got here... everybody did absolutely their own thing as far as literacy... Nobody ever talked to each other... So we've tried to develop some common strategies [for] instruction... trying to learn a little bit more about what reading strategies kids need to know in order to better comprehend what they read." The focus on teachers collaborating to learn together was reflected as well in another teacher's comment that she'd been meeting with colleagues to "define for ourselves what is literacy instruction... what does it involve?"

Across the six schools we see that discussions about math instruction tended to be narrower compared to literacy. It was primarily in literacy professional communities that teachers engaged in any dialogue about fundamental pedagogical issues. In this way the function, as well as the form, of these subject-specific professional communities differed.

CONCLUSION

The school's professional community is a dimension of school leadership and management that focuses on the collective rather than individual formal or informal leaders. A school's professional community can contribute to the work of leading and managing instruction – potentially providing opportunities, encouragement, and support for teachers in their efforts to improve their classroom practice. However, the configuration of these communities may differ depending on the school subject.

Our account shows that teachers' professional communities around math and literacy instruction are distinct in several ways. In terms of the form of the professional community, teachers communicate more frequently, and with more colleagues, about literacy instruction than about math instruction, as demonstrated by network densities, indegree centrality score averages, observations of meetings and casual conversations, and teachers' own reports. Functionally, these communities also differ. Discussions in each professional community centre on different topics, and different types of teachers tend to be sought out for advice in each subject area. These structural and functional differences between teachers' professional communities around math and literacy point to the relative strength of literacy professional communities in these six schools.

REFERENCES

Abercrombie, N., Hill, S., & Turner, B. S. (1995). *The penguin dictionary of sociology*. Retrieved August 30, 2004, from www.xreferplus.com

Barley, S. R. (1986). Technology as an occasion for structuring: Evidence from observations of CT scanners and the social order of radiology departments. *Administrative Science Quarterly, 31*, 78-108.

Borgatti, S. P., Everett, M. G., & Freeman, L. C. (2002). UCINET for Windows: Software for Social Network Analysis [Computer software]. Harvard: Analytic Technologies.

Bryk, A. S., & Schneider, B. (1996). *Social trust: A moral resource for school improvement*. U.S: Department of Education Office of Educational Research and Improvement.

Burt, R. S. (1992). The social structure of competition. In N. Nohria & R. G. Eccles (Eds.), *Networks and Organizations: Structure, Form, and Action* (pp. 57-91). Boston: Harvard Business School Press.

Coburn, C. E. (2005). Shaping teacher sensemaking: School leaders and the enactment of reading policy. *Educational Policy, 19*(3), 476-509.

Drake, C., Spillane, J. P., & Hufferd-Ackles, K. (2001). Storied identities: Teacher learning and subject-matter context. *Journal of Curriculum Studies, 33*(1), 1-23.
Grossman, P. L., & Stodolsky, S. S. (1995). Content as context: The role of school subjects in secondary school teaching. *Educational Researcher, 24*(8), 5-11, 23.
Ingersoll, R. M. (2003). Who controls teachers' work? Power and accountability in America's schools. Cambridge, MA: Harvard University Press.
King, J. A., & Weiss, D. A. (1995). Thomas Paine High School: Professional community in an unlikely setting. In K. Seashore Louis & S. D. Kruse (Eds.), *Professionalism and community: Perspectives on reforming urban schools* (pp. 76-104). Thousand Oaks, CA: Corwin Press.
Lewicki, R. J., & Bunker, B. B. (1996). Developing and maintaining trust in work relationships. In R. M. Kramer & T. R. Taylor (Eds.), *Trust in organizations: Frontiers of theory and research* (pp. 114-139). Thousand Oaks, CA: Sage.
Little, J. W. (1990). The persistence of privacy: Autonomy and initiative in teachers' professional relations. *Teachers College Record, 91*(4), 509-537.
Lonnquist, M. P., & King, J. A. (1995). Changing the tire on a moving bus: Barriers to professional community at Whitehead School. In K. Seashore Louis & S. D. Kruse (Eds.), *Professionalism and community: Perspectives on reforming urban schools* (pp. 133-159). Thousand Oaks, CA: Corwin Press.
McLauglin, M. W., & Talbert, J. E. (2001). *Professional Communities and the Work of High School Teaching.* Chicago: University of Chicago Press.
Mishra, A. K. (1996). Organizational responses to crisis: The centrality of trust. In R. M. Kramer & T. R. Taylor (Eds.), *Trust in organizations: Frontiers of theory and research* (pp. 261-287). Thousand Oaks, CA: Sage.
Raywid, M. A. (1995). Professional community and its yield at Metro Academy. In K. Seashore Louis & S. D. Kruse (Eds.), *Professionalism and community: Perspectives on reforming urban schools* (pp. 45-75). Thousand Oaks, CA: Corwin Press.
Rollow, S., & Bryk, A. S. (1995). Catalyzing a professional community in a school reform left behind. In K. Seashore Louis & S. D. Kruse (Eds.), *Professionalism and community: Perspectives on reforming urban schools* (pp. 105-132). Thousand Oaks, CA: Corwin Press.
Rowan, B. (2002). Teachers' work and instructional management, part 1: Alternative views of the task of teaching. In W. K. Hoy & C. G. Miskel (Eds.), *Theory and research in educational administration* (Vol. 1, pp. 151-168). Greenwich, CT: Information Age Publishing.
Rowan, B., Raudenbush, S. W., & Cheong, Y. F. (1993*). Contextual effects on the self-efficacy of high school teachers.* Stanford, CA: Center for Research on the Context of Secondary Teaching, School of Education.
Seashore Louis, K., & Kruse, S.D. (1995). *Professionalism and community: Perspectives on reforming urban schools.* Thousand Oaks, CA: Corwin Press.
Seashore, Louis, K., Kruse, S. D., & Bryk, A. S. (1995). Professionalism and community: What is it and why is it important to urban schools? In K. Seashore Louis & S. D. Kruse (Eds.), *Professionalism and community: Perspectives on reforming urban schools*, Thousand Oaks, CA: Corwin Press.
Siskin, L. S. (1990). *Different worlds: The department as context for high school teachers.* Stanford, CA: Center for Research on the Context of Secondary Teaching, School of Education.
Siskin, L. S. (1991). *School restructuring and subject subcultures.* Stanford, CA: Center for Research on the Context of Secondary Teaching, School of Education.
Siskin, L. S. (1994). *Realms of knowledge: Academic departments in secondary schools.* Washington DC: Falmer Press.
Spillane, J. P. (in progress). The practice of elementary school leadership: How the subject matters.
Spillane, J. P., & Burch, P. (2004). The institutional environment and instructional practice in K-12 schools: "Loose coupling" revisited. In B. Rowan (Ed.), *New institutionalism in education* Albany: State University of New York Press.
Stodolsky, S. S. (1988). *The subject matters: Classroom activity in math and social studies.* Chicago: University of Chicago Press.

Talbert, J. E., & McLaughlin, M.W. (1994). Teacher professionalism in local school contexts. *American Journal of Education, 102*(2), 123-153.

Talbert, J. E., McLaughlin, M. W., & Rowan, B. (1993). Understanding context effects on secondary school teaching. *Teachers college record, 95*(1), 45-70.

Weiss, D. A., Seashore Louis, K., & Hopkins, J. (1995). Dewey Middle School: Getting past the first stages of restructuring. In K. Seashore Louis & S. D. Kruse (Eds.), *Professionalism and community: Perspectives on reforming urban schools* (pp. 160-184). Thousand Oaks, CA: Corwin Press.

AFFILIATIONS

Page Hayton Lee and James P. Spillane
Northwestern University,
USA

NEIL DEMPSTER

CHAPTER 5

Leadership for Learning: Some Ethical Connections

INTRODUCTION

In this chapter I draw on research conducted in Queensland, Australia, and recent writing in the field of ethics in education to discuss a number of ethical issues if school principals are to connect aspects of their leadership with learning. My sources show that school principals say they are working in an increasingly complex ethical environment, especially since the broad political and policy movement called 'new managerialism' has held ubiquitous sway with western democratic governments (OECD, 2002; Hargreaves, 2000; Leithwood and Riehl, 2003; Leithwood, 2005; Groundwater-Smith and Sachs, 2002). The effects of managerialism are evident in the work of researchers such as Begley (2006), Begley and Johansson (2003) and Lacey (2006) which shows that the contemporary ethical environment contains tensions, many of which are attributable to managerialist reforms. Our work in Queensland, Australia substantiated this claim by showing that principals believe that they are under competitive pressures to produce improved student performance so that school reputation is enhanced to aid marketing to an increasingly discerning set of educational consumers (Dempster, Freakley & Parry, 2002). Managerialist reforms have increased the powers of governments in education by centralising curriculum and assessment control, setting standards for teachers and leaders while at the same time increasing the school leader's responsibility for managing the delivery of improved outcomes locally (Matters, 2005; Ehrich, Cranston & Kimber, 2005). As a result, there is no doubt that principals face many troublesome ethical issues, and some frequently.

I focus in the first part of the chapter on three types of troublesome issues only - issues that have much to do with the principal's role in leading learning. I do this, first, because a principal's decisions about staff, resources and professional development are concrete expressions of what he or she values about learning; second, because they are perennial issues which no principal can avoid; and third, because the decisions made about these

J. MacBeath and Y.C. Cheng (eds.), Leadership for Learning: International Perspectives, 81–99.
© *2008 Sense Publishers. All rights reserved.*

matters have direct and indirect effects on staff and students. The three types of troublesome issues are:

- the fair treatment of difficult or underperforming staff members;
- the equitable allocation of resources for learning and teaching; and
- the just provision of support for professional development opportunities for teachers.

I discuss these three types of issues using a number of fictionalised case accounts gathered during the study referred to above (Dempster, Freakley & Parry, 2002). My purpose is to show that reaching ethically defensible decisions rests firmly on the values a principal brings to an issue and a sound knowledge of different ethical approaches to those decisions.

In the second part of the chapter, I use explanations offered by principals to examine different decision routes. The use of intuition, I suggest is intrinsic to all ethical decision making routes but should not be employed without the use of other supporting processes.

In the final part of the chapter, I outline three critical measures associated with difficult decisions, measures which can contribute to leadership sustainability. These measures require a conscious understanding by principals of their own values and the networks of support they need as they grapple with worrying matters. I conclude by arguing that principals need to continue to learn about the way they make decisions if they are to sustain themselves as trusted leaders of learning over time.

THREE TYPES OF DIFFICULT ETHICAL ISSUES

I turn first to the most troublesome of all ethical issues with which principals deal, the matter of difficult and underperforming members of staff (Dempster, Freakley & Parry, 2002)

Fair Treatment of Difficult or Underperforming Members of Staff

If schools say they hold high expectations of teachers and students, it is critical when members of staff are underperforming or being decidedly difficult that action is taken. Indeed, Leithwood (2005) and Silins and Mulford (2002) go so far as to say that good leaders maintain high standards of professionalism and ensure that teachers are well prepared and supported in the crucial work of teaching and learning. That said, when underperformance is identified, or when 'bloody mindedness' occurs and children are being affected, what to do about it is clearly an ethical issue. Should a

LEADERSHIP FOR LEARNING: SOME ETHICAL CONNECTIONS

principal opt for a developmental route for the member of staff concerned, or should reprimand or dismissal be the avenue taken. The first case account I offer places this dilemma right on the principal's desk and shows that the values a leader brings to the table and the context of each and every case always figure prominently in any decision reached.

Case Account (a). 'It Doesn't Make Me Feel Good but What Was I To Do?

Noel Roberts is the principal of a large secondary school. One of his Mathematics teachers had recently experienced a mild heart attack but had returned to work upon recovery. Back at work the teacher continued to be plagued by ill health and was not performing satisfactorily. Noel placed him on diminished work performance after a considerable struggle over deciding what to do. Noel explains his thinking in his own words:

> He did not engage with the students. He wrote stuff on the blackboard and the kids were rioting. The kids who wanted to learn were told to come down to the front, and the rest could go down the back and play merry hell.

While Noel had to decide what to do about the situation, he was concerned about the well being of the teacher. But as he said:

> It was a very difficult decision to place this man on diminished work performance. The teacher lost face and everyone knew about it even though we tried to keep it confidential. This teacher was having a miserable time. He was ill and in his fifties. When he should have been looking at a fairly comfortable existence, if you dismiss him, you've virtually taken away his source of income, his self-esteem, or whatever little self-esteem he had left. He couldn't change jobs. He had nowhere to go. And, you could ruin his whole life. You could end up destroying him. So it was a dilemma.

But, Noel was also concerned about his responsibility to the students. As he explained:

> The teacher is there to do a job. He's affecting the lives of 150 to 200 kids, having a critical effect on their lives, and he's not accepting his responsibilities. It was nothing against the person. I couldn't tolerate it, because he's there to do a job.

Following the decision, Noel decided to help the teacher to get a medical discharge. The teacher did not like this at all and claimed that he was being unfairly treated. Within a month, he died of a heart attack whilst writing on the blackboard. "I think", Noel reflected, "that my actions contributed to his heart attack. It doesn't make me feel good. But what was I to do?"

DISCUSSION

While the decision taken by the principal might be seen by some as heartless, it was based, consciously or unconsciously on a commitment to the moral purpose of education, that is: educators are about making things better, not worse for their students. When this was obviously not happening, as the principal believed was the case, he felt that a decision had to be taken in the students' interests rather than in the interests of the teacher. The fact that the teacher's illness may have contributed to his underperformance did not justify doing nothing. The source of this decision is to be found in consequentialist ethical theory. In short, the principal determined that the consequences of taking no action would have resulted in many lives being affected. Taking action against the teacher affected one life. Consequentialist ethics is quite utilitarian, seeking the greatest good for the greatest number as one of its key justifications. Was the decision taken right, fair, just and good? As with most ethical issues, decision makers have to live with the aftermath of the decisions they make as well as the knowledge that different decisions are always possible and justifiable.

The second case account also deals with diminished work performance and includes two of the decision options available to a principal – dealing with underperformance by development or by dismissal. In this case, the person concerned was a Head of Department (HOD) in a large secondary school, and a member of the school's senior management team. The principal, Simon Brown, would have felt some loyalty to the HOD because of their professional relationship.

Case Account (b). 'Would You Like to Know My Decision Now or After Your Operation?'

Simon recalls the background to the problem of diminished work performance in these terms:

> After I'd been here a couple of years and everyone had got to know me, the entire staff of this department asked for a meeting with me. I knew it was something to do with the Head of Department because of lingering doubts that I had about her performance. Upon receiving advice, I informed the HOD that I'd been requested to have the meeting and that I was going to go ahead with it. I promised to let her know at the end of the meeting every single thing that happened and

we'd plan together what to do about it. I went ahead with the meeting and everyone gave me about five pages of complaints they had about this particular person. I shared the complaints with her very quickly after the meeting and we decided to bring this out in the air altogether. So we took everyone away for a day and explored the nature of the complaints and how people were feeling. We also explored what people thought would make an ideal Department. We came away from that day with a lot of stuff and a range of action plans. We worked away at them pretty solidly. After about four months, we decided to conduct a review to take stock of where we were. The outcome was that there was a slight improvement amongst some staff and a small number were now 50-50 about the HOD. Nevertheless, a large number still felt very negative towards her.

The attitude amongst some staff members was: 'I don't care what she does I'm not going to forgive her and I'm going to undermine her as long as I can'. I had to decide what to do about this. It was clearly becoming quite urgent.

Simon arranged another interview with the Head of Department to discuss the results of the review and to communicate to her what action ought to be taken. The day before the interview the Head of Department was diagnosed with level 4 cancer and needed to have an urgent operation within the next 2-3 days. On arriving at the interview, the Head of Department said:

> Well this is my last day. I have to go for the operation next Monday. I'll let you know as soon as I can how I'm going. But before I go, can you tell me what you've decided.

Simon reported his reply and his reflection on it in the following words:

> I thought that I could either lie to her or I could tell her the truth. I didn't want to lie, so I asked her if she would prefer to know the decision after her operation. She insisted that she be told now. I had to tell her that although there had been a slight improvement she would be placed on diminished work performance. I asked her if she would like to know more about the process and what it would mean for her. So we sat down and went through all of that. Deep down, I had a real conviction that she would never make the grade.

DISCUSSION

On the way to his final decision, Simon had already employed a developmental strategy with his HOD. In a sense, this was 'Plan A' and it was based on an 'ethic of care'. When this did not yield the results he might have hoped for, he moved to 'Plan B'. When an 'ethic of care' prevails, the decision maker is sensitive to the importance of relationships and does all in his or her power to maintain these in difficult circumstances. This was the option pursued through the planning day and the four month period of 'grace'. The data collected at that point showed that there was still insufficient improvement in performance and other action was then necessary. This brought into focus the underlying value in cohesive staff relations that Simon obviously held strongly. As a result, he moved to place the HOD on diminished work performance because her actions were considered to be having negative effects on the performance of the teaching staff. Again, as in Case Account (a) the greater good for the greater number prevailed, notwithstanding the surgical operation the HOD needed. Consequentialist ethics therefore, was the source of the final decision and the value at its core was staff teaching effectiveness. Again, as in the first Case Account, when there were likely to be effects on staff and ultimately students, a hard line was taken.

The third Case Account I use involves a difficult member of staff and a situation not uncommon in schools where principals have the authority to grant leave.

Case Account (c). 'Holding a Gun at Your Head'

Lou Adams is the principal of a large government secondary school. He describes the issue in the following way:

> I'm not sure how popular I was with one of my staff members recently. She's a very committed mathematics teacher, and has been with us for two years. She wanted to go on a holiday with a girlfriend for the first term next year. It was to be unpaid leave but I couldn't replace her. So I didn't approve her leave.

He explained the factors that influenced his decision as follows:

> I took into account that she had been a very conscientious teacher and a good staff member. I also took into account that she taught Maths and that if I didn't approve the leave she'd probably resign and get a position in a private school. I also had to be careful about the messages I would send out.

In an interview to discuss the application, Lou pointed out to the teacher that while the trip would be very good for her personally, he believed that the continuity of teaching for the kids was more important. He explained that she was asking for leave to take a holiday, not sick leave, not maternity leave nor stress leave. He also explained that he would not be able to replace her. The next day the teacher submitted her resignation, whereupon Lou immediately arranged for another meeting with her. He reversed his decision and approved her leave. He explained his decision as follows:

> I made it clear to the teacher that I didn't believe that she had a really valid reason for leave. Nevertheless, she had been a very conscientious teacher and I said that I wanted her to stay in the government system. Basically I reversed my decision because I believed that she was a good Math teacher, and knowing that Mathematics teachers are so hard to get in government schools, I would have hated to lose her to a private school.

DISCUSSION

This case brings decisions based on three ethical theories into play. For the principal's initial decision, he sought recourse to the bureaucratic rules relating to leave, namely that unpaid leave is given to those in need for bereavement, personal illness (when sick leave has been exhausted), maternity or family support. Unpaid leave for a holiday was not normally considered justifiable. When decisions are based on rules or procedures and justified by them, they are consistent with deontological (or duties based) ethical theory. However, the teacher reacted as the principal suspected she might and handed in her resignation. The reversal of the decision was based on a combination of consequentialist ethics and an ethic of care. Allowing her to go meant that he would maintain a relationship with a good teacher in the future and that her expertise would not be lost to schools such as his. It appears that his overriding value was loyalty to his sector of education or perhaps it was a strong antipathy towards his competitors in the private school sector. Why he chose the deontological route in the first place, when he ultimately acceded to the request is open to debate. His change of heart would have been as likely to send out a 'message' to others more unfavourable than the initial decision not to approve the leave. Was his decision a good example of leading for leaning? The answer in the short-term is 'No' as students' interests did not figure at all in the outcome. In the longer-term, the answer may be 'Yes' because a good Mathematics teacher would not be lost to government school children.

What we learn from the three cases dealing with difficult or under-performing staff is that there is no guaranteed right response to ethical issues. Nevertheless, there is evidence when a hard line on staff performance is taken, that it is the interests of other staff members and students which prevail. However, the third Case Account points to some of the 'fallout' that is possible when decisions are changed or reversed in the interests of one or other of the parties.

Having addressed the most difficult type of ethical issues faced by principals, I move now to discuss a second set of troublesome matters. These deal with the fair and equitable allocation of school resources, decisions which are directly connected with teaching and learning.

THE FAIR AND EQUITABLE ALLOCATION OF RESOURCES

In educational environments particularly in secondary schools where subject departments are often in competition with each other for their share of school budgets, the school leader needs to be seen as dealing fairly with all. The following Case Accounts show how three principals handle the matter. I provide a discussion of these cases after the presentation of all three.

Case Account (d). 'Transparent Budget Processes'

Phil Jacobs is the principal of a large secondary school. He is acutely aware that the processes used in determining the budget are often the subject of argument in schools. Phil explains how he handles this issue:

> When we're allocating resources, I have a process in my school where other people make most of the decisions about where funds should be spent. I just monitor allocations and expenditure to make sure there's equity. I make sure the process is such that it's very transparent. The Heads of Department and co-ordinators put their priorities down and we all sit around a table and hash it out. I'm just the Devil's Advocate who is prepared to argue with everyone. When it gets really tight and they're getting down to the priorities they really want, that's when I play the Devil's Advocate. That's how I manage the process by making it open, and everyone knows what's going on and everyone's got a copy of everyone else's priorities. So no one can say, "Hey, we didn't know about this.

Case Account (e). 'Open and Collaborative Budget Processes'

Brad Lennon is the principal of a large secondary school in a low socio-economic area. Like many principals, Brad feels that some of the hardest issues at his school are in allocating resources. This is partly because the school does not have a great deal of discretionary funding from the government and partly because it is unable to demand too much of its parent body. In his words:

> We can't ask parents for any exorbitant contributions here - say $60 - $70 per year. That's the upper limit, and that has caused some difficulty for many parents.

Brad also reported that every three years he undertakes a complete budget review to ensure that particular patterns of resource allocation do not become entrenched. He does this through a survey of priorities followed by open discussions in which "everything is up for grabs".

He argues that 'consensus building' is one of the hardest roles for a Principal and it comes into stark relief whenever there are conflicts over budget allocation. Many teachers and Heads of Department defend their territory vigorously and parents criticise particular allocations from the point of view of their children's subject choices. At the end of the day, Brad says that it is the Principal who needs a defensible resource allocation process and this is more likely to occur when the process is "open and collaborative". And as Brad says:

> This means that sometimes my views get 'rolled' because someone has greater knowledge than I have. For example, we've just spent approximately $40,000 on new photocopiers. I've got a Registrar here with more expertise in this sort of area than anyone else, so I was able to stand right back from that allocation decision. That's the sort of shared leadership I'm trying to get.

Case Account (f). 'Neither Grace nor Favour'

Van Debden is the principal of a primary school. Van believes that the allocation of funds to different sections of the school exercises the minds of all principals.

He asks: "How should this be done?" and describes his approach as follows:

> All the time I'm trying to come up with a better budgeting model. But you know, I am definitely not a person who sits here and allocates money on a grace and favour basis. There is a finance committee made up of the Heads of Department and therefore the school community sees this group as being empowered and having ownership

of the budget process. Now you could say, *well that's a very cunning way of shifting the blame from yourself.* But I believe that it's a question of my commitment to valuing people and to enrolling them in the distribution of our resources.

DISCUSSION

In the three cases above, each Principal sought to share the decision-making process so that resource allocation was seen as collaborative, consensual and transparent. Avoiding being placed in a position where patronage or special pleading are the bases upon which funds are allocated was considered essential by all three leaders. Indeed the sharing of responsibility for the determination of priorities and collective decisions about resource usage seem to be valued strategies more likely to produce decisions which are perceived as 'fair' by the school community. Moreover, because a committee is involved, teacher and student needs are more likely to be in the foreground. At the same time, the engagement of groups of staff members in this process is felt to be an important way of connecting middle managers and teachers to significant aspects of the school's operations. Moreover, the lessening of frequently felt tensions over budgeting and funds allocation creates conditions of trust within a school community. By opening the process to many more eyes than those of the Principal, the ethics of school money management are enhanced.

Although it could appear as though these three principals might be 'ducking' budget responsibility by giving it to others, each has retained a key role which allows an ongoing contribution to credible fiscal processes. For one, it is a probing role as Devil's Advocate, for the second it is the difficult task of 'consensus building' while for the third, it is the review and development of the school's budgeting model. How widespread the use of shared leadership for resource allocation decisions is, is unknown, but it seems to offer an approach which has the capacity to take the 'heat' out of what has often been regarded as a principal's annual nightmare. More importantly, by connecting key members of staff with the school's finances, the principal is showing faith in his or her colleagues' abilities to produce decisions which are in staff and student interests. A much stronger sense of ownership and potential commitment to the school's priorities are therefore likely to result.

Whilst the allocation of resources will always test the approach to decision-making taken by principals, funding for staff professional development creates its own share of troublesome decisions.

LEADERSHIP FOR LEARNING: SOME ETHICAL CONNECTIONS

JUST PROVISION FOR STAFF PROFESSIONAL LEARNING

In this part of the chapter I provide two case accounts involving the expenditure of funds on staff professional development followed by a discussion of the decisions taken.

Case Account (g). 'Paid Professional Development'

Robbie Robertson is the principal of a large secondary school. He recognises that supporting particular staff members to attend professional development activities can pose problems. This is particularly so when fees are involved. Robbie described the following situation after the recent appointment of his registrar:

> This was a tricky one. The registrar wrote me a letter and said she wanted me to send her on a public sector management course. It was $4000. That was a "big ask" when you look at the dollars in a professional development bucket in a school this size. I said to myself, "I applied to do this course last year and the Department wouldn't pay for me. So, I decided I would not be paying for her."

> This was a natural response. Then I thought that I shouldn't stop anyone else because of my negative experiences. So, I gave it some serious thought. I took it home and talked to my wife about it and I spoke to a couple of colleagues. I then went through in my mind how I might justify sending her by asking myself some questions. Did she need to have a greater level of skill because our school was amalgamating with another and would this course provide her with those skills? I rang a couple of other principals and the advice from my colleagues was negative.

> Then I was in a quandary. I rang the Public Sector Management Commission to get its view, which of course was positive. So one view was pushing me towards saying yes but other information was pushing me to say no.

> Eventually I had to decide. I wrote back to the registrar and thanked her for her memo saying that I was looking into it and that I was hopeful to be able to support her. I said that I was going to explore the content of the course to see if it would meet her needs. I did this formally because she had given me a formal note. When I had gathered more data, I realised that the course wasn't going to meet her needs. So I spoke to her about my concerns and what other courses

were around. I also indicated that I didn't have any problems putting significant funds towards her professional development because I felt that she did require some assistance to develop the high level skills needed in our new circumstances.

However, she decided that she would not proceed and I wondered if I had helped her to reach her decision. In the end I didn't actually have to say no. I think that consciously or unconsciously, I worked the two of us towards that decision.

DISCUSSION

As can be seen from the account above, the principal was faced with an issue which took some time to resolve. He wrestled with his own intuitive view before setting it aside as he sought views from others. In fact, he forced himself to take a contrary position as he gathered information about the usefulness of the proposed program. Eventually, his tactics enabled the registrar to withdraw her request based on the information her principal had been able to assemble. This case shows how time consuming such a decision can be. It might well be argued therefore, that the principal should have 'bitten the bullet' and withheld approval right at the outset. In short he could have run with his intuition. That he did not was probably due to his concern for a working relationship which would be critical as they moved to amalgamate two schools. Automatically, he appeared to be employing an ethic of care as the backdrop to his approach. Was the decision just? In the circumstances, it seems that both parties concluded that it was.

Case Account (h). 'The Weekend Retreat'

Katherine Vincent had been newly appointed as the principal of a large primary school. She had an administration team consisting of two deputies and a registrar. She had been considering whether to take this team away for a strategic planning weekend led by an outside facilitator. Allocating and justifying the expenditure of funds on an exercise for administrators alone troubled her. At the time, she commented:

So we were going to take the administration team away for a weekend for which the accommodation costs would be about $2000. I also looked at the price of a facilitator. The cost was going to be about $1000 per day. I had to decide if we would have the facilitator for two days. But the perception, if it got out to the community and to the staff, would be that I was going to 'blow' $2000 on a facilitator. I tried to balance up the benefit to the administration team of the weekend and to the school long-term, against the flak that I could get from the staff and community on one night away for $4000. They could have perceived it as a 'booze up'.

Katherine eventually decided that she would take the administration team away for its planning weekend, but not before she had discussed the matter with her district director. She did this for a number of reasons, but mainly to get an external view on her decision. In her own words:

> I just explained my concern to him that some staff members wouldn't understand a retreat's worth. And he said to me, "Well are you going to share the outcomes with them?" That helped me think of ways to make sure I avoided any problems. So I wrote an article in the newsletter to parents. I told the staff up front. I told them why we would be going on the weekend. I said we would communicate the outcomes at meetings. I told the community and I was honest. I told them I would be paying a facilitator.

Katherine concluded that she always felt better about a decision about which she was honest, where she didn't have to 'whitewash' something or put a 'spin' on it.

DISCUSSION

The outcome from this case begs the question of Katherine, "Are there circumstances when she does have to 'put a spin' on something or 'whitewash' it? I assume from her words that there are. But space does not allow me to list some of the situations in which a principal's ethical elasticity might be stretched. The case also suggests that there will always be situations in which principals have control of discretionary professional development funds and where they have the final decision on expenditure. Was the decision to take the school's management team on the retreat just? The fact that the principal was honest does not necessarily mean that a just decision was reached. More information about the proportion of the professional development budget taken by the retreat would have been necessary, as would information about the claims on the budget made by teachers. After all, the usual purpose of a professional development budget is to ensure that opportunities are available to teachers to improve their knowledge and skills for the benefit of their students. A justification on these grounds, rather than on the basis of 'honesty' would have provided a stronger rationale for the retreat for all concerned.

In summing up this part of the chapter, it is instructive to note that the two cases of funding for professional development had the principal as the sole arbiter of the final decision. Other principals I have observed employ strategies involving groups of key teachers. Sharing the leadership and management of professional development funds with members of staff takes the onus off principals and subjects professional learning programs to peer review. Such a process makes allocations transparent and the outcome of consistent procedures rather than individual preference. In many institutions, the leader is able to withhold a limited quantum of funds for strategic purposes or for contingencies. No one would deny the need for a principal to have the wherewithal to respond to unanticipated professional development or planning issues. But in the interests of managing perceptions about the fairness of allocations, peer review and decision-making processes for the bulk of a school's professional development budget, are desirable.

DIFFERENT DECISION-MAKING ROUTES

In this part of the chapter, I examine what a number of Principals do as they work towards decisions which they feel are ethically defensible. In the Case Accounts cited so far, different routes to resolution were followed. These 'routes' can be regarded as strategies or tactics, but however they are viewed, my analysis of how leaders reach decisions tells me that they all start from a 'first impulse' or intuitive position upon learning about a particular situation. There is also evidence that this 'impulse' arises spontaneously from the values each individual holds. The important attribute that principals, as final arbiters need, is the acknowledgement that their 'first impulse' should be tested in the light of other views and information relevant to the case. The spontaneous part of this process is non-rational, the testing part must be. When this is understood, principals are able to adopt the open-ness of stance or cognitive flexibility (Leithwood, 2005) that is essential to perceptions of fairness amongst those who have vested interests in a decision (Harris & Chapman, 2002). Indeed, there is supportive research showing that school leaders build trust and respect for their decisions when they enrol trusted and respected others during the decision-making process (Duignan, 2003; Harris & Chapman, 2002).

I use three examples from principals themselves to illustrate the 'first impulse' starting point for ethical decisions and the follow-up strategies contemplated.

LEADERSHIP FOR LEARNING: SOME ETHICAL CONNECTIONS

Case Account (i). 'Eating Healthy Food'

Lorraine Smith's first impulse when confronted with her new school's Tuck Shop or Canteen inventory was to get rid of the junk foods on offer. In her words:

> The Tuckshop presented me with a really worrying issue because junk food is all that is sold. It's full of fat and sugar. I would never have believed when I was a young mother 20 years ago that junk food at school would be difficult to fix. I just can't believe it. The money rolls in from its sale, and we desperately need the money. But so far, I've done nothing. Making a change would involve a lot of talk with the community. It would involve a lot of talk with the Parents and Citizens Association and other parent groups. But, I felt I needed to build relationships first. So that's how I have justified my lack of action after four months in the school. All I have done is to drop a few little hints at meetings about healthy food. That's all I've done! It's going to be a very hard one for me. But I think healthy eating is very important.

Case Account (j). 'Being Ethically Pragmatic'

Helene Charles had been appointed to a fairly traditional primary school, one without much internal student achievement monitoring. She believed that this was a situation needing change even though the teachers felt very uncomfortable about it. After all, they argued, on external tests, the kids' results had been pretty good for a long time.

For Helene, the ethical issue was how she could press for a more professional assessment program without jeopardising staff morale. As she says:

> It's a balance between people's comfort and where we should be going. Nothing is absolutely black or white. However, I think you know what's the right thing to do and that's the direction you are striving to achieve. Sometimes you can't get there as quickly as you would like. Sometimes you've got to go in the direction but be pragmatic by lowering the benchmark a little bit. Okay, I'll give in on that part but I won't give in on the direction that I'm setting.

Case Account (k). 'Depersonalising a Decision'

Sam Panini is a Principal who has recognised the limitations of his 'first impulses' even though he knows that these frame his immediate reaction to most issues involving difficult staff members. He admits that the personal will always intrude but he argues that:

> What you have to do is de-personalise it. It is very easy to say, 'I really can't stand that person. She gives me a bad time. Wouldn't it be great to get rid of her. That's the initial temptation, absolutely. My ethics, my conscience and my Catholic guilt come in when I ask myself, 'Am I doing the right thing?' You have to have a basis for decision-making, and the basis can't be a personal preference when you are a school Principal. Therefore you go to a question such as, 'Is this person contributing or not contributing to the general good of the school?'

Case Account (l). 'The Right Decision'

Katherine Jordan is the principal of a primary school. She says that she does not have any problems in making decisions. But according to Katherine, "making the right decision is another matter". However, she says that she "knows" when the right decision has been made.

> When the decision feels right, I think you feel right. I think inside you say, this is the right decision. I make mistakes like everybody else. But when I make a decision, I make it thinking I am doing the right thing by whatever parties are involved. And so when I have made the decision, I don't feel badly.

Case Account (m). 'A Cooling Off Period'

Greta Hillbreck is the principal of a primary school. She received advice from a colleague that her school had been openly criticised by an educational advisor at a recent meeting of school principals. She recalls the incident and her initial feelings:

> I was initially furious. I was really angry. I thought the advisor had been stupid and unethical and that I would 'have a go at her.'

After this initial reaction, Greta paused and reflected on the situation. She knew that she should not deal with a situation like this when she was angry. She decided to 'sleep on it' and give herself time to gather relevant information. She decided to find out what other principals at the meeting knew as she had heard only one opinion. She felt that she needed to make sure that the facts were right before deciding on her course of action. She also decided to ask the education advisor to come and see her to ask what she had said.

"I decided", Greta reflected, "to give myself time to cool down in order to deal with the matter in a rational manner."

DISCUSSION

The four cases I have described show clearly that the personal views of principals cannot be divorced from the situations they encounter. Ethical maturity is in evidence however, when school leaders put aside their intuitive responses to ensure that a more measured journey towards a decision is taken. That measured journey is aided by delaying tactics, by changing tasks, by accepting that there are steps along the way to an ultimate goal, but in all cases, the 'first impulse' of the leader is put on hold while broader perspectives on the ethical issue are canvassed. That said, my analysis tells me that it is unlikely that an experienced Principal will implement a decision with which he or she does not feel at personal ease. Without the decision feeling right, fair, just and good, it is too difficult to sleep soundly at night.

SUSTAINING LEADERS OF LEARNING

In the final part of the chapter I argue briefly that there are at least three support mechanisms to which principals should have access if they are to sustain themselves emotionally and professionally throughout their careers as leaders of learning.

First they need access to a mentor for conversations about personal and professional values (Fullan, 2002; Southworth & Weindling, 2002). It is through disclosure in the company of a respected colleague that positions are challenged, reinforced or forged anew. Without this kind of access, it is difficult for school leaders to develop the necessary understanding of their own values (Begley, 2006) which are the source of their 'first impulses' or their intuition about what is ethical.

Second, they should have well developed avenues for immediate support when urgent ethical issues arise. Our research has shown (Dempster, Freakley & Parry, 2001) that this is most often found in larger schools in the principal's administrative team. But it can be found in respected senior officers or in trusted partners or colleagues at a distance from the school. What is essential is a network of support on demand so that the Principal is not alone in tackling what has to be done to deal with troublesome matters fairly and expeditiously. This leadership support does not come in a package on appointment. It has to be deliberately acquired, because without it, principals, as a group, more so than most, are susceptible to the debilitating effects of emotional stress (Lacey, 2006).

Third, they need opportunities for reflection (Begley, 2006; Gurr, Drysdale & Mulford, 2005) in the company of others who face similar circumstances so that experiences can be shared, insights gained and future practice enhanced. These professional learning opportunities should also be used to bring ethical theory and practical resolution together. Understanding what is theoretically possible acts as a helpful predictor of future action and can provide warm comfort to leaders trying to remain calm, patient and rational while others around them are emotional and irrational. An understanding of ethical theory in action provides a strong platform for the kind of informed decision-making essential to long-term leadership.

CONCLUSION

This chapter has used case accounts provided by principals themselves to examine a number of difficult ethical issues as they attempt to establish some of the important conditions for students' learning. It has shown that while ethical theory can be used as a source for different resolutions, there will always remain alternative outcomes that are equally warranted in the eyes of one or other of the affected parties. How a decision is reached by an ethically mature leader is almost as important as the decision itself. Different strategies or tactics provide opportunities for all voices to be heard while putting aside the principals' personal preference or 'first impulse'. Finally, to ensure that principals are able to sustain themselves, knowing that the next ethical encounter is 'just around the corner', it is imperative that they have mentors and support networks ever ready to offer assistance. Leading learning isn't easy but part of the solution is found in ethically defensible decisions that help to create just conditions for staff and students.

REFERENCES

Begley, P. (2006). Self-knowledge, capacity and sensitivity: prerequisites to authentic leadership by school principals. *Journal of Educational Administration, 44*(6), 570–589.

Begley P., & Johansson, O. (Eds.). (2003). *The ethical dimensions of school leadership.* Dordrecht, Boston: Kluwer Academic Publishers.

Dempster, N., Freakley, M., & Parry, L. (2001). The ethical climate of public schooling under new public management. *International Journal of Leadership in Education, 4*(1), 1–12.

Duignan, P. (2003, September). *Formation of capable, influential and authentic leaders for times of uncertainty.* Paper presented at the Australian Principals' Association Conference, Adelaide.

Lacey, K. (2006). *Exploring sustainability in school leadership*. Jolimont, Melbourne: Incorporated Association of Registered Teachers of Victoria.

Matters P. N. (2005). Future school leaders: Who are they and what are they doing? Expect the unexpected! In P. L. Jeffrey (Compiled), *AARE 2005 international education research conference papers* [Conference of the Australian Association for Research in Education, December 2005]. Melbourne: AARE.

Ehrich, L. C., Cranston, N., & Kimber, M. (2005). Academic managers and ethics: a question of making the 'right' decision. In A. Brew & C. Asmar (Eds.), *Higher education in a changing world: Proceedings of the 2005 Annual International Conference of the Higher Education Research and Development Society of Australasia (HERDSA)* (pp. 133–140). NSW, Australia: The University of Sydney.

Fullan, M. (2002). The role of leadership in the promotion of knowledge management in schools. *Teachers and Teaching: Theory and practice, 8*(3/4), 409–419.

Gurr, D., Drysdale, L., & Mulford, B. (2005). Successful Principal Leadership: Australian case studies. *Journal of Educational Administration, 43*(6), 539–551.

Groundwater-Smith, S., & Sachs, J. (2002). The activist professional and the reinstatement of trust. *Cambridge Journal of Education, 32*(3), 341–358.

Hargreaves, A. (2000). Four ages of professionalism and professional learning. *Teachers and Teaching: Theory and Practice, 6*(2), 151–182.

Harris, A., & Chapman, C. (2002). *Effective leadership in schools facing challenging circumstances.* London: National College of School Leadership.

Leithwood, K. (2005). Understanding successful school leadership: Progress on a broken front. *Journal of Educational Administration, 43*(6), 619–629.

Leithwood, K., & Riehl, C. (2003). *What do we already know about successful school leadership?* AERA Division: A task force on developing research in educational leadership. Retrieved from http//www.cepa.gse.rutgers.edu

Organisation for Economic Cooperation and Development (OECD), Centre for Educational Research and Innovation. (2002). *Education at a glance: OECD indicators* (2002 ed.). Paris: Author.

Silins, H., & Mulford, B. (2002). Leadership and school results. In K. Leithwood & P. Halinger (Eds.), *Second international handbook of educational leadership and administration* (pp. 561–612). Dordrecht: Kluwer.

Southworth, G., & Weindling, D. (2002). *Leadership in large primary schools: Executive Report.* London: Esmee Fairbairn Foundation.

AFFILIATIONS

Neil Dempster
Griffith University,
Australia

DAVID FROST AND SUE SWAFFIELD

CHAPTER 6

Researching LfL through an International Collaborative Project

School effectiveness research showed us that the ethos of the school can make a difference to learning outcomes and later that positive leadership can create the organisational conditions associated with effectiveness (MacBeath & Mortimore, 2001). However, at the beginning of this century there was still a great deal to be understood about the relationship between leadership and learning. A number of researchers in the fields of educational leadership and school improvement were expressing frustration at policy initiatives that seemed to be supported by school effectiveness research. Those in the English speaking countries who had already experienced the performativity culture and the new managerialism that it supports exchanged their views with those in the Scandinavian countries who were fearing that they would be led down the same path. The global trend was towards the reduction of the concept of learning to successful performance in standardised tests and the reduction of the concept of leadership to the implementation of national reforms by headteachers or principals exercising 'firm leadership'. It was time to rethink what we meant by learning, what we meant by leadership and the relationship between the two, particularly in educational contexts. A series of informal conversations prepared the way for a research project dedicated to the exploration of these fundamental questions.

DEMOCRATIC LEARNING: THE CHALLENGE TO SCHOOL EFFECTIVENESS

The Carpe Vitam Leadership for Learning project[1] launched during the 15th International Congress for School Effectiveness and Improvement (ICSEI) at Copenhagen in January 2002 had two important characteristics: first it would meet the challenge of a performativity culture by examining school leadership and its relationship to learning across different cultures and national systems; second, it would conduct itself according to a set of shared democratic values. These values rested on a commitment to distributed forms of leadership and learning. At the ICSEI conference researchers from the UK, USA, Norway, Denmark and Austria were able to coalesce around this expression of values and they were subsequently joined by like-minded colleagues from Greece and Australia.

From the outset the project was conceived as an alternative to the dominant school effectiveness paradigm which, together with neo-liberalist ideology underpinned the increasingly global standards agenda. We wanted to construct an antidote to the approach to the influence of 'new public management' (Ferlie, Ashburner, & Pettigrew, 1996; Moos, 2004) where community members are reframed as consumers and educational purposes are reduced to measurable outcomes that are subject to target-setting. We were sympathetic to those critics (see for example Elliott, 1996; Fielding, 1997) who argued that the emphasis on measurable outcomes in school effectiveness research supports a narrow view of educational purposes and the desperate pursuit of test scores distorts the concept of learning. The Carpe Vitam project would enable us to explore leadership, learning and their inter-relationship independently of this dominant discourse, providing schools with encouragement to explore alternative perspectives.

INTERNATIONAL COLLABORATION

The research team consisted of university academics from cities in seven countries: Australia, Austria, Denmark, Greece, Norway, UK and USA. There were representatives from both Seattle on the west coast of America, and Trenton, New Jersey on the east coast. These eight sites did not constitute a sample in the normal sense of the term; rather they were included because of the personal connections made through past collaborations in which John MacBeath was a common factor and because of shared values and priorities. The particular characteristics of these team members and the nature of the schools to which they had access played a significant part in shaping the project. The Danes and Norwegians for example had been experiencing the creep of 'new public management' and saw the project as an opportunity to identify leadership practice that accords with their strongly entrenched democratic traditions. They wanted to articulate a vision of schooling that was based on Dewey's ideas about education and citizenship before they were swept away by the force of 'the global trend of market orientation and standardisation' (Moos & Møller, 2003, p. 360). In contrast, colleagues from New Jersey were motivated in part by the need to bring fresh thinking to the seemingly intractable problems of the urban public schools that have become the victims of the significant opting out of the state system on the part of those parents who have the economic power to do so (MacBeath, 2004). The fact that there were eight different policy contexts represented within the project enabled us to use contrast as a resource in our research and learning although we did not see the project as belonging within the comparative tradition per se.

Members of this international research team brought to the project their experience of work in leadership and school improvement in eight quite different contexts as well as different intellectual traditions and research methodologies. Our deliberations as a team were necessarily challenging: our stated values ruled out the imposition of a standardised methodology for example and required a great deal of flexibility and sensitivity to cherished ways of working. Our premise was that the very different nature of these sites would of itself generate a cross-national dialogue and a quality of collaboration that would enhance our understanding of the connections between leadership and learning. We sought to embrace the differences in language and culture rather than see them as problems.

Our regular research team meetings held in a variety of cities around the world were characterised by discussion of the developing policy contexts in the participating countries. We also discussed data gathering strategies such as the surveys we conducted twice during the life of the project. The design of these instruments and their translation into different languages was particularly challenging because terms such as 'middle manager' that are commonplace in the UK are not recognised in some of the other countries. As the project matured, the focus on data gathering strategies tended to be overshadowed by discussion about, and detailed planning of, conferences and other networking events. This discursive process based on critical dialogue was the key to the success of the project and is discussed in more detail below.

AN ECLECTIC AND EMERGENT METHODOLOGY

The values that had shaped the conception of the project led inevitably to the belief that whatever insight could be gained had to be the product of co-inquiry: researchers and practitioners working together to test out ideas in the challenging contexts of schools. Each of the eight local research teams invited three urban schools to join the project as active participants on the basis that they were also committed to the values we had expressed at the outset of the project.

A key element of the project design was the allocation of a 'critical friend' to each school. Their role was to establish a dialogue with key players in the school and provide support for innovation and the development of practice that corresponds with the espoused project values. Drawing on the experience of other projects in which critical friends had worked alongside researchers (MacBeath, Schratz, Meuret, & Jakobsen, 2000;

Swaffield, 2004), the intention was to build a relationship of trust such that teachers would feel supported in their analysis of current practice and feel confident in venturing into new ways of thinking about their roles as learners and leaders.

The commitment to the democratic values we had subscribed to at the outset of the project led inevitably to ongoing debate about methodology and the continuous reshaping of our strategies and techniques. We came to describe the methodology of the project as 'eclectic and emergent' (Frost & Swaffield, 2004), one that reflected the differing research traditions which each research team brought to their work with schools, but also our commitment to sharing our practice as researchers and to collective learning about research methodology as we progressed deeper into the process. A key theme of our discussions was the relationship between knowledge and action. Some members of the team had worked within the action research tradition; some were wedded to the concept of 'co-inquiry', others preferred to talk of 'action learning'.

In spite of this diversity, the project began with a degree of agreement about common research strategies across the eight sites, but leaving plenty of room for local diversity. The common data gathering at the start of the project included a questionnaire administered to school leaders, teachers and students, a series of interviews with principals and teachers, pupil and principal shadowings and focus group meetings with parents. In addition the schools were encouraged to generate their own 'portrait' as a means of sharing information about themselves with other participating schools and as a process of self-reflection and evaluation (Fischman, 2001; Lawrence-Lightfoot & Hoffmann-Davis, 1997; Schratz & Löffler-Anzböck, 2004). This rich package of data served a number of purposes including making an assessment of leadership practice and organisational capacity within the participating schools, supporting each school's developmental endeavours, and feeding into the discursive process afforded through the international conferences. The data were also drawn upon later in the project to inform our meta-analysis.

The questionnaire told us about the differences in perceptions about the school as it is and how people would like it to be. The instrument had a double-sided structure, with each of its forty or so items requiring two responses – one indicating a perception of importance or value, the other indicating the respondent's perception of the extent of actual practice (MacBeath, Frost, & Swaffield, 2005). The exercise thus constituted a 'tin opener' (MacBeath, 2002), the data providing starting points for dialogue within and across schools, turning the many areas of ambiguity to positive benefit in exploring consensus and acknowledging difference.

Although these common data gathering strategies had been agreed it was understood that local teams would decide how best to support the schools and document the development of practice. In spite of the variation in approach at local level the coherence of the project depended on the method of analysis. Our challenge was to achieve sufficient comparability in methodology to allow for a valid meta-analysis. In order to do this we resolved to share accounts of our practice as researchers as we progressed through the project so that we might become sufficiently conversant with each other's methodologies to borrow and adapt research tools and strategies. During the final stages of the project we produced reflective accounts of our methodologies in each site and these were judged against an agreed set of criteria for robustness. Final reports from each site enabled the Cambridge team to conduct a meta-analysis that informed the theoretical insights and outcomes we presented for debate in our final international conference.

It would be misleading however to see the Carpe Vitam LfL project as purely a data-led research project. This project's most distinctive characteristic is the way it provided the stimulus and scaffolding for discourse about leadership and learning across national and cultural boundaries.

THE PROJECT AS A DISCURSIVE PROCESS

The project was fomented in the context of an international critical debate about policy and practice. Shared democratic values underpinned a collaborative design in which researchers and practitioners from across the world sought to reclaim and reframe the concepts of leadership and learning; the link between the two would be explored experientially within the constraints of the global policy environment and the challenges of urban schooling. In order to pursue these goals we needed strategies and tools.

A key strategy was a series of international conferences hosted by the research partners. These were typically three-day residential conferences for all the researchers, representatives from all of the participating schools, and the critical friends. Ideas were introduced through a series of presentations by visiting speakers including Lorna Earl, Louise Stoll, Archie McGlyn, Judith Warren Little, Mats Ekholm, Per Fibæk Laursen, Ciaran Sugrue, David Perkins and by members of the research team. Practitioners displayed materials depicting aspects of their schools and presented their perspectives on leadership for learning. Workshops, sometimes with national groups, sometimes with cross-national groups, enabled participants to engage in the process of reflection.

As the process gathered momentum there were fewer expert presentations and more sharing of practice and debate about values, ideas and principles. These discussions were structured and scaffolded using tools such as the 'desk top graffiti' or 'vignettes of practice'. Practitioners began to form links that led to networking between schools in very different places. Some teachers provided glimpses of practice that were seized upon by other participants and taken back to their schools to be adapted and used for transformational purposes. Part of each international conference was a programme of visits to local schools to investigate leadership for learning practice at first hand, an activity that became increasingly structured as the project progressed.

At the final conference in Athens we were able to clarify and codify what we had learnt, and debate the finer points of our conceptual framework, as well as continue the sharing of practice and the forming of collaborative links.

The project could be viewed as a discursive process, a form of inquiry that was nourished by theoretical frameworks and by the gathering of data, but one which is essentially dialogical. The dialogue took place not only in the tightly structured international conferences but also at local and regional levels when schools met to share practice and, in some cases, engage in joint work. In the London context, for example, the three schools joined forces to organise a professional development day that involved all the staff from each school in a day of workshops about learning. Ironically perhaps some of this local dialogue took place during the international conferences which provided opportunities to spend quality time in deep reflective discussions with colleagues from the same school - something which seemed difficult to do in the busyness of everyday life.

Dialogue also took place when individuals or small groups made links with other project schools in a different countries, often involving visits. For example, all of the teachers from one of the Danish schools spent a week with the three London schools; members of the senior leadership team from a UK associate school in Stevenage visited Trenton and led workshops for teachers both in the school and on a training course for aspiring principals. Such face-to-face networking is understandably limited by the constraints of intercontinental travel but it was augmented by the use of email through which teachers exchanged materials and accounts of practice. This tends to work best when people have already established personal relationships through face-to-face meetings. The electronic dimension was taken a stage further with a virtual conference in the final year of the project.

To say that the project involved dialogue on a number of different levels does not necessarily add up to a process that can be described as discourse.

The capacity to build a coherent set of ideas depended on a range of discursive activities that were nourished by both data and theory and that were shaped and structured through the careful and deliberate use of a range of tools and strategies. Our collective understandings were the product of this process. We did not see the dialogue as serving the purpose of the validation of the outcomes of data analysis, but rather we saw it as the process of meaning-making that was an essential characteristic of our methodology.

A key strategy that ran throughout this discursive process giving it focus and shape was the development of a set of principles for practice.

PRINCIPLES FOR PRACTICE

Part-way through the project we began to develop a set of principles for practice as a device to sharpen the focus of our collective reflection and clarify our understanding of leadership for learning. The idea of 'principles for practice' was loosely based on that of 'principles of procedure' (Stenhouse, 1975 after Peters, 1959). Principles of practice are statements in which values are embedded, and are sufficiently concrete to enable a group of people to clarify and refine their visions of ideal practice. It was emphatically not intended that the principles for practice should be used as a normative checklist against which to measure performance; rather they constitute an expression of pedagogical aims.

We presented the first draft of the principles at the beginning of the third international conference, held in Copenhagen. They provided a backdrop to the conference and were explicitly addressed in a series of workshops. Discussion activities were structured in a way that enabled everyone to critique the principles and contribute to their development. Through these workshops and subsequently through research team meetings and the virtual conference we were able to revise, re-order and re-word the principles for the final conference in Athens. At this conference the debate about the principles became more robust, incisive and critical, enabling the research team to develop a final version that reflects, as clearly as any such device can, a consensus within the project. The discursive process through which the principles came into being is indicated by the diagram in Figure 1. The discursive process depicted is grounded in democratic values and the moral purpose of education. The relationship between the principles, professional practice, data and theories is an iterative and interdependent one. The principles are not only an outcome of the project – an expression of our collective understanding about leadership for learning and our commitment to its realisation in practice – but also a tool to enable us to develop that understanding. They also provided the research team with an analytical tool used at the conclusion of the project as a framework for the meta-analysis of reports from each of the eight research sites.

Figure 1: Developing Principles for LfL Practice through a Discursive Process (MacBeath, Frost, Swaffield, & Waterhouse, 2006)

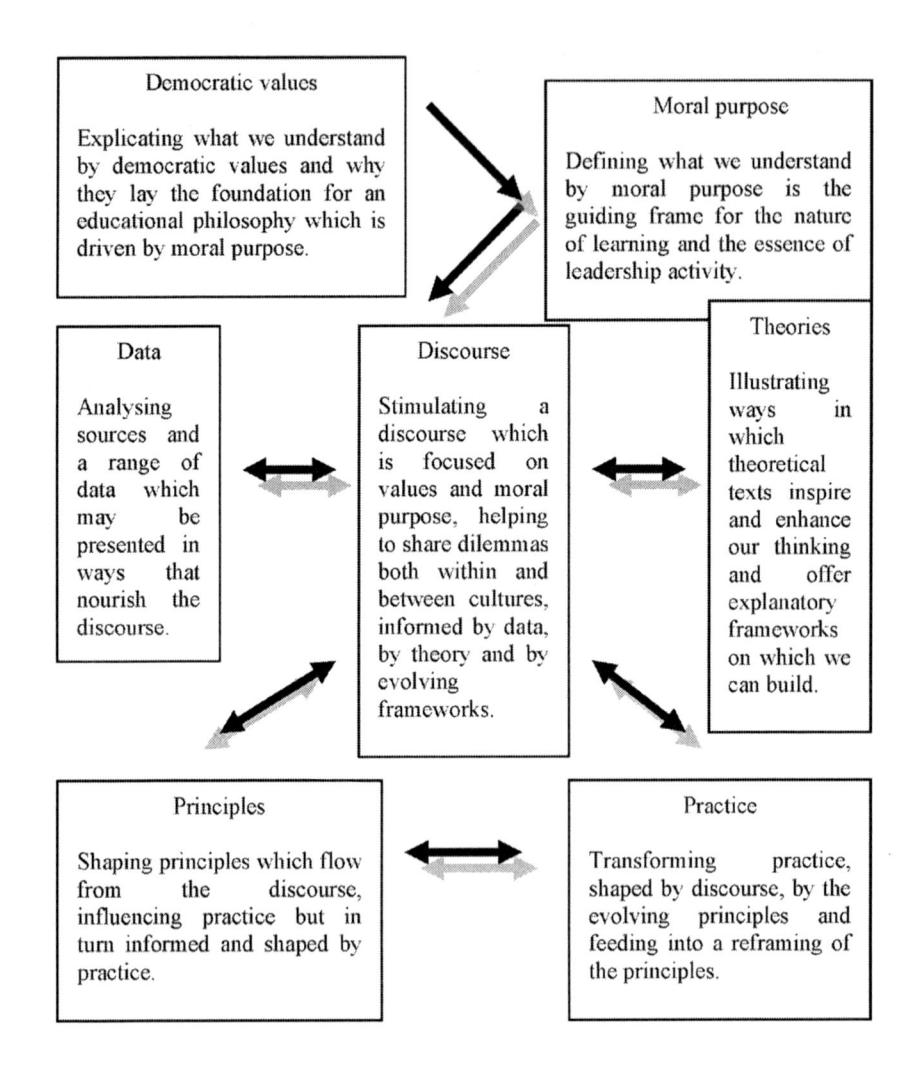

Democratic values

Explicating what we understand by democratic values and why they lay the foundation for an educational philosophy which is driven by moral purpose.

Moral purpose

Defining what we understand by moral purpose is the guiding frame for the nature of learning and the essence of leadership activity.

Data

Analysing sources and a range of data which may be presented in ways that nourish the discourse.

Discourse

Stimulating a discourse which is focused on values and moral purpose, helping to share dilemmas both within and between cultures, informed by data, by theory and by evolving frameworks.

Theories

Illustrating ways in which theoretical texts inspire and enhance our thinking and offer explanatory frameworks on which we can build.

Principles

Shaping principles which flow from the discourse, influencing practice but in turn informed and shaped by practice.

Practice

Transforming practice, shaped by discourse, by the evolving principles and feeding into a reframing of the principles.

The process through which we arrive at principles for practice is portrayed here through the grounding of values and moral purpose and the ways in which these nourish the discourse, helping to contextualise the data and inform the theory. All of these are portrayed as forms of activity, explicating, defining, stimulating, analysing, shaping and transforming – the essential elements of learning and of leadership.

THE PRINCIPLES

The principles for practice developed through the Carpe Vitam project are expressed in Figure 2 below as five broad statements, each of which is expanded by five or six more specific statements. The full statement of principles is included in the Appendix.

Figure 2: Principles for Practice – Five Statements

Principles for Practice – Five Statements

Leadership for learning practice involves:
    maintaining a focus on learning as an activity
    creating conditions favourable to learning as an activity
    creating a dialogue about leadership and learning
    the sharing of leadership
    a shared sense of accountability

It should be noted that the five principles are interrelated but presented as five separate statements to facilitate understanding and discussion. We now discuss each principle in outline, illustrating with data from the Carpe Vitam project schools.

MAINTAINING A FOCUS ON LEARNING AS AN ACTIVITY

This first principle is the one on which all others rest, and reflects a commitment to making learning the over-riding priority in school life. It may seem unnecessary to emphasise the central importance of learning, but the familiarity of the word and the different ways it is used can prove problematic. In the language of governments, learning is often taken as synonymous with attainment as measured by tests. In popular conception it is what happens in classrooms as the result of teaching, often with the idea of a curriculum being 'delivered' by a teacher and 'received' by pupils.

By contrast, our principles for practice are built on the idea of learning as an activity. This is not the purely cognitive activity of individual students, but also social activity involving all members of the school community in the widest possible range of transactions and locations. Learning is assumed to involve the development of understanding, practical capability, meta-cognitive awareness, and the ability to learn how to learn, as well as dispositions such as resilience and curiosity. Learning occurs in the flow of interaction among members of the learning community and therefore has social and emotional dimensions that are inseparable from the cognitive. This is where the connection between learning and leadership becomes so apparent, as learning is enhanced through opportunities to exercise leadership. For example, when children teach one another or collaborate to support each other's learning, the development and expression of human agency and moral purpose impels learning and discovery.

The word 'focus' in the expression of this first principle is key because, regardless of the national context, the everyday discourse within schools is shaped by policy pressures and by the demands of organisational convenience, so that learning can cease to be the main consideration. Maintaining the focus on learning has to be worked at and be the paramount concern of leadership. The project surveys clearly indicated that a commitment to maintaining a focus on learning grew in strength during the life of the project, but remained a challenge. Nevertheless, it is clear that working to maintain the focus on learning is profoundly satisfying and intrinsic to teachers' professional identity. Evidence from an Australian school, for example, indicates a developing enthusiasm for learning, stimulated by a professional discourse amongst the staff.

> ...we're actually talking about how kids are learning (and) talking about how we're learning in the classroom with the kids as well.

The effort to maintain the focus on learning came also from the systems in which schools operate. For example in the US East context, the District Superintendent adopted an explicit, district-wide goal that professional development should be focused directly on learning. He saw this as a tangible demonstration of his belief that conversations about learning on the part of administrators and teachers are important planks of a transformation strategy.

> We're also doing it in the contracts that we've negotiated ... increased time and opportunities built into the school day, for teachers to meet to facilitate dialogue and planning.

Principals played key roles in maintaining the focus on learning. There was evidence from the US West context for example which indicated how principals model learning, provide a vision of learning and manage systematic change. One principal was described as having a 'strong and definite focus on learning and how to meet the difference in disposition, orientation and learning preferences both of students and teachers'.

CREATING CONDITIONS FAVOURABLE TO LEARNING AS AN ACTIVITY

The second principle follows naturally from the first. If there is to be a focus on learning as activity, there is a need to work on the conditions that nurture this fragile entity and provide opportunities for the learning capacity to grow. This is as much about culture building as it is about the design of the physical environment and the use of appropriate pedagogic strategies.

Across the project teachers shared their knowledge, offered critical friendship to one another, critiqued students' work and observed in one another's classrooms. The development of cultures of trust and tolerance of difference enabled them to open up their practice to the scrutiny of others without feeling threatened. There was evidence from some project schools of deep learning conversations developing in open and critically friendly environments. It was possible to see how collaboration grows organically, and cultures are built from the bottom up. For example, an Austrian school reported that in the flow of everyday work like-minded teachers sought out allies, exchanging experiences and materials. However, gravitating towards attuned colleagues reduces the opportunities for engaging with those holding contrary value positions, different views of teaching and learning, and divergent practices. The leadership challenge is to be bold enough to invite conflict, believing that schools grow as much through vigorous debate as through easy consensus.

One of the Norwegian project schools was newly purpose-built to reflect the kind of learning that educators hoped would take place there. The open physical spaces were designed to encourage easy communication and informal conversations among staff and students, and to build the ethos of learning. In a London school the deputy headteacher pointed to the communal staffroom in which teachers from different departments worked side by side, exchanging ideas, 'sowing the seeds of more formal planning', and giving impetus to leading learning. How communication flows through a staff is a condition that underpins learning at student, teacher and senior leadership level. This was highlighted in one Australian school where it was said, prior to the arrival of the new principal, 'nobody knew how anyone did anything. It was all done by word of mouth, ad hoc and by the seat of your pants'. The recognition of this communication lacuna gave rise to trans-disciplinary learning teams, designed to increase the learning exchange across the school, recognising that changing the professional mindset is a necessary prelude to changing the student mindset. In the Second Chance School in Athens there were many opportunities for teachers and students to reflect on the nature, skills and processes of learning. For example, teachers meet weekly to discuss how students learn and to share problems, and seminars are organised to include other 'second chance' schools. Students have opportunities to focus on the 'how' of learning using tools that stimulate thinking and provoke learning conversations. Teachers routinely seek students' opinions on their learning and on how they think they can learn better.

Towards the end of the project the extent to which school cultures nurtured distributed learning was tested by the questionnaire item: *The culture of our school encourages everyone to be a learner*. Responses indicated considerable variation in perceptions of progress both between and within national contexts. For example in US East the variation was between 17 and 38 per cent while in Norway it ranged from 26 to 83 per cent. Data from interviews help to explain some of this variation. In the high scoring Norwegian school teachers reported that everyone was encouraged to exercise initiative and to take responsibility. This was made possible by senior leadership providing the scope for staff to share their thinking and to experiment with new ideas. In the other two schools teachers reported less support from the principal and senior leadership team in allowing proactive initiatives in leadership for learning.

CREATING A DIALOGUE ABOUT LEADERSHIP FOR LEARNING

The third principle lays emphasis on dialogue, whose Greek roots (dia logos) remind us of a particular kind of conversation – a search for shared meaning and common understanding. This principle is concerned with the link between leadership and learning which is fore-grounded when we go beyond the tacit, taken-for-granted assumptions about both leadership and learning and make our perceptions and beliefs about them visible and explicit. A powerful strategy to support this is collegial inquiry in which staff and students raise questions about pedagogy and gather data to fuel collective reflection. In many cases the Carpe Vitam project survey data provoked this kind of process but it was taken forward most powerfully where teachers and principals drew upon their partnerships with their local university and were engaged in award-bearing investigations leading to Certificates, Masters degrees and Doctorates.

Involvement in the Carpe Vitam project stimulated systematic reflection on the link between leadership and learning in other ways. For example in US East vice-principals from across the District were invited to participate in a programme of 'strategic inquiry' aimed at investigating how leadership and learning interact. Participants worked in teams visiting each others' schools and conducting a series of interviews and observations. A Greek principal described how the individual voices that had existed in the school before the Carpe Vitam project 'came together', and staff began to have systematic discussions about school improvement with a focus on learning and leadership. While much of what was said was not new, discussions brought to the fore latent ideas that were not only being discussed in new ways but accepted and applied in the classroom practice. Progress made was attributed in large part to the influence of the critical friend who acted as a catalyst for the school to discover, in the principal's words, 'the paradise that was actually around us'.

Whilst examples of dialogue about leadership for learning were quite rare, much more apparent was evidence of learning-centred dialogue in which the link to leadership may, or may not, be inferred. In the following US West example the link is not explicit but beneath the statement lies an implicit leadership function of the working group.

> The question of focus and purpose led to the decision to form a working group of teachers and administrative staff to examine student performance, student opinions of learning and climate in the school, and staff perception of student learning and leadership.

The creation of a working group in this Seattle school arose from the dialogue about leadership for learning between schools and across national boundaries. It came through exposure to different ways of thinking, exemplary vignettes of practice in other places and workshop forums which created opportunities to engage critically. This is reflected in the report from the US West team which describes the development of relationships and the nature of the dialogue over the course of the project, 'moving from local description to cross-national understanding'.

The second tranche of survey data gathered in the final year of the project told us something about progress in relation to the dialogue about leadership for learning. The responses suggested that although some schools had made great strides it remains a significant challenge. In a pressured environment where deep or 'authentic' learning can become submerged, the evidence points us to the conclusion that it can only be kept alive if there is the kind of visionary and subversive leadership that facilitates the dialogue discussed here. This implies principals, headteachers, senior leadership teams and district superintendents with the will, courage and resilience to draw all members of their learning communities into the dialogue.

THE SHARING OF LEADERSHIP

Infusing all five principles is a view of leadership as activity rather than the functions of particular leadership roles or positions of status. Principals and headteachers had brought their schools into a project that explicitly valued shared leadership, but for many schools this proved to be a challenging proposition, particularly where there had been long established hierarchies of responsibility.

In the Carpe Vitam project schools it was evident that senior leadership teams created structures that encouraged wider participation in school development and allowed informal and incipient leadership to have fuller expression. An Australian principal remodelled his school by breaking it into four sub-schools, each with a focus on leadership for curriculum and learning. While this structural change recognised and affirmed the informal leadership that already existed, it nevertheless signified a change in mindset.

> (We) have a philosophy that everyone in our school is a leader ... whether they're a classroom teacher or someone in admin, right through to the principal. But staff involved in our learning teams have been leaders ... they've selected curriculum ... we have learning team leaders as well that play specific roles and call meetings...

How the principle of shared leadership played out in different cultural contexts was an enduring subject of discussion among project participants. The traditionally flatter organisation of schools in Norway and Denmark seemed to encourage broader participation than in Austria, Greece, the US and England where more hierarchical structures dominate. For many schools shared leadership is about working together, teamwork, and collaboration, but it is the interplay of strong leadership from the top and leadership as distributed that emerges as a recurring paradox in the Scandinavian data. One Danish principal reflected:

> I must provoke, be direct in order to build an appropriate working environment. Leadership should be visible. People must be clear that we have a leader, a vision, and that things are not always straightforward and easy. ... As a principal, I have to be a leader of the department leaders, and not just a member of the 'leadership team'. Some have been unhappy with my role as a 'head leader', thinking instead that I should be an ordinary member of this group. In some ways I've become very alone, working in isolation.

The inclusion of young people within distributed leadership was a major theme in Carpe Vitam and prompted, for example, a Seattle principal to focus upon student voice for his doctoral study. '(The) argument that students could make a significant contribution to the teaching and learning affairs of the school was compelling to me and the other members of our team.'

Comments from a Danish student illustrate how the pedagogic culture in some project schools gave students freedom and responsibility for their learning.

> The independent responsibility for learning makes me inclined to learn more... We choose what we want to work with on our own, but the teachers keep tabs on you if you start reducing the demands you make on yourself.

Within the student group, it was said, members helped to uphold a kind of self-discipline, putting pressure on 'lazy' members; leadership was characterised as 'spontaneous' and 'shared'. Another student said: 'If somebody gets a good idea in relation to the task or has some kind of insight beforehand, it seems natural that he or she takes on the leadership for a period'.

In some project schools, for example in London, student leadership was fostered through the allocation of special roles such as being a mentor to younger students or being a representative on the School Council. This culture of student leadership was echoed in Brisbane where respondents explained that student leadership opportunities arose from a cultural shift caused by a more systemic focus on learning. This had led to a virtuous circle of increased pupil attendance, greater student engagement, and more opportunities for authentic learning.

The data from the various sites suggested that 'shared leadership' is something that principals, teachers and students increasingly aspire to but is understood quite differently in different settings. In some instances it is understood in the sense of delegation, while in others it is seen in more bottom-up terms, as initiative spontaneously exercised and as teamwork. In conference workshops we offered tools such as the 'Leadership Density Grid' to enable groups of staff to identify growth points in the pursuit of shared leadership. These workshops reminded us of how deeply embedded conceptions of leadership are, and the time it takes for new forms of shared leadership to emerge and become established in thinking and practice.

FOSTERING A SHARED SENSE OF ACCOUNTABILITY

Accountability is a particularly problematic concept, rooted as it is in political structures and with redolent connotations that evoke strong responses in different cultures. In discussions at our international conferences it aroused vigorous debate, reflecting in part the enormous variation across the project in school colleagues' experience of accountability. To some the word suggested the dutiful report of levels of measured attainment to political masters; to others it was something more collegial.

Many participants emphasised the importance of various forms of internal accountability. For example, a principal from US East saw accountability as being primarily concerned with the collaborative evaluation of the quality of students' work.

> Once a month at grade level meetings teachers bring examples of student work and we discuss them. Teachers have good conversations about student work, both within and across grade levels.

At a Norwegian school a feature of their approach to accountability was to invite parents in to observe classroom practice, helping to foster a dialogue about the nature of the educational experience the school offers. In a Greek school accountability was described in terms of responsibility for actions taken that teachers owe to one another.

These three different examples all focus on internal accountability, to students, parents and colleagues. Complex relationships between internal and external accountability began to emerge. For example, it was reported that in the US East involvement in the project had clarified the importance of a focus on learning and the conditions for learning as a counterbalance to a focus on statutory standard assessments alone. This had given the impetus to developing a shared approach to internal accountability as a precondition of accountability to external agencies. A major theme in the UK context was the tension between the external pressure created by the 'standards agenda' and the more professional imperatives. Some teachers felt a sense of embattlement and ambivalence about accepting responsibilities for leadership in such a climate. In Austria accountability demands assumed a lower profile than in the US or UK but were described as a pressure exerted by external authorities rather than from the school itself, and as an unwelcome exigency of the changing political landscape.

As with other aspects of the leadership for learning principles there is evidence of gradual movement from very different starting points to some common ground. What came to be held in common is that, however accountability is understood, it has to confront top-down expressions of accountability that disempower teachers. When there is strong internal support and conviction as many of these Carpe Vitam schools report, there is resilience and vitality to tell the school's story in their own register and in terms of their own core values.

CONCEPTUALISING LFL AS AGENTIAL ACTIVITY

The principles for practice are framed by a theoretical model in which the main pillars are that both leadership and learning are conceived of as 'activities' linked by the common concept of 'agency'. The idea of learning as activity has its intellectual underpinnings in socio-cultural theory in which people learn through membership of 'communities of practice' (Wenger, 1998). A key idea within this way of thinking about learning is 'participation' (Sfard, 1998) which implies that learning requires engagement with activity. Engeström's work on activity theory has built on the legacy of Vygotsky and Leont'ev to show how activity in pedagogical scenarios is mediated through tools such as language (Edwards, 2005). The idea of leadership as activity draws upon similar theoretical resources. Peter Gronn's account of leadership rests on a theory of action which draws heavily on activity theory (Engeström, 1999) which supports the view that leadership is a collective phenomenon in which things happen as a result of 'conjoint agency'. The notion of activity bridges the gap between agency and structure and is 'present in the flow of activities in which a set of organisation members find themselves enmeshed' (Gronn, 2000, p. 331).

The idea of leadership as a distributed activity has been explored empirically by James Spillane who emphasises that leadership is the product of collective interaction between people (Spillane, 2006). In the Carpe Vitam project we saw many examples of developing practice which reflects this way of conceptualising leadership.

What links learning as activity and leadership as activity in our framework is the concept of human agency. This concept proved quite problematic, particularly for some of the practitioners in the project. It may be a concept used quite routinely within the field of social theory but it is perhaps less familiar in professional communities. Put simply, human agency is about the capacity for intentional action and the knowingness that enables us to monitor our own actions. It is what singles us out from other animals. Arguably, to be fully human is to exercise choice and have a degree of control over the goals and processes that constitute our lives. This is not to deny the very real constraints, both material and ideological, that social structures present, but Anthony Giddens' structuration theory suggested a less deterministic view of action. He argued that social structures are necessarily recreated in the moment of action and so human agency becomes a source of bottom-up power. Social structures still constrain the way human beings act and think, but agency acts upon those social structures to reshape them (Giddens, 1984). Within the Carpe Vitam project we saw how the purposes of leadership and learning are realised when human agency is allowed to flourish. Indeed we came to understand that both leadership and learning are optimised when they become part of the same process.

CONCLUSION

The Carpe Vitam Leadership for Learning project was established to try to reinvigorate the debate about leadership, learning and the link between the two. In addition we wanted to develop a way of working that would constitute an alternative to the school effectiveness tradition, one in which democratic values could be defended in the context of a policy environment that seemed to have eroded these. Those of us who participated in the project may well feel that we have been able to reclaim and reframe the concepts of leadership and learning as activities that foster and extend human agency, but the important question now concerns the extent to which the project can have impact beyond those directly involved. Traditionally we might expect a project to publish 'findings' and 'recommendations' for policy and practice but in this project we want to offer a legacy of a different form.

At the conclusion of the project we published the key ideas and principles for practice in a very accessible format (MacBeath, Swaffield and Waterhouse, 2006). We hope that this brief, illustrated account of the discursive process referred to above, will inspire others to enter into similar partnerships to pursue the link between leadership and learning for themselves.

NOTES

[1] An international research and development project funded for three years until December 2005 by the Wallenberg Foundation in Sweden, with further financial support from participating countries. The project was directed from the University of Cambridge by John MacBeath, and co-directed by David Frost and Sue Swaffield. Team leaders in other countries were: George Bagakis (University of Patras, Greece), Neil Dempster (Griffith University, Brisbane), David Green (Centre for Evidence Based Education, Trenton, New Jersey), Lejf Moos (Danish University of Education), Jorunn Møller (University of Oslo), Bradley Portin (University of Washington) and Michael Schratz (University of Innsbruck).

Further details are available at: http://www.educ.cam.ac.uk/carpevitam

REFERENCES

Edwards, A. (2005). Let's get beyond community and practice: The many meanings of learning by participating. *The Curriculum Journal, 16*(1), 49–65.

Elliott, J. (1996). School effectiveness research and its critics: Alternative visions of schooling. *Cambridge Journal of Education, 26*(2), 199–224.

Engeström, Y. (1999). Activity theory and individual and social transformation. In Y. Engeström, R. Mietten, & R-L Punamäki (Eds.), *Perspectives on activity theory*. Cambridge: Cambridge University Press.

Ferlie, E., Ashburner, L., & Pettigrew, A. (1996). *The new public management in action.* Oxford: Oxford University Press.

Fielding, M. (1997). Beyond school effectiveness and school improvement: Lighting the slow fuse of possibility. In J. White & M. Barber (Eds.), *Perspectives on School Effectiveness and School Improvement.* London: Institute of Education.

Fischman, G. E. (2001). Reflections about images, visual culture, and educational research. *Educational Researcher, November,* 28–33.

Frost, D., & Swaffield, S. (2004). *The leadership for learning (Carpe Vitam) project: An eclectic and emerging methodology.* Paper presented within the symposium, 'The Leadership for Learning (Carpe Vitam) project' at the 17th International Congress for School Effectiveness and Improvement, Rotterdam January 6th–9th.

Giddens, A. (1984). *The constitution of society.* Cambridge: Polity Press.

Gronn, P. (2000). Distributed properties: A new architecture for leadership. *Educational Management and Administration, 28*(3), 317–38.

Lawrence-Lightfoot, S., & Hoffmann-David, J. (1997). *The art and science of portraiture.* San Francisco: Jossey-Bass.

MacBeath, J. (2004). Democratic learning and school effectiveness: Are they by any chance related? In J. MacBeath & L. Moos (Eds.), *Democratic learning: The challenge to school effectiveness.* London: Routledge/Falmer.

MacBeath, J., Frost, D., & Swaffield, S. (2005). Researching Leadership for Learning in Seven Countries (The Carpe Vitam Project). *Education Research & Perspectives, 32*(2), 24–42.

MacBeath, J., Frost, D., Swaffield, S., & Waterhouse, J. (2006). *Leadership for learning: Making the connections.* Cambridge: University of Cambridge, Faculty of Education.

MacBeath, J., & Mortimore, P. (2001). *Improving school effectiveness.* Buckingham: Open University Press.

MacBeath, J., Schratz, M., Meuret, D., & Jakobsen, L. (2000). *Self-evaluation in European schools: Story of change.* London: Routledge.

McBeath, J. (2002). *The self-evaluation file: Good ideas and practical tools for teachers, pupils and school leaders.* Glasgow: Learning Files Scotland.

Moos, L. (2004) Introduction. In J. MacBeath & L. Moos (Eds.), *Democratic learning: The challenge to school effectiveness.* Routledge/Falmer.

Moos, L., & Møller, J. (2003). Schools and leadership in transition: The case of Scandinavia. *Cambridge Journal of Education, 33*(3), 353–370.

Peters, R. S. (1959). *Authority, responsibility and education.* London: Allen and Unwin.

Schratz, M., & Löffler-Anzböck, U. (2004). The darker side of Democracy: A visual approach to democratising teaching and learning. In J. MacBeath & L. Moos (Eds.), *Democratic schools, democratic learning: The challenge to school effectiveness and improvement.* London, Routledge/Falmer.

Sfard, A. (1998). On two metaphors for learning and the dangers of choosing just one. *Educational Researcher, 27*(2), 4–13.

Spillane, J. (2006). *Distributed leadership.* San Francisco: Jossey-Bass.

Stenhouse, L. (1975). *An introduction to curriculum research and development.* London: Heinemann.

Swaffield, S. (2004). Critical friends: supporting leadership, improving learning. *Improving Schools, 7*(3), 267–278.

Wenger, E. (1998). *Communities of practice.* Cambridge: Cambridge University Press.

APPENDIX 1

THE CARPE VITAM LEADERSHIP FOR LEARNING PROJECT

Principles for practice

1. Leadership for learning practice involves maintaining a focus on learning as an activity in which:
    1.a. everyone[1] is a learner
    1.b. learning relies on the effective interplay of social, emotional and cognitive processes
    1.c. the efficacy of learning is highly sensitive to context and to the differing ways in which people learn
    1.d. the capacity for leadership arises out of powerful learning experiences
    1.e. opportunities to exercise leadership enhance learning

2. Leadership for learning practice involves creating conditions favourable to learning as an activity in which:
    2.a. cultures nurture the learning of everyone
    2.b. everyone has opportunities to reflect on the nature, skills and processes of learning
    2.c. physical and social spaces stimulate and celebrate learning
    2.d. safe and secure environments enable everyone to take risks, cope with failure and respond positively to challenges
    2.e. tools and strategies are used to enhance thinking about learning and the practice of teaching

3. Leadership for learning practice involves creating a dialogue about LfL in which:
    3.a. LfL practice is made explicit, discussable and transferable
    3.b. there is active collegial inquiry focussing on the link between learning and leadership
    3.c. coherence is achieved through the sharing of values, understandings and practices
    3.d. factors which inhibit and promote learning and leadership are examined and addressed
    3.e. the link between leadership and learning is a shared

concern for everyone

3.f. different perspectives are explored through networking with researchers and practitioners across national and cultural boundaries

4. Leadership for learning practice involves the sharing of leadership in which:
4.a. structures support participation in developing the school as a learning community
4.b. shared leadership is symbolised in the day-to-day flow of activities of the school
4.c. everyone is encouraged to take the lead as appropriate to task and context
4.d. the experience and expertise of staff, students and parents are drawn upon as resources
4.e. collaborative patterns of work and activity across boundaries of subject, role and status are valued and promoted

5. Leadership for learning practice involves a shared sense of accountability in which:
5.a. a systematic approach to self-evaluation is embedded at classroom, school and community levels
5.b. there is a focus on evidence and its congruence with the core values of the school
5.c. a shared approach to internal accountability is a precondition of accountability to external agencies
5.d. national policies are recast in accordance with the school's core values
5.e. the school chooses how to tell its own story taking account of political realities
5.f. there is a continuing focus on sustainability, succession and leaving a legacy

AFFILIATIONS

David Frost and Sue Swaffield
Faculty of Education, University of Cambridge,
UK

NOTES

[1] 'Everyone' includes students, teachers, teaching assistants, headteachers/principals and the school as an organisation.

LARRY SACKNEY AND CORAL MITCHELL

CHAPTER 7

Leadership for Learning: A Canadian Perspective

In Canada, education is in the portfolio of provincial rather than national governments, and yet the educational reform scene has been remarkably similar across the country. Over the past two decades, it has followed a typical trajectory: from school effectiveness to transformational leadership to accountability to learning communities. As each new wave of reform has swept across the schools, ripples from previous initiatives continue to wash up on educators' desks. This reform environment has presented teachers and administrators with a complex array of changes, some compatible but many conflicting.

In his analysis of the reform movement in Canada, Levin (2001) concluded that most mandated reforms were poorly designed and not well implemented. Moreover, a majority of the reforms were too inflexible to meet local conditions, were poorly resourced, created teacher opposition, were modified to suit varying political pressures, and were often abandoned before they had a chance to bear fruit. In a reform environment of this character, school leaders and administrators face the daunting task of integrating the various policy changes in ways that build strong, vibrant supports for learning in schools and among educators. This chapter explores this task context with respect to five broad sets of challenges: learning communities, teacher capacity, administrator learning, school councils, and accountability trends.

LEARNING COMMUNITY MODELS

As in many other parts of the world, learning communities have become the dominant goal for school improvement initiatives across Canada. The received wisdom of this model is that, as educators reflect on the consequences of their practice, develop and experiment with new practices, and share effective practices with one another, they build greater capacity to solve difficult educational problems and to create exciting learning climates and improved learning outcomes for students (Harris, 2002; Mitchell & Sackney, 2006; Stoll, McMahon, & Thomas, 2006). The reality, however, usually lags somewhat behind (in many cases far behind) the rhetoric. One reason for this unfortunate state of affairs is that the learning community model represents a marked departure from the traditional isolationist character of teaching. Second, many of the existing models and practices have been developed outside Canada and imported into Canadian schools with uncertain results. Third, the learning community literature does not offer clear pathways for administrators to follow as they attempt to implement the model in their schools. These issues present school leaders with serious challenges as they attempt to create learning community models and practices that are informed by local contexts, realities, capacities, and values.

The learning community model requires educators to make a collaborative effort to improve learning outcomes for students. This collaborative enterprise asks educators, for example, to learn with and from colleagues, to describe and discuss their pedagogical challenges and educational concerns, and to share information and resources (Mitchell & Sackney, 2006). The effect of such collegial relationships is to open teachers' practices to the scrutiny of their peers and supervisors, but shining a collective spotlight on individual practice can feel quite threatening, especially to those whose practices might appear to warrant some improvement. To make the collegial activity more than a superficial presentation of so-called "best practice," a considerable level of trust needs to exist among colleagues and between teachers and leaders. Trust, however, is a tricky thing to establish, and it is even more difficult to sustain for the long term (Sergiovanni, 2005). For leaders in Canadian schools, the challenge is exacerbated by a political climate of mistrust of the profession by the public (Stein, 2001), which can cause teachers to retreat behind closed doors and to open for public attention only that which is likely to look good in the press. This is not an impossible challenge for leaders to meet, and we have witnessed many school principals and teacher leaders building sufficient trust in their schools to entice teachers to work with one another on a deep level and to garner the benefits of improved teaching and learning. But this challenge demonstrates the complex character and entangled context within which leadership for learning operates.

In Canada, the usual method for helping educators to create learning communities has been to introduce them to models that have been developed elsewhere, usually from other countries. Workshops, for example, have been held in many jurisdictions across the country in the practices of the Dufour and Eaker (1998) model. We have found that educators in general and school leaders in particular are unable to transfer the model into a set of school processes that actually make a difference in the learning (and the lives) of teachers and students. Furthermore, the model does not offer a theory of learning communities that is grounded in an epistemology that leaders and teachers can understand. It is a recipe approach to building professional learning communities, reminiscent of the effective schools research in the 1970s and early 1980s. Our experiences with school districts attempting to implement that research literature taught us that recipes do not work; each school is unique and to impose the same template results in uneven implementation and wasted effort (Sackney, 2007). We have noticed this same problem in a number of school districts that we have recently observed as they attempt to implement the learning community model. The momentum is not there, and leaders have not found a way to make the model a priority in their schools or to have an impact on teaching and learning.

We have noticed this to be the case with any model that is presented as an intact set of principles, procedures, and practices. This outcome appears to be a consequence of the content-laden character of such professional development opportunities, which fails to engage leaders in an intense examination of what it means to be a learning community, what good teaching and learning look like, how their leadership affects the work of teaching and learning, and what they can do to build a vibrant learning climate for teachers and students. This level of critical reflection is essential for school leaders to come to a sense of learning as a vital life process that cannot be forced or directed but that can be engaged, fostered, encouraged, and channelled by a supportive and inviting learning environment. This profound shift in perception is precisely what is needed to move leaders away from recipes and models and toward a deep engagement with learning across the school.

Such a shift in perception implies that bringing a learning community into reality cannot be done by relying on a prescribed set of processes and procedures. Almost all the recent literature (e.g., Bolam, McMahon, Stoll, Thomas, & Wallace, 2005; Huffman & Hipp, 2003; Louis, 2006; Mitchell & Sackney, 2006; Stoll, Fink, & Earl, 2003) makes it abundantly clear that the development of a learning community is context-specific and that recipes are not only unavailable, but they are also undesirable. Leaders face the difficult task of building a culture of inquiry, learning, and continuous improvement that reflects and responds to the specific conditions that exist within the school and that honours and supports the people who populate it (Fullan, 2006). We have found that, in successful schools, learning leaders know the people, the organizations, the communities, and the contexts; they ask questions rather than provide answers; and they know what is happening with teaching and learning. Most importantly, they find ways to release the creative energy of teachers and students, for this is the force that fosters experimentation and that breathes life, excitement, and enthusiasm into the learning environment for students and for teachers. This implies, of course, that leaders are comfortable with ambiguity, that they are more interested in learning than in outcomes, and that they trust teachers and students to work their magic in the classrooms. It also implies that leaders see leadership as being distributed where it can arise from many different sources.

TEACHER CAPACITY

The foregoing discussion implies that the challenges of building learning communities are intimately connected to the question of teacher capacity. The learning community model represents a paradigm shift with a focus on constructivist pedagogy, teacher as learner, collaborative work environments, data-driven decision making, and systemic awareness. These conditions require skills and abilities that do not always come naturally to teachers and that are not typically included in teacher education programs. Consequently, leaders are faced with the challenge of providing learning opportunities for the teaching staff that will prepare them to function within this paradigm.

To build a learning community requires that teachers focus collectively on student learning, reflective dialogue, and collaboration that moves beyond the bound of the classroom (Bolam et al., 2005). To facilitate such collective activity, certain structural arrangements are necessary: time to meet, interdependence, trust, and respect. But the issue is more than structural; it is also professional. Elmore (1995), for example, has argued that school improvement initiatives usually fall short for two reasons: "(1) they require content knowledge and pedagogical skill few teachers presently have, and (2) they challenge certain basic patterns in the organization of schooling" (p. 366). Although Elmore made this observation more than a decade ago, his recent work (2004) continues the theme that teachers generally lack the skills or capacity to work in teams or to generate continuous improvement in teaching and learning. Watkins (2005) agrees that "resources – such as trust and respect, teachers having knowledge and skills, supportive leadership and socialization – are more critical to the development of professional community than structural conditions" (p. 191).

When we ask teachers to use learning-centred teaching, we are asking them to engage in fewer classroom tasks, to do less telling and have students do more discovering, to do more design work and more modelling, to create climates for support and interaction, and to use a variety of learning strategies. We have found that teachers in high capacity learning schools have incorporated many of these practices but that teachers in low capacity learning schools have not (Sackney & Mitchell, 2006). In many cases teacher training does not prepare them to work collaboratively and in more student-centred learning environments.

Both Reeves (2006) and Marzano (2003) state that professional teaching practices have an enormous impact on student achievement, but a huge gap exists between professional development about effective teaching practices and actual implementation of the practices. In a study of more than 1500 classroom observations, Reeves (p. 101) found the following instructional profile:

- Clear learning objectives: 4%
- Worksheets: 52%
- Lecture: 41%
- Monitoring with no feedback: 22%
- Students required to speak in complete sentences: 0%
- Evidence of assessment for learning: 0%
- Evidence of bell-to-bell instruction: 0%
- Fewer than one-half of the students engaged: 82 %

Our work (Sackney & Mitchell, 2006) has found similar results with low learning-capacity classrooms. This result is especially problematic in light of Marzano's finding that about 67% of student achievement variance can be accounted for by the effect of individual teachers. He states, "It is clear that effective teachers have a profound influence on student achievement and ineffective teachers do not. In fact, ineffective teachers might actually impede the learning of their students" (p. 75). If teachers are to meet Reeves' and Marzano's challenge to be better educators, then educational systems need to ensure that teachers have the capacity to teach in ways that helps students to learn. Teachers need a certain level of knowledge about their subject matter, but they also need the pedagogical knowledge of how to teach that subject in ways that excite and engage their students.

Hopkins, Harris, and Jackson (1997) contend that building capacity for improved teaching and learning requires certain conditions to be in place at the school and classroom level. At the school level, they argue for a commitment to staff development, involvement of stakeholders in school policies and decisions, transformational leadership approaches, effective coordination strategies, focus on inquiry and reflection, and a commitment to collaborative planning activity. At the classroom level, the necessary conditions are authentic relationships, rules and boundaries, planning and resources, teacher's repertoire, pedagogic partnerships, and reflection teaching. Working upon both sets of conditions simultaneously, they argue, has the potential to build capacity within and across the system.

Our observations of school people who are building learning communities in their schools have demonstrated that the changes are more profound than simply gaining access to new instructional strategies. As the focus on learning deepens, we have seen educators begin to examine their professional roles and, in many cases, to reconstruct their professional identities. Although each individual works through this process differently, the general movement is toward an understanding of their personal responsibility for the collective good of the school (Mitchell & Sackney, 2007). But this shift requires teachers to release some attachments to their primary teaching assignment. For example, many teachers come to see themselves as *school* teachers rather than as *classroom* teachers, with an attendant shift in focus from *one group* of students to *all* students. Because this new identity broadens the scope of their commitment, some teachers have been worried about their ability to stay in close touch with the students in their classrooms. Successful school leaders understand that the profound changes in professional identity bring losses as well as opportunities, and they find creative ways of helping educators to acknowledge, articulate, and deal with the losses (Bridges, 1997). This type of reflection frees teachers to move through the losses, to integrate new roles with past commitments, and to gain a deeper understanding of what it means to be an educator.

PERSONAL PROFESSIONAL LEARNING

In many jurisdictions in Canada, the current emphasis on learning communities has reconstructed the role of school leaders as facilitators of student and professional learning and as co-creators of shared purposes and common understandings. This role represents a shift from the traditional administrative domains of policies, procedures, and regulations, but the traditional topics continue to sit at the centre of most leader preparation programs. In Ontario, for example, the Principal's Qualifications Program (Ontario College of Teachers, 2001), which is the primary pathway for leadership preparation in the province, is dominated by topics relating to management, decision-making, policies, and legalities. Although topics related to teaching and learning are present, they are not central in the curriculum. This example is repeated in most other provinces of Canada, which leaves leaders on their own to find professional development that equips them to put learning at the centre of all school operations and decisions.

Of equal concern is the lack of attention in most school jurisdictions to ongoing professional education for school administrators. In many cases, classroom teachers are the primary targets of the expectations and opportunities for ongoing learning, and there appears to be an implicit assumption that the formal leaders (particularly the principals) have sufficient skills, abilities, and knowledge to perform their tasks. We have found some examples of individual workshops and seminars that target school leaders, but we have found very few examples of ongoing professional development that is designed specifically for school leaders or that carries an expectation that school leaders should and will continue to engage in professional learning. This failure to provide explicit, focused, ongoing professional development for school leaders is one of the most worrisome findings from our investigations into leadership for learning.

In spite of this bleak picture of institutionally delivered professional learning, we have found some school principals and many teacher leaders who seek out formal and informal learning opportunities and who invest their own time and money to participate. Although we have found more teacher leaders than principals making these personal investments, we have found that school principals work at finding materials, resources, opportunities, and time that can enable teacher leaders to access relevant professional development. We have also found many school principals who stay abreast of new educational initiatives and innovations through their administrative networks and personal reading. Although this is an informal approach to professional development, it has been helpful in introducing new ideas and moving information around in the school.

In an environment with a focus on learning, leadership is about developing other leaders. Hargreaves and Fink (2005) and Fullan (2006) argue that leaders cannot accomplish everything on their own. Instead, if they are to attain sustainable leadership, they need to develop leadership capacity in others. Fullan sees capacity building as a core activity of leaders. He states, "Capacity building . . . is multifaceted because it involves everything you do that affects new knowledge, skills, and competencies; enhanced resources; and strong commitments" (p. 85). He adds that capacity building is a term that has made a big difference and is known by everyone from "the premier to classroom teachers" (p. 87).

Our work with learning community schools suggests that the cutting edge of professional development for school leaders is in preparing them to create school cultures where teaching and learning are at the centre of every discussion, every decision, every plan, and every initiative. Although this seems like an obvious statement, we have not found this focus to be evident in most schools or to be on most leadership agendas. Instead, we have found school leaders to be more concerned with accounting than with learning, with control than with teaching, with compliance than with risk-taking, and with public relations than with student experiences. From our perspective, the best way to create schools with vibrant learning climates is to re-educate school leaders, to bring them to a deep engagement with and appreciation for the excitement of true learning. Professional development for leaders needs to take them into new, interesting, and challenging territory, to push them to consider the effects of their own practice on the educational experiences of others, and to engender in them a sense of excitement as they learn something of value. If leaders do not feel this excitement, if they do not personally experience the transforming power of learning, they are ill-prepared to bring forth school cultures that fully engage the learning potential of teachers and students.

SCHOOL COUNCILS

The current emphasis on improved teaching and learning has been accompanied in many Canadian jurisdictions by the creation of school councils that enable parental involvement in school governance and operations. In Ontario, for example, school councils have been mandatory for all publicly funded schools since 1997, and implementation and refinement of the councils have been moving forward since that time. As part of the ongoing process, the Ontario Ministry of Education (2002) published a guide for school council members, which defined the purpose of school councils as being "to improve student achievement and enhance the accountability of the education system to parents" (p. 2.2) and which established the right of school councils "to express their views on any issues that are important to them" (p. 2.2). With this guide, the Ontario ministry positioned parents and school councils to play a key role in school planning, decision-making, and improvement. But it raises the question of what role parents want to play and/or are prepared to play. Although we have not found school councils to interfere inappropriately in school operations, we have found that school leaders face some deep challenges in building strategies for authentic and effective participation of parent groups and school councils.

One of the most serious challenges facing school leaders is that of equitable representation of parents on school councils. When we meet with school councils and other parent groups, we usually sit at the table with mostly white, middle-class, educated parents. Even in schools with an ethnically diverse student population, the representatives on the school council come from the same substratum of society. These members have spoken to us of their frustration at being unable to entice other parents to join the school council or to become involved in school processes, and we have found them and the school principals to be well-intentioned. But the problem remains: how do school leaders bring to the table the parents who feel uncomfortable in a school that is led predominantly by well-educated middle-class people? This is a challenge that has yet to be successfully met in most schools in which we have observed, even in learning community schools.

A second challenge lies with the capacity of parents and school council members to move beyond the interests of their own children and to embrace the interests of all children in the school. Most parents originally become involved in school councils and school activities to enhance the experiences of their own children, but as part of the school council they are asked to focus on the collective good. We have witnessed some progress on this front, especially in schools that function as strong learning communities. Some school leaders, for example, rotate parent volunteers through a host of different school activities, classrooms, grade levels, groups, and events so that they become familiar with many different students and gain an understanding of the array of learning opportunities and challenges evident in the school. Other leaders provide workshops and training sessions for parents and school council members that introduce them to the wonders and responsibilities of working with other people's children. With these and other strategies, school leaders have been remarkably resourceful in helping parents and school council members to gain an attachment to children from other families and to come to a sense of their obligation to all the students in the school, as well as to their own children.

ACCOUNTABILITY

In spite of considerable rhetoric about improving the learning outcomes for students, the current accountability environment places greater emphasis on student performance than on student growth and development. In Ontario, for example, most public accountability of education is situated in the annual province-wide literacy and numeracy tests conducted by the Education Quality and Accountability Office (for details, see http://www.eqao.com/). Although few other provinces have such a heavy institutional presence in academic testing, each province links school accountability and improvement expectations to large-scale test results (Ben Jaafar, 2006). This trend has been justified with the contention that common standards and performance-based accountability systems provide necessary benchmarks against which schools can be judged (Leithwood, 2004). This configuration of accountability has generated a nation-wide movement toward centrally controlled outcomes-based curricula, standards of teacher quality, and targets for student achievement. In Western Canada, for example, the provincial education ministers meet regularly to ensure that standards and curricula are similar.

This shift towards centralization and the specification of common standards has been accompanied by accountability mechanisms that designate and hold schools and school districts responsible for the learning outcomes in their jurisdictions. In a review of school improvement across Canada, Sackney (in press) found that governments are mandating performance-based goals, targets, timelines, monitoring procedures, and reporting to stakeholders. In some provinces (e.g., Alberta), schools have to submit their improvement plans for approval to the district board and then to the Ministry of Education. Other provinces are crafting similar requirements. At present, Saskatchewan appears to be the lone holdout, but even in that province a continuous improvement framework has been developed and mandated for use. The problem from our perspective is that common standards, large-scale test results, and tightly controlled central monitoring are more concerned with student performance than with student learning, and this approach to accountability fails to capture the excitement and enthusiasm that comes with real learning. School leaders, therefore, face the challenge of finding measures of student achievement that address authentic learning and of generating broad understanding of and support for this type of accounting.

One strategy for meeting this challenge is for leaders to shift the discourse away from accountability and toward assessment. Educators agree that assessment is a powerful tool for discovering what students know and are able to do, but there is considerable confusion over what *assessment* actually means or what it should look like. Earl (2006) has done considerable work in repositioning assessment as a tool for learning rather than as a mechanism for accountability. She defines assessment as having "three intertwined but distinct... purposes – *assessment for learning, assessment as learning*, and *assessment of learning*" (p. 6, italics in the original). We see Earl's work as marking an important shift in the configuration of assessment. Because of the early stages of this work, the new representation of assessment has not yet found its way into accountability discourses and practices, but we see this as the necessary step that will help to reclaim accountability and assessment for learning purposes.

A second strategy for meeting the challenge is to redefine accountability from a Canadian perspective. Ben Jaafar (2006) participated in two pan-

Canadian studies investigating the constructions and effects of educational accountability policies, from which she and her colleagues "concluded that Canadian educational accountability is best described as a hybrid model of results-oriented EBA [economic-bureaucratic accountability] and process-oriented EPA [ethical-professional accountability]" (p. 64). Her subsequent analyses position the Canadian perspective as "inquiry-based accountability" (p. 69), in which all measures, including large-scale and classroom-based assessments, are seen as entry points into professional discussions about learning experiences, opportunities, outcomes, and desires, which can be used to inform and direct attention and action so as to achieve the greatest learning benefits for all students. This approach to accountability is consistent with the goals of learning-centred leadership, but it is not an approach that is commonly acknowledged or valued in the accountability literature. We therefore see a need to reconstruct the discourse to raise the profile and the status of inquiry-based accountability.

CONCLUSION

What is becoming evident across Canada is that leadership for learning is positioned in rhetoric about improvements in teaching and learning but is entangled in provincial expectations for performance planning, monitoring, and reporting. In most provinces, this expectation is played out by requiring schools to collect and interpret data, develop action plans in consultation with the school council, and subject the subsequent implementation to central approval and monitoring. This approach to accountability positions school leaders as managers of the development, implementation, and reporting enterprise rather than as role models of authentic learning and great teaching. It also positions them not as partners of the teaching force but as superiors to the teachers and scrutineers of their work. This latter role is most evident in Ontario, where all teachers must undergo a periodic formal appraisal by school administrators. While this practice has not traveled across the country, it is symptomatic of a general push for greater teacher accountability to meet common standards of professional practice and to improve student achievement on common tests.

What remains unknown is whether central governments in Canada will move to greater school accountability policies if schools do not meet the goals and performance targets set for them. At present, there are few, if any, direct consequences associated with poor performance for individual teachers, schools, or districts, but some literature is beginning to float the notion of putting "positive pressure" on schools that do not show achievement gains over a period of time (e.g., Fullan, 2006). Additionally, we are starting to see writing that argues for reducing inequities in school learning, with this outcome being attached to leadership responsibilities but with no articulation of the consequences associated with the task (e.g., Ontario Ministry of Education, 2003).

We fear that, although the notion of learning communities has permeated the Canadian educational landscape, the recipe approach taken in many school jurisdictions may have caused the concept to have peaked in many schools. We are starting to see waning attention to developing learning communities. We believe that teachers and school leaders are not aware of the epistemology behind learning communities. In Saskatchewan, for example, the continuous assessment framework is now front and center in government policy, but school leaders have not figured out how to use the concepts in their search for improved learning. Furthermore, teachers feel that the new push means that some other things have to drop out. Sackney (2006) argues that, unless each new initiative is embedded in a systemic approach to reform, where each new policy coheres with other policies and where each initiative has beneficial impacts at the classroom level, teachers are unlikely to see any meaning in the initiative. If they fail to find meaning, they are unlikely to invest time and effort into the initiative. In Canada, we have yet to see this shift in approach.

To approach educational reforms systemically requires a holistic, ecological view of the school as a living organism (Mitchell & Sackney, 2000). This perspective brings attention to the totality of patterns, connections, relationships, interactions, and mutual influences that emerge among people and the forces that impinge on them. Furthermore, it requires a type of leadership that may not be readily available in many schools because it means that educators must make a profound shift in how we think about, talk about, and value learning. From our perspective, if leadership is truly for learning, then leaders are filled with the energy that comes from learning something new, interesting, challenging, and exciting, and they create school environments that infuse their colleagues, students, and other community members with the same energy.

Over the years of our research, we have found a few schools to have this character, where the embedded philosophy enshrines a type of professional identity and a set of relationships that place learning at the center of every activity, structure, plan, function, decision, interaction, conflict, objective, or outcome; where each individual is valued as a person with capacities, histories, and interests to be respected and honoured; and where people undertake the hard work of constructing exciting, authentic, supportive learning moments. This philosophy is not an easy one to develop or to follow, but we have found it to be possible. Too often, leaders and teachers are content with being good, but good is simply not enough. We have been fortunate to find some school leaders in Canada who dare to be great. We wish that leadership preparation programs and institutional contexts would empower more leaders across the country to follow their example.

REFERENCES

Ben Jaafar, S. (2006). From performance-based to inquiry-based accountability. *Brock Education, 16*(2), 62–77.
Bolam, R., McMahon, A., Stoll, L., Thomas, S., & Wallace, M. (2005). *Creating and sustaining professional learning communities*. Department for Education and Skills. Research Report RR637, University of Bristol. Retrieved March 16, 2007, from www.eplc.info
Bridges, W. (1997). *Managing transitions: Making the most of change*. London: Nicholas Brealey.
DuFour, R., & Eaker, R. (1998). *Professional learning communities at work*. Alexandria, VA: ASCD.
Earl, L. (2006). Assessment – a powerful lever for learning. *Brock Education, 16*(1), 1–15.
Elmore, R. (1995). Teaching, learning, and school organization: Principles of practice and the regularities of schooling. *Educational Administration Quarterly, 31*, 355–37.
Elmore, R. (2004). *School reform from inside out*. Cambridge, MA: Harvard Education Press.
Fullan, M. (2006). *Turnaround leadership*. San Francisco: Jossey-Bass.
Hargreaves, A., & Fink, D. (2005). *Sustainable leadership*. San Francisco: Jossey-Bass.
Harris, A. (2002). School improvement: What's in it for schools? London: Routledge/Falmer.
Hopkins, D., Harris, A., & Jackson, D. (1997). Understanding the school's capacity for development: Growth states and strategies. *School Leadership and Management, 17*(3), 401–411.
Huffman, J. B., & Hipp, K. K. (2003). *Reculturing schools as professional learning communities*. Lanham, ML: Scarecrow Education.
Leithwood, K. (2004). *Educational accountability: Issues and alternatives*. Briefing notes prepared for Saskatchewan School Boards Association, Regina, SK.
Levin, B. (2001). *Reforming education: From origins to outcomes*. London: Routledge/Falmer.
Louis, K. S. (2006). Changing the culture of schools: Professional community, organizational learning, and trust. *Journal of School Leadership, 16*(5), 477–489.
Marzano, R. (2003). *What works in schools: Translating research into action*. Alexandria, VA: ASCD.
Mitchell, C., & Sackney, L. (2000). *Profound improvement: Building capacity for a learning community*. Lisse, The Netherlands: Swets & Zeitlinger.
Mitchell, C., & Sackney, L. (2006). Building schools, building people: The school principal's role in leading a learning community. *Journal of School Leadership, 16*(5), 627–640.
Mitchell, C., & Sackney, L. (2007). Extending the learning community: A broader perspective embedded in policy. In L. Stoll & K. S. Louis (Eds.), *Professional learning communities: Divergence, depth and dilemmas* (pp. 30–44). Berkshire, UK: Open University Press.
Ontario College of Teachers. (2001). *Principal's qualification program*. Retrieved March 16, 2007, from http://www.oct.ca/teacher_education/additional_qualifications/principals_qualification/
Ontario Ministry of Education. (2002). *School councils: A guide for members*. Retrieved March 16, 2007, from http://www.edu.gov.on.ca/eng/general/elemsec/council/council02.pdf
Ontario Ministry of Education. (2003). *Building pathways to success Grades 7-12*. Retrieved March 16, 2007, from http://www.edu.gov.on.ca/eng/document/reports/pathways.pdf
Reeves, D. (2006). *The learning leader: How to focus school improvement for better results*. Alexandria, VA: ASCD.
Sackney, L. (2006). *Systemic reform for sustainability*. Paper prepared for Saskatchewan Learning, Regina, SK.

Sackney, L. (2007). History of the school effectiveness and improvement movement in Canada over the past 25 years. In T. Townsend (Ed.), *International handbook of school effectiveness and improvement* (pp. 167–182). Dordrecht, The Netherlands: Springer.

Sackney, L., & Mitchell, C. (2006, June). *Learning community classrooms*. Paper presented at the annual conference of the Canadian Society for the Study of Education, York University, Toronto.

Sergiovanni, T. (2005). *Strengthening the heartbeat: Leading and learning together in schools*. San Francisco: Jossey-Bass.

Stein, J. G. (2001). *The cult of efficiency*. Toronto, Ontario: Anansi.

Stoll, L., Fink, D., & Earl, L. (2003). *It's about learning [and it is about time]*. London: Routledge/Falmer.

Stoll, L., McMahon, A., & Thomas, S. (2006). Identifying and leading effective professional learning communities. *Journal of School Leadership, 16*(5), 611–623.

Watkins, C. (2005). *Classrooms as learning communities: What's in it for schools?* London: Routledge.

AFFILIATIONS

Larry Sackney
University of Saskatchewan,
Canada

Coral Mitchell
Brock University,
Canada

GEORGE K. T. ODURO

CHAPTER 8

Promoting Learning in Ghanaian Primary Schools: The Context of Leadership and Gender Role Stereotypes

INTRODUCTION

The totality of a child's development depends largely on the quality of learning activities in which he or she engages in an educational context. In Ghana, it is the belief of many that quality primary education is fundamental to a child's successful transition into responsible adulthood. Primary education covers a period of six years, and has two levels. The first level (*Lower Primary*) caters for children aged from 6-8 years. Children at this stage fall between Piaget's pre-operational learning category where children's imagination flourishes, and language becomes a significant means of self-expression, and early concrete operational categories of learning where children understand and apply logical operations to facilitate objective and rational interpretation of their experiences. The second level *(Upper Primary)* covers ages 9-11. At this stage, children learn to understand the basic concepts of conservation and many other scientific ideas (Berger, 2000). Children require an atmosphere that offers them the opportunity to reflect, think creatively, find out things for themselves to satisfy their curiosity, ask questions, criticise, solve problems, observe, view information critically, and assimilate new knowledge (The Republic of Ghana, 2002, p.27).

Generally, primary education in Ghana seeks to provide children with the basic skills they need to read, write, and manipulate basic numbers - skills that form the foundation for subsequent education and future life skills outside the school environment. In addition to the development of skills in reading, writing and arithmetic, primary education in the country seeks to socialize children by developing in them sound moral attitudes, appreciation of their cultural heritage and identity, the ability to adapt constructively to the changing local environment and the development of good citizenship (ibid). Thus the skills developed in primary school are seen as vital to the future of Ghana's children.

Through primary school education, children learn and are inspired to develop creative and critical thinking, environmental consciousness, a sense of nationhood, good citizenship, self-reliance, dignity of work and patriotism (Mensah, 2001). Educating children, then, has multiple impacts on their present and future lives, which extend to the society in which they live and its future generations. In this light, Ghana has, since the enactment of her 1961 Education Act, sought to make quality primary education accessible to all children (Antwi, 1992). Article 38 (Clause 2) of the country's 1992 Constitution, for example, guarantees the educational rights of children in the country: *'the Government shall, ... draw up a programme for ... the provision of free compulsory and universal basic education'*. Similarly, Section 8 (sub-section 1) of Ghana's Children's Act, (Act 560), provides that *No person shall deprive a child access to education ...'*. A number of initiatives have been put in place to ensure that such a promise is fulfilled. Among these initiatives are the introduction of capitation grant aimed at removing monetary hindrances to children's access to school education and the introduction of free food programme (these are discussed later).

While these interventions have increased pupil enrolment in the primary school, it raises a question related to quality teaching and learning. I argue in this chapter that increasing pupils' access to education is meaningless unless it is linked up to quality teaching and learning. This argument is critical when one considers that African leaders, including Ghana, have resolved to enhance capacity for sustainable development through the New Partnership for Africa's Development (NEPAD). NEPAD's determination to Africanize strategies for accelerating development has required new ways of enhancing pupil learning to ensure that products of the school system meet international standards. Moreover, with the country's policy of decentralization, the public has become increasingly interested in what goes on in school, making the school more accountable to the tax payer. We need to find answers to questions such as: What happens to Ghanaian children while they are in the classroom? What challenges do children grapple with in the process of engaging in learning activities? To what extent have headteachers and teachers been able to provide the required leadership for achieving quality in pupil learning? Does gender representation in school leadership matter in the process of enhancing pupil learning in Ghanaian primary schools?

THE GHANAIAN CHILD AND LEARNING CHALLENGES

In discussing the effect of school leadership and gender stereotypes on learning in Ghanaian primary schools, it is essential that we understand the Ghanaian child. We need to know the processes through which the child acquires knowledge, develops attitudes and acquires skills. This is crucial because the provision of education will be meaningless if that education does not serve the interests of the child.

The Ghanaian child, like any other child elsewhere, learns new things from what they see around them, what they hear around them and from what they do. At home, in school and within the larger society, children tend to emulate behaviours of adults whom they consider as their role models. As Nicaky and Brooklyn (1997, p1) put it, 'when a person has a role model, they look up to that special someone, adoring them, wanting and trying to be everything that person stands for'. Within the school, literature is replete with evidence to show that teachers' values, beliefs, and attitudes tend to influence the character formation of the children they teach. Writing from the perspective of British schools, for example, Dean (1995, p.37) reminds primary school heads that the 'school affects the way children develop' and stresses 'Children are not only affected by their peer groups in school. They also use older children and teachers as models'. They learn from experiences that come their way and from 'the values of those around'. From the reactions they receive from others to their behaviour, as well as in conversation, children begin to develop their own sets of values. Everything that happens to children contributes to the type of adult that they will want to become. Learning in children can therefore be promoted when educators provide opportunities for them to make maximum use of their sense organs as illustrated in Figure 1:

Every child in the classroom has the potential to develop his or her learning capacities through the sense of touch, hearing, seeing, smelling and tasting. This is only possible however if the school creates the enabling environment for the child to learn. Providing support for children's learning in the classroom is essential because the child in Ghanaian schools encounter many learning-related challenges.

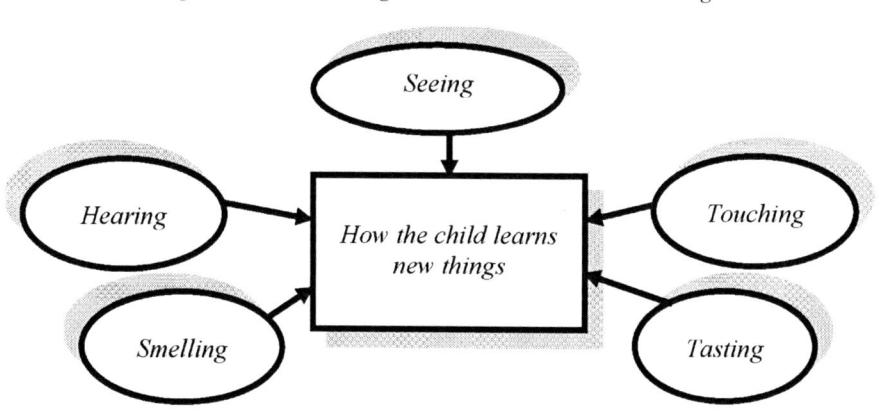

Figure 1. Senses through which the child learns new things

GEORGE K. T. ODURO

THE GHANAIAN CHILD'S LEARNING-RELATED CHALLENGES

Challenges faced by the primary school child in the process of learning are numerous. These challenges may be seen from health-related, emotional, and socio-economic perspectives.

A. Health-related challenges

Issues of health and safety in Ghanaian primary schools are a source of challenge for most children, especially in rural areas. Some people in the country hold the opinion that schools, unlike the mining industries or manufacturing companies, are a minimum risk to health and safety, hence not much concern should be given to this aspect of school life. Yet, some conditions within the school pose a threat to the health of children. Schools grapple with health cases related to malaria, nausea and vomiting, fainting, diarrhoea and stomach ache. Moreover, teachers who should attend to these health-related problems in the school tend not to be capable of doing so. In the rural areas especially, schools rarely keep well-equipped first-aid boxes. Consequently, children who fall ill are often asked to go home for treatment. In situations where access to a hospital or clinic is very difficult, such practice can prove to be disastrous.

Central to the health-related challenges is malnutrition and infection which adversely affects the physical growth of children. Paediatricians agree that when children are not properly fed, their mental growth suffers (Child-to-Child Trust, 1993. p.61). In 2005, the Reproductive and Child Health Unit of the Ghana Health Service (GHS) reported that children need good nutrition to enable them to succeed in their learning activities (reproductive and Child Health Unit, Ghana Health, 2005, p.54). Children who live in congested urban slums characterized by high population density, lack of proper drainage and sanitation are prone to health-related problems resulting from malnutrition. For example, a study* aimed at addressing nutritional problems of children in Kenyan slums, in the capital of Ghana, Accra, Nima, Sodom and Gomorrah and Chorkor, found that 86.2% of school children were stunted in their growth. Another study conducted in rural and urban slums in Ethiopia, found that 3% of the children had severe Protein-Energy Malnutrition SASPEN, 2003-2004).

Health-related tasks of the school are therefore critical. Headteachers and teachers are required to ensure that food prepared and sold to children in the school is well prepared. Schools also have the responsibility to create conditions that minimise the possibility of injuries. In the event of a pupil sustaining an injury, teachers are required to provide first aid before referring the case to medical practitioners.

Another health-related challenge which faces the child stems from the effect of the HIV/AIDS pandemic. In Ghana, like other African countries, children become orphans as a result of AIDS. A study of orphan children in the Eastern Region of Ghana, found that children orphaned by AIDS often do not get quality care from their extended family. 'While 93% of them were cared for by the family, the quality of such care was often low' (Ghana Human Development Report, 2004, p.68). Without proper care, such vulnerable children are compelled to engage in sex either for money or for emotional comfort. For example, a 2004 study of 20 primary schools and 12 junior Secondary Schools in the Bawku East District of the Upper east Region of Ghana showed that 'almost 30% of ... AIDS orphans ... have had sex more than once, compared to about 10% for all school children' (ibid).

B. Emotional challenges

Although, the laws of Ghana protect the rights of the child to life and survival, and both parents and teachers value the life of the child, children are maltreated in various ways. At home, experiences of divorce or other forms of broken homes which deny children access to parental attention (from the father and mother under the same roof) are a source of emotional challenge to children. Those who suffer most are girls who are often denied access to parental guidance and counselling on matters that are unique to girls. Related to this denial are restrictions associated with children's exploration of nature.

In Ghana, parents tend to be over-protective of their children and therefore do not allow them to engage in play activities that will encourage them to explore the environment and extend their horizons. Where play is encouraged the child is limited by cultural expectations constraining what he or she can say during play activities, especially if what the child says affects the adult. With such limitations, the child's analytical thinking tends to be suppressed. A personal observation of the author's own three children over a period of one year (2004 – 2005), as shown in Box 1, suggests strongly that children in Ghana are able to analyse critically issues they observe when they are encouraged to talk.

Box 1: Children develop critical mind when they talk at play

One day while the children were playing at the back of my bedroom, the eldest Paa Kwesi (7 years) played the role of a father (apparently imitating how I behave towards them at home), while the other two Kofi-

> Quakyi (5 years) and Akua (3 years) played the role of children. They demonstrated to my surprise how I occasionally shouted at them when they failed to study and played the organ and how I occasionally threatened to punish anyone of them who injured him or herself when playing. What was more challenging was when Kofi (5 years) analysed my behaviour by using the metaphor of a dog's reaction to someone running. He quizzed his brother and sister as follows: 'Paa Kwesi, wo nhu se Daddy te se okraman? Se wo di agoro na wo hwe ase a, na obe bow o. Okraman nso, wo tu amirika na wo hwe ase a, na obe ka wo' (literarily meaning, 'Paa Kwesi, don't you think that Daddy behaves just like a dog? When we play and injure ourselves, he threatens to punish us. Similarly, when we run during play and fall down, the dog tries to bite us'.

By Ghanaian cultural standards, any adult responding to the dialogue in Box 1 would have condemned my son's utterance as improper, but I saw it as an opportunity to learn how children develop critical thinking. When I probed further into Kofi's observation, I realized that the boy felt I was not being fair to him. He did not understand why instead of pitying him when he got injured while playing, I should become annoyed and threaten to punish him. The boy would not have been bold enough to demonstrate such an analytical reasoning in an environment in which children are discouraged from expressing their opinions. Children develop the habit of asking probing questions that help them to gain understanding of things they find confusing when they are encouraged to talk and play. Headteachers and teachers need to accept that 'one of the best instincts and skills young children bring to school is the desire and ability to talk. ... They must therefore be given enough opportunities to talk' (Asant, 2000, p.32).

C. Socio economic challenges

Closely linked to health-related and emotional challenges is socio-economic challenge. Gaining access to, and enrolling in, school does not guarantee a child's sustained learning activity. Many enrolled children fail to complete the six years of primary school, dropping out after only a year or two (Casely-Hayford, 2002a). Studies by the Ghana Education Service (GES) confirm that *poverty*—resulting in parental inability to support their child's education—*is the single greatest cause of school drop-out*, as reported by 42% of out-of-school children interviewed in 1997 (Boakye et al., 1997). Moreover, many parents—particularly poor parents working in subsistence agriculture in rural settings—expect their children to stay home to work on the family farm.

With the introduction of the capitation grant and the government's free food programme, the scale of school drop-out has improved considerably. For example, whereas in 1997, a study by the Ghana Education Service found that about 50% of all children enrolled in primary school (30% of girls and 20% of boys) were not completing the full six years, by 2004/05, the Ministry of Education reported that 78.7% of pupils had completed primary school. Nonetheless, these figures also reveal that more than half a million pupils leave primary school too soon. Those who remain in school are also compelled by poverty to absent themselves from school regularly.

Traditionally, Ghanaian social systems provided a type of welfare system where 'crisis in the nuclear family may lead to kin and occasionally non-kin child fostering' (Republic pf Ghana, 19992, p.18). Yet, in recent times, socio-economic changes, such as increased urbanization, have aversely affected extended family support. Traditional social structures which in the past catered to the development of children, are increasingly breaking down. Community support in times of need is also in decline. We now have a situation where poor family income compels children to engage in menial jobs to raise money to meet school related costs such uniform and additional textbooks which the capitation grant does not cover. Along the streets in Accra, one finds primary school children selling a variety of items under a scorching sun. This situation is challenging to headteachers who have to constantly devise ways which ensure that children attend, and remain, in school. This is not helped, however, by an imbalance in the teacher-pupil ratio.

D. The challenge Pupil-teacher Ratio

The learner (pupil) – teacher ratio (PTR) is another source of challenge, particularly in rural deprived areas. In the northern part of the country, for example, the PTR in 2004/05 ranged between 40 and 57—considerably higher than the national average of one teacher for every 32 pupils. Large class size makes it difficult for teachers to take into consideration individual differences. The case of one district in the central region of Ghana: Komenda-Edina-Eguafo-Abrem (KEEA) district, as illustrated in Table 1, exemplifies the problem related to primary school teacher supply in the country.

As shown in Table 1, PTR in this district is 41:1 which is far above the national norm of 32:1. This situation results in a practice where needy children, especially those who are very shy, are often denied the individual attention they require from their teachers. The district ratio illustrated in the

Table would be even be higher if we were to concentrate on the number of trained teachers in the district. This is because out of 423 Primary School Teachers in the district in 2002/2003, 138 (32.6%) were untrained. Trained teacher retention across the country, especially in disadvantaged districts such as the KEEA is a problem because rural communities lack decent accommodation, social services such as electricity, hospitals and other social amenities. As a result, large numbers of untrained teachers are recruited to fill teaching vacancies. Table 2 presents a regional distribution of trained and untrained primary school teachers in the 10 regions of Ghana in 2004/2005:

Table 1: Primary School Pupil-Teacher Ratio by Circuit in KEEA District, 2002/2003

Circuit	Pupil's Enrolment	Total No. of Teachers	Pupil Teacher Ratio
Agona	2866	61	47:1
Ayensudo	2508	58	43:1
Elmina	4981	126	40:1
Kissi	2435	59	41:1
Komenda	2975	70	43:1
Ntranoa	1635	49	33:1
Total	17400	423	41:1

Source: UNICEF & Republic of Ghana, 2004:98

Table 2: Trained and Untrained Teachers

Region	Trained Teachers Male	Trained Teachers Female	Untrained Teachers Male	Untrained Teachers Female
Ashanti	4,999 (66.3%)	4,201 (94.0%)	2,543 (33.7%)	270 (6.0%)
Brong Ahafo	3,453 (55.1%)	1,350 (80%)	2,813 (44.9%)	322 (19.3%)
Central	2,300 (54.6%)	2,012 (85.3%)	1,916 (45.4%)	347 (14.7%)
Eastern	4,355 (71.7%)	3,515 (93.1%)	1,715 (28.3%)	260 (6.9%)
Volta	3,997 (84.0%)	2,367 (94.0%)	759 (16.0%)	152 (6.0%)
Greater Accra	1,502 (90.7%)	3,733 (98.9%)	154 (9.3%)	40 (1.1%)
Western	2,463 (49.1%)	1,645 (79.6%)	2,588 (50.9%)	422 (20.4%)
Northern	2,550 (47.4%)	754 (72.9%)	2,830 (52.6%)	281(27.1%)
Upper East	1,152 (64.2%)	643 (84.7%)	642 (35.8%)	116(15.3%)
Upper West	916 (74.2%)	508 (87.6%)	318 (25.8%)	72 (12.4%)

Source: Ministry of Education, Science and Sports, EMIS Project, 2005)

Challenges such as those mentioned in the paragraphs above are critical in the school's efforts to promote quality teaching and learning. They have partly contributed to the poor performance of pupils in the country's criterion referenced tests (CRT). Increasingly, the school has been blamed for pupils' poor performance making the attainment of quality education a major concern on government agenda. This is reflected in Section 6.6 of the Government's 2004 White Paper on the Anmuah-Mensah' Report reviewing the country's 1987 Educational Reform Programme (ERP). It observes that:

> The system, pouring out every year hundreds of thousands of unskilled, unemployable and rather young Ghanaians onto the after-school world of work, has been run by Ghana Education Service which regrettably has been unable, for a decade and a half, to correct its manifest defects and turn it around. Both the system and its management need fundamental changes, and government has accordingly decided not to tinker with marginal adjustments to it but to carry out a radical reform of it. (p.14)

In addressing these problems, quality assurance strategies such as, firstly, a Performance Monitoring Test (PMT) and a School Performance Appraisal Meeting (SPAM) have, since 1998, been used as tools for monitoring teaching and learning outcomes in primary schools. Secondly, district teacher support teams (DTST) have been set up to facilitate improvement in the quality of teaching and learning. Thirdly, a Whole School Development Programme (WSDP) was introduced as a strategy for mainstreaming all interventions for the achievements of quality education. In spite of these measures there is still a general dissatisfaction with the management of teaching and learning at the basic level (MoEESS, 2002). Why is it that in spite of all the primary school improvement interventions, achieving quality in teaching and learning at the basic level continues to be a problem in Ghana?

ENHANCING PUPIL LEARNING: THE MISSING INGREDIENT

With the introduction of the ¢30,000.00 *per* pupil capitation grant, which according to newspaper reports has increased pupil enrolment in schools, and the free food policy of government which seeks to attract and retain pupils in school, one might have been tempted to conclude that these interventions would solve the problem related to pupils' learning. While not denying the positive impact of the capitation grant and the free-food policy on the expansion of access to basic school education, increased enrolment in schools *per se* does not of itself promote learning. Achieving quality in teaching and learning goes beyond quantitative expansion in the number of primary schools, increase in the number of school buildings and changes in the structure of our school system. As Gyekye (2002) argues,

> The desire or enthusiasm to access school education in order to acquire knowledge, skills, and new tools of analysis, is one thing; to actually succeed in acquiring them and showing evidence in having acquired them in concrete terms is quite another ... The quality of the products of an institution or a programme is often evidenced in the quality of performance of the products Gyekye (2002, p.28).

We need to acknowledge that the process of achieving quality teaching and learning requires effective leadership, both at the school and classroom levels. We need a quality of leadership that will effectively manage increasing enrolment, manage change and innovation, create environments conducive to learning and teaching and provide the needed professional support for teachers and pupils.

THE LEADERSHIP ROLE OF HEADTEACHER IN ENHANCING PUPIL LEARNING

The primary task of school leadership is to create an environment in which learning can flourish. International literature on school effectiveness and improvement agrees that a school's success is largely influenced by the manner in which the headteacher perceives and performs his/her work Sammons et al., 1985, MacBeath and Mortimore, 2001). In Ghana, the results of a 2005 DfID-sponsored research jointly carried out by researchers from the University of Cape Coast and the University of Sussex suggest that good school leadership can indeed counterbalance the relationship between poverty and low educational outcomes (Kutor, Forde, Asamoah, Dunne & Leach, 2005).

Yet, in sub-Saharan Africa, the Commonwealth Secretariat in 1990 observed that, though school heads, especially in deprived communities, carried primary responsibility for creating an effective educational environment, many of them were overwhelmed by the task, because strategies for training and supporting them were largely inadequate. Fifteen years after the Commonwealth Secretariat's observation, Kutor et al., 2005) suggest that the quality of school management in Ghana tends to be better in high achieving schools typically found in urban areas but not in rural areas. The researchers observe that attainment of the millennium goal of eradicating poverty in Africa will depend largely on the ability of school leaders to transform their schools and promote systematic quality education, so closing the gap between rural deprived areas and the urban more privileged communities.

Headteachers in Ghana perform varied tasks. While some of their tasks are routinely carried out, others are situational. The nature of their tasks is reflected in comments such as *'at times, the head himself does not know what his task will be the next moment'* (Oduro, 2003, p.159), and *'in fact, what I do in a day cannot be spelt out at one sitting'* (ibid). For analysis sake these tasks can be classified into two categories: *direct pedagogical tasks* (DPT) and *non-direct pedagogical tasks* (NPT). The former include tasks which relate directly to teaching and learning, such as supervising teachers' lesson preparation and delivery, handling classes and provision of teaching/learning materials. For example, supervision of teaching and learning is an important leadership task performed by primary school headtecahers in Ghana. It involves vetting teachers' lesson notes, providing professional guidance and requires monitoring of classroom practice. Supervision is a task that the Ghana Education Service (GES) has long identified as a viable means by which public (government funded) schools could catch up with the superior performance of private (non-government) schools. A 1998 report of the GES Council on the re-structuring and operations of the GES, for instance, notes, *'the private schools with less qualified and less trained teachers perform better than public schools. The major reason is the more effective supervision (my emphasis) in private schools'* (GES Council, p.20, iem 6.9).

Non-direct pedagogical taskes (NPT), by contrast, refer to duties, which indirectly affect teaching and learning. As Dean (1995, p.104), writes, every school has a number of tasks to be carried out which are not part of the teaching processes. The major NPT tasks identified with Ghanaian heads include supervising the process of cleaning and tidying the school campus, ensuring that vendors of food who come into the school compound maintain hygienic practices, inspecting building projects and performing office work among others. One problematic aspect of the headteachers' NPT activities is the health-related roles they are required to perform, such as ensuring that food prepared and sold to pupils is hygienically prepared. As one head explained *'if the children don't take in good food, it affects their health so even though I'm not a health inspector, I have to see to it that the food they prepare is well cooked'*. Besides, headteachers are responsible for creating conditions that minimise the sustenance of injuries and general illness among pupils as well as staff.

As headteachers' leadership role is to rearrange the multiplicity of tasks while also supervising teaching and learning, school improvement is unlikely to be realised without a sustained training programmes for headteachers. This is fundamental because people appointed to headship positions in our basic schools are insufficiently prepared for their leadership tasks.

Recommendations based largely on seniority in 'rank' and 'experience' appear to be the main criteria for appointing headteachers. To become a headteacher, one should have had experience in the classroom as a teacher. An official of the Ghana Education Service (GES) explained the processes involved in appointing headteachers as follows:

> The headteachers are appointed from the teachers in the district. To qualify for appointment as headteacher, you must be a principal superintendent or anybody of a higher rank if he chooses to be in the classroom.

In deprived rural areas where it is difficult to get principal superintendents to accept posting to schools, a senior superintendent or superintendent is appointed as the substantive head. The process of appointment, according to this official, starts with recommendation from the aspirant's circuit officer, in his own words:

> The circuit supervisors will ensure that actually the person being nominated has proven leadership skills, has sound financial management, the person is morally right, disciplined, approachable, and knowledgeable. The person must be capable of solving problems and when these recommendations are made to the director, a panel is constituted and he is brought before the panel for an interview.

Closely linked to the question of training, is the question of whether the practice of headteachers performing the dual role of leading the school and teaching classes contributes to quality leadership. This practice is common in schools, in rural areas, where there are problems related to staffing or where pupil enrolment is very low. At a 2005 DfID-funded Needs Analysis Workshop involving 120 primary school headteachers drawn from 6 out of the 10 regions of Ghana, all the participants complained about workloads involved when they combined their leadership roles with classroom teaching. The argument as to whether headteachers should be assigned classes is not peculiar to Ghana. Dean's (2001, p.83 reprinted) review of Mortimore *et al.*'s UK–based study of deputy headteachers, for example, provides a parallel to this. Her review shows that the heads had conflicting feelings about their role as classroom teachers. On one side, 'they felt it was an advantage in many ways' because 'it enabled them to continue having direct contact with pupils and to provide an example for colleagues'. On the other hand, the deputy heads 'felt that the dual role put pressure on them because they had too little time to get to know all the children and parents and to support colleagues'. This view supports the argument that the headteacher's additional role as a classroom teacher adversely affects the extent to which he or she is able to guide the overall process of teaching and learning at school level.

Making primary heads substantive classroom teachers is, in my view, inimical to school improvement, while at the same time depriving pupils of the right to a full time teacher. In most cases, pupils are left on their own in the classroom while the head attends to other non-teaching tasks. Left on their own, such classes are often characterised by purposeless noise, fighting and bullying. In a 2003 study of headteachers, Oduro observed that headteachers tried to control the situation by occupying pupils with class exercises. In most cases, headteachers set as many exercises as they could, especially in mathematics, on the chalkboard for the pupils to complete on their own. In other cases, the class prefect was asked to occupy the pupils with singing and story telling. In yet other instances, children were asked to go out and play outdoor games. The boys played football while the girls played 'ampe (an indigenous outdoor game for girls). These issues are impacted on in substantive ways by the gender imbalance among the pupil population and in the staffing of schools.

PROMOTING LEARNING: THE CONTEXT OF GENDER STEREOTYPES

Gender issues have become critical in advancing education for all children in Africa (UNICEF, 2005, p.1) To promote gender balance in primary education, Ghana's Ministry of Education, with financial support from Development Partners, established a Girls' Education Unit (GEU) within the Ghana Education Service (GES) in 1997. The GEU was tasked with the responsibility of increasing the national enrolment of girls in primary schools to equal that of boys by the year 2005. Additionally, the Unit was charged with developing strategies that would reduce the drop-out rates for girls in primary schools from 30% to 20%. The co-ordinating role of the GEU was to facilitate, network, influence, focus, plan, evaluate, collect and disseminate data on good practices with a view to improving the enrolment and retention of girls in school.

In spite of these policy interventions, the 2004/2005 national Gender Parity Index (GPI) remains 0.93 for Primary School, which according to UNICEF, is still far below the goal of 1.00 (ibid). Disparities in enrolment rates exist across the ten regions, 'with the three northern regions registering the lowest average girls primary school participation rate of 43.4%. (SACOST, University of Education, Winneba, 2005, p.9-10). Girls, especially those in the rural areas, also encounter a number of challenges in school. Circumstances in some schools, especially those located in rural areas, are such that girls in primary six are between the ages of 15 and 17. At that age, girls have special physiological and psychological problems for which they need experienced female staff in whom they can confide and receive advice. Handling of issues related to menstruation, as an example, is a common problem girls encounter. This could be understood within the Ghanaian cultural context where issues of menstruation and other sex-related matters affecting girls are expected to be handled by women, and those affecting boys handled by men. This belief has, over the years, developed in the minds of traditional women through socio-cultural conditioning to such an extent that the traditional rural school girl is likely to be embarrassed by any experience of menstruation while in school and will be shy to tell her male headteacher or male teachers than she would with a female teacher or headteacher. Such daunting experiences, in some cases, lead to girls dropping out of school.

To address this situation, female representation in primary school teaching and leadership is critical. Yet, in Ghanaian rural schools females are under-represented. This under-representation of women in leadership roles affects girls' attitude to learning as it does not provide them with role models. In a Leadership Needs Analysis Workshop sponsored by the Department for International Development (DfID), all 240 primary headteachers acknowledged that it was important that girls in rural schools are taught by some female teachers. Yet they were divided as to whether females should be posted to rural areas. This corroborates the results of Oduro's 2003 small-scale study in which some headteachers argued for the posting of females to rural schools because *'rural school enrolment comprises both girls and boys,* and the *fact that some problems that affect girls in the school would be best handled by female teachers'*. Others however opposed the posting of female teachers to deprived rural schools because they thought women could not cope with the difficult life there. The fear that women teachers might not get marriage partners of their choice is one of the common reasons for female under-representation: *"If you're a female teacher, you should not be posted to the interior part because there're problems there. Sometimes, they may get there and may out of necessity marry to a man who already has two wives; they're compelled to give in because ladies are weak"* (Oduro, 2003, p.151). One male headteacher observed, *'my experience tells me that when they come from the training college and posted to the rural areas, the people that they meet do not help them to get the right partners'*.

While it is true that life in the rural areas is difficult, it remains a puzzle and a challenge to policy makers why girls in the rural areas should not be granted the opportunity to enjoy the same role model as girls in urban schools. The failure to attract female teachers to rural areas, discriminates against girls and perpetuates the rural urban divide. Considering that females constitute more than 51% of the total population of Ghana of which a majority live in the rural areas (Smua-Sekyi, 1998), the need for female headteachers in such areas is of critical importance. As long as the distribution of female headteachers and teachers remains highly skewed in favour of urban primary schools to the disadvantage of rural schools, female role stereotyping will persist and thereby make the GES' efforts at creating equal opportunities for all children to obtain quality education even more difficult to achieve.

CONCLUSION

The foregoing discussions underscore the significant role that the school system plays in promoting learning among children in primary schools. Children learn best when there is quality of leadership that creates the optimum conditions for learning and teaching. Children learn best when there is a recognition of children as persons with a right to be respected and treated as unique individuals. This is central to the Children's Rights Convention (CRC) which explicitly obliges everyone to respect the dignity of children as members of the human community. School leaders in Ghana can promote children's sense of acceptance when they treat all children without discrimination and when children know that the classroom teacher pays particular attention to him or her during the teaching and learning process. Children learn new things faster when those involved in school leadership encourage them to see the mistakes they make during the learning process as opportunities for further learning. When the learning environment is made conducive for children to engage in talking and they are encouraged to learn by playing, they are more likely to develop their creativity.

To make headteachers and teachers more confident in promoting learning among children, gender issues should be given priority attention in the appointment of headteachers and posting of trained teachers. Equal weighting should be given to females and males in distributing leadership responsibilities in schools in rural areas. Moreover, efforts should be made to build leadership capacity in primary schools by investing more into the preparation of primary school headteachers enabling them to develop the right attitude and skills for effectively managing the learning challenges faced by their pupils.

REFERENCES

Antwi, M. K. (1992). *Education, Society and Development in Ghana.* Accra: Unimax Publishers.
Amuah-Sekyi, E. T. (1998). 'Ghana: Education for Girls'. Presentation at the Women's Centre at Eastern Wasgington University (May, 1998).
Asante, K. (2000). Teaching English in the Primary School. In Owolabi, J. (2000). *Teaching the Ghanaian Child*, Accra: Afolabi Publishers.
Berger, K. S. (1995, 2000). *The Developing Person. Through Childhood.* USA: Worth Publishers.
Boakye , J. (1997). Synthesis of Research on Girls' Education in Ghana. *The Ghana Teachers'Journal*, 2,21–27.
Bush, T. & Jackson, D. (2002). A preparation for School Leadership. In Belmas (October 2002). *Educational Management and Administration.* London:Thousand Oaks & New Delhi: SAGE.
Child-to-Child Trust (1993). *Child for Health.* UK: Werner.
Dean, J. (1995). *Managing the primary school* (2nd ed., 2001). London: Routledge.
Ghana Human Development Report. (2004). Breaking The HIV/AIDS Chain: A Human Development Challenge. Ghana: UNDP, UNFPA.
Kutor, N., Forde, L.D., Asamoah, A., Dunne, M., & Leach, F. (2005). *School life: Gendered experiences in Junior Secondary Schools in Ghana.* Printed in Ghana: DFID and University of Sussex.
MacBeath, J. (2003). The Alphabet Soup of Leadership. Inform. Number 2. Leadership for Learning: The Cambridge Network.
MacBeath, J. & Mortimore, P. (2001) *Improving School Effectiveness*, Buckingham, Open University Press.
Mensah, J. A. (2001). 'Community Support for Girl-Child School Attendance in Ghana: The Case of Winneba in the Central Region of Ghana. An Unpublished Master of Philosophy Thesis. University of Cape Coast.
Ministry of Education, Youth and Sports (2004). White Paper on the Report of the Education Reform Review Committee, MOEYS: Accra.
Nickay, P., & Brooklyn, N. Y. (1997). A Strange Model. Retrieved from http://www.teenenk.com/Past/1997/8686.html
Oduro, G. K. T. (2003). Perspectives of Ghanaian Headteachers on Their Role and Professional Development: The case of KEEA District Primary Schools. Unpublished Thesis. Cambridge.
Reproductive and Child Health Unit. (2005) *Annual Report.* Accra: Ghana Health Service (GHS).
SACOST, University of Education, Winneba (2005). *Bridging The Gap:Linking School and the World of Work*, Winneba: UEW.
Southworth, G. (1995). Talking Heads: An Investigation into Primary Heads in the 1990s. UK: University of Cambridge Institute of Education.
The Republic of Ghana. (2002). Meeting the Challenges of Education in the Twenty First Century. Report of the President's Committee on Review of Education Reforms in Ghana. Accra: NCTE.
United Nation's Children's Fund (UNCEF) and Republic of Ghana (2004). *Ghana Education Service School Mapping Report -2004.* Accra.
UNICEF & Republic of Ghana. (2004). *Ghana Education service School Mapping Report – 2004.* Komenda-Edina-Eguafo-Abrem (KEEA) District. Accra.

AFFILIATIONS

George K. T. Oduro
University of Cape Coast
Ghana

BILL MULFORD

CHAPTER 9

Learning About School Leadership in Australia

INTRODUCTION

Previous chapters have highlighted the diversity of school governance arrangements and the breadth of tasks and responsibilities facing school leaders wherever they are working. This chapter focuses on the role of school leadership in enhancing student learning and other schooling outcomes. It draws on Australian research to examine the policies and conditions under which school leaders are likely to be able to exercise this role most effectively.

There are formidable conceptual and empirical challenges in establishing the links between school leadership and school outcomes. A wide range of different factors – including resource levels, teachers' knowledge and skills, curriculum structure and student background – are potentially important in shaping student outcomes. School leadership influences these factors and is influenced by them in ways that are difficult to conceptualise and measure. Nevertheless, an extensive research base supports the view that leadership is of critical importance in effective schooling. This chapter draws on, and is limited by, a recent review of Australian research literature (Mulford, 2007) in the area[1] in reaching this conclusion.

In what follows, the review of recent Australian literature starts where it matters most in schools, that is, with evidence on student outcomes and the differences among different groups of students. Aspects of school leaders' work that shape the extent to which they are able to enhance student learning are then discussed. Following this discussion, a summary is presented of research on the impact of school leadership on student learning. Building on these discussions, the chapter concludes by examining the research on interactions between school leadership and other influences on student learning. It is in these last multi-dimensional approaches, which reflect the complexity of schools, that we find the strongest grounds for informing policy and practice.

STUDENT OUTCOMES: LEVELS AND DIFFERENCES AMONG STUDENTS

In brief, it can be concluded that it <u>does</u> matter which Australian school a student attends and how that school is organised and led. Student academic achievement, academic self-concept and engagement and participation in school and then further study and/or work have been shown to be linked to teacher and school practices, that is, practices that that can be influenced by school leadership.

Australian students score in the top group of OECD countries in PISA (Thomson *et al.*, 2004b), although the spread of scores is 'greater than would be considered desirable in relation to our national aspirations' (Thomson *et al.*, 2004a, p. 13). Rothman and McMillan (2003) found that approximately one-sixth of the variation in achievement scores in literacy and numeracy in Australia could be attributed to differences between schools. A little more than half of this between-schools variance could be explained by differences in student composition and the organisational climate of the school.

Using the PISA database, Marks and Creswell (2005) found that state differences in achievement among Australian secondary school students were larger than generally assumed and could not be attributed just to socio-economic-status (SES) and demographic factors (such as Indigenous status, region and grade level). The authors argued for research on the administrative and policy configurations responsible for such results. Some studies have explored aspects of these configurations, such as pupil grouping practices, school-average-achievement, support structures, and use of family social capital. Using detailed information from the records of 5,500 Tasmanian Year 10 students and multi-level modelling techniques, Lamb *et al.* (2001) found large social, gender and school differences in levels of study. Of particular note were that higher SES resulted in being in the top level English and mathematics classes, girls outperformed boys in English and attendance at private non-Catholic schools resulted in higher performance. Further, Lamb and Fullarton (2002) found that classroom differences accounted for over one-quarter of the variation in Australian TIMMS student mathematics achievement. Significant differences were found by types of student grouping practices, with students in higher bands or tracks receiving substantial gains in achievement. For students in the bottom band it was found better to be in a school that did not stream or track.

PISA (OECD, 2001), including the Australian results, has found that on average those students who liked school perform better than those who do not. The aspect of student engagement found to be most closely associated with reading performance was their ability to control the learning process.

While there was no single factor that explained why some schools or countries had better results, school policies and practices that tended to be associated with success, after taking account of other observed school and home background factors, included teacher expectations of student performance, teacher morale and commitment, school (not teacher) autonomy, positive teacher-student relations, and a good disciplinary climate.

ACER's longitudinal surveys of Australian youth (Marks *et al.*, 2001; Fullarton, 2002) have also stressed the importance of student engagement with school. They found that a high engagement at the school level even moderates the negative effects of SES and indigenous status. Provision for, and encouraging students to participate in, a broad range of school activities was found to lead to a student's closer connectedness to the school community as well as have flow-on effects to more academic parts of the curriculum.

From surveys of 5,150 Year 8 and 10 students from all three school sectors in Tasmania, Hogan and Donovan (2005) found significant relationships between students' subjective agency and academic outcomes, as well as a range of social capital outcomes such as sociability, trust in others, collaboration, being a good student, and participation in community groups. Hogan and Donovan (2005) believe that not to measure such broader outcomes of schooling 'underestimates the net contribution that schools make to individual wellbeing and aggregate social utility' (p. 100).

Using the representative sample of Australian 15-year-olds in the original PISA data base and multi-level modelling, Marsh (2004) found that academic self-concept depends not only on a student's academic accomplishments but also the accomplishments of those in the school the student attends. The effect of school-average-achievement was significantly negative and the size of these negative effects did not vary significantly across states and territories. Placement of high achieving students in academically selective schools and academically disadvantaged children in regular classrooms was found to result in lower academic self-concept.

As well, Wilson's (2002) qualitative 25 month study of a co-educational, comprehensive high school situated in the western suburbs of Sydney identified 24 cultural dimensions which impacted upon student participation. Only eight of these factors were found to have an enhancing impact, including sympathetic and structured teacher support and school leaders who model behaviours of openness and inclusion. Wilson (2002) concludes that it is 'only by including students as meaningful participants in the learning community of their school are we likely to resolve issues of decreasing motivation and academic performance amongst young people in the secondary school years' (p. 98).

THE WORK OF SCHOOL LEADERS

This section focuses on aspects of school leaders work that shape the extent to which they are able to enhance student learning. Effective distributed middle manager leadership has been found to be collaborative, facilitative, supportive, motivating, and focused on student learning and improvement. However, there would seem to be little professional learning provided specifically for the role.

A. Workload and job satisfaction

While the majority of Australian school principals say that they suffer role expansion, increasing overload, ambiguity, conflict and stress, they are also highly satisfied. The exception to this high level of satisfaction is in many small rural schools. Contextual pressures are seen to arise from poor funding, and limited support from governments.

Rapid top down change and accountability pressures also worry principals. Within the school, principals are frustrated by demands that find them spending time on administrative and managerial matters rather than the preferred relationships, strategy and educational. Values held by successful principals have been found to include being ethical, authentic, consultative issues and demonstrating integrity, compassion and an ability to promote staff ownership. Successful principals are also transformational, especially through their ability to show concern for individuals and build relationships, rather than by being visionary and inspirational. Aspects of the principals' role, such as performance management, professional learning, ICT use, and position redesign, are more likely to succeed if they are based on a professional and cooperative approach rather than a hierarchical and bureaucratic model.

The effects of distributed leadership based on role (heads of department, curriculum middle managers and teachers in model, or 'lighthouse', schools) have been researched in Australia. From interviews with 26 heads of department (HOD) in two government and two non-government NSW secondary schools, Deece (2003) found that, given the ambiguity and time constraints of the HOD role, their leadership needs to be collaborative and facilitative. However, little professional learning support was found, especially for the preferred approach of working with and/or observing others or the development of the required interpersonal and teamwork skills.

White's (2001) research involving 46 staff from all levels in three metropolitan Melbourne secondary schools underscores the leadership potential of curriculum area middle managers. He found middle managers draw from a portfolio of four leadership approaches - instructional leader, curriculum strategist, learning area architect, and administrative leader. What was most important for success was that middle managers create a learning area culture that is focused on student learning and improvement and which is collaborative in its operations and motivating for teachers and students alike.

In a rare longitudinal study, Wildy and Wallace (2002) examined the subsequent leadership effects of 10 teachers who worked in lighthouse schools involved in restructuring reforms. Those who moved to other schools carried their ideas and experience with 'something akin to missionary zeal' (p. 15). However, these researchers conclude that while importing lighthouse teachers into new schools is an important strategy to ensure the spread of educational reform, also needed is a supportive context where there is a critical mass of reform-minded leaders.

A recent Australian Education Union (AEU, 2005) survey of principals in all Australian public schools (N = 1,104, which represents a 16% response rate) indicated: heavy and increasing workload, with 85% of principals working between 45 and 65 hours in an average week, and over the past three years the workload was seen to have increased 'a lot' (76%); in terms of funding and resources schools were seen to be 'worse off' by 40% of principals; and, major priorities for additional funding were more help for individual students (80%), building maintenance and improvement (75%), more teachers (70%), more administrative and support staff (60%), and more welfare support.

A number of these results are similar to earlier studies in Queensland and Victoria. In Queensland, Cranston and Ehrich (2002) found role overload, ambiguity and conflict were characteristic, principals would prefer to spend more time on strategy and relationships rather that administrative management but 80% were satisfied with their role. The publication in 2004, of *The Privilege and the Price - a Study of Principal Class Workload and its Impact on Health and Well Being* (Victoria DET, 2004) highlighted a range of issues around the capacity of school leaders to cope with a much enlarged role. In the survey:

- 75% of respondents agreed that 'there is so much work to do, I never seem to get on top of it';
- 80% of principals agreed that they frequently 'come home too tired to do some of the things I like to do';
- 47% of principals and 36% of assistant principals have had 'a medical diagnosis which connects any health problems (they have) to their work as principal class officers';

- mean hours worked per week reported by principals were 60 and by assistant principals 58; and
- 78% of principals and 80% of assistant principals rated their job most of the time as being 'High Stress'.

Interestingly, despite the report's findings about the negative impact of the job on family life and health "principals and assistant principals almost overwhelming love their job. They think of themselves as privileged to have such an important and rewarding vocation" (Victoria DET, 2004, p.8).

B. Principals in small, rural schools

Small, rural schools bring their own challenges. From extensive interviews with four novice principals in small, rural, Western Australian government schools, Wildy and Clarke (2005) found challenges included the smallness of the school in isolated, conservative communities, heavy teaching responsibilities and beginning their first appointment as a principal with little preparation for leadership. The researchers concluded that in a context of high accountability, limited resources and rapid change, there is a serious disjunction between teaching and leadership roles in such schools that will make the role less and less attractive.

Through interviews and observation, Lester (2003) examined the situation faced by 12 teaching principals in remote rural Queensland communities. Leadership was found to be a juggling act involving a number of tensions and dilemmas. The tensions included those among management, sole and instructional leadership, and between principal and community educational knowledge. Dilemmas were found between staff development and dismissal as well as principal and community educational vision. The school community and professional support mechanisms were found to play a central role in resolving these tensions and dilemmas.

C. Values in leadership

Research on values in leadership is well represented in the Australian educational leadership literature. From five case studies of Brisbane Catholic secondary college principals and the values that underscore their leadership behaviour and how these values are formed, Branson (2005) developed and tested an instrument for helping principals to visualise and comprehend relationships between their principalship behaviours and personal values. Use of the instrument resulted in an increased self-confidence in the principalship. Using questionnaires and interviews of staff from an independent Queensland secondary school undergoing change in pastoral care arrangements, Chittenden (2004) found a link between ethical leadership and the success of the pastoral care programme. However, it was also found that there was a need for staff ownership and managerial consultation for any changes in structure and organisation to be accepted.

Dempster *et al.* (2004) found that even though Queensland principals have well meaning intentions and find their feet in one of three ethical camps (absolutist, relativist and ethic of care), by and large, they exhibit contradictions in their ethical reasoning and conflicts with their own personal and professional values. Employing interviews, observation and document analysis, McGahey (2002) explored school leaders' beliefs and philosophies in the formation of a moral community in nine NSW Catholic schools. Leaders were found to play a key role in this dialogue, especially when they were authentic, a person of integrity and ensured all voices were heard. Swann (2001) reports the results from previous research to argue the importance of leader compassion.

However, using a questionnaire with a stratified sample of 367 (73% response rate) Victorian principals, Collard (2004) concluded that principals were far from a homogenous group in term of their self-images. Independent boys' school principals were found to be most attuned to conservative images of themselves as solitary and autonomous leaders. Men from government secondary schools were found to most likely to view themselves in traditional bureaucratic terms, whereas female leaders were most attuned to collaborative images, particularly if they came from primary or girls' schools. Identification with images of 'leading learner' or 'advocate for children' was found to decrease with school size.

D. Transformational leadership

Another area of leadership examined in recent Australian educational journals relates to transformational school leadership, that is leadership involving individual support, building a culture and supporting structure of working with and through others, a school vision, high expectations for performance, and intellectual stimulation. From a questionnaire completed by 19 Victorian government school principals and 192 of their raters, Gurr (2002) confirmed a tendency for principals to use a transformational style. Raters, but not principals themselves, were more likely to perceive women using transformational leadership than men although there were no differences by type and level of school. However, using research from previous studies with 370 principals, Collard (2002) argues that there was a need to recognise that gender is mediated by other factors, such as diverse social, system and institutional cultures.

From a questionnaire study of 124 teachers from 12 Sydney metropolitan secondary schools, Barnett *et al.* (2001) investigated the relationships between transformational and principal transactional leadership behaviours and teacher and school learning culture outcomes. It was found that only the transformational characteristic of individual concern was associated with teacher satisfaction, willingness to give extra effort and favourable perception of leader effectiveness. On the other hand, vision/inspiration was found to have a negative association with student learning culture and excellence in teaching. It is suggested that a visionary/inspirational principal may actually distract teachers from concentrating on teaching and learning.

In a follow up study, Barnett and McCormick (2003) conducted interviews with principals and 11 teachers from schools where the principal has been perceived by teachers as a transformational leader, with characteristics of individual concern and vision. The results reinforced the importance of principals building relationships and therefore the value of individual concern but not vision.

E. Information Communication Technology (ICT)

Other Australian studies have examined the principal's performance management, role in ICT and role redesign. Employing interviews with 31 Victorian government school principals, Mongan and Ingvarson (2001) found support for performance management. However, to be fully acceptable, a new model would be needed. This model would need to have a strong focus on the professional learning and growth of the principal, school and organisational improvement, cooperation and teamwork rather than competition, emphasis on longer term as well as shorter term goals, regular constructive feedback, and transparent processes.

Gurr and Broadbent's (2004) Victorian study of 21 government school principals and 24 Catholic school teachers who held leadership positions found that, although at an early stage of development, ICT had fundamentally changed their work. An example was the use of e-leadership meetings in digital space. More specifically, Schiller (2003) surveyed 217 (62% response rate) Newcastle school principals on their use of, competency with and skills acquisition in ICT. While it was found that many principals now recognise the critical role that they play in facilitating the implementation of ICT in their schools to improve teaching, learning and administrative processes, considerable variation was found in use, competence and skill acquisition. The authors called for greater professional development in the area.

F. Role redesign

Through an analysis of various case studies of the redesign of the principalship, Blackmore *et al.* (n.d.) identified five ways in which the processes of redesign were beginning to be undertaken: sharing pedagogical knowledge construction; sharing responsibility and resources to provide greater access and equity; setting up co-principalship for a family friendly workplace; multi-campus restructuring; and, developing community-based leadership (such as in Indigenous communities). Those that focussed firstly on the question of a principal's work were much more limited in their effects than where it is part of a larger enterprise with a coherent and meaningful ethical and political purpose. They also note the limitations of those redesigns which do not eventually get to a prime focus on students' learning.

SCHOOL LEADERSHIP AND STUDENT LEARNING

In brief, the research shows that the principal has an important role to play in successful Australian schools and how they are run (such as in the approach to decision-making and planning). Success is more likely when the schools are collegial, consultative, collaborative, involve partnerships, and matters are shared and owned by stakeholders. Small, rural schools offer particular challenges in this regard. Finally, schools and their leaders have available an increasing range of quality, publicly available surveys and other data sources to inform their decision making and planning.

The principal has been found to be important for a successful school. Employing questionnaires and site visits in 19 new government schools in five states, Collier (2001) found a common need for new schools to quickly establish their credibility. Consultative principals, collaboratively developed foundational documents, and a distinctive identity through innovatory practices were all found to be important for establishing success. Wood's (2005) case study of an outer metropolitan Catholic secondary college in South Australia found that a number of characteristics were important in moving the school from serious decline to strong success. These included a determined planned effort, shared and owned by stakeholders who have identified with and relate reform to their unchangeable core beliefs. The roles of the principal and leadership were found to be pivotal here, especially in the building of relationships and partnerships with the internal and external environments.

Dinham (2005) found both positional and distributed leadership to be key factors in 50 successful school sites (departments and teams) in 38 NSW secondary schools. Success was based on standardised test results, public examinations, nominations from various stakeholders, and improvement over time ('value-added' measures). From observation, interviews and document analysis emerged a set of seven principal leadership attributes and practices. Core was a focus on students, learning and teaching. Other categories were: external awareness and engagement; a bias towards innovation and action; a relationship emphasis and personal qualities such as being honest, trustworthy, compassionate, communicative, and a good listener; building expectations and a culture of success; supporting teacher learning, and developing a sense of common purpose and collaboration.

More specifically, particular approaches to school decision making and planning have been shown to be related to enhanced learning. At a broad level, an analysis of Australian policy documents on school-based management by Lingard *et al.* (2002) demonstrated that it is a contested concept. Tensions between centralising and decentralising were found to continue, as did those between the market and equity/social justice objectives. From survey responses from 15 Tasmanian high schools (124 teachers and 1,181 students), Mulford *et al.* (2004) found that where decision making is perceived by teachers as collegial, collaborative and consultative and providing adequate opportunities for participation it will be more likely to lead to positive student perceptions about their school and teachers, as well as perceptions about relationships and their own performance, than where decision making is top-down, executive or does not foster widespread involvement. Complementing these results, it was found that where teachers identify the main sources of school stress as lack of support from management, poor leadership and ineffective decision making processes, students are much less favourably disposed towards their teachers or their own engagement and performance.

Hatton (2001) provides a case study of school development planning (SDP) in one small rural disadvantaged NSW primary school. It was found that while SDP that is collaborate and genuinely focused on classroom life proved to be a rewarding process for staff and had a positive effect on student outcomes, the link between SDP and increased efficiency was not proven, especially in relation to effective community involvement. Case studies based on observation, document analysis and interviews in four remote and rural WA schools by Clarke and Wildy (2004) further illustrate the cultural complexity of small school leadership and its involvement in decision making and school planning.

Increasingly schools and their leaders have available a range of quality, publicly available surveys to inform their decision making and planning (see the entire volume 11, number 2, 2005 edition of *Leading & Managing*). For example, Silins and Mulford (2005) detail the development of one of the first valid and reliable measures of organisational learning in schools that employed survey results from over 3,700 Tasmania and South Australian teachers and principals. Organisational learning was found to consist of four embedded factors: trusting and collaborative climate; a shared and monitored mission; taking initiatives and risks; and, ongoing, relevant professional development.

INTERACTIONS BETWEEN SCHOOL LEADERSHIP AND OTHER INFLUENCES ON STUDENT LEARNING

Other Australian research has come closer to the reality faced by schools and their leaders by exploring the complexity of links among leadership, school external and internal environments and improved student learning. The Queensland School Reform Longitudinal Study (Queensland DEA, 2001) of 24 schools over a three-year period found that the development of professional learning communities within schools is associated with greater use of more productive classroom pedagogies by teachers. More specifically, the data demonstrated strong links between three key variables and more frequent use of productive classroom pedagogies: the degree of teachers' collective responsibility for student learning, the overall level of professional learning community operating within a school and the strength of leadership on pedagogy. Productive school leadership was also found to include a high focus on a culture of care, a strong commitment to a dispersal of leadership and involved relationships amongst the school community, and a high focus on supporting professional development and learning community.

From a three-year study of 24 Queensland schools involving classroom observations and interviews with teachers and principals, Hayes et al. (2004) detail three case studies that focus on leadership practices. They found that dispersed, involved, productive leadership supported the achievement of both academic and social outcomes through a focus on pedagogy rather than management, a culture of care and related organisation processes, including being fully cognisant of Education Department policies and directives whilst not feeling unduly bound by them.

A report edited by Cuttance (2001) on school innovation emphasises the importance of principal, teacher and student leaders, developing a culture of sustained innovation from the local or school level and leadership as a focused action, culture building and an organisation-wide process of learning. The lessons from this study included that effective innovations are grounded in learning teams of teachers, are based on whole-school understandings and beliefs, employ distributive leadership, use rigorous data-based scrutiny of what is done, and have a principal who focuses on teaching and learning.

An Australian whole-school revitalisation initiative, the Innovative Design for Enhancing Achievements in Schools (IDEAS) Project (Andrews & Crowther, 2003) was underpinned by a framework for enhancing school outcomes (strategic foundations, cohesive community, infrastructure design, school-wide pedagogy, professional supports), an implementation strategy (initiating, discovery, envisioning, actioning, sustaining) and parallel leadership (teacher and administrator). An independent evaluation of a 12 school national trial of IDEAS (Chesterton & Duignan, 2004) found positive impacts on teachers in terms of pedagogical reflections and discussion, collaboration, decision making, and morale and some early beginnings to changes in teacher practices, considerable shift in the leadership paradigm away from power of position, but little in the way of improved learning outcomes for students.

Voulalas and Sharpe (2005) conducted interviews with 22 Sydney metropolitan principals who had been identified by District Superintendents as taking action to help their schools become learning organisations. Although leadership was seen as a key factor in transforming schools, respondents lacked a clear understanding of learning organisations. Traditional school structures and cultures, lack of implementation time and difficulty in obtaining the support of staff and parents were seen as the major barriers to implementation.

In contrast are the results from a two-year case study and questionnaire study involving 96 South Australian and Tasmanian secondary schools, including over 5,000 students and 3,700 teachers and their principals (see Silins & Mulford, 2004 for a summary). The Leadership for Organisational Learning and Student Outcomes (LOLSO) research found that leadership that makes a difference is both position based (principal) and distributed (administrative team and teachers). But both are only indirectly related to student outcomes. Organisational learning (OL) involving three sequential development stages (trusting and collaborative climate, shared and monitored mission and taking initiatives and risks) supported by appropriate and ongoing professional development is the important intervening variable between leadership and teacher work and then student outcomes. That is, leadership contributes to OL, which in turn influences what happens in the core business of the school – the teaching and learning. It influences the way students perceive how teachers organise and conduct their instruction, and their educational interactions with, and expectations for, their students.

The South Australian and Tasmanian research found that students' positive perceptions of teachers' work directly promote their participation in school, academic self-concept and engagement with school. Student participation is directly and student engagement indirectly (through retention at school) related to academic achievement. School size is negatively, and socio-economic status and student home educational environment are positively, linked to these relationships. LOLSO has developed a well-defined and stable model accounting for 84% of variance in student engagement, 64% of student academic achievement and 87% of organisational learning.

Two recent Australian studies linked to the ongoing eight-country International Successful School Principals (SSP) Project (Gurr *et al.*, 2005) reinforce the complexity of the links among leadership, school internal and external environments and a range of improved student learning (see Box 1).

Box 1: Leadership and school success

Based on three in-depth case studies of successful principals leading successful Victorian schools, Gurr *et al.* (2003) found that principals have a key role in the success of schools broadly and, in particular, on student outcomes. While each of the principals had different personalities and interpersonal styles, they all were expert at working with and through others to improve their schools. They had a significant impact on student learning through a number of key interventions that focused on teaching and learning and building professional commitment and capacity.

Based on detailed case studies of five Tasmanian successful principals and their schools, Mulford and Johns' (2004) results parallel those of Gurr *et al.* (2003). They present a new model for examining successful school principalship (see Figure 1). The interactive and sequential model is set within a context that includes community and system understandings and requirements. It then focuses on the principal's values, which link to individual and school capacity and the development of a school vision. The context and principal's values represent the 'why' and the individual and school capacity and vision represent the 'how' of successful leadership. The model then progresses to the 'what', or outcomes of successful leadership, which include teaching and learning, a range of academic and non-academic student outcomes and community social capital. These three foci are linked by evidence-based monitoring and critical reflection, which, if warranted, lead to change and/or transformation of the why, how and/or what.

BILL MULFORD

KEY ISSUES AND CHALLENGES

What have we learnt about school leadership in Australia? What seem to be promising policies and conditions for making school leaders most effective in improving school outcomes? The research on Australian educational leadership reviewed in this chapter suggests that:

- leadership is a key factor in successful schools;
- leaders contribute to student learning indirectly through their influence on other people, organisational capacity and context;
- leadership that enhances staff and student learning takes account of a combination of contextual, individual (self and others), organisational, outcome, and evaluative/accountability factors over time; and
- a great deal depends on which of these areas the leader chooses to spend time and attention. As a single input by a leader can have multiple outcomes, they need to be able to see the whole as well as the individual factors and the relationships among them over time.

The conditions and policies under which school leaders can exercise this role most effectively include:

- a rebalancing of the relationship between the political and bureaucratic and the professional that gives greater weight to the professional;
- much less emphasis on the organisational or managerial than has previously been the case - there is very little evidence to link such an emphasis to either improved school or student outcomes;
- avoidance of 'the great man or woman' theory of leadership;
- ongoing, relevant supportive professional learning; and
- data and other sources of information that provide schools with valid, reliable and easily administered ways of monitoring performance, diagnosing student learning difficulties, and implementing appropriate strategies.

Particular leadership practices seem to be more effective in promoting improved student outcomes in schools:

- values held by successful principals include being ethical, authentic and consultative and demonstrating integrity, compassion and an ability to promote staff ownership;
- successful principals provide individual support, develop organisational culture (working with and through others to build professional commitment and capacity that focuses on teaching and learning), and provide

structure, vision, expectations for performance and intellectual stimulation. However, there is a need for staff ownership for any changes in school structure and organisation to be accepted; and
- distributed leadership is vital for school success, especially where it is collaborative, facilitative, focuses on student learning and improvement, is motivating for teachers and students alike, and develops a critical mass of reform-minded staff.

Successful school reform is all about development – leaders' action and professional learning programmes need:

- to first get the personal/interpersonal, distributed leadership, collective teacher efficacy or trusting and collaborative climate 'right';
- once the personal/interpersonal is 'right' then it can be used to focus on the educational/instructional, including having a shared and monitored mission; and
- once the educational/instructional is 'right' and there is confidence in what the school is doing and why it is doing it, then the leaders and school can move to focus development/learning/change, including working with others schools in a 'nested' model.

The context for leadership and school reform must be taken more into account with variables such as Education Department policies and practices, school location, school size, and home educational environment having been shown to have a clear interactive effect on leadership, the school and student outcomes.

A key overall priority is broadening what counts as good schooling – students' achievement in a knowledge society is increasingly being seen as wider than the cognitive/academic and involving both quality and equity. Not to measure the broader outcomes of schooling underestimates the net contribution that schools make to individual well-being and the wider society.

Finally, the research and knowledge base on how school leadership interacts with a wide range of other factors to enhance student learning needs to be strengthened. Although this chapter was able to draw on a wide range of Australian research studies, this is a challenging area of work that needs on-going support, the development of new conceptualisations and empirical approaches, and close interaction with the fields of policy and practice.

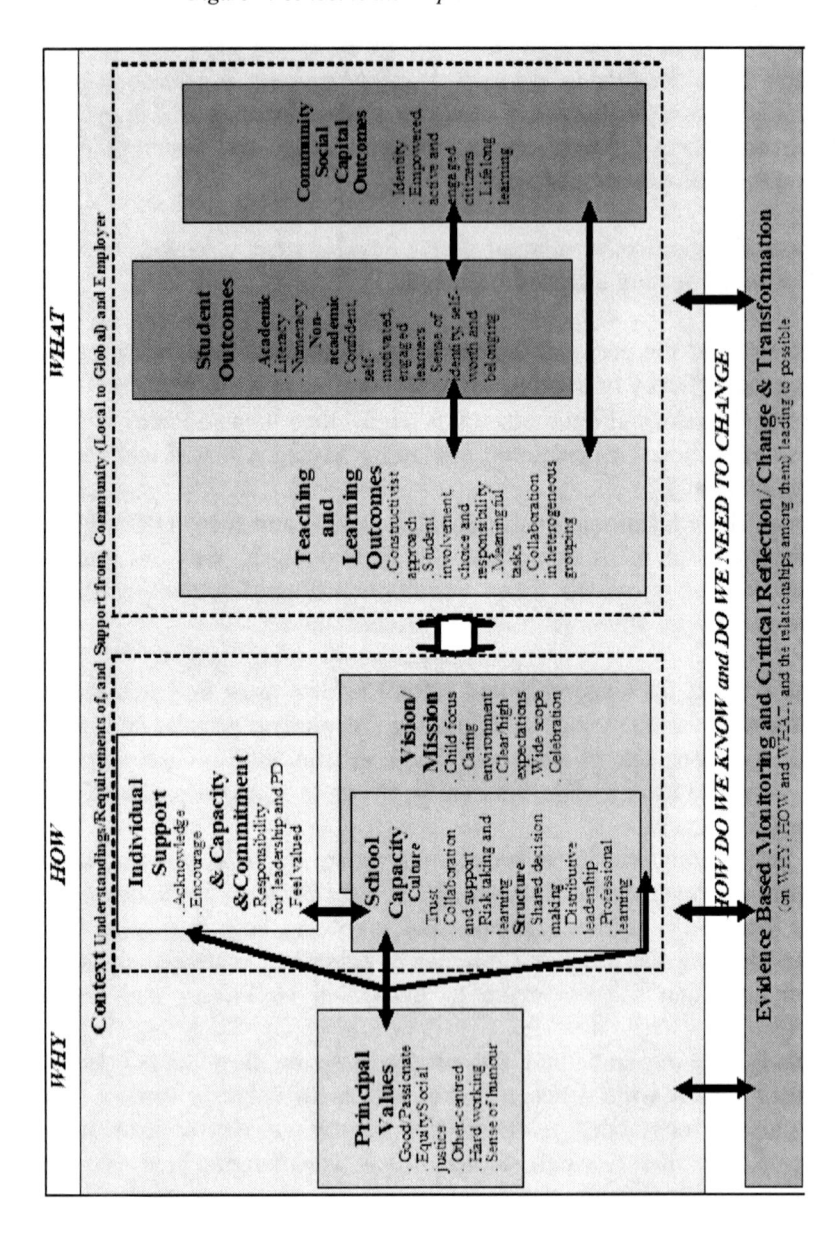

Figure 1: School leadership and student outcomes

NOTES

[1] This review reports on the last five years (2001 – 2005) of four major Australian-based educational journals. These journals comprise two general educational journals, the *Australian Journal of Education* and the *Australian Educational Researcher*, and two journals more targeted to the area, *Leading & Managing* and the *Journal of Educational Administration*.

REFERENCES

AEU (2005). National principals' committee state of our schools survey 2005. Melbourne: Australian Education Union.

Andrews, D., & Crowther, F. (2003). 3-dimensional pedagogy: The image of 21st Century teacher professionalism. In F. Crowther (Ed.), Teachers as leaders in a knowledge society. Deakin, Victoria: Australian College of Education Yearbook. Retrieved from http://www.dest.gov.au/sectors/school_education/publications_resources/profiles/schooling_issues_digest_motivation_engagement.htm

Barnett, K., McCormick, J., & Conners, R. (2001). Transformational leadership in schools: Panacea, placebo or problem? *Journal of Educational Administration*, 39(1), 24–46.

Barnett, K., & McCormick, J. M. (2003). Vision, Relationships and Teacher Motivation: A Case Study. *Journal of Educational Administration*, 41(1), 55–73.

Blackmore, J., Thomson, P., Sachs, J., & Barty, K. (n.d.). Which school? Who applies? An investigation of the shortage of applicants for the principalship. ARC research report.

Branson, C. (2005). Exploring the concept of values-led leadership. *Leading & Managing*, 11(1), 14–31.

Chesterton, P., & Duignan, P. (2004). Evaluation of the national trial of the IDEAS Project. Canberra: DEST.

Chittenden, A. (2004). Ethical leadership in the context of structural and organisational change in pastoral care. *Leading & Managing*, 10(1), 77–102.

Clarke, S., & Wildy, H. (2004). Context counts: viewing small school leadership from the inside out. *Journal of Educational Administration*, 42(5), 555–572.

Collard, J. (2002). Leadership and gender: time for critical analysis. *Leading & Managing*, 8(2), 100–109.

Collard, J. (2004). Learners, initiators, servants: The self-images of Victorian principals in the 1990s. *Australian Educational Researcher*, 31(3), 37–56.

Collier, J. (2001). Market niche in new state schools. *Leading & Managing*, 7(2), 151–162.

Cranston, N., & Ehrich, L. (2002). Overcoming sleeplessness: role and workload of secondary school principals in Queensland. Leading & Managing, 8(1), 17-35.

Cuttance, P. (Ed.). (2001). School innovation: Pathways to the knowledge society. Canberra: Department of Education, Training and Youth Affairs.

Deece, A. (2003). The leadership capabilities and decision-making of the secondary head of department. *Leading & Managing*, 9(1), 38–51.

Dempster, N., Carter, L., Freakley, M., & Parry, L. (2004). Conflicts, confusions and contradictions in principals' ethical decision making. *Journal of Educational Administration*, 42(4), 450–461.

Dinham, S. (2005). Principal leadership for outstanding educational outcomes. *Journal of Educational Administration*, 43(4), 338–356.

Fullarton, S. (2002). Student engagement with school: Individual and school-level influences. Camberwell: Australian Council for Educational Research. Longitudinal Surveys of Australian Youth. Research Report No. 27.

Gurr, D. (2002). Transformational leadership characteristics in primary and secondary school principals. *Leading & Managing*, 8(1), 78–99.

Gurr, D., & Broadbent, D. (2004). Interaction between ICT and school leadership. *Leading & Managing, 10*(1), 18–31.

Gurr, D., Drysdale, L., & Mulford, B. (2005). Successful principal leadership: Australian case studies. *Journal of Educational Administration, 43*(6), 539–551.

Gurr, D., Drysdale, L., Di Natale, E., Ford, P., Hardy, P., & Swann, R. (2003). Successful school leadership in Victoria: Three case studies. *Leading & Managing, 9*(1), 18–37.

Hatton, E. (2001). School development planning in a small primary school: Addressing the challenge in rural NSW. *Journal of Educational Administration, 39*(2), 118–133.

Hayes, D., Christie, P., Mills, M., & Lingard, B. (2004). Productive leaders and productive leadership: Schools as learning organisations. *Journal of Educational Administration, 42*(5), 520–538.

Hogan, D., & Donovan, C. (2005). The social outcomes of schooling: Subjective agency among Tasmanian adolescents. *Leading & Managing, 11*(2), 84–102.

Lamb, S., & Fullarton, S. (2002). Classroom and school factors affecting mathematics achievement: A comparative study of Australian and United states using TIMSS. *Australian Journal of Education, 46*(2), 154–171.

Lamb, S., Hogan, D., & Johnson, T. (2001). The stratification of learning opportunities and achievement in Tasmanian secondary schools. *Australian Journal of Education, 45*(2), 153–167.

Lester, N. (2003). Primary leadership in small rural school communities. *Leading & Managing, 9*(1), 85–99.

Lingard, B., Hayes, B., & Mills, M. (2002). Developments in school-based management: the specific case of Queensland, Australia. *Journal of Educational Administration, 40*(10), 6–30.

Marks, G., & Creswell, J. (2005). State differences in achievement among secondary school students in Australia. *Australian Journal of Education, 49*(2), 141–151.

Marks, G., McMillan, J., & Hillman, K. (2001). Tertiary entrance performance: the role of student background and school factors. Camberwell: Australian Council for Educational Research, Longitudinal Surveys of Australian Youth, Research Report No. 22.

Marsh, H. (2004). Negative effects of school-average-achievement on academic self-concept and comparison of the big-fish-little-pond effect across Australia states and territories. *Australian Journal of Education, 48*(1), 5–26.

McGahey, V. (2002). Espousing moral community in Catholic schools: sensing the spirit in school leadership. *Leading & Managing, 8*(1), 60–77.

Mongan, J., & Ingvarson, L. (2001). Managing performance: A review of the performance management programme for principals in Victorian state schools. *Leading & Managing, 7*(2), 181–197.

Mulford, B. (2007). Overview of Research on Australian Educational Leadership 2001-2005. Melbourne: Australian Council for Educational Leadership ACEL Monograph.

Mulford, B., & Johns, S. (2004). Successful school principalship. *Leading & Managing, 10*(1), 45–78.

Mulford, B., Kendall, L., & Kendall, D. (2004). Administrative practice and high school students' perceptions of their schools, teachers and performance. *Journal of Educational Administration, 42*(1), 78–97.

OECD (2001). Knowledge and skills for life: First results from PISA 2000. Paris: OECD.

Queensland Department of Education and the Arts (2001). The Queensland school reform longitudinal study: teachers' summary. Brisbane: The State of Queensland. Australia, Department of Education and the Arts.

Rothman, S., & McMillan, J. (2003) Longitudinal Surveys of Australian Youth Research Report Number 36. Australia: Melbourne Australian Council for Educational Research.

Schiller, J. (2003). Successful interventions: The Australian primary principal as key facilitator in ICT integration. Refereed paper accepted for "The second wave of ICT in education", a conference of the Asia-Pacific Chapter of the Association for the Advancement of Computing in Education (AACE), Dec 2-5, Hong Kong, 2003. To be published in the internationally distributed AACE Digital Library http://www.aace.org/dl/

Silins, H., & Mulford, B. (2004). Schools as learning organisations: effects on teacher leadership and student outcomes. *School Effectiveness and School Improvement, 15*(3–4), 443–466.

Silins, H., & Mulford, B. (2005). Organisational learning questionnaire: Quality evidence. *Leading & Managing, 11*(2), 46–54.

Swann, R. (2001). Ecocentrism, leader compassion and community. *Leading & Managing, 7*(2), 163–183.

Thomson, S., Cresswell, J., & De Bortoli, L. (2004a). PISA in brief from Australia's perspective: Highlights from the full Australian Report. Camberwell: Australian Council for Educational Research.

Thomson, S., Cresswell, J., & De Bortoli, L. (2004b). Facing the future: a focus on Mathematical literacy among Australian 15-year-old students in PISA 2003. Camberwell: Australian Council for Educational Research.

Voulalas, Z., & Sharpe, F. (2005). Creating schools as learning communities: Obstacles and processes. *Journal of Educational Administration, 43*(2), 187–208.

Victoria, Department of Education & Training. (2004). The privilege and the price: A study of principal class workload and its impact on health and well-being. Melbourne: Human Resources Division, DET.

White, P. (2001). The leadership of curriculum area middle managers in Victorian government secondary schools. *Learning and Managing, 7*(2), 131–150.

Wildy, H., & Clarke, S. (2005). Leading the small rural school: The case of the novice principal. *Leading & Managing, 11*(1), 43–56.

Wildy, H., & Wallace, J. (2002). Lighting the way: School restructuring and the movement of people and ideas. *Leading & Managing, 8*(1), 1–16.

Wilson, S. (2002). Student participation and school culture: A secondary school case study. *Australian Journal of Education, 46*(1), 79–102.

Wood, M. (2005). A marketing study of school self-awareness: Moving from serious decline to strong success. *Leading & Managing, 11*(1), 57–67.

AFFILIATIONS

Bill Mulford
University of Tasmania
Austra

DAMING FENG

CHAPTER 10

Leadership Strategies for Learning Improvement: Cases from Mainland China

INTRODUCTION

Today, the improvement of student learning is still one of the priorities for school leadership though requirements for the role of school leaders in the 21st century are intensifying (Tomlinson & Feng, 2001). In the last decades, a compelling body of empirical evidence has demonstrated the significant effects of school leadership on school conditions and student learning (Leithwood, Aitken, & Jantzi, 2006, p. 59-60). On the other hand, leadership for learning, particularly for student learning is likely to be one of key elements in government requirements or professional standards for school leaders in most western countries. For example, the Standards for School Leaders developed by the Interstate School leaders Licensure Consortium, in the United States requires school leaders to promote "the success of all students by facilitating the development, articulation, implementation, and stewardship of a vision of learning", placing "student learning as the fundamental purpose of schooling", and ensuring that "barriers to student learning are identified, clarified, and addressed" (Sergiovanni, 2001, pp. 25-27). The same expressions or implications can be identified in the Leadership Development Framework of the National College for School Leadership, in England (NCSL, 2001) and the dimensions and competencies of school leadership of the Australian Principals Centre, Victoria, Australia (Davis, 2003).

THE CHINA CONTEXT

Compared with the landscapes in western countries, China presents a different picture. Although the requirement of leadership competency fostering student learning is not new for China's school leaders (State Education Commission, 1991), such a requirement has still been seen as an ideal goal, not yet the reality. The primary reason for this is that little is known about the linkage between leadership performance and improvement of student learning because very little empirical research has been conducted in China's schools thus far (Wu, 2000, pp. 27-28; Li, 2005, p. 12). As one attempt to explore the linkage between leadership performance and learning improvement in China, this chapter aims to identify key strategies of leadership which contribute to student learning through documentary analysis in three schools. Developments in Shanghai Zabei No. 8 Middle School, Lanzhou No.10 Middle School, and Yangsi Middle School, described by a number of authors (Chen, 2003; Zhang, 2004; Ni, 2006) as exemplifying successful learning – centred leadership. An analysis of these publications and other supportive materials, offers insights into the improvement of learning in these three schools but also lays particular emphasis on identifying the key strategies of leadership which underpin that success. Specifically, it attempts to answer the question 'what are the key strategies of leadership that contribute to improvement of student learning?' And to provide policy makers and schools leaders with recommendations which are worth considering.

TYPICAL CASES OF LEARNING IMPROVEMENT IN DISADVANTAGED SCHOOLS

The focus of this chapter is the learning improvement in the Shanghai Zabei No. 8 Middle School, Lanzhou No. 10 Middle School, and Yangsi Middle School as the stories of these three schools chosen to illustrate factors which account for their success, and with wider application.

A. Schools had been disadvantaged schools before their improvement took place.

Traditionally, a disadvantaged school in China referred to the lowest performing school among ordinary schools, in which at least four major characteristics could be observed: (a) lack of sufficient funding and necessary equipment for normal operation; (b) a majority of students from low socioeconomic status families, low academic achievers with low self-esteem and low motivation due to repeated experiences of failure in school; (c) most teachers having low levels of confidence in improving students' achievement and lacking skill in instruction; and (d) the focal point of school leadership as keeping order rather than improvement in the quality of learning. Paralleling China's economic development and increasing resourcing of education in 1990s, the first of these four factors has been removed in recent years but the other three are still in existence.

According to Peter Mortimore, the effective school is "one in which students' progress further than might be expected from consideration of its intake." (Mortimore, 1998, p. 258), in other words of these four factors an effective school should add extra value to its students' outcomes in comparison with other schools serving similar intakes (Sammons, 1999, p. 76). The most convincing cases of learning improvement should therefore not be drawn from the elite magnet schools or selective schools, but rather from the disadvantaged schools. The No. 8 Middle, No. 10 Middle, and Yangsi Middle had been typically disadvantaged schools before the improvement of their student learning took place.

B. The improvement of student learning in these schools has been widely acknowledged.

The practices of learning improvement in No. 8 Middle, No.10 Middle, and Yangsi Middle are well-known and the most influential cases widely acknowledged in China. The case of No. 8 Middle School was highlighted by the Ministry of Education in 1994 (Liu, 2005) and has been influential in rebuilding the quality of disadvantaged schools in China since the 1990s, through conferences, symposiums, and publications all with a focus on No. 8 Middle School. Since 1995, a number of disadvantaged schools in different parts of China have emulated the strategies of No. 8 Middle to improve their student learning with achieved satisfying results (Chen, 2003, pp. 19-21). The case of No.10 Middle was identified in 2000 as a successful example of learning improvement and was named in 2001 as a "Model School" by the Municipal Government of Lanzhou. In 2004 learning improvement in No.10 Middle was published and celebrated in leadership workshops for disadvantaged schools in inland China (Xie, 2005). Similarly, the case of Yangsi Middle was recommended in 1999 by the provincial government of Jiangsu Province. In the last decade, more than 400,000 educators have made study visits to Yangsi Middle School since it has been widely known as one of the most successful schools in the region (Zhang, 2005; Ni, 2006, p. 145).

C. School leaders play the crucial role in promoting improvement of student learning

Throughout the process of improving learning in these three schools, school leaders have played the crucial role in restructuring, establishing guiding beliefs, developing innovative pedagogies, implementing positive appraisal, fostering school-based teacher development, and making full use of external resources. In acknowledgement of their contributions, the leaders of these three schools have been awarded honourable titles by government and professional organizations. The principal of No. 8 Middle was given the title of National Excellent Educator in 1994 and Municipal Excellent

Principal in 1999. The principal of No. 10 Middle was awarded the National May-Fifth Labor Medal in the late 1990s. The principal of Yangsi Middle was given the title of National Excellent Educator and Provincial Excellent Principal in 1990s. (Chen, 2003, p. 21; Xie, 2005; Ni, 2006, p. 146)

COMPARATIVE PICTURES BEFORE AND AFTER IMPROVEMENT

As mentioned above, the three schools examined in this chapter had been disadvantaged schools before improvement took place. In 1989, the issue of disadvantaged schools was first placed on the agenda of State Education Commission (SEC, renamed the Ministry of Education in 1998). Ten years later, the Ministry of Education issued an important policy document entitled *Reinforcing the development of disadvantaged schools and making every school work in large and medium cities*. This document put forward initiatives aimed at improving the quality of disadvantaged schools by introducing changes in funding, governance, policies of enrolment, human resource distribution, and teacher development (MOE, 1998). What happened in these three schools has therefore to be seen in that policy context.

A. The No. 8 Middle

No. 8 Middle is an inner-city school located in Shanghai, a modern metropolis. The school community, Zabei District, is one of poorest socio-economic communities in the city. The statistics and psychological measurements gathered from 1986 to 1987 reveal a profile of a typically disadvantaged school (Wang, 1993, pp. 283-285; Chen, 2003, p. 2; Xiong & Yu, 2005, pp. 749-750) (see the left column of Table 1). Supported by the local educational authority, in 1987 this school started its project aimed at improving the effectiveness of teaching and the quality of learning in the school. By the end of 1980s, there was clear evidence of improvement as shown in Table 1 (right hand column) (Chen, 2003, p. 4, p. 19; Xiong & Yu, 2005, pp. 761-762; Liu, 2005) (see the right column of Table 1).

B. The No. 10 Middle

No.10 Middle is a school located in Lanzhou, a city in inland China with a low level of economic development. Most students come from the families of low socio-economic status. In 1996 No. 10 Middle was identified as a typically disadvantaged school by the local education authority and by dissatisfied stakeholders (Guo, 2004; Zhang, 2004, pp. 37-50; Xie, 2005) (see the left column of Table 1). In that year, the school was involved in the three-year program of rebuilding disadvantaged schools launched by the municipal government of Lanzhou. Leaders of No.10 Middle School capitalised on this opportunity and positive encouragement from the education authority to develop a shared vision with leadership strategies aimed at fostering teacher development, student learning, and a caring school culture. In 1998 the school gained the Quality Improvement Award of Lanzhou followed by an Excellent Quality Award in 2001 and was named a Model School in 2001 (Guo, 2004; Zhang, 2004, pp. 88-100) (see the right column of Table 1).

C. The Yangsi Middle

Yangsi Middle School is a school in the rural area of Jiangsu Province. It was a school with many features typical of disadvantaged schools in 1980s. Equipment and facilities for teaching and learning were out of date. Most teachers had little confidence in improving their students' learning. Most students had not experienced success in their primary education and were potential dropouts, They were typically low academic achievers and at high risk. Most were from farmers' families, of low socioeconomic status and little formal educational background (see the left column of Table 1). In the decade between 1991 and 2001 Yangsi Middle School became known as a successful school for at risk students with two key slogans – "No child cannot be taught" and "Everybody can learn well". In 2002, Yangsi Middle was named as a provincial Model School in Jiangsu Province (Ni, 2006, pp. 1-2, 145-146; Zhang, 2005).

Table 1: The different situations before and after improvement in three schools (VII, X and Y)

	Before	After
Student learning	Out of 35 middle schools in the district, the student average score of this school in entrance examination for middle school was at the bottom while the ratio of student criminality was at the top. (VIII) Out of 17 middle schools in the district, student average scores in this school in entrance examination for middle school was at the bottom but the ratio of student criminality was at the top. (X)	Out of 35 middle schools in the district, the student average academic achievement in this school rose from the bottom to the middle range while student criminal cases dropped from the top level down to zero. (VIII) Out of 17 middle schools in the district, the student average academic achievements in this school rose from the bottom to the first three. (X)

Before	After
About 50 per cent of the students were failing in academic learning. (Ys)	Among schools in the same community, student average academic achievement in this school is at the top. (Ys)
One-third of students failed to be promoted from grade to grade when they were in elementary schools. (VIII)	Among neighbouring schools, student behaviour in this school is in first place. (VIII, X, Ys)
Only 22 per cent of the graduates of this school passed the final standardized test. (VIII)	Proficiency of the students at this school in English listening comprehension, fast reading and comprehension, and oral expression is higher than that of students from ordinary schools in the district. (VIII)
Only 16 percent of the graduates in this school passed the final standardized test. (X)	
Most students were not in the habit of preparing for lessons before class. (VIII, X, Ys)	Nearly 100 per cent of the graduates in this school passed the final standardized. (VIII, X, Ys)
Most students were not in the habit of reviewing lessons after class. (VIII, X, Ys)	Students tend to participate confidently in various academic events and contests confidently. (VIII, X, Ys)
Only 11 per cent of the students were in the habit of completing their homework without copying from others. (VIII)	91 percent of the students are in the habit of completing their home work without copying from others. (VIII)
Most students had no confidence that they could succeed in passing final standardized test. (VIII, X, Ys)	More than 90 per cent of the students express satisfaction with their school. (VIII)
Most students had little motivation for learning. (VIII, X, Ys)	Most have confidence that they would succeed in passing final standardized test. (VIII, X, Ys)
10 per cent of the students had completely lost heart in their learning and adult life in the future. (VIII)	Most of the students are in the habit of preparing lessons before class. (VIII, X, Ys)
Only 10 per cent of the students expressed satisfaction with the school. (VIII)	Most of the students are in the habit of reviewing lessons after class. (VIII, X, Ys)
Most of students exhibited low self-esteem, particularly in classroom work. (VIII, X, Ys)	Most of students exhibit high self-esteem. (VIII, X, Ys)
	Students unprecedentedly won the third place in an English contest in competition with ordinary and high performing schools in the district. (VIII)

	Before	After
Other conditions at the school	Teacher Most teachers had little interest in professional development and pedagogical improvement. (X) Most teachers had little confidence in improving their students' learning. (VIII, X, Ys) 20 per cent of the teachers were unqualified. Leadership The focal issue of school leadership was not improvement of quality in learning but simply keeping order. (VIII, X, Ys) There were no systematic rules and norms of school management. (VIII, X, Ys) Equipment and facilities Equipment and facilities for teaching and learning were out of date. (VIII, X, Ys) School-parent collaboration Few parents had knowledge of techniques designed to assist children's learning at home. (VIII, X, Ys) There was little collaboration between school and parents. (VIII, X, Ys)	Teacher Most teachers have confidence in improving their students' learning. (VIII, X, Ys) Most teachers are qualified in teaching. (VIII, X, Ys) Leadership The focal issue of school leadership has shifted from school order to the continuous improvement in teaching and learning. (VIII, X, Ys) Rules and regulations fostering student learning have been developed. (VIII, X, Ys) Equipment and facilities Most parts of equipments and facilities for teaching and learning have been replaced. (VIII, X, Ys) School-parent collaboration The school provides parents with knowledge of techniques to assist children in learning at home through special support programmes. (VIII, X, Ys) There is a Parent Consultative Committee seeking ways to share parenting skills in assisting children in their learning. (VIII, X)
Social recognition	The school was identified as a typical disadvantaged school. (VIII, X, Ys)	The school is given the title of "Model School". (VIII, X, Ys) Improvement of student learning was recognised by the Ministry of Education. (VIII & X) Improvement of student learning was recognised by the provincial government of Jangsu. (Ys)

DAMING FENG

KEY LEADERSHIP STRATEGIES CONTRIBUTING TO LEARNING IMPROVEMENT

Through documentary accounts in these three schools a number of leadership strategies may be identified.

A. Sharing guiding beliefs with school members

"Guiding beliefs" refers to a series of shared assumptions and ideas among students, teachers, support staff, school leaders, and parents. These address the cardinal questions in school life, such as, what is the ultimate meaning of education? Can every teacher change the destiny of at risk students? What is the most valuable experience in a teacher's career? To establish these guiding beliefs and to foster confidence in improvement of student learning, the leaders of these three schools employed a range of differing strategies to raise teachers' level of confidence and optimism. Through a process of continuing dialogue, Jinghai Liu, the principal of No.8 Middle encouraged teachers and support staff to embrace the belief that "The ultimate meaning of education is to help children pass through the fog in their life to find themselves". The vision for school staff is captured in these two affirmations - "It is essential for educators to believe that every student has the potential to be successful", and "One of the most important responsibilities for educators is to teach children learning how to learn and learning to strive for success". Liu persuaded students and parents to believe that "Success is not the exclusive privilege for someone. Rather, it is an equal right that belongs to everybody", and "The precise meaning of success is not a high score on a test. Rather, the term 'success' should refer to a person's relative progress in comparison with his past" (Chen, 2003, p. 35; Xiong & Yu, 2005, p. 754).

In the No. 10 Middle School, Dewen Zhang, the principal developed, in collaboration with his staff, a Three-Year Strategic Plan for School with student learning as its primary focus. In the process of developing the Plan, the vision was captured in the two statements -"It is the greatest virtue for a teacher to show love towards disadvantaged or at risk students" and "The most valuable experience in a teacher's career is to change the destiny of disadvantaged or at risk students". (Zhang, 2004, p. 63; Xie, 2005).

In Yangsi Middle School in the first week of every school year, teachers and students make presentations, sharing their experiences and stories from the previous year, with their peers and, in particular with children new to the school. The topics of the presentations which remain constant are "No child cannot be taught" and "Everybody can learn well". Linsen Cai, the principal of the school initiates these activities endorsing the guiding belief that every student has the chance to improve on his or her learning in

Yangsi Middle School as long as he or she has a positive attitude to achievement (Zhang, 2005).

B. Establishing high expectations based on understanding of prior achievement

The research findings of effective schools conducted in 1970s and 1980s revealed that high expectations for all students promote improvement in student learning (Edmonds, 1986; Hopkins, 1987, Levin, 1988; Brook, Nomura, & Cohen, 1989). However, previous experience in disadvantaged schools in China showed that high expectations didn't work if individual students could not see tangible evidence of substantial progress (Chen, 2003, p. 53). Thus, the leaders of these three schools recognized that the high expectations should take into account where students were in their learning. With students at risk, therefore, consideration needed to be given to standardized testing, ensuring that students were not striving for goals that were too ambitious and potentially demoralising. With this in mind, the leaders of these three schools encouraged teachers to know what students were capable of and set targets accordingly.

C. Playing the role of head developer in developing innovative pedagogies

To have students see their progress and improve their low self-esteem, leaders of No.8 Middle, No.10 Middle, and Yangsi Middle worked with their teachers at every grade level to develop innovative pedagogy in order that every classroom became a place where the individual's needs for achievement and positive experiences could be met. In No.8 Middle, a task team headed by Principal Liu developed pedagogy with the following four characteristics (Chen, 2003, p. 184-185; Liu, 2005):

a. *Adjust the starting point*: A teacher knows and understands the current level of achievement of individual students by interviewing students and their parents, checking students' previous homework, engaging in quizzes before class, and the question-answer sessions during class work. The teacher will suggest starting points for individual students at the beginning of a semester. Given the fact that most of students at the No. 8 Middle are low academic achievers with low self-esteem, starting points are usually more modest than general national curriculum standards.

b. *Moderated pace*: To minimize the chance of frustration and maximize the chance of success teachers adjust the pace of learning for students who may experience difficulties in keeping pace with normal requirements. In this way, students with learning difficulties enjoy more opportunities to experience progression and success in the learning.

c. *Varied activities*: It is easy for at risk students to become distracted if a teacher's presentation lasts 15 minutes or more. Thus, it is important for teachers to shift the format of teaching and learning from time to time, providing students with interactive student-student activities.

d. *Quick feedback*: Teaching (by teacher) – doing and practising (by students) – checking and correcting (by teacher) – identifying problems and problem solving (by the teacher together with students) is a basic cycle in every classroom session. Through this quick feedback, teachers or students can together identify problems in their teaching or their learning so as to improve their work. Through quick feedback students are able to set an immediate view of their progress in learning. An essential factor in rebuilding their confidence in learning over time.

In similar fashion innovative pedagogies have been developed in No. 10 Middle and Yangsi Middle. These pedagogies create opportunities for, and experience of, success. In these three schools leaders are the investigators and champions of innovative pedagogies.

In Yangsi Middle School, teachers led by Principal Cai developed an innovative pedagogy described as "Teaching after learning" and "Instant exercises" (Ni, 2006, pp. 19-21):

a. *Teaching after learning*: As at risk students are often distracted and do not pay attention to the teacher, they have difficulty with their homework. Instead of the traditional approach, "teaching after learning" means spending no more than a minute in presenting learning objectives and academic requirements and providing students with a planned work sheet. After a three-minute briefing, the teacher asks students to complete the work sheet. Students read the materials related to the worksheet and study relevant sample questions and answers in textbook before they fill in the work sheet. The teacher then makes his/her rounds while students are studying textbooks and doing worksheet by themselves. After this stage, the teacher encourages students to identify their problems and to find the solutions independently by communication and questioning with their peers. At the end of this stage, the teacher provides the necessary guidance and summarises at the end.

b. *Instant exercises*: This refers to a fifteen-minute stage immediate after the teacher's summary. Students complete another worksheet with the purpose of reinforcing and practising what they just learned and understood in the previous stage. Individual students can do either a part of work (compulsory) or all parts of work (optional) based on individual's current level of achievement.

Evidence from research conducted in the last few decades demonstrates that engaging low-achieving students in a challenging curriculum can produce positive academic and social outcomes (Levin, 1988). Similarly, the pedagogy of "Teaching after learning" and "Instant exercises" can engage low-achieving students and help students learn how to learn and how to self-regulate over time.

D. Developing formative assessment

Leaders of No. 8 Middle, No. 10 Middle, and Yangsi Middle Schools worked with their teachers to develop assessment designed to encourage students' learning. This helps in four ways (1) students recognize the relationship between their endeavours and improved learning outcomes; (2) students learn to attribute failure in learning to insufficient input, insufficient previous knowledge, or inappropriate methods rather than low intelligence; (3) students learn how to identify problems, how to analyze errors, and how to adjust the goals for their further learning; (4) students learn to respect each other (Liu, 2005). To ensure that teachers apply innovative pedagogies and formative assessment in their teaching, autocratic leadership style has had to give away to a more democratic leadership style. Usually, it is easy for leaders to ask subordinates to change but find it difficult to change themselves. This was something recognised by the leaders of these three schools, resulting in a change in their leadership style. In addition, leaders of the schools initiated performance-related pay by restructuring incentives. A special allowance rewarded teachers who had made efforts to use innovative pedagogies and formative assessment (Chen, 2003, pp. 251-254; Zhang, 2004, p. 65; Zhang, 2005).

E. Leading school-based teacher development

To prevent at risk students' failure and to improve their learning and self-esteem, disadvantaged schools need well trained teachers who are able to teach effectively in non-traditional ways, who can tailor traditional curricula to the learning needs of individual students, and deal with disciplinary and truancy problems. In China's universities and teacher training institutions, there are very few sophisticated training programs able to meet the complex needs of individual teachers from disadvantaged schools. On the other hand, it is futile for China's disadvantaged schools to impose strategies gleaned from western countries, particularly from the U.S. As Donnelly (1987) describes it, successful programs in America "separate at-risk students from other students, they relate work to education, are small, have low student-to-teacher ratios, and provide counseling and supportive services." Such an approach is too costly for

China's schools. Given the circumstances prevailing in China, leaders of No. 8 Middle, No. 10 Middle, and Yangsi Middle School have collaborated with experts in teacher education to develop school-based professional development. Among these approaches are "team study", "micro study with peers" and "co-authored script".

a. *Team study:* Teachers who teach the same subject at the same grade get together once a week to analyze issues emerging from classroom practice and to discuss the possible solutions to negative student attitudes and unhelpful peer relationships. The priority for the coming week will then be identified. School leaders usually participate in this study in different teams so as to provide teachers with the necessary support and understanding (Ni, 2006, pp. 176-177).

b. *Micro study with peers*: The school videotapes a ten-minute episode of a teacher's class selected by the teacher herself and shows it with colleagues in the same department to discuss and analyze advantages and disadvantages of the teacher's teaching evidenced by this ten-minute extract, so as to find ways of furthering teachers' skills and repertoire. (Chen, 2003, p.6; Xiong & Yu, 2005, p. 760).

c. *Co-authored script*: The school encourages every teacher to display a selected script for a 45-minute class session. This script is circulated among his or her colleagues in the same department. Each teacher who receives the script is required to revise or refine the original script based on his or her values, perspectives, and understanding of teaching and learning. The script may be revised and refined many times before it is finally passed back to its original author weeks later. It is helpful for the original author (particularly for a teacher at his or her early service stage) to read and understand the revised and refined script in which other teachers' intelligence and experiences are embedded. Later, the school will collect all of the co-authored scripts as materials to be shared commonly (Wen Hui Daily, 2006a, p. 12).

F. Making full use of external resources

With continuous improvement in China's economy, both central and local governments have established special foundations for disadvantaged schools in the last decade. For instance, the central government in 1995 established a special foundation for disadvantaged schools in inland China, providing disadvantaged schools in 852 less developed counties with approximately 1.6 billion US dollars invested by the year 2000 (Li, 2003, p. 251). In another development, the governments of east coastal cities intend to establish special foundations themselves for local disadvantaged schools.

As the most developed coastal city in China, Shanghai, for example, had invested 1.1billion US dollars of extra funding for 194 local disadvantaged schools from the year of 2002 to 2005 (Wen Hui Daily, 2006b, p. 12). Leaders of No. 8 Middle, No. 10 Middle and Yangsi Middle made use of this funding to renovate the school building, to fit classrooms and laboratories with necessary equipment, and to pay for professional development (Zhang, 2004, p. 77, 82; Ni, 2006, pp. 76-77).

Recently, inter-district support programs have been initiated and specific ways of implementing the programs have been developed by some local governments. By way of inter-district partnership, inter-district internship, inter-district mentoring, and inter-district volunteering, leaders of No. 8 Middle and No. 10 Middle had the opportunity to promote teacher development at their schools (Zhang, 2003, p. 60; Wang & Su, 2004; Wen Hui Daily, 2006a, p. 11).

In the process of improving learning, the leaders of these three schools have also developed supportive programs for parents. In No. 10 Middle, Principal Zhang organized a children's education workshop to share successful experiences with parents. Through the experience of the workshop, a partnership between parents and teachers was built (Zhang, 2003, p.85). The No. 8 Middle School set up the parental council at school level, parental teams at grade level, and parental volunteers at class level in order to help the school develop a secure and supportive climate within the school (Xiong & Yu, 2005, p. 760).

RECOMMENDATIONS

In this chapter, the publications and other supportive materials describing the process and outcomes of learning improvement in these three schools have been examined. As a result, six key strategies of leadership that contribute to improvement of student learning were identified. For the practitioners in the field of educational leadership, the following recommendations based on the cases of these three schools strategies are worth considering.

For policy makers, improving learning for disadvantaged and at risk students should be given priority. According to the 1990 *World Declaration on Education for All*, all children, "shall be able to benefit from educational opportunities designed to meet their learning needs" and "an active commitment must be made to remove educational disparities." (UNESCO, 1990) It is imperative for governments to provide disadvantaged and at risk students with opportunities for improvement in their learning. The cases presented in this chapter suggest that success in learning improvement for disadvantaged and at risk students requires a positive and supportive external environment in which governments can play a leading role.

The recommendation for institutions providing leadership development is that leadership strategies identified in this chapter are likely to prove helpful in developing appropriate training programs for school leaders in disadvantaged schools. School leadership, rather than government policy, is the most crucial factor for improved student learning. While policies and initiatives backed by fiscal support at system level are crucial in promoting improvement, these won't work in any substantive way if effective and appropriate leadership strategies at individual whole school level don't match them well. In the final analysis it is leadership strategies at site level that count.

School leaders, particularly principals, need to consider the leadership style that they should adopt in fostering student learning. In China, Principal Accountability has been in place since the late 1980s (Xiao, 1994, p. 67). The principal is thus the final decision maker as well as the person who is ultimately accountable (Wu, Feng, & Zhou, 2000, p. 84; Wu, 2002, p. 63). For years, many principals have tended to adopt an autocratic leadership style because the "authority-compliance" approach comes easily in controlling, demanding, and ensuring top down compliance. Yet, such a leadership style does not appear to contribute to the enhancement of student learning (Feng, 2003, 2005). Not surprisingly, the key strategies identified in this chapter won't work until such autocratic leadership styles are abandoned. The stories of three schools demonstrate the value of innovative pedagogies and formative assessment within a democratic leadership style. It is impossible for a leader to work collaboratively with their teachers in leading the way to success in an autocratic environment.

A final recommendation for leaders of disadvantaged schools is to pay careful attention to learning how to learn. As Marge Scherer writes:

> One current debate is about the definition of a "highly qualified teacher." Policymakers argue about what matters more----content knowledge, knowledge of instructional techniques, or knowledge about how students learn---but they rarely note that all three kinds of knowledge are necessary for a *highly qualified* teacher to possess. (Scherer, 2006)

What does this mean for classroom practice? Dewen Zhang, the principal of No. 10 Middle points out that students are at risk for different reasons. It may be down to inappropriate learning habits and learning strategies, low self-esteem, a low level of motivation, or little interest in specific subjects. To identify the current needs of every student and help him or her to overcome his or her major barriers to learning, we need not only skilful and knowledgeable practitioners but also patient, responsive, and caring teachers with a loving heart (Zhang, 2004, p. 91).

In motivating teachers to work hard, school leaders have been, for years, familiar with two motivational rules. One is "what gets rewarded gets done" and the other is "what is rewarding gets done." However, Sergiovanni reminds us that there is an alternative rule: "What we believe in, and what we feel obligated to do because of a moral commitment, gets done. Again, it gets done, and it gets done well, without close supervision or other controls." (Sergiovanni, 1992, p. 27) In short, it is the motivational rule of "what is good gets done." If school leaders believe that Sergiovanni (1992) is correct, far more attention will have to be given to tapping the moral source on which teachers can draw and bringing the moral imperative into play in improving learning for students at risk.

NOTES

The author would like to acknowledge the support of the PhD Programme Scholarship Fund provided by East China Normal University in 2007.

REFERENCES

Brook, J., Nomura, C., & Cohen, P. (1989). A network of influences on adolescent drug involvement: Neighborhood, school, peer, and family. *Genetic, Social, and General Psychology Monographs, 115*(1), 303–321.

Chen, D. (2003). *Liu and successful education*. Beijing: International Cultural Publishing Company.

Davis, B. (2003). Developing leaders for self-managing schools: The role of a principal center in accreditation and professional learning. In P. Hallinger (Ed.), *Reshiping the landscape of school leadership development: A global perspectives* (pp. 145–162). Lisse: Swets & Zeitlinger Publishers.

Donnelly, M. (1987). At risk students. *ERIC Digest Series No. 21*. Clearinghouse on Educational Management Eugene. Available: http://www.ericdigests.org/pre-928/risk.htm

Edmonds, R. (1986). Characteristics of effective schools. In U. Neisser (Ed.), *The school achievement of minority children: New perspectives* (pp. 93–104). Hillsdale, NJ: Lawrence Erlbaum.

Feng, D. (2003). Restructuring and reinventing the Principal Responsibility System. *Theory and Practice of Education, 23*(1), 34–37.

Feng, D. (2005). Restructuring the principal accountability in China. *Exploring Education Development, 25*(1), 26–29.

Guo, W. (2004). *A principal is the flag of a school*. Retrieved January 10, 2004, from http://www.xtyz.com

Hopkins, D. (1987). *Improving the quality of schooling: Lessons from the OECD international school improvement project*. London: The Falmer Press.

Leithwood, K., Aitken, R., & Jantzi, D. (2006). *Making schools smarter: Leading with evidence*. California: Corwin Press.

Levin, H. (1988). Accelerated schools for disadvantaged students. *Educational Leadership, 44*(6), 19–21.

Li, J. (2005). *Positive research on headmasters' leadership and school efficiency*. Jinan: Shangdong People's Publishing House.

Li, L. (2003). *Talking about education: Interview with Li Lanqing*. Beijing: People's Education Press.

Liu, J. (2005). Success from initiatives and efforts. In L. Ma (Ed.), *A wise conversation with sixty principals* (pp. 8–14). Shanghai: Shanghai Educational Publishing House.
National College for School Leadership. (2001). *Leadership development framework*. Nottingham.
Ministry of Education (MOE). (1998). Reinforcing the development of disadvantaged schools and making every elementary and middle school works in large and medium cities. Retrieved from http://www.bjsupervision.gov.cn/zcfg/
Mortimore, P. (1998). *The road to improvement: Reflections on school effectiveness.* Lisse: Swets & Zeitlinger Publishers.
Ni, G. (2006). *Yangsi Middle School, as I see it.* Nanjing: Hehai University Press.
Sammons, P. (1999). *School effectiveness: Coming of age in the twenty-first century.* Lisse: Swets & Zeitlinger Publishers.
Scherer, B. (2006). What teachers want. *Educational Leadership, 63*(6), 7.
Sergiovanni, T. J. (1992). *Moral leadership: Getting to the heart of school improvement*, San Francisco: Jossey-Bass Publishers.
Sergiovanni, T. J. (2001). *The principalship: A reflective practice perspective.* Boston: Allyn & Bacon.
State Education Commission. (1991). *The prerequisites and requirements for the principal position.* Tianjin: Tianjin Educational Publishing House.
Tomlinson, H., & Feng, D. (2001). The new requirements for headteachers in the 21st century. *Instruction & Management, 12*(10), 3–6.
UNESCO. (1990). *World declaration on education for All* (1st printing). New York. Retrieved from http://www.cies.ws/PaperDocuments/PDF/WorldDaclarationonEducationForAll.pdf
Wang, M. (1993). *The well-known pilot programs of educational reform in China.* Qingdao: Qingdao Ocean Press.
Wen Hui News Report. (2006a, January 12). Achievements of the rebuilding disadvantaged middle schools project in Shanghai. *Wen Hui Daily.*
Wen Hui News Report. (2006b, January 11). Achievements of the rebuilding disadvantaged middle schools project in Shanghai. *Wen Hui Daily.*
Wu, Z. (2000). *Educational administration.* Beijing: People's Education Press.
Wu, Z. (2002). *Theory and practice of school management.* Beijing: Beijing Normal University Press.
Wu, Z., Feng, D., & Zhou, J. (2000). *Educational administration: A new framework.* Shanghai: East China Normal University Press.
Xiao, Z. (1994). *School management studies.* Beijing: People's Education Press.
Xie, W. (2005, December 14). Dewen Zhang: The principal of the fourteenth middle school. *Modern Education News.* Lanzhou.
Xiong, M., & Yu, B. (2005). *A history of educational explorations and experiments in modern China.* Jinan: Shandong Educational Publishing House.
Zhang, D. (2004). *Providing good education for every student.* Beijing: Education & Science Publishing House.
Zhang, J. (2005, May 11, 13, 17, 18). Interpreting what happening in Yangsi Middle School. *China Education Daily,* 4. Retrieved from http://hi.baidu.com/

AFFILIATIONS

Daming Feng
East China Normal University,
China

BRADLEY S. PORTIN, MICHAEL S. KNAPP, MARGARET L. PLECKI AND MICHAEL A. COPLAND

CHAPTER 11

Supporting and Guiding Learning-focused Leadership in US Schools

INTRODUCTION

It is a difficult, yet exciting, time to be an educational leader in the US. So much is expected of school leaders, district (or other local education authority) officials, local board members, or even teachers who are assuming formal or informal leadership responsibilities. State educational leaders operating at some distance from the classroom face the same high expectations, along with the demands of guiding an entire educational system towards improved performance. The climate of high accountability underscores the weight of the expectations facing all these leaders.

One of the most consistent concerns for elementary and secondary education in the US is the unresolved challenge of ensuring equitable learning opportunities for all students. While gains have been reported in many of our country's most challenged schools, the issues associated with consistent access to high quality teaching and learning opportunities still remain (Togneri & Anderson, 2003).

This is not a uniquely American problem but one experienced in many countries. However, each national context provides their own historical, cultural, and political reasons for student achievement patterns. In adding to this volume, it is our intent to inform the cross-national dialogue about expectations for student learning and how leaders (formal and informal alike) can influence a school's or system's capacity to support high quality teaching and learning.

While many factors influence and contribute to student learning (with special emphasis on the instructional capacity of the teachers who work with students), leadership in all its forms contributes in important ways to the learning process (Leithwood and Riehl, 2003). It remains a challenge to conceptualize how to connect leadership practice with student learning, and then mobilize others' energies and commitment accordingly. This challenge implicates not only individual leaders, operating from their respective vantage points in a complicated system, but all of them together. *How are they to bring their collective efforts to bear on the task of improving learning for all students?* And it also implicates a larger set of actors whose actions guide or support leadership practice. *How do they create conditions that prompt and enable leaders to constructively influence learning outcomes?*

THE LENS OF LEARNING-FOCUSED LEADERSHIP

The starting place for our inquiry into learning-focused leadership is based in certain assumptions. One, already suggested, is that student learning takes pride-of-place in any consideration of the purposes of schools. If students are not making progress in expected ways, it becomes a matter of public and policy concern.

We do not, however, limit learning-focused leadership to the domain of student learning, but also acknowledge that schools have larger learning agendas (Knapp, Copland, & Talbert, 2003). These include the improvements in practice and capacity building necessary for the professionals in the school to continuously sharpen their practice. In addition, organizations themselves face opportunities to adapt and change to meet the expectations placed on them. This represents a form of organizational learning that can feed the context for student learning.

The central point is that educational leadership is ultimately concerned with learning. Efforts to improve leadership practice, therefore, imply helping leaders to more effectively address questions of learning improvement. In this respect, we are building on a line of thinking that we and others have been engaged in over the last five years in which the connections between leadership activity and learning events have been more systematically conceptualized and empirically studied.[1]

In this chapter, we extend that thinking by clarifying certain aspects of the exercise of leadership that seem essential to the productive connections between leadership and learning improvement and by painting a more specific picture of conditions and activities that affect leaders' work. Here, we make the further assumption that these conditions and activities occur at various levels of the educational system, especially at state, district, and school levels, and that their *joint influence* is what matters most to the exercise of leadership. We also make the assumption that effective leadership is intimately connected to a specific local and state context, and that broad principles can guide the leaders' work only up to a point. From there on, the matter rests with local politics, site-specific relationships, and the leaders' responsiveness to the particulars of the communities they serve.

The model presented here is one that conceptualizes leadership for learning in three interacting arenas. Visually, the model is represented in figure 1. Figure 1 represents three interacting sets of activities and conditions that we suggest have an influence on learning-focused leadership. At the center is the exercise of learning-focused leadership located primarily (but not exclusively) at the school level. Leadership practice may be exercised by a host of school personnel in a distributed manner (Spillane, 2006) or located in traditional principal roles. This exercise of learning- focused leadership relies on what leaders bring to the work, what they learn from engaging with feedback, and the potential direct and indirect ways they might influence teaching and learning within a school.

Figure 1. Activities and Conditions that Shape Learning Š focused Leadership

Policy Environments:
Federal-state-local activities that affect resources, set reform expectations, and allocate authority

Leadership Support System:
State-local activities that seek to direct, support, improve and assess leadership practice

The Exercise of Learning-Focused Leadership

What leaders bring to Š and learn from Š their work

Leadership practice

Potential influences on student, professional, and system learning

Feedback on learning, improvement efforts, and performance

(Figure reprinted with small alterations from Knapp, Copland, Plecki, & Portin, 2006, p. 2)

Given the intent to exercise learning-focused leadership, particular kinds of activities are implicated in any strategy oriented toward the improvement of teaching and learning. For example, these might include:

• ***Redefining leadership roles and responsibilities.*** School and district leaders reconstruct or assume redesigned leadership roles that keep matters of learning improvement in the foreground as a central, collective responsibility.
• ***Using data, evidence, and feedback.*** Leaders at all levels generate, access, and use information that helps them pinpoint learning needs, imagine

solutions, describe the operation of programs, and assess performance. Of particular importance are various forms of *feedback* to leaders concerning their own and others' efforts to address learning agendas.

- ***Focusing resources on learning:*** Local and state leaders allocate—which often means *reallocating*—resources that directly support the learning of students, teachers, and others, while managing the politics of (re)allocation accordingly. In addition, rather than treating resources as fixed quantities, they pay particular attention to *developing* resources, especially the human resources—the teaching staff and instructional support personnel who are in a position to serve the full range of students' learning needs.

As we consider the exercise of learning-focused leadership in schools, current efforts to ensure equity and access to high quality teaching and learning (as well as the attendant achievement measures) imply a larger system of support and guidance. In this chapter, we are largely locating our analysis in the system of publicly-funded state education in the US, in this case, the school and school district system which serves most students in the US. One step removed, other activities at the state and local level take aim at the way leaders think about and approach their work, thereby guiding or supporting leaders towards a more learning-focused forms of practice, by:

- ***Developing future leadership capacity.*** As part of formal preparation programs, recruitment initiatives, or "homegrown" leadership development arrangements inside school districts, a new generation of teacher leaders, school administrators, district officials, instructional improvement coaches, or an agency's leadership cadre can be identified and nurtured. All of these are required, individually and in context, to take learning improvement seriously and understand what it means.
- ***Providing direction or models for leaders' daily work.*** Certain state and local policies and practices communicate what is expected for leaders' work—e.g. through widely promulgated leadership standards, specifications for leadership positions, and arrangements for administrator supervision. Though they often don't, these communications about leaders' work can speak clearly and forcefully about learning-focused leadership practice.
- ***Supporting the ongoing professional learning of practicing leaders.*** Arrangements of many kinds, from individual mentoring or coaching to formal professional development sessions, teach individuals or leadership teams what it means to focus energy more centrally on learning improvement.
- ***Establishing leadership evaluation systems.*** Arrangements for generating evaluative data about leadership performance, either as formative

guidance for the leaders' growth or summative judgments about their accomplishments and capacity, can serve to highlight and guide learning-focused aspects of leaders' practice.

Schools and districts sit within larger policy contexts—local, state, and federal—each of which shape how schools are funded, expected outcomes and accountability measures, and licensure and authorization (among other policy concerns). These policy activities have important implications for leaders' work, even though they are not primarily aimed at leadership practice. These activities occur in three environments:

- *The authorizing environment,* generated by governance arrangements (at all levels), collective bargaining and the contractual agreements it produces, and the interaction among educational stakeholders within and around these arrangements.
- *The resource environment,* including the sources of funds and human resources, and also the infrastructure for gathering information on and for the schools, as well as rules governing the use of these resources.
- *The reform policy environment,* comprising the forces and conditions created by state and federal policies aimed at enhancing the quality of schooling, such as standards-based reform policies.

In numerous ways, these actions in the policy environments invite or command the attention of educational leaders. While the particular policies that come to the fore reflect many interests, a concern for the quality of learning may be infused into the debate and interplay that produces these policies. At a minimum, it implies taking a hard look at what these policies might mean for leaders' ability to focus their energies on learning improvement; at best, participants in policy environments can coalesce around actions that will make leaders' job easier.

SUPPORT AND GUIDANCE FOR LEARNING-FOCUSED LEADERSHIP

These broad categories of activity elicit questions about what people or groups located in different positions within states, districts, or schools actually do in attempting to guide or support leadership practice focused on learning improvement. This section provides a few, illustrative examples of activities that are occurring at the school, district support, and policy levels.

In schools, a relatively small number of educators are involved in the leadership of the school, but more than the formal administrators (principal, assistant principal) may participate in activities that broaden the concept of "leadership" and focus it on matters of teaching and learning in classrooms, as illustrated by the activities in Table 1.

Table 1. *Illustrative Activities at the School Level that Prompt or Support Learning-focused Leadership*

Embedded in the exercise of learning-focused leadership itself	Aimed at guiding or supporting leadership practice
• *Role redefinition*: Establishing teams within the school which take on instructional leadership responsibilities • *Information use*: Setting up systems for teachers to examine student work in relation to grade-level expectations and state standards • *Resource reallocation*: Reallocating time so that teachers can work together on instructional planning	• *Leadership development*: Identifying teachers with leadership potential and nurturing their growth as a future instructional leadership cadre • *Direction for leaders' daily work:* Adopting school-specific statements about what is expected of all who exercise leadership • *Support for leaders' professional learning:* Creating regular occasions for leaders in the school to engage in new learning about high quality teaching • *Leadership assessment systems*: Developing a 360-system for gaining regular feedback on the principal's and other leaders' effectiveness

At the school district (local authority) level, a different set of individuals come into play, occupying positions that are generally defined in terms of administrative functions—personnel, budget, transportation, community relations, school administrator supervision, and so on—only some of which are formally related to teaching and learning. Left to their own devices, their work will often have little to do with learning improvement, but through intentional action by leaders strategically placed within the central office can develop new ways of relating to schools, implied by the activities, that concentrate effort and attention on learning improvement goals (Table 2).

A more dispersed set of actors participate in the policy environments that affect local educational leaders' work. The organizational and political cleavages between State Education Department, governor's office, legislature (both houses), State Board of Education, and other players (e.g., professional Standards Board) will often mean that common ground is hard, or even impossible, to find. Yet separately and, when possible, together, these players have the capacity to make a focus on learning prominent and the implications of this apparent for forms of leadership support. As Table 3 suggests, the ability to form new learning environments is determined by a mix of policies at state level.

Table 2. Illustrative Activities at the District Level that Prompt or Support Learning-focused Leadership

Embedded in the exercise of learning-focused leadership itself	Aimed at guiding or supporting leadership practice
• *Role redefinition:* Creating managerial support roles to remove some aspects of the routine work of the principalship and enable more of a learning focus • *Information use:* Creating or locating informational tools for school leaders • *Resource reallocation:* Making teacher professional development, linked to identified learning agendas, a resource priority	• *Leadership development:* Developing a "leadership pipeline" strategy for the district, in conjunction with a local provider, that seeks to "grow" personnel through various stages of leadership careers • *Direction for leaders' daily work:* Adapting state leadership standards in ways that reflect local learning improvement priorities • *Support for leaders' professional learning:* Creating a local leadership induction/ mentoring program, parallel to teacher induction and mentoring • *Leadership assessment systems*: Creating learning-focused criteria to guide leadership assessment within the district

Table 3. Illustrative Activities in the State Policy Environment that Affect Leaders' Ability to Focus on Learning Improvement

Aimed at guiding or supporting leadership practice	Aimed at broader policy, not specific to leadership, yet with major implications for learning-focused practice
• *Leadership development:* Ensuring that principal licensure standards are keyed to learning improvement goals • *Direction for leaders' daily work:* Publicly promoting instructional leadership and related aspects of learning-focused leadership as a central responsibility of local educational leaders • *Support for leaders' professional learning:* Investing state dollars in periodic professional development for practicing leaders (e.g., to promote instructional leadership), especially for school leaders in their first three years • *Leadership assessment systems*: Linking leadership assessment to explicit, learning-focused standards for leadership practice	• *Authorizing environment:* State governing bodies creating occasions for cross-department conversation about learning goals • *Resource environment:* Creating incentives that encourage the relocation of staff to better serve unmet student needs • *Reform policy environment:* Allowing districts flexibility in defining the indicators of success in achieving state standards-based reform goals

Not shown in any one of these tables is the potentially reinforcing effect that activities in one area and at one level of the system can have on each other. The enduring challenge is one of finding coherent, sustainable ways to join forces across jurisdictional or positional boundaries, and across levels in the system, in the service of learning-focused leadership and leadership support.

STATE AND LOCAL ACTIVITIES THAT SEEK TO SUPPORT AND IMPROVE LEADERSHIP PRACTICE

A different set of activities, one step removed from the immediate exercise of leadership in schools, has equally profound consequences for the prospects of effective leadership with a learning agenda and a concern for the development of individual teachers in classrooms. These activities aim at leadership practice itself—how principals and leadership team members go about their daily work. As shown in Figure 2, these activities at district and state levels include:

- *Activities to develop future leadership capacity*: Efforts mounted as part of formal preparation programs, recruitment initiatives, or "homegrown" leadership development arrangements inside school districts, to identify and nurture the next generation of teacher leaders, school administrators, district officials, instructional improvement coaches, or an agency's leadership cadre.
- *Activities that provide direction or models for leaders' daily work:* Explicit communication of expectations for leaders' work, through such means as widely promulgated leadership standards to leadership position specifications or supervisory expectations.
- *Support for the ongoing professional learning of practicing leaders:* Arrangements of many kinds, from individual mentoring or coaching to formal sessions aimed at teaching groups or teams of leaders new things about their work.
- **Leadership assessment systems:** Arrangements for generating evaluative data about leadership performance, either as formative guidance for the leaders' growth or summative judgments about their accomplishments and capacity.

In principle, these four sets of activities have much to do with how schools and school systems are led and ways in which leadership may evolve. Even though, in practice, relatively little may be done to take advantage of them or to connect them with one another, *these activities comprise a potentially powerful set of conditions for guiding and supporting learning-focused leadership practice.*

This second set of leadership support activities is often intimately connected to the first. Consider, for example, district instructional reform initiatives that target the development of principals' instructional leadership capacity as a central piece of a strategy for improving teaching and learning.[2] In such instances, the medium for improving leadership practice is immersion in the problem of teaching and learning itself. In the view of some observers, such an immersion is the only way to ensure that leaders at all levels of the system gain enough expertise and maintain sufficient "presence" in instructional reform matters to make a difference in the quality of teaching. In such instances, leaders learn by doing, and by receiving various degrees of guidance as they do so.

Figure 2. Activities that Seek to Support and Improve Leadership Practice

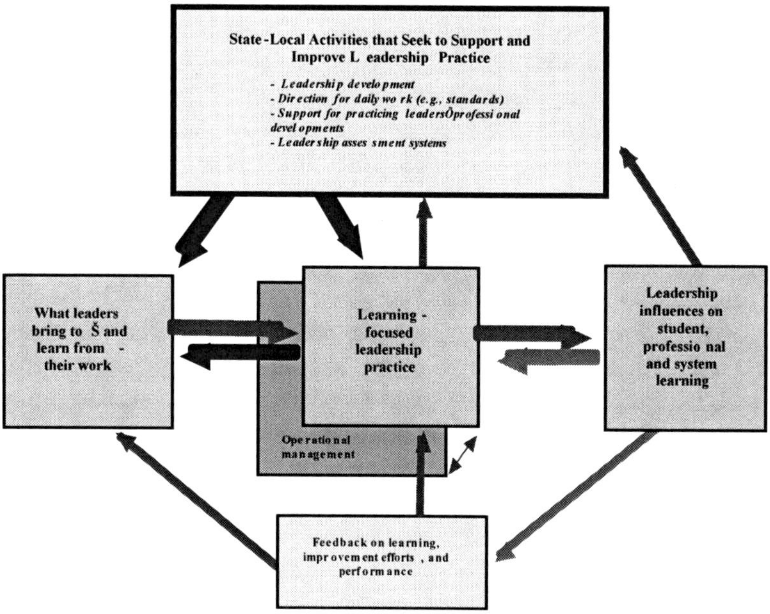

(Reprinted from Knapp, Copland, Plecki, & Portin, 2006, p. 24)

A closer look at these four components of leadership support demonstrates how, separately and together, they may exert influence on leaders to undertake learning improvement agendas.

Development of aspiring leaders for formal and informal, learning-focused roles.[3] Leaders move into leadership roles, both formal and informal, through a series of state and local actions that determine who exercises leadership and what they are supposed to know for this purpose. For one thing, recruitment processes, formal preparation, and (re)certification, along with selection, hiring, and assignment arrangements, bring particular individuals into administrative positions in school and district settings. Often reflecting some set of leadership standards, the criteria that operate in these developmental processes may highlight aspects of leadership work, roles, and responsibilities directed at learning improvement.[4] A similar, though less formalized set of processes tend to operate in the development of teacher leaders and other individuals who assume non-administrative leadership positions, with parallel implications for the *distributed* exercise of learning-focused leadership.

Directing leaders' daily work towards learning improvement. Various actions at state and local levels offer specific direction to practising leaders and leadership teams. For one thing, explicit leadership standards, increasingly embraced by both states and districts, provide broad statements of desirable practice for leaders.[5] Specific expectations appear in hiring agreements, job descriptions, and collective bargaining contracts, not to mention the directives that occur in the process of leadership supervision (where this function is conceived of as organizational control). In principle, expectations for leadership practice from all these sources can (though they generally don't) emphasize learning improvement as a central—indeed, the central—business of leaders' daily work.

Support for the ongoing professional learning of practicing leaders. Given the wide range of demands on contemporary educational leaders, no practicing leader could learn everything he or she needed to know before taking on such roles. While joining forces in distributed leadership arrangements may appear to mitigate this problem, even teams of leaders have lots to learn about effective collective practice aimed at learning improvement.[6] The sources of support for ongoing professional learning—among them, mentoring arrangements, professional development of various kinds, the formative aspects of leadership supervision (where this function is conceived as a supportive activity), feedback from leadership assessment systems (if conceived of as serving a formative purpose), and interactions with networks of peers—assume a great deal of importance. To the extent that these sources offer concrete help with frameworks and techniques for pursuing learning improvement goals, they may encourage or equip many leaders to assume a more learning-focused approach to leadership.

Assessment of leadership practice.[7] Without some form of feedback on their work, leaders and leadership teams—not to mention their supervisors or others who oversee leadership practice—are left guessing as to the actual effects of leaders' efforts and whether these have anything to do with learning improvement. While astute leaders are likely to be gathering informal feedback all the time, the development of formal leadership assessment systems can offer a systematic way to gauge what leadership activities accomplish and how they might be improved. Traditionally, narrowly conceived performance evaluation approaches have tended to rate practicing leaders on measures such as incidence of parental complaints or aggregate achievement scores for the school or district. Yet as the sophistication of such systems grows, so does their potential application to the learning-related aspects of leadership.[8] Coupled with an explicit intention to inform leaders' own efforts, such systems are an important complement to the "inquiry and action cycle" described earlier.

Leadership development (both pre-service and in-service), direction, support, and assessment are closely related to one another—at least they can be—if leaders at state and local levels try to maximize the synergies among them. Linking leadership standards that explicitly target learning improvement to leadership assessment systems, for example, represents one potentially powerful way that leaders in the state-local system of schooling can begin to encourage more connections between leadership practice and learning outcomes. Coupled with job descriptions that articulate a leader's responsibilities for student, professional, and system learning, standards and assessments can begin to weave a reinforcing web of support for learning-focused practice (this will also include contractual agreements or other ways of codifying and communicating intentions for leaders' work).

Reconsidering support for improving leadership practice in and around the school. In principle, what is done to develop, direct, support, and assess leadership comes from many sources—the district central office and board, the state education agency, professional associations, local universities, and external organizations, to name a few of the most obvious sources. All of these interact with one another in ways that directly affect whether and how leaders focus on improving learning. Once again, we can ask: what is the character of available leadership development opportunities in preparation pipelines or in the practice of leadership? How much, if at all, do these opportunities sensitize leaders or other potential leaders to learning-related issues? Does the district central office visualize a role for itself in increasing the leadership capacity of the school? In what ways are leadership standards considered (if at all) by state and local policymakers and, if so, do these standards explicitly highlight the leaders' responsibilities for learning improvement?

Traditional modes of preparation have fallen under pointed critique, of late (Levine, 2005), for their relatively weak, and sometimes nonexistent, system of support for the improvement of leadership practice. A robust image of leadership development and support can point the way towards more powerful forms of preparation.

ENTRY POINTS FOR ENABLING LEARNING FOCUSED LEADERSHIP

Emerging practices and some more established ones, in educational systems that show signs of improvement (at least, as indicated by test score performance), suggest the following six entry points in the process of nudging educational systems toward a greater and better supported focus on learning improvement:

1. *Establishing a clear and public focus on learning improvement priorities for students, professionals, and the system as a whole.* Here, leaders are in a position to put all of these learning agendas on the table and to encourage action that creates mutual reinforcement among them.

2. *Reconceiving leadership roles so that they emphasize learning improvement, take full advantage of the collective capacity of staff, and still manage basic operational needs of schools and districts.* Here, working together, district and school staff have numerous ways to distribute responsibility for important tasks such as instructional leadership. They can do so differently at elementary, middle, and high school levels, if attention is paid to the level-specific meaning of these leadership roles.

3. *Informing leadership action with data and inquiry that relates to learning needs, performance, and conditions supporting learning.* Here, state and local leaders can do much more to prompt "cycles of inquiry" in schools, district central offices, and state agencies and as they do so encourage "cultures of inquiry" in these settings. Building robust data infrastructures and investing in efforts to help leaders develop "data literacy," broadly construed, will help support these cycles of inquiry.

4. *Aligning people, money, and time as closely as possible with learning improvement priorities.* Because funds, staff, and time do not always bear a close relation to learning improvement priorities, there are many opportunities to bring them more into line, though doing so will often generate active political resistance or simply need to work against the weight of

traditional practice. Reallocating funds and staffing incentives to support high-needs schools are especially important, as is the configuration of time that will support joint planning and professional learning.

5. *Providing leaders with regular feedback about their work in relation to learning improvement priorities, combined with regular opportunities to learn about and from their work.* In a much more fine-grained way than annual assessments of student learning provide, leaders in a variety of school and district positions can benefit from assessment feedback, both formal and informal, helping them know how to improve their practice. The goal of improving leadership practice is more likely to be achieved when the feedback is tied to opportunities for further professional learning in the context of daily work (e.g. through mentoring systems).

6. *Combining clear guidance for leaders with sufficient room to exercise discretion over matters related to learning improvement.* State and local governing bodies and others who define what educational leaders are expected to do have substantial opportunities to communicate more explicitly the centrality of learning improvement in leaders' work. But the message needs to be accompanied by attention to the degree of discretion leaders need to carry out this responsibility.

These entry points are only illustrative, and they are not based on a complete and irrefutable evidence base about the development and ultimate effectiveness of learning-focused practice. There is much we have yet to learn about how to encourage and support these leadership practices, yet the logic is clear and compelling, and emerging evidence and images of possibility suggest that the logic is sound.

We close with a hope and a caution. The hope is that these ideas prompt further efforts to connect different leaders' efforts with one another, especially across levels in the system, in pursuit of a more coherent web of support for strong, learning-focused leadership in schools and school districts, The caution is that we avoid placing unrealistic expectations on educational leaders, as if they were solely responsible for the learning of the nation's young people. And we also caution that partial solutions—that attend to one kind of supportive condition while ignoring another—may set the stage for leaders, and those they lead, to fail. Information without resources, new roles without authority to act, learning-focused leadership activity without feedback on it—all may fall short of the promise that lies in the attempt to renew and refocus leadership practice in education.

NOTES

This chapter draws on the work of a research team at the University of Washington at the Center for the Study of Teaching & Policy (CTP), commissioned by The Wallace Foundation to conduct research related to an unfolding leadership improvement initiative. The chapter builds on ideas discussed in the monographs and conference papers (Knapp, Copland, Plecki, & Portin, 2006; Knapp, Swinnerton, Monpas-Huber, Portin, Marzolf, Plecki, & McCleery, 2005; Knapp, Plecki, Alejano, Portin, Feldman, Copland, & Boatright, 2005) and contains material previously published in: Knapp, M. S., Copland, M. A., Plecki, M., Portin, B., & Colleagues. (2006). *Leading, learning, and leadership support*. Monograph published by the University of Washington CTP with support from The Wallace Foundation.

NOTES

[1] See: Knapp, M. S., Copland, M. A., & Talbert, J. E. (2003). *Leading for learning: Reflective tools for school and district leaders*. Seattle, WA: Center for the Study of Teaching & Policy, University of Washington; Knapp, M. S., & Associates (2003). *Leading for learning sourcebook: Concepts and examples*. Seattle, WA: Center for the Study of Teaching & Policy, University of Washington; Copland, M. A., & Knapp, M. S. (2006). *Leadership for learning: Reflection, planning, and action*. Alexandria, VA: Association for Supervision & Curriculum Development. Our thinking in these reports and book parallel the argument of Stoll, L., Fink, D., & Earl, L. (2003). *It's about learning (and it's about time): What's in it for schools?* London & New York: Routledge Falmer. Some aspects of the connections between leadership and learning outcomes have been studied, for the most part, in investigations of the effects of principal leadership—see reviews of this knowledge base in Hallinger, P., & Heck, R. H. (1996). Reassessing the principal's role in school effectiveness: A review of empirical research, 1980-1995. *Educational Administration Quarterly*, 32(1), 5-44; Leithwood, K., & Riehl, C. (2003). *What do we already know about successful school leadership?* Chicago, IL: American Educational Research Association.; Leithwood, K., Louis, K. S., Anderson, S., & Wahlstrom, K. (2004). *How leadership influences student learning*: New York: The Wallace Foundation. A large-scale study of these matters is now underway, guided by a team from the University of Minnesota and the Ontario Institute for Studies in Education (OISE) at the University of Toronto.

[2] New York Community School District 2 exemplified one of the early attempts to mount this kind of capacity building effort aimed at principals (see Fink & Resnick (2001), Developing principals as instructional leaders., *Phi Delta Kappan*, 82, 598-606. See also, Resnick, L., & Glennan, T., (2002), Leadership for learning: A theory of action for urban school districts, in Hightower et al. (Eds.), op. cit.

[3] See Portin, B., Alejano, C., Knapp, M. S., & Marzolf, E. (2006). *Redefining roles, responsibilities, and authority of school leaders*. Seattle, WA: Center for the Study of Teaching & Policy, University of Washington..

[4] See Murphy, J. (1992). *The landscape of leadership preparation: Reframing the education of school administrators*. Newbury Park, CA: Corwin Press. See also: Davis, S., Darling-Hammond, L. LaPointe, M., & Meyerson, D. (2005). *Developing successful principals: A review of research*. Stanford, CA: Stanford Educational Leadership Institute.

[5] Leadership standards may be adopted by state or local government based on widely promulgated standards, such as those of the Interstate School Leaders Licensure consortium (ISLLC), or they may be developed by professional associations as guidance or advice to members of the profession, as in the case of the standards of the National Association of Elementary School Principals (NAESP)—see Murphy, J., (2005). Unpacking the foundations of the ISLLC standards and addressing the concerns of the academic community. *Educational Administration Quarterly*, 41, 1, 154-191; National Association of Elementary School Principals (2002), *Leading learning*

communities: Standards for what principals should know and be able to do, Alexandria VA: Author.

[6] See argument in Portin et al., 2006, op. cit., regarding school leaders' learning; a recent investigation into distict-level leaders' learning—while in the midst of exercising leadership—appears in Swinnerton, J. A. (2006), *Learning to lead what you don't (yet) know: District leaders engaged in instructional reform.* Unpublished doctoral dissertation. Seattle, WA: University of Washington.

[7] See Portin, Feldman, & Knapp, 2006, op. cit.

[8] Various elaborated systems are currently being proposed—see Reeves, D. (2004), *Assessing educational leaders*, Thousand Oaks, CA: Corwin Press. Examples of sophisticated and comprehensive leadership assessment systems now being instituted at state and local level are described in Portin, Feldman, & Knapp, 2006, op. cit. Developmental work is underway at Vanderbilt University to create a new generation of leadership assessment tools.

REFERENCES

Knapp, M., Copland, M., Plecki, M, & Portin, B. (2006, April). *Improving learning-focused leadership in complex educational systems: The role of evidence, resources, and authority to act.* Symposium presented at the annual meeting of the American Educational Research Association, San Francisco, CA.

Knapp, M., Copland, M, & Talbert, J. (2003). *Leading for learning: Reflective tools for school and district leaders.* Seattle, WA: Center for the Study of Teaching & Policy, University of Washington.

Knapp, M., Swinnerton, J., Monpas-Huber, J., Portin, B., Marzolf, L., Plecki, M., & McCleery, J. (2005, November). Strengthening leadership in schools, districts, and states: Data-based practice, leadership roles and authority, and district governance. Interactive Symposium presented at the University Council for Educational Administration Annual Conference, Nashville, TN.

Knapp, M., Plecki, M, Alejano, C., Portin, B., Feldman, S., Copland, M., & Boatright, B. (2005, November). Strengthening leadership in schools, districts, and states: Resource allocation, leadership assessment, and high school transformation. Interactive Symposium presented at the University Council for Educational Administration Annual Conference, Nashville, TN.

Leithwood, K., & Riehl, C. (2003). *What do we already know about successful school leadership?* Chicago: American Educational Research Association.

Levine, A. (2005). *Educating school leaders.* Washington, DC: The Education Schools Project.

Spillane, J. P. (2006). *Distributed leadership.* San Francisco: Jossey-Bass.

Togneri, W., & Anderson, S. (2003). *Beyond islands of excellence: What districts can do to improve instruction and achievement in all schools.* Washington, DC: The Learning First Alliance and the Association for Supervision and Curriculum Development.

AFFILIATIONS

Bradley S. Portin, Michael S. Knapp, Margaret L. Plecki and Michael A. Copland
University of Washington,
Seattle,
US

OON-SENG TAN

CHAPTER 12

Problem-Based Learning: Some Insights into Pedagogical Leadership and Administrative Challenges

INTRODUCTION: A SINGAPORE GLIMPSE

Most leaders and policy makers know that for a nation to succeed we need to encourage members of the society to strive to realise their fullest educational potential. The nature of education and its curricula has implications not only for the quality of life but also for national development (Tan, 2003). Many nations are currently grappling with their national educational agendas so as to align curriculum practices with the need for national and global survival and growth. In Asia, the need to refine education systems to foster creative thinking, entrepreneurial spirit and lifelong learning has been repeatedly articulated. The daily news is flooded with discussions of the knowledge-based economy (KBE), the rapid proliferation of IT, information accessibility, new industrial and business challenges, and changing political and social landscapes. For example in Singapore, the *Straits Times* on 12 November 2002 carried the headline: "Panel on workers wants school reforms". The article referred to a high-level panel advocating the reform of the education system, starting at the secondary school level, in order to propel the Singapore economy into the future.

Educators today need to assume new roles, as designers of a new learning environment. The Committee on Singapore Competitiveness observed that over the last three decades Singapore has had a successful education system that supported a production-based economy (Ministry of Trade and Industry, 1998). However it added, to "improve the longer-term competitiveness of Singapore, we should refine our education system to help foster creative thinking and entrepreneurial spirit among the young" (p. 86). It recommended that three major components of the education system should be addressed: (i) the content of the curriculum, (ii) the mode of delivering this curriculum to students, and (iii) the assessment of performance.

The Economic Development Board similarly emphasised that for "our knowledge-based economy to flourish, we will need a culture which encourages creativity and entrepreneurship, as well as an appetite for change and risk-taking" (1999, 3). It further argued that it is not good enough to have an education system that prides itself on developing people with strong competencies in analytical, systematic and systems thinking without an imaginative approach to new competencies. In Singapore, for example, the concern with "keeping pace with changes in the world" has been repeatedly reiterated by the Ministry of Education (*Straits Times*, 31 July 1997, p. 1) revisiting a theme articulated almost a decade ago. The desired outcomes of education for post-secondary students were at that time redefined to include qualities such as the ability to think, reason and deal confidently with the future; to seek, process and apply knowledge; innovativeness; a spirit of continual improvement; a lifelong habit of learning; and an enterprising spirit in all undertakings (Ministry of Education, 1998, 4).

The aim of *Manpower 21: Vision of a Talent Capital*, the strategic blueprint for developing Singapore's manpower, is to turn Singapore into a place "where people use their talents to create value; where entrepreneurs abound and thrive; and in which people can develop and multiply their potential through continuous learning and participation in meaningful jobs. It is a centre of ideas, innovation, knowledge and exchange; a place with a strong culture of continuous learning for lifelong employability" (Ministry of Manpower, 1999, 18). The report noted that the rationale for lifelong learning is convincing, but it observed that "the majority of our working population do not pursue any form of training" (p. 24). Dr Tony Tan, Deputy Prime Minister of Singapore, observed that education is in need of a major overhaul; in fact, he noted that incremental change is not the way forward as it would simply "aggravate the problem of perpetuating practices that should be jettisoned if a country is to move ahead" (*Straits Times*, 2002, p. H2). Corollaries of the above concerns include changing the mindsets of both the present and the future generations in learning to learn, the need for continuous learning, assuming personal responsibility for one's own learning, and embracing new approaches to learning that equip individuals with relevant competencies. Tan (2003) shows how changes through quantum-leap innovation differ from incremental changes, which result from perpetuation of existing processes. This is illustrated in Figure 1. Tan's model parallels Hargreaves and Fink's (2005) argument for sustainable leadership, for deep learning and real achievement. The idea of innovation in the KBE is to discard something not because it is not producing results but because, though it may be efficient, it is not necessarily effective in today's climate. We are often caught in the paradigm of producing more of the same. Do we really need to reinvent our educational practices to meet the challenges of the KBE?

The challenge is indeed for educators to design new learning milieux and curricula that really encourage motivation and independence so as to equip students with learning, thinking and problem-solving skills. Hargreaves (1994, 2003) noted the need for teachers and schools to educate young people in skills and qualities such as adaptability, responsibility, flexibility and the capacity to work with others. Our paradigms may be correct, but if we do not believe that we can move on and succeed in that paradigm then we would once again be stuck. Teachers need to believe that innovation in education is both necessary and practical and that, whether as teachers or school leaders, they can be entrepreneurial in experimenting with new approaches to learning.

Hargreaves and Fink (2005, p. 28) noted that "It is easy to advocate more instructional leadership, to insist that all educational leaders should become leaders of learning. It is harder to make leadership for learning a practical reality. And it is hardest of all to do this in policy and reform climates that repeatedly pull the plug on leaders' efforts to achieve depth and breath of learning in their systems and their schools."

Tan (2003) proposed that education in the KBE should involve:

- encouraging lifelong learning (learning throughout life)
- fostering lifewide learning (transfer of learning across contexts and disciplines)
- assuming greater personal responsibility for one's learning
- learning how to learn from multiple sources and resources
- learning collaboratively
- learning to adapt and to solve problems (i.e. to cope with change)

The philosophical underpinnings of learning-centred leadership have been actualised in some ways by the attempts of educational policy makers, educational leaders, researchers and practitioners in the recent policy initiative entitled "Teach Less, Learn More" (TLLM). The Ministry of Education (2007) articulated TLLM in these words:

"Teach Less, Learn More is about teaching better, to engage our learners and prepare them for life, rather than teaching more, for tests and examinations. TLLM aims to touch the hearts and engage the minds of learners, to prepare them for life. It reaches into the core of education – why we teach, what we teach and how we teach."

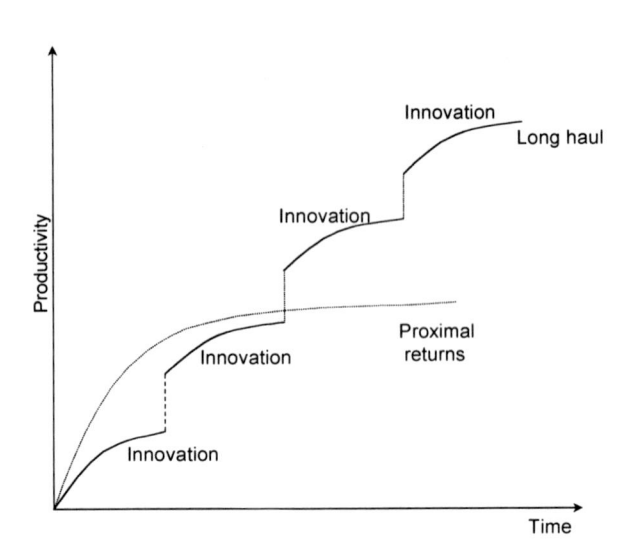

Figure 1. Model of quantum-lead innovation

It calls for "more: for the learner, to excite passion, for understanding, for the test of life" and "less: to rush through the syllabus, out of fear of failure, to dispense information only for a life of tests."

It calls for "more: the whole child, values-centric, process and searching questions" and "less: of the subject, grades-centric, product and textbook answers."

It calls for "more: engaged learning, differentiated teaching, guiding, facilitating and modelling, formative and qualitative assessing, a spirit of innovation and enterprise" and "less of drill and practice, one-size-fits-all instruction, telling and set formulae standard answers".

Tan, Ee, Lee & Lam (2007) collated a collection of reports on curriculum innovation, in which schools had demonstrated that they had embarked on research more prolifically than ever before. Major approaches used in some of the innovation included programmes and approaches such as "Habits of Mind", "Teaching for Understanding", "Problem-based learning" and a range of integrative approaches. Problem-based learning has been found to be an effective innovation as a result of learning-centred leadership in schools at various levels of its operation (Tan, 2002, 2004a; Tan, Tham & Hoe, 2005).

PROBLEM-BASED LEARNING CURRICULUM: PARADIGM SHIFT IN PEDAGOGICAL POLICY

The term *curriculum* refers not only to intended learning outcomes but also to the environment created to bring about these outcomes. Looking at a curriculum thus involves consideration of all the experiences that individual learners have in a programme of education (Parkay & Hass, 2000) as well as the design of the learning environment (Tan, 1994).

Tan (2000c) argued for a curriculum shift of three foci of preoccupation as illustrated in Figure 2. Traditional programmes of education and training have an over-preoccupation with content. What is important is a shift towards designing more real-world problems as catalysts around which learners engage in a process of actively working on unstructured problems. This necessarily calls for a problem-based approach to the curriculum. It has been argued that by using "real-life" problems as a focus learners would really learn how to learn. Boud and Feletti (1997) argued that Problem-Based Learning (PBL) is the most significant innovation in education. It suffices at this stage to say that by having real-life problems (rather than content) as focal points, with students as active problem solvers and teachers as mediating coaches, the learning paradigm shifts towards achievements that are seen as apposite to a knowledge-based era. Margetson (1994) noted that a PBL curriculum helps promote the development of lifelong learning skills in the form of open-minded, reflective, critical and active learning. Furthermore, it has been observed that PBL curricula can better facilitate the acquisition of problem-solving, communication, teamwork and interpersonal skills – attributes that are also sought after by industry.

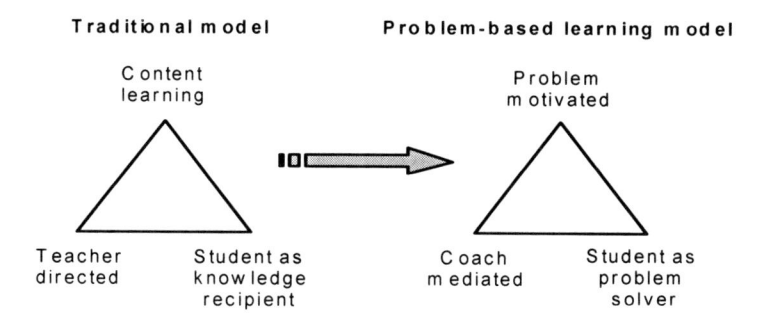

Figure 2: A Model of Curriculum Shift

Arguments dealing with what counts as knowledge are not new. We can define the need for content knowledge as "knowing what" and for process knowledge as "knowing why and how", borrowing Schon's idea of *The Reflective Practitioner*. The argument is for the teaching of processes and the use of real-world scenarios in learning. The implications for teaching and learning are that teachers should be:

- designers of learning
- facilitators and mediators of learning

It is then a matter not of how much content we disseminate in our classrooms but how we engage students' motivation and independent learning that is important. In PBL, the design of real-world problem scenarios is crucial and the problems act as triggers for self-directed and collaborative learning. If we want to develop greater entrepreneurship, students need to learn to take greater ownership of their learning – making knowledge their own. However, we should not underestimate the challenge that this presents to teachers and to school leaders who are faced with the difficulty of handling large numbers of students who are schooled with the mindset of dependence, addicted to digested information and didactics, often coming to classroom learning with inadequate reading skills. Yet, learning to learn and lifelong learning are important goals and it is clear that there will be increasing demands in the future for workers to be able to read more intelligently and critically and to write and communicate confidently.

As facilitators and mediators of learning, our role is to teach heuristics, provide scaffolding, connecting students to the milieu of knowledge available in texts, as well as through various other sources, and with discrimination in accessing the World Wide Web. Nor should this be seen as simply an individual pursuit as the design of learning environments must include opportunities for the development of collaborative learning.

Methods of assessment will also have to change. In Singapore teachers and students are heavily preoccupied with examinations. Charles Handy (1994) described what he called the Macnamara Fallacy as something like this: We measure what is easily measured and disregard what we cannot easily measure. Then we presume what can't be measured as unimportant, and we assume what can't be measured as non-existent. He described this as suicidal. Many of the competencies and process skills that are most needed and valuable cannot be easily measured. Examinations that primarily test content knowledge are deemed as most reliable and objective, but the assessment of content knowledge alone may lack validity in today's world.

Eraut (1994), for example, highlighted that, whilst a written syllabus may acknowledge skills such as "communication" and "learning to work in teams" as basic and important, in reality the learning processes used do not cater to these developments. Writing a good essay on "interpersonal skills" does not necessarily reflect knowledge about people, or working with people in real life situations.

In today's world of knowledge and participation, assessment should be more about learning rather than selection. Diversification of assessment appears to be essential to broadening learning, and implementation of more innovative learning methods such as PBL and project work need to be complemented by more holistic reviews of the curriculum and evaluation.

We also need the practicality and the know-how – otherwise we will be caught up in plenty of discussions, seminars and workshops without translating things into action and without really bringing about change.

In this Internet era, how we learn is what we learn. The question is - Are we designing the learning environment and facilitating learning in ways that motivate students to learn in ways that empower them for tomorrow? Or are we escaping the responsibility of tomorrow by evading changes in our practices?

PROBLEM-BASED LEARNING PEDAGOGY

Problem-based learning (PBL) focuses on the challenge of making students' thinking visible. Like most pedagogical innovations, PBL was not developed on the basis of learning or psychological theories, although the PBL process embraces the use of meta-cognition and self-regulation, but from grounded practice. PBL is recognised as a progressive active-learning and learner-centred approach in which unstructured problems (real-world or simulated complex problems) are used as the starting point and as the anchor for the learning process (Tan, 2004b; Tan 2007).

In recent years, PBL has gained new momentum as a result of several developments. The first is the increasing demand to bridge the gap between theory and practice. This demand is particularly evident in medical education (Balla, 1990a, 1990b). Norman and Schmidt (1992) found that PBL enhances the transfer of concepts to new problems, the integration of concepts, intrinsic interest in learning, and learning skills. Albanese and Mitchell (1993) showed that, compared with traditional teaching approaches, PBL helps students in knowledge construction and reasoning abilities.

The second factor is the accessibility of information. Educators have always recognised the value of using problems to stimulate learning and thinking, but when to pose a problem as well as the nature and scope of the problem have been limited by the learner's lack of knowledge and of accessibility to information. Thus, problems were usually given only after the dissemination of knowledge and were often delimited by what was already taught. However, the advent of Internet technologies has ushered in new possibilities with PBL.

Thirdly, the emphasis on real-world competencies, such as skills in independent learning, collaborative learning, problem solving, and decision making, provides a strong rationale for adopting PBL. Glasgow (1997) argued that the real world is filled with problems, projects, and challenges, thus creating a "curriculum that reflects this reality makes sense" (p. 14).

Fourthly, developments in learning, psychology, and pedagogy appear to support the use of PBL. For example, research on memory and knowledge points to the importance of memory not only as a series of associations but, more importantly, as connections and meaningful coherent structures (National Research Council, 1999). We now know more about "novice" learners and "expert" learners. We can develop better individual learning by providing opportunities for acquisition of procedures and skills through dealing with information in a problem space and learning general strategies of problem solving. From the pedagogical perspective, PBL derives a great deal from constructivist theories of learning (Schmidt, 1993; Savery & Duffy, 1995; Hendry & Murphy, 1995). In PBL approaches, understanding is derived from interaction with the problem scenario and the learning environment. Engagement with the problem and the problem inquiry process create cognitive dissonance that stimulates learning, and so knowledge evolves through collaborative processes of social negotiation and evaluation of the viability of one's point of view. Meta-cognitive strategies and self-regulation are therefore integral aspects of PBL processes.

PBL approaches in a curriculum usually include the following characteristics (Tan, 2003):

- The *problem* is the starting point of learning.
- The problem is usually a *real-world* problem that appears unstructured. If it is a simulated problem, it should be as authentic as possible.
- The problem calls for *multiple perspectives*. The use of cross-disciplinary knowledge is a key feature in many PBL curricula. In any case, PBL encourages the solution of the problem by making use of knowledge from various subjects and topics.
- The problem challenges students' current knowledge, attitudes, and competencies, thus calling for identification of learning needs and *new areas of learning*.

- *Self-directed learning* is primary. Thus, students assume major responsibility for the acquisition of information and knowledge.
- *Harnessing of a variety of knowledge sources* and the use and evaluation of information resources are essential PBL processes.
- Learning is *collaborative, communicative and cooperative*. Students work in small groups with a high level of interaction in peer learning, peer teaching, and group presentations.
- Development of inquiry and problem-solving skills is as important as content knowledge acquisition for the solution of the problem. The PBL tutor thus facilitates and coaches through questioning and cognitive coaching.
- Closure in the PBL process includes synthesis and integration of learning.
- PBL also concludes with an evaluation and review of the learner's experience and the learning process.
- The goals of PBL include content learning, acquisition of process skills and problem-solving skills, and lifewide learning. The term *lifewide learning* lays emphasis on skills such as self-directed learning, independent information mining, collaborative learning, and reflective thinking. Lifewide learning entails the acquisition of competencies that can be transferred across various life and work situations. The skills learned are applicable to learning in a new discipline or learning to do something new.
- In many PBL approaches, the student confronts a situation where he or she needs to accomplish an objective, and where the means (i.e., the information, process, and actions to be taken) is something new or previously unknown to the student. In many ways, the pedagogy of PBL helps make visible or explicit the thinking and the richness of the cognitive structuring and processes involved.

A problem triggers the context for engagement, curiosity, inquiry, and a quest to address real-world issues. Figure 3 illustrates what goes on in the mind of the learner (cognition) and the probable changes in behaviour (learning) that are triggered by the problem.

The challenge in diversifying educational methods is to design learning through the effective use of problems. Depending on the nature of the discipline, the goals of the curriculum, the flexibility of cross-disciplinary integration, and the availability of resources (e.g., time, infrastructure, information systems), problems can be used appropriately, strategically, and powerfully. PBL also provides a structure where innovations such as e-learning can be incorporated (Tan, 2007).

MAKING PBL HAPPEN: CONTEXT OF INNOVATION AND LEADERSHIP

In the case of PBL, leadership for learning acquired meaning in an institution where PBL was being explored. In researching PBL Tan (1994) noted the way in which lecturers designed curriculum that paid little attention to the needs of the learner and what learners could be empowered to do. Using Oliva's model (1992) with considerations given to (i) The Learner, (ii) The Society and (iii) The Subject Matter, Tan found in his survey with 65 academic staff that only 27% of them gave high ratings (on a Likert Scale) to the learner as a most important focus while 65% rated highly the amount of consideration given to subject matter. In other words, staff tended to be preoccupied with what they were to teach and invested a large part of their energies, deliberations and concern on issues of content knowledge. This finding concurred with Ramsden's (1992) that the needs of learners and how they learn were not given sufficient attention. Tan argued for the need to "create opportunities for students to commit themselves to a learning task and learn by doing", further noting that "what is probably more important is the need for case studies, problem-based learning and simulations of real-life situations" (Chong, 1995, p. 3).

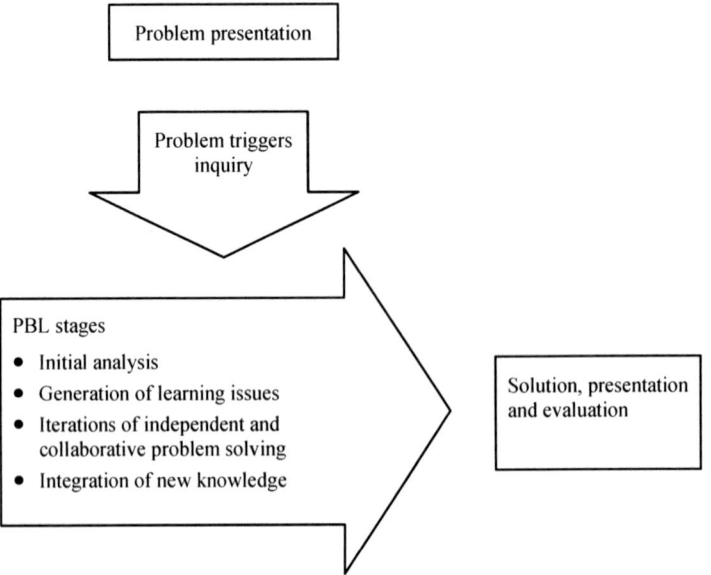

Figure 3 illustrates the key components in the PBL process.

```
        ┌─────────────────────┐
        │ Problem presentation │
        └─────────────────────┘
                  │
         ┌────────▼────────┐
         │ Problem triggers │
         │     inquiry      │
         └─────────┬────────┘
                   ▼
┌──────────────────────────────┐
│ PBL stages                   │
│ • Initial analysis           │      ┌──────────────────────┐
│ • Generation of learning     │─────▶│ Solution, presentation│
│   issues                     │      │ and evaluation        │
│ • Iterations of independent  │      └──────────────────────┘
│   and collaborative problem  │
│   solving                    │
│ • Integration of new         │
│   knowledge                  │
└──────────────────────────────┘
```

Source: Tan, O. S. (2003, p. 32) Problem-based Learning Innovation: Using problems to power learning in the 21st century. Singapore: Thomson Learning

On the basis of these macro-developments the initiative for a problem-based learning approach was conceived, resulting in the eventual setting up of the Temasek Centre for Problem-based Learning (PBL). The centre was set up "to meet the challenges of preparing students for the world of dynamic change" by adopting "a new academic architecture" that featured problem-based learning (Tan, 2000a, 2000b). The philosophy of the centre was "to establish a culture of inquiry, enterprise and meaningful student learning" through the use of PBL. It was envisaged that PBL would benefit students by developing problem-solving acumen, integrated knowledge-based and lifelong learning. Through PBL students were expected to attain greater self-motivation, develop higher order thinking skills, teamwork and communication skills (Albanese & Mitchell, 1993; Boud & Feletti, 1997; Tan, Little, Hee & Conway, 2000). The Centre serviced the institution by providing opportunities for staff to be trained in PBL through workshops, forums, open lectures and exchanges with PBL experts. Through the Centre teachers were exposed to workshops which included: Introduction to PBL, Design of PBL Problems, Facilitation in PBL, Curriculum Development in PBL and Assessment in PBL. Selected staff were sent to various international PBL centres such as those at the University of Southern Illinois, University of Maastricht, Newcastle University, University of Samford and the Illinois Mathematics and Science Academy. The Centre also provided consultation to the various schools for curriculum development, consultation, research and development in PBL. The Centre also acted in collaboration with the local and international centres to exchange and advance the practice of PBL. One of the accomplishments of the Centre was to host the Second Asia-Pacific Conference on Problem-based Learning which saw over 140 paper presentations and some 500 local and overseas delegates.

Reflecting on leadership for learning it is important to note that several awareness issues pertaining to positioning the innovation have proved to be essential in bringing about change and meeting needs. By positioning we mean taking note of the following.

Global Trends. Leaders need to be aware of global and regional trends that may be related to what they want to do. This will help to rationalise and articulate their project for learning.

National Agenda. Leaders are cognisant of national agendas and priorities not only for being politically astute but they also recognise that small project or micro-level initiative which is fulfilling a particular national priority can actually take off much faster than top-down reform.

Know the State-of-the-Art. Leaders commit to a project to advance good practices or a field of knowledge and take a stand that whatever changes in policies may happen they intend to work on it because their loyalty is one of improving a particular practice in a field they are committed to.

Commitment to Change. An educational development project in particular is about a commitment to change underpinned by sound educational beliefs or philosophy.

Beyond Educational Justification. It is vital for leaders to look for more than just an educational justification. Previous educational research has not always convinced everyone. Multi-prong justifications such as those pertaining to economics and social impact help.

Consistent Championship. It is important for leaders to consistently champion and advance a good idea over a period of time. Projects do not just happen with a one-off idea.

Build a Team of People. Innovation teams can be formed by assignment but when leaders have an informal collaboration with a large team it is much easier for things to take off.

Collaborative International Network. Having a network of people locally and internationally who share the same interests can be very helpful even though they may not be part of the project team.

I was privileged to see the implementation of PBL in a context where the administration and management gave it full support and advocated the use of PBL as the anchoring philosophy for professional training and education. The piloting and implementation also won national recognition when together with a number of colleagues we won an "Innovator Award" for co-pioneering PBL as an innovation in education. What was gratifying about the award was not so much our initiatives as educators but the fact that The Enterprise Challenge Award from the Prime Minister's Office recognised an educational innovation - problem-based learning.

To meet the challenges of the knowledge economy a S$10 million fund was established in 1999 under the auspices of the Singapore Prime Minister's Office to provide "venture capital" for innovative and enterprising projects. Known as The Enterprise Challenge the goal is to fund innovations that could create new value or significant improvement in public services in Singapore. As director of the institution's PBL centre then, I had the opportunity to work with course teams, undertake staff development work and monitor student feedback in PBL initiatives across various disciplines and levels.

On reflection I note two major milestones that epitomize the importance of looking out for, and, seizing opportunities so that a project can be strategically positioned and be implemented. The first involved an organisational level strategic planning session where a management retreat was held to "re-invent" education. This led to a search for a new academic architecture. The second was the cognisance of the national initiative – The Enterprise Challenge (TEC). An educational project did not initially appear to fit the bill required of TEC. The TEC was an "initiative to bring out the Silicon Valley spirit inside the Public Service" and deliverables had to be measurable in terms of cost-saving and enterprise of a more inventive nature. Of the seven projects which obtained funding in the year 2000, six were technologically related. One was a biotechnology project that impacted directly on environment enhancement; two were information technology projects; and three were high-tech systems design and development. The assessment criteria for the TEC is one of the most rigorous of award criteria as it is not only a matter of funding but also that of the highest recognition of innovation then. In conjunction with this TEC award the implementation team received a research and innovation grant to fully pilot PBL in one of its courses. It was a 10-month intensive project to develop a prototypical curriculum with templates for course development, facilitators' and learners' packages, assessment and comprehensive evaluation.

In getting the TEC funding the project was delimited to one particular course. The purpose was to be able to focus, define and delimit the scope of the project for measurement and evaluation. Educational development projects, unlike industrial or management projects, tend not to have a clear boundary and are often too multi-faceted. By choosing just one course it was easy to articulate the scope, resources, time line and realistic deliverables. It was also important to know clearly what the funding body wanted. In the case of the TEC award I had to appear before a final panel that comprised the Permanent Secretary of the Ministry of Manpower, chief executives from the public and private sectors and senior staff from the Office of the Prime Minister. And had to focus on three things: originality, feasibility and benefits.

Some of the key lessons pertaining to organisation and planning for leadership in learning may be summarised as follows:

Conviction and Clarity of Purpose. A strong conviction and clear idea of what you want to change helps provide the meaning and motivation without which there will be little momentum for organisation and planning.

Well-developed Ideas and Mental Models. It takes time to develop an idea which is then embedded in mental models and communicated to others.

Visualise the Feasibility and Benefits. It helps in project planning to have the end in mind and to visualise the outcomes and benefits.

Systems Thinking and Systematic Thinking. Planning and organisation involve a constant awareness of the holistic aspect of the project as well as detailed planning.

Singapore is well known for its efficiency in many spheres of government, public and commercial services and work. Education is no exception and generally projects are well organised and planned.

CHALLENGES OF LEADERSHIP IN LEARNING

Whilst a culture of strong planning, systems thinking and systematic thinking helps provide the foundation for projects to be effectively set in train, implementation and sustaining momentum are never easy. What are the major obstacles? The first pertains to dealing with paradigms and mindsets. PBL involves a rather radical change and whilst its philosophy and rationale seem convincing, people are generally highly sceptical as they do not know how it will work. As mentioned previously, the Temasek Centre for Problem-based Learning provided staff development in areas of PBL design, facilitation, curriculum development and assessment. Furthermore, course teams embarking on PBL worked with PBL staff to develop their curriculum. It should be noted however that PBL was new to both staff developers and teaching staff and, as a consequence, major gaps were experienced in skills of curriculum design, facilitation and assessment.

The other obstacles were related to existing systems and processes. Whilst top-management support may be given there are often bulky systems already in place that needs to be changed. PBL innovation also requires breaking the impasse and surmounting the barriers of many entrenched academic policies and systems. The teacher's roles in PBL is very different. Thus items in the standard student feedback form included things such as "clarity of explanation" yet PBL entails getting students' to seek and obtain their own solutions or explanations. The approach we adopted, therefore, was one of educating and helping peers become informed. While in this case the scheme had won a national recognition and therefore has strong negotiating cachet. Nevertheless. greater cognisance of the larger intertwining systems was still essential and building collaboration and encouraging ownership were critical. Owing to the fact that PBL was prescribed as a viable alternative, surveys of lecturers' perceptions were generally positive. Nevertheless surveys and monitoring of student feedback produced mixed results. Whilst these quantitative data were helpful in gaining a broad picture the most valuable sources of insights however were qualitative.

WHAT ARE SOME INSIGHTS AND LESSONS FOR LEADERSHIP IN LEARNING?

The Uncertainty Principle. In a culture where planning and systematic thinking prevail, the very strength of project planning becomes a major weakness. I learned the hard way to propagate what we may call the uncertainty principle. In PBL all we know is that we are practising things characteristic of PBL but we are really not so sure if we are achieving some of the intended outcomes. As mentioned above this has implications for systems of evaluation which have to be changed as we are not measuring the same things as previously. The example given was student feedback. Like the uncertainty principle the presence of such uncertainties however do not necessarily mitigate the value of the project. Accepting the uncertainty principle is a necessary part of innovation.

Practical and Systems Barriers. The experiences with this project point to the fact that de-skilling and re-skilling are essential to the practice of PBL. The lack of PBL skills was one factor responsible for many of the implementation problems. There were many practical problems that were related to one another. In addition to the issue of requisite skills, related problems were the lack of resources such as time, administrative support, space and materials. In spite of all the planning, PBL resources for students, the design of problems, availability of rooms for PBL-type discussions and support staff were often lacking at one time or another. Sometimes staff were caught in a vicious cycle where the lack of time, support and resources led to poor quality at each successive stage of implementation. Furthermore the systems that were in place were not change-friendly. In fact the more efficient the current system the greater it is as a barrier to change. There is a need to embrace flexibility on the part of the custodians of the system and it is here where leaders of learning have to win collaboration and promote ownership of new ideas through strategic communication.

Mindset and Value Barriers. The PBL project involved mindset change in academic staff and students as well as administrators. People naturally feel more secure, comfortable and confident with familiar of ways of teaching and learning and changes are bound to be initially resisted. While staff training and plenty of preparation were needed to overcome psychological barriers there are however more deeply embedded obstacles that are sometimes difficult to surmount. In teaching and learning one will find that barriers which have to do with values and belief systems that go deeper than psychological barriers. This is especially difficult in Asian culture where people are less inclined to articulate their beliefs and personal philosophy about what they feel strongly about. Resistance sometime results in paying lip service or "conspiracy of the least", namely, doing enough just to get by. There are no easy solutions to such resistance; the positive approach is to establish niches of success cases to showcase and convince people of the true value and benefit of the project. This is why the idea of recruiting champions for a project is important for a project to take off.

The Whole is More than The Sum of Its Parts. The PBL project experienced student resistance in the initial stages of implementation. If we had relied on initial responses alone to decide whether or not to proceed the project would never have taken off. Similarly there were many parts that were not optimised when change was taking place. A holistic approach and systems perspective were more helpful in addressing the diverse barriers or problems that cropped up.

Leadership in learning involves taking the multiple perspectives of informed learning, scholarship and cognitive and emotional commitment. Just as Milo learnt in The Phantom Tollbooth that the only failure is not to try, we should be adventurous in our learning and in taking the lead.

REFERENCES

Albanese, M., & Mitchell, S. (1993). PBL: A review of the literature on its outcomes and implementation issues. *Academic Medicine, 68,* 52–81.

Balla, J. I. (1990a). Insight into some aspects of clinical education, I: Clinical practice. *Postgraduate Medical Journal, 66,* 212–17.

Balla, J. I. (1990b). Insights into some aspects of clinical education, II: A theory for clinical education. *Postgraduate Medical Journal, 66,* 297–301.

Boud, D., & Feletti, G. I. (Eds.). (1997). *The challenge of problem-based learning* (2nd ed.). London: Kogan Page.

Chong, E. (1995). *Recess: Education the next wave.* Singapore: Temasek Polytechnic.

Eraut, M. (1994). Developing professional knowledge and competence. London: Falmer Press.

Glasgow, N. A. (1997). New curriculum for new times: A guide to student-centered, problem-based learning. Thousand Oaks, CA: Corwin Press.

Handy, C. (1994). The empty raincoat: Making sense of the future. London: Hutchinson.

Hargreaves, A. (1994). *Changing teachers, changing times.* London: Cassell.

Hargreaves, A., & Fink, D. (2005). Sustainable leadership. New York: Taylor & Francis.

Hendry, G. D., & Murphy, L. B. (1995). Constructivism and problem-based learning. In P. Little, M. Ostwald, & G. Ryan (Eds.), *Research and development in problem-based learning, 3: Assessment and evaluation.* Newcastle: Australian Problem Based Learning Network.

Lee, O. K., Ee, J., & Tan, O. S. (2006). *Educational research with a calling: 20 years of ERAS.* Singapore: Educational Research Association of Singapore.

Margetson, D. (1994). Current educational reform and the significance of PBL. *Studies in Higher Education, 19,* 5–19.

Ministry of Education. (1998). *The desired outcomes of education.* Singapore: Author.

Ministry of Education. (2007). *Teach less, learn more.* Singapore: Author.

Ministry of Manpower. (1999). *The manpower 21 report.* Singapore: Author.

Ministry of Trade & Industry. (1998). *Committee on Singapore Competitiveness.* Singapore: Author.

National Research Council. (1999). *How people learn: Bridging research and practice.* Washington, DC: National Academy Press.

Oliva, P. F. (1992). *Developing the Curriculum* (3rd ed.). New York: Haper Collins Publishers.

Parkay, F. W., & Hass, G. (2000). *Curriculum planning: A contemporary approach* (7th ed.). Boston: Allyn & Bacon.

Ramsden, P. (1998). *Learning to lead in higher education.* New York: Routledge.

Savery, J. R., & Duffy, T. M. (1995). PBL: Instructional model and its constructivist framework. *Educational Technology, 35,* 31–7.

Tan, O. S. (1994). Curriculum development for the 21st century: A model and perspective for course designers. *Temasek Journal, July*, 34–41.
Tan, O. S. (2000a). Reflecting on innovating the academic architecture for the 21st century. *Educational Developments, 1*(2), 8–11.
Tan, O. S. (2000b). Intelligence enhancement and cognitive coaching in problem-based learning. In C. M. Wang, K. P. Mohanan, D. Pan, & Y. S. Che (Eds.), *TLHE symposium proceedings*. National University of Singapore.
Tan, O. S. (2000c). Reflecting on innovating the academic architecture for the 21st century. *Educational Developments, 1*, 8–11.
Tan, O. S. (2002). Project management in educational development: A Singapore experience. In C. Baume, P. Martin, & M. Yorke (Eds.), *Managing educational development projects: Maximising impact* (pp. 153–169). London: Kogan Page.
Tan, O. S. (2003). Problem-based learning innovation: Using problems to power learning in the 21st century. Singapore: Thomson Learning.
Tan, O. S. (2004a). Students' experiences in problem-based learning: Three blind mice episode or educational innovation. *Innovations in Education and Teaching International, 41*(2), 169–184.
Tan, O. S. (Ed.). (2004b). *Enhancing thinking through problem-based learning approaches: International perspectives*. Singapore: Thomson Learning.
Tan, O. S. (Ed.). (2007). *Problem-based learning in e-learning breakthroughs*. Singapore: Thomson Learning.
Tan, O. S., Little, P., Hee, S.Y., & Conway, J. (Eds.). (2000). *Problem-based learning: Educational innovation across disciplines*. Singapore: Temasek Centre for Problem-based Learning.
Tan, O. S., Tham, Y. C., & Hoe W. M. (2005). Singapore's leading STAR (Special Talents and Achievement Recognition). *The Specialist Schools and Academies Trust Journal of Innovation in Education, 3*(3), 13–17.
Tan, O. S., Ee J., Lee, Y. P., & Lam, K. (Eds.). (2007). *Teach less, learn more (TLLM) school-based curriculum innovation: Research reports*. Singapore: Ministry of Education.

AFFILIATIONS

Oon-Seng Tan
National Institute of Education
Nanyang Technological University
Singapore

GIOVANNA BARZANÒ AND FRANCESCA BROTTO

CHAPTER 13

Leadership, Learning and Italy: A Tale of Atmospheres

Our 'tale of atmospheres' is about teachers facing leadership challenges for learning. On the one hand, we look at 'seeds of leadership for learning' in a nationally-devised initiative involving headship trainees engaging in online communities, and on the other a local professional development experience with a network of schools in which we see the interplay of varying tensions behind attempts to grow collaborative cultures. The stage setting is the national scenario of school autonomy, one that has promised much but delivered much less. Bureaucratic mindsets continue to pervade the system, demanding 'results' from schools but often lending a deaf ear to the authentic voices which teachers and pupils try to express. 'Faint lights on the horizon' might be the sub-title of our tale, although the sailing is rough and the keel unsteady.

SETTING THE SCENE

In Italian educational culture, leadership has a strong symbolic value. Traditionally speaking, leadership at school level has always been associated with the head, the frontline person who is in charge of the school as an establishment. With the most recent legislation (2000) having introduced school autonomy, giving headteachers the status of *dirigenti scolastici* and the responsibilities of high rank civil servants, the formal (and symbolic) weight of heads has been enhanced. This is even more so if we consider that the Italian *istituto scolastico* (the school establishment which falls under the responsibility of one head) is in most cases a cluster of schools with buildings on a variety of sites.

Since 1974 Italian schools have been officially governed by a complex structure, composed of a governing body and a number of other collegial bodies. This structure was devised in order to guarantee *collegialità*, meaning distributed collective decision-making rather than a collaborative culture of "professional collegiality" (Frost et al, 2000, p.22). School heads in Italy are in fact "inserted into an organization with a decision making process that is widely distributed among various components, [both] internal organizational players and external social powers" (Summa, 2003, p.16), making the intertwining levels of responsibility in the governance system extremely complex.

Collegialità, then, is in the norm enacted bureaucratically (Brotto, 2003a) and in often "contrived" forms (Hargeaves, 1994), and in many circumstances represents a missed opportunity for distributed leadership and collaborative professional learning. Thus, the contexts within which leadership is practiced in Italian schools may seem not only demanding, but even paradoxical when seen through the eyes of a foreign observer.

In a context still dominated by the symbolic power of authority, teachers experience contradictions in finding their own voices as leaders and learners, whether in their classroom activity, as members of a profession or as future heads themselves. Despite the 'teaching freedom' they enjoy, established by the Italian Constitution and reinforced by Union contract, in practice teachers struggle with school autonomy (Associazione TreeLLe, 2006). Without 'teaching freedom' through which teachers exercise their sense of agency (whether in relation to their pupils, their colleagues, the school, the community or the system as a whole) leadership for learning may be something of a misnomer. As reported elsewhere in this book we see leadership as an activity embedded within which is the concept of agency (MacBeath, 2006b, p.39) forming "the bridge between leadership and learning" (Frost, 2006, p.2).

In this chapter we present a summary of two professional development experiences involving teachers coming from the ranks of roughly 1900 headship trainees due to take up headship positions in September 2007, together with others who participated in a residential activity organised by the 30-school STRESA school network in the Province of Bergamo (Lombardy). Its focus was on responsibility for learning and where that locus of responsibility falls.

The data that we analyse here come from pilot surveys which give voice to the participants who engaged in professional development activities. These examples are given because these voices highlight two things; on the one hand, a growing awareness of leadership issues and of actions that would be needed to 'make a difference' to learning within a school environment; on the other hand, perceptions (or hopes) of possibilities for self-efficacy, however difficult this may be within the Italian situation. In reporting these voices, we treat them as acts of agency, as speech acts (Searle, 1969), a form of intentional action with the potential to induce other action. The STRESA network "summer school" experience not only throws into relief conflicting attitudes to a theoretically learning-rich opportunity, requiring a high degree of personal engagement, but also reflects how actively sharing experience through a collaborative culture presents an exceptional challenge to very many teachers, and is at best only a sporadic activity in most Italian schools.

VOICES OF TRAINEE HEADS OVER THE WEB: LEADERSHIP (?) FOR LEARNING?

Preparing for headship in Italy: current developments

School heads in Italy are appointed by the Ministry of Education on the basis of a nationally devised but regionally managed competition. Recent legislation in 2007 has opened the competition to qualified teachers with five years of experience, instead of the seven that had been mandated since 2001, so modifying competition and recruitment procedures (see Appendix). This procedure has lightened the load of would-be heads when compared to the very tough selection process of trainees previously undergoing pre-service development (2006-2007). The nature of the competitive process has left at least a third of Italy's 10,000 plus *istituti scolastici* with either unqualified acting heads or temporary *reggenze* (two school establishments being run by the same *dirigente scolastico*) with another two-thirds with heads on the brink of retirement (DiSAL, 2006). These new procedures, and other current fast-track competitions exclusively reserved for acting heads, are expected to solve the shortage problem.

The headship trainees we shall report on below are those involved in the 2006-2007 *Corso – Concorso Ordinario* training programme.

Looking at leadership-related threads on the CCO online forums

As in all recent centrally-devised professional development and education schemes involving large numbers of participants in the world of schooling (teachers, non-teaching staff, school heads and students), the *Corso – Concorso Ordinario* (CCO) headship trainees are engaging in a blended-learning environment using the Puntoedu platform run by the National Agency for the Development of School Autonomy (http://www.indire.it). Among others, these are forums and virtual classrooms to contribute to and communities to share in. A certain amount of the work on the platform is part of a bureaucratic requirement and once the training period is over, further access to the relative section is denied. This means that whatever form of interactive community may arise in the process it is time limited and if there is to be any community leadership in the future it would need to be kept alive by other means.

Data from the pilot study involving hundreds of CCO headship trainees from all over the country (June 2006 – early January 2007) filled over 600 pages of discussion with 40 plus leadership threads on issues such as leadership identity, roles and styles; education policy, headship and leadership; leadership and school autonomy; leadership and change; leadership and management; leadership and the school as a learning organization; leadership and pupil learning; empowerment and team leadership; leadership and accountability; leadership and quality; professional development for leadership; transformational leadership; distributed-related concepts of leadership.

The contributions were screened for their understandings of the background policy environment and wider context, for their summary perceptions, portrayals and metaphors of school leadership (Serpieri, 2002), for their citations of leadership literature, for their underscoring of facets of learning and for their explicit or implicit linking of leadership and learning. Here we provide only some insight on what these future heads have said on these matters.

THE CHALLENGES OF LEADING (FOR LEARNING) IN AN ITALIAN AUTONOMOUS SCHOOL

While the words of many CCO prospective heads appear promising, this does not imply that their schools will necessarily become havens of learning-centred leadership. When school autonomy was introduced, one of its sternest critics, Luisa Ribolzi (1997, p.12) portrayed the position of Italian heads as living a paradox similar to that of the "man supposed to find a black cat in a dark room on a moonless night", having to "guarantee system outcomes that have yet to be defined, in the absence of parameters to measure them and being clueless as to how to act to change them". Nonetheless, at the time there were high hopes that autonomy could break consolidated and rigid patterns so as to foster "a creative and flexible combination" of everything that constitutes an intentional learning environment (Cerini, 1997).

Ten years down the road, there is a widespread view that "our schooling system does not have the ability to be a growth factor for the country and its people" (Antonelli, 2006) and that "school autonomy 'taken seriously' [should be] refocused on powerful educational tasks, rather than on accessories [...]. Autonomy to engage in research should thus be centre-stage [for schools] with organizational development at the service of what takes place in the classroom" (Cerini, 2006). A recent countrywide survey conducted amongst deputy heads and *funzione strumentale*[1] showed only "moderate acceptance as to how school autonomy has been implemented", their relative disillusionment depending also on the lack of political support for its development (Fischer et al., 2006, p.163). In these years, it may be said; the pictures of the "legal school" (as in legislation and policy documents) and of the "real school" (with its impoverished resources and daily strife) appear to have been developed in two different darkrooms.

Thus, turning the "real school" into the "clean, wholesome and welcoming learning-friendly environment for all" that Ornella, one of the CCO trainees, wishes for, is the foremost challenge facing Italian practitioners at this time. This is particularly true if we consider, for instance, that the funds transferred to schools in support of autonomy in order to run their everyday business were cut by 49% between 2001 and 2006 with even more drastic cuts in the following year in the funding of supply teachers to cover temporary absences. Moreover, the complexity of the governance system in Italian schools in these and other matters makes decision-making daunting. Thus, even if the "global challenge" of "standardization and control" (Bottery, 2004) hangs in air as more of a virtual threat in the policy documents than as a concrete reality for future headship, this is only some consolation in the immediacy of the other "global challenge" of "commodification and fragmentation" with schools competing in a quasi-market, which two-thirds of Italian teacher leaders and heads see as inevitable in a situation of demographic standstill (Fischer et al, 2006) – as is the case in Italy.

LEADERSHIP

There is comparatively little literature available in Italian on educational leadership, either by Italian authors or in translation. In recent years, attempts have been made to introduce practitioners to educational leadership research from other cultural contexts through professional development initiatives and free online materials in Italian (Brotto, 2003b, 2004). As Giovanni, one of the CCO forum participants stated, Italy is paying the price of the "lack of a significant link connecting policy, research, innovation and professional development". Moreover, the research perspective in the country has been generally grey (1.1% GNP) when compared to the EU average (1.9% GNP: EU19, 2004), this being especially true in education (Drago, 2006).

Given a lack of first-hand access to educational leadership literature or research the majority of these prospective heads see themselves as wanting to act within a range of 'leaderships' that are perceived as conceptually related or overlapping: 'distributed', 'collaborative', 'participative', 'transformational', 'sustainable', 'strategic', 'relational/co-operative', 'moral', 'democratic', 'resonant (primal)', 'receptive', 'inspirational', 'reflexive', drawing mainly on North American authors such as Hargreaves, Sergiovanni and Goleman – the latter two being available in translation – in addition to one an Italian author's work on, 'reflexive leadership', Vitulllo.

Although there are fine theoretical distinctions among these various definitions (Spillane, 2006, 22 – 25, for example), these are less apparent and more confusing for these trainee principals in search of an identity and trying to answer the question what sort of leader can *I* be? One of the participants, Stefania, makes a distinction between "*stare con*" ('being with') and "*essere per*" ('being for'), her aspiration for leadership seen as 'being with', marked by "contagious" listening, empathy, teamwork and sense-making, allied with 'being for' as mutual empowerment and service. If leadership for learning requires "a sharing of leadership" (MacBeath, 2006a:38) there is some reassuring evidence that these future heads appear at least to be thinking along these lines.

SEEDS OF LEADERSHIP FOR LEARNING?

"When people grasp a sense of their own agency, they may take initiative to draw attention to something meaningful" (MacBeath, 2006b, p.43). For CCO headship trainees leadership for learning implied making explicit their own differing conceptions of learning. Four main categories emerged:

1. learning is system and context dependent as well as being a factor of systemic survival and development;
2. learning is a lifelong and lifewide experience, which needs to contribute to reflective and creative practices of multilevel citizenship;
3. learning is an epistemological and narrative event, interpreting and modelling reality as a social construct;
4. learning is not just to look for solutions, but to put oneself in a research perspective learning to ask the right questions.

Although these features correlate with one another, we can examine these singly, matching a few of the trainee voices from the online community to each of these four categories (see Table 1) so as to highlight the 'seeds' of leadership for learning which are implicit in these accounts.

Haridimos Tsoukas (2005, p.70) writes, "as well as being institutions, organized contexts are *practices*" and from a "gnosiological point of view", participating in a practice means "sharing in its narratives" of examples, metaphors, experiences, thoughts. In presenting these voices, their use of metaphor, their aspirational language, their sense of values, we have tried to capture something of the 'ethos' of their discussion and what they hope to 'be' in spite of a policy context which may well inhibit the flowering of their sometimes high flown ideals. If, however, we were to take all of the voices of these CCO trainee heads and subject them to quantitative analysis, we might be disappointed by the relative lack of awareness of leadership as being related to learning. We have, so as to speak, picked the cherries out of the fruitcake. Yet, if we see these various thematic threads as slices of that fruitcake, we may take a more optimistic stance, remembering how the separate flavours of the fruit and nuts mellow together in the cake tin in the weeks before we eat it at Christmas.

SETTING THE SCENE FOR TEACHER LEARNING: VOICES FROM THE STRESA NETWORK SUMMER SCHOOL

Can professional development activities support the development of leadership for learning? The second experience described here raises some interesting issues with regard to teachers' discussion of leadership for learning in the context of a residential training module, held in June 2006, in which 179 teachers participated.

The context and the promoter

The course was the sixth edition of a recurrent activity organised at the end of every year by the "STRESA Network" (STRumenti per l'Efficacia della Scuola e l'Autovalutazione), an association of some 30 primary and lower secondary schools (accounting for 3,215 teachers and 2,7818 pupils in 2006-2007). The Association was founded in Lombardy in 1998 with the purpose of planning and implementing school self-evaluation for school improvement. Over the years, the need to integrate and support self-evaluation through robust, creative research and professional development activities for teachers and heads had become increasingly evident to the network's steering group. In the Italian educational scenario, high stakes accountability does not exist and even external evaluation has not yet resulted in any fruitful initiative, despite many (unsuccessful) attempts (Domenici, 2005). Nor has there been national promotion of self-evaluation as is the case, for instance, in England (MacBeath, 2006a). So, self-evaluation faces a considerable challenge if it is to become a genuine tool for improvement and if it is to become internalised in the day-to-day work and affections of teachers. If it is to raise self-awareness and prove useful in framing and confronting crucial issues arising from every day school life, it must belong to teachers and be close to their needs, independently of any official external demand.

Table 1: Trainee Voices from the Online Community in Four Categories

1. Learning in relation to system and context	For Adriana, Giancarlo and Pasquale, many current dirigenti scolastici respond "inadequately to the needs of learning-centred leadership", not being themselves "guides for learning" or not role-modelling what it might mean to be part of a "comunità formativa" ('learning community'). Mario pleads the case for "pupil learning as the core issue in any discussion on leadership or accountability". Annalisa, Annamaria and Rossella discuss leadership in system terms of "what is needed to make the school a learning organization Nino insists on "building possibilities for 360-degree collaboration with the outside world", in order to improve outcomes in pupil learning. Guido highlights how externally defined models of quality have made his school "something like a big railway station (not in Italy) or an international airport, in which the trains and planes all leave on time [...] but whose 'organizational culture' only marginally impacts on the quality of teaching".
2. Lifelong and lifewide learning for multilevel citizenship	Anita focuses her contribution on the ability we should have to be "self-challenging in a continuous learning process", issuing from our readiness to listen to others and to become reciprocally interdependent. Maria sees headship as having a daily diet of "paideia and Bildung". Fiorenza believes the only way to face the challenges of "the so-called 'liquid society' (Baumann), the 'risk society' (Beck) and the 'global society' (Goldsmith)" is to engage in cooperative learning in order to activate the "dynamics of citizenship and of lifelong learning." Alfonso underscores the "high cultural traffic" marking 'today's school as a social world', thus requiring "an anthropological" perspective in its learning practices.

3. Learning as a narrative event and social construct	Elisabetta, Stefania and Silvia concur in arguing the case for interpretive "autobiographical and narrative" approaches in professional learning, whether self-directed or related to teachers. Maria Teresa shares an Italian summary she has made of a paper on social capital presented by Robert Putnam to the 2004 OECD Education Ministers' meeting in Dublin, using as its title the African proverb: "you need a village to raise a child", calling to mind an interweaving of voices as well as efforts and responsibilities. Some metaphors used by the future heads in their portrayals of leadership: "being in the other's belly" (a "Gestalt perspective" by Anita); "boundary walking" and "border crossing" (Andrea, after Scurati); a "ferryman" (Teresa, after Lagrasta); in the words of Nestor to his son in Homer's Iliad (Rosa): "learn to use multiple intelligences, to oppose the use of force, to nurture a capacity for foresight, to think densely and to recognize opportunities").
4. A research perspective learning to ask the right questions	Turning a school into a "research community is not just an ideal model for teachers, but it has to apply to heads as well" (Mauro). Giuseppina adds that "if learning is important for teachers […], it is even more so for someone who must lead a learning organization" and this someone is "a person who might not always have the right answers but knows what questions to ask himself and to ask others". Clara speaks of the need to fathom "what isn't there" through "negative capability". Francesca hopes for more "black box" thinking as less attention, perhaps, should be paid to the exclusively rational and intentional views of organizational life, recognizing the importance of its "mythical, sense-touching, blurred, ambiguous and paradoxical qualities"

Charts filled with numbers and cold figures do not say very much to Italian teachers who are, by tradition sceptical of any forms of evaluation (Losito, 2007), at least when there is a lack of space, time and support for interpretation and development of ideas. With this in mind the network began to launch seminars, workshops and research groups for teachers and heads together in which different viewpoints could be shared (Barzanò, 2002). While such activities initially targeted the technicalities of self-evaluation, following what was seen as most relevant by teachers and heads, they gradually developed into more "philosophical" forums, focusing on the big question emerging from self-evaluation analyses. For example, 'Why are there such large differences between classes with regard to how pupils view their teachers, when in fact teachers are working towards very similar objectives? What does feedback mean? Why do children often think that the feedback and the reward they get from teachers is unsatisfactory?

Underpinning this development is a belief that school improvement cannot be achieved when learning is focused only on pupils. The involvement of teachers themselves and the school as a whole is a fundamental to the whole initiative (MacBeath, 2006b). This led to the conviction that what we needed to establish was 'a learning scene' in which teachers' narratives could be valued adequately, could be and generative of new thinking and link to wider narratives about social change and globalisation (Goodson, 2003).

So the STRESA network "summer school" became a main arena where the trickiest questions arising from data analysis could be discussed and plans made for initiatives to tackle them. It consists of residential modules lasting three days, each usually hosting some 150-200 teachers. Every year the "summer school" is focused on a different topic, clustering together a series of crucial questions. In order to maximise the impact on individual schools, it was agreed that participants could be partially sponsored (70%) by the network when they enrolled in large groups from the same school (at least 8). Participants are seen as "explorers", of meanings, of encounters, and attitudes in relation to the selected topic. They work intensively in plenary or in groups following the official agenda. However, as is typical of residential courses, they can are also able to benefit from "a third time": the more emotional and less formal one where they can share the full life of three days, letting feelings, ideas and proposals emerge at their own pace (Claris and Cancelli, 2006).

The activities

The 2006 edition's overarching topic was "the responsibility of teachers and heads in the teaching-learning process". Some of the underlying questions were: how do we constructively face pupils with their failures? To what extent do we have to change our assessment criteria on the way, according to the needs of the context? How do we balance our own principles with the need to adapt them to children's interests? Are we prepared to sometimes "cheat" on legislative requirements in the interests of children? Teachers and heads attended a preliminary plenary section on theory, where the concept of "responsibility" was discussed from different perspectives through talks given by a philosopher, a psychoanalyst, an orchestra conductor, an expert on educational organisations and an expert of business organisations. Then they worked for a full day in self-coordinated modules of 10-15, aimed at sharing their experiences and discussing their implications. The work groups' task was to present the assembly with their considerations and perspectives, using different communication styles. Results led to a meaningful variety of lively feed-back reported in the assembly. This included:

- PowerPoint presentations, in which responsibility was defined making use of metaphors, ironic sketches or comics illustrating typical school dilemmas;
- Analysis of conflicts occurring with teacher colleagues and pupils, requiring long term approaches in apparent contradiction with the need for immediate results;
- Musical performances (guitar) including songs and pace exercises underlining the ups and downs of moods and burdens of responsibility;
- Drama performances illustrating typical scenes of school life.

Two drama performances were particularly interesting and give the idea of the learning ethos. The first was performed by a group of eight heads who acted in different roles and represented the typical scene of a new foreign child placed in a problematic class in the middle of the school year. The performance, with its touch of irony combined with warm passion, elicited an intense involvement of the audience and offered a precious opportunity to frame the headteacher/teacher relationship from different viewpoints; eight heads performing in front of their teachers about school problems was, for Italian teachers, an unusual learning situation. The second performance was a witty representation of a case where every one was blaming someone else for something going wrong and for which they were all partly responsible. It was given in the middle of the plenary room and stimulated a complaint by the participants on the course itself – for a few minutes the whole audience did not realise it was a joke!

Inside the learning atmosphere

In the spirit of a continuous self-evaluation process, the network is used to undertaking an evaluation of its activities. The 2006 summer school edition was the object of a particularly intense evaluation process, more deeply and with more revealing instruments than the usual cursory questionnaires. Its rationale was considered by the network members unusually brave, both in relation to the topic and the nature of the very testing questions which it aimed to address, together with the broad "unorganised" space left to the participants themselves. In addition to the usual questionnaire, including both tick-box and open ended questions, in-depth interviews and informal conversations together with 'thick descriptions' were undertaken by professional researchers, appointed by the network. While the quantitative data collected led to the expected appreciation of the course in most of its aspects, qualitative data provided more sophisticated and significant information.

The 2006 course was attended by 179 participants (67 newcomers) of which 177 returned the questionnaire. 162 participants answered the question: "Can you describe a particular feeling you experienced in this course, a moment when you felt touched?" This generated a variety of observations and comments in addition to the 35 participants who took part in individual or collective interviews.

The teachers' perceptions emerging from the data collected proved informative and formative for a number of reasons: they offered a test bed for the course rationale and its future development but even more telling they opened a window on teacher learning, and what it implied for their professional work and identity. The majority of the comments, both from the written observations and from interviews were about the learning adventure, determined by the topic as well as by the way of working and the course ethos For the purposes of this brief analysis only two broad categories are considered: discovery accounts and critical comments. Here are some meaningful examples selected among the "discovery accounts":

> I feel it as a privilege... being able to work not only with children, but also with adults, with whom you can share professional ideas and even more... matching your experience with others is interesting and involving: I feel very enriched! (Marta, Interview).

> It's my first time at the summer school... I was curious: why are we listening to an orchestra conductor? Why do we have so much time on our own in small groups? Now I start to understand: the passion that the conductor spoke about is the same I put in my own work! And if I have time to discuss this with colleagues I will go back home ready to put ideas into practice... (Rossella, Interview)

> I left home with the idea that I would have never been able to participate actively in a debate: I was not brave enough "to come into play". Suddenly this feeling changed. Why? Thanks to the nice words of the speakers? No! Listening, listening and listening: not with my

ears, but entering into people, being able to dig into the depth of their beauty. Everything changed because people showed themselves, their inner feelings. I was enriched by them. (Valeria, Written comment).

I go back home with a sense of belonging to the teacher category having been reinforced. I'm proud to be a teacher after having met so many colleagues of such breadth and depth. (Camilla, Written comment)

The topic is intriguing but difficult. Last year I was scared... the course was about "feedback and reward"... difficult lectures, a lot of quotes. Philosophy, science... even poetry! I kept asking myself: " What will the impact of all these things be on my work?" Yet during the year, once all the ideas had settled down inside my self, I realised how many things I had learnt and how I could mirror my experience into many ideas I had never met before... indeed through my own experience! (Michele, Interview)

These positive quotes are no more than a small sample but their tone makes them sound like popular adverts extolling customer satisfaction. What is noteworthy in these examples, however, is the way they unravel important aspects of teachers' attitudes, relevant to understanding their needs and professional scope for learning. When we read behind the enthusiasm, we discover that lying behind these affirmations lie scarce opportunities for teachers to develop their professional identity in the course of their normal work. What all these accounts share is a sense of surprise and wonder when facing experiences which, according to the most literature on professional development should be routine for all good education professionals (Eraut, 1994, Goodson, 2003, MacBeath, 1998). There is an abundance of research and theoretical texts which lay emphasis on sharing experiences "in depth" with colleagues, discovering richness and hidden treasure (Marta, Rossella), learning how to listen (Valeria), reflecting on their learning (Michele). It is striking to think that Michele, an experienced fully qualified teacher who proves to be open to reflection, has finally met the opportunity to become aware of how his own learning works. How can he deal with children's learning every day if he himself is not aware of his own learning?

While it would appear that these teachers have over time internalised the diminished public value accorded to the teaching profession, what emerges from behind the screen is a "new pride" (Camilla). Many participants alluded to this self-discovery, opportunities to feel proud of themselves both as individual professionals and collective profession.

Critical comments bring to light further aspects of how teachers interpret their opportunities to learn:

> Like my colleague I had difficulties in the group. We spoke for three hours about sharing ideas and experiences and at the end the strongest personality decided. We were short of time and he was the one who said what had to be presented. I did not agree with what my colleagues were saying, but I kept silent. What I think is very different, but luckily I could share it with my room mate during the night! (Paola, Interview)

> I appreciated the group work, but I would have preferred a real coordinator, rather than one selected by the group itself. A person more aware of the objectives and the group dynamics would have been more effective (Annamaria, written comment).

> I think that in a course most of the time should be given over to the speakers, our maestri. I like listening to them. The group work would have been more effective if it had not only been based on our experience, but on more input by the speakers. I would have preferred a more skilled coordinator (Stefano, written comment).

> Last year there were more suggestions and inputs by the speakers… It was a bit light this year! I would have liked more input. This morning we spent three hours talking with colleagues in the group. In the past years it was only an hour, there were more talks (Marina, Interview).

There were far fewer critical comments than discovery accounts, there being generally positive observations. However, these comments show how a group of teachers and heads have difficulty in taking on board the responsibility of their learning through more autonomous agendas. Above all they are looking for *maestri*, great lecturers who can 'give lessons'. They are open to learning, but they feel more comfortable with a traditional pattern. As Marilena explained in an interview, "I like the idea of being a pupil for once. I like learning, going back to school, attending lessons." Some teachers are reluctant to share their experiences with colleagues and seem to indicate that colleagues' ears are not qualified enough to listen to the story they have to tell. What these teachers have in mind is a more hierarchical view of learning in which someone is transmitting and someone else is receiving.

This quick journey into the voices of some Italian teachers does not obviously intend to provide a detailed portrait of what the perspectives for leadership for learning are. The STRESA network summer school is, to some extent, a privileged learning scene for education professionals. Unlike other professional development contexts it benefits from the stability and continuity offered by the network's history. Participants in the course are motivated; they know from their own experience or from colleagues' accounts what the style of the network is and what they can expect. However, they are still surprised to discover that a deep sharing of their experience with colleagues may result in a successful exercise. They are still not familiar with the idea that at the core of their profession today there should be continuous learning, "critical, penetrative, thoughtful, and ruminative [...], that engages people's feelings and connects with their lives" (Hargreaves and Fink, 2006, p.53). To use a gastronomic metaphor, they could be sophisticated wine connoisseurs, who can distinguish and appreciate different brands, yet they look at wine with wonder and they enjoy it with the naïve pleasure of someone who has always drunk only beer. This gives an idea of how finding good and convincing opportunities to learn may be challenging and complex for teachers. On the other hand, some teachers do not even dream of being active and reflexive in their learning, as revealed in an interview with Clara: "Some teachers are very good at reading books. One year they implement one book, the next another one. If the second says the opposite from the first it does not matter: it is written in a book, it must be done!"

These teachers' voices indicate clearly how important, but complex, it is to create contexts in which they can see from the outside and appreciate their own professional competence.

Experiences such as the STRESA network summer school show that meaningful learning events can be implemented successfully, but connecting these events and creating a stable active learning environment around teachers is a difficult task.

CONCLUDING REMARKS

The voices of the participants in the two examples described reflect different kinds of learning ethos emerging from attempts in Italy to create contexts which root the idea of leadership for learning in the discourses and practices of education professionals. The idea itself is of growing interest in the Italian educational arena, although it has always to be set in a policy context where the aim is one of improving pupil performance results - *successo formativo* Nonetheless, it finds its way into national initiatives, such as the *corso-concorso* forums illustrated above, and other professional development activities which target teachers through blended learning. It has also inspired several local experiences which have been able to benefit from more stable audiences in long-term projects, as is the case of the STRESA network.

However, implementing leadership for learning in a broad sense in Italy appears to be more complex than expected. A diehard traditional bureaucratic mind frame at the governance level, together with the lack of investment in educational research, makes the task arduous, to say the least (Drago, 2006).

The risk is also that frameworks launched with the best intentions, intended to be rich in their implications and possible developments, may produce only overarching 'labels', deceiving with 'appearance' more than 'substance'. In the case of the corso concorso for headship, the stimulating dialogue taking place among the trainee heads is only superficially monitored, attention being paid to whether or not they perform their mandatory tasks rather than to what they really have to say – as such an opportunity lost to research which potentially might involve researchers and practitioners in working, thinking and planning together. Moreover, once the formal part of the training is over, access to the platform is withdrawn and the further "official support" available only comes in the form of sporadic top-down interventions, with little evidence of a genuine and on going response to real needs.

On the other hand, the STRESA network experience shows how establishing a systemic fruitful learning environment for teachers is also complex. As the Italians say: *una rondine non fa primavera* ("one swallow doesn't make it summer"). Individual events may be successful in themselves, but producing a real culture of learning among teachers is a different story altogether, the ordinary life of most practitioners still being far removed from the intensive and reflective opportunities to learn. In addition, several teachers appear to stay anchored to the hierarchical learning patterns they experienced as students.

Indeed what these examples underline is the need to nurture, through continuous monitoring and feeding, those broad arenas where discussions, reflections and experiences may cross each other and grow. In other words, leadership for learning requires a continuous reinventing of the scene, while carefully and sensitively observing what is happening. This is the challenge we are facing.

NOTES

[1] *Funzione strumentale* teachers are contractually recognized, but have an unstable and hybrid profile, and are perceived as a fragmentary and temporary reply to a structural problem (Armone, 2001) related to a lack of middle management in Italian schools. They are teacher coordinators that have honed skills in organisational planning, project design, team building and leading, ICT, evaluation methodology and knowledge of the local community within Italian autonomous schools.

2 The authors would like to thank Silvia Zanoni for her help in processing the questionnaires and Giorgia Galano and Emiliano Grimaldi, research students at the University of Naples for conducting the interviews.

REFERENCES

Antonelli, G. (2006). *FRAMES – Idee per la scuola che verrà*. [Online]. Available: http://www.scuolaer.it.
Armone, A. (2001). Una possibile mappa formativa per le Funzioni Obiettivo. In IRRE Emilia Romagna, L. Lelli, and I. Summa (Eds.), *Professionalità docente per l'innovazione*, pp. 151-164. Naples: Tecnodid.
Associazione TreeLLe. (2006). Per una scuola autonoma e responsabile. *Quaderni TreeLLe, 5*.
Barzanò, G. (2002). School Self-evaluation Towards a European Dimension. *European Journal of Teacher Education, 25*(1), 83-102.
Bottery, M. (2004). *The challenges of educational leadership*. London: Chapman.
Brotto, F. (2003a). Collegiality and School Leadership: reflective enquiry within the Tuscan action-research team. *The Enquirer, autumn*, 3-8.
Brotto, F. (2003b, February, 17-18). *Una selezione degli Atti del Convegno 'Collaborative Leadership, Change through Exchange: Visions and practices of leadership for learning*. Carrara. [Online]. Available: http://www.edscuola.it/archivio/comprensivi/materiali.html.
Brotto, F. (2004, November, 20). Atti del Convegno *'Self-Evaluation and Schools: Whose Leadership?'* Milan. [Online]. Available: http://www.edscuola.it/archivio/comprensivi/materiali.html.
Cerini, G. (1997). *Autonomia scolastica: un decreto prêt-a-porter?* [Online]. Available: http://www.edscuola.it/cerini.html.
Cerini, G. (2006, December, 1-2). *Se la riforma fosse una ballata popolare...*. Paper presented at the FRAMES Project Conference, Martin Sicuro, San Benedetto del T.
Claris, S. & Cancelli, S. (2006). *Ritratto in formazione*. [Online]. Available: www.retestresa.it.
DiSAL – Dirigenti Scuiole Autonome e Libere. (2006). *Contratto Dirigenti Scolastici*. [Online]. Available: http://www2.tecnicadellascuola.it.
Domenici, G. (2005). Valutazione in gioco: moda o risorsa?. In C. Scurati (Ed.), *Strutture di professionalità per la dirigenza scolastica*. Brescia: La Scuola.
Drago, R. (2006, November, 22). *La dirigenza scolastica nel quadro del declino del sistema scolastico italiano e della sua gestione*. Paper presented at the DiSAL Annual Conference, Chianciano.
Eraut, M. (1994). *Developing Professional Knowledge and Competence*. London: Falmer Press.
Fischer, L., Fischer, M.G., & Masuelli, M. (2006). *Le figure organizzative emergenti fra gli insegnanti della scuola italiana*. Turin: L'Harmattan Italia.
Frost, D. (2006). *Why is the concept of agency so important in Leadership for Learning*. Paper presented at ICSEI 2006, Fort Lauderdale, Florida, USA.
Frost, D., Durrant, J., Head, M., & Holden, G. (2000). *Teacher-led school improvement*. London & New York: Routledge Falmer.
Goodson, I. (2003). *Professional knowledge, Professional lives*. Maidenhead: Open University Press.
Hargreaves, A. (1994). *Changing teachers, changing times: Teachers' work and culture in the postmodern age*. London, Cassell.
Hargreaves, A., & Fink, D. (2006). *Sustainable leadership*. San Francisco: Jossey-Bass.
Istituto Nazionale di Statistica – ISTAT (2007). *Statistiche sulla scuola*. Rome: ISTAT.
Losito, B. (2007). Il sistema nazionale di valutazione. In G. Cerini & G. Spinosi. *Voci della scuola*. Naples: Tecnodid.
MacBeath, J. (1998). *Effective school leadership: Responding to change*. London: Chapman.
MacBeath, J. (2006a). *School inspection and self-evaluation: Working with the New Relationship*. London: Routledge.
MacBeath, J. (2006b). A story of change, growing leadership for learning. *Journal of Educational Change, 7*, 33-46.
Ribolzi, L. (1997). Dirigere e governare non soltanto gestire. *Autonomia e dirigenza, VI* (1-2), 11 – 14.
Searle, J.R. (1969). *Speech Acts: An essay in the philosophy of language*. Cambridge: Cambridge University Press.

Serpieri, R. (2002). *Leadership senza gerarchia*. Naples: Liguori.
Spillane, J. P. (2006). *Distributed leadership*. San Francisco: Jossey-Bass.
Summa, I. (2003, February, 17-18). *La leadership collaborative*. Paper presented at the International Leadership Conference 'Collaborative Leadership, Change through Exchange: Visions and practices of leadership for learning', Carrara.
Tsoukas, H. (2005). *Complex knowledge: Studies in organizational epistemology*. Oxford: Oxford University Press.
Ufficio Scolastico Provinciale di Bergamo (2006). *Materiali corsi per dirigenti scolastici*. [Online]. Available: http://www.bergamo.istruzione.lombardia.it/riccione/riccione.htm.
Varchetta, G. (2005). Contesti ambigui e apprendimento adulto. In A. Fontana & G. Varchetta (Eds.), *La valutazione riconoscente*. Milan: Guerrini e Associati.
Vitullo, A. (2006). *Leadership riflessive*. Milan: Apogeo.

APPENDIX: THE CURRENT RECRUITMENT PROCEDURE IN ITALY FOR SCHOOL HEADS THROUGH NATIONAL COMPETITIONS (2007)

1. Qualified teacher applicants with five years of experience are screened in a pre-selection phase through objective testing;
2. admitted candidates sit for a written examination and an oral examination-interview;
3. the qualifications and experience in the academic, professional and cultural fields are evaluated on a point scale for candidates successfully completing the second phase;
4. a ranking is determined on the basis of the results of the previous phases and a predetermined number of candidates are then admitted to a headship training programme;
5. training for headship;
6. awarding of an initial 3 – 5 year contract by Regional education officers to the new heads, or dirigenti scolastici as they are called, and their appointment to any school in the region requiring a head, with their first year in office as a probationary year;
7. permanent status in headship through renewable contracts generally ensues.

AFFILIATIONS

Giovanna Barzanò
Ufficio Scolastico Regionale Lombardia, Ministero della Pubblica Istruzione
Italy

Francesca Brotto, Direzione Generale Affari Internazionali, Ministero della Pubblica Istruzione
Italy

JORUNN MØLLER

CHAPTER 14

Living with Accountability and Mandated Change – Leadership for Learning in a Norwegian Context

The focus on learning in educational policy documents is often linked to an analysis of the leadership and governing structures of schools. The leadership discourse has changed dramatically during the last fifteen years. One thread is moving away from the linear, technological approach, in which leadership is conceived of as a means to bring about pre-determined ends. However, while the new discourses move away from leadership as control, we are now witnessing an increase in external control over schools. In other words, tensions and contradictions connected to the way school leadership is being conceptualized can be identified, and there is a need to explore how recently introduced accountability systems are influencing both the focus of the work as a principal, the discourse of leadership for learning and approaches to leadership development.

The chapter will discuss the relationship between different forms of accountability and school leadership in a Norwegian context. The analysis draws upon and compares findings from two studies. The first is a case study on successful school leadership (Møller et al., 2005). The second is an action research project which aimed at exploring leadership for learning (Møller, 2007c). Both studies demonstrated new ways of conceptualizing leadership as distributed practice that extend well-beyond individual roles. In addition, they serve as examples of how professional accountability is established locally. Implications for leadership development will be discussed.

THE NORWEGIAN CONTEXT

Norway, as well as the other Nordic countries, has invested more than other nations in the education sector. The educational level is high and the state school is highly regarded by the public (Telhaug, Mediås, & Aasen, 2006, p.278-279). Norwegian educational policy has intended to create both equal and equitable life conditions for all social groups, regardless of social background, gender, ethnicity and geographical location. More than 95% of the cohort is enrolled in ordinary classes in public schools[1]. The Education Act stipulates that all activity should be carried out in accordance with fundamental democratic, humanistic and Christian values[2], and that education should uphold and renew the national cultural heritage to provide perspective and guidance for the future. Culturally the population of Norway is fairly homogeneous, with a small indigenous Saami minority mostly in the North (0.2% of the pupils use the Saami language at school). In addition there are between 10 000 and 15 000 Norwegians of Finnish descent in the counties of Troms and Finnmark. Many of them use their own language. Due to recent migration, the student population in Norwegian schools is changing, and becoming more multicultural and multilingual. By the end of 2005 the immigrant population constituted approximately 390 000 persons or 8.3 % of the total population. A large majority of the immigrants have settled down in the area around Oslo (Norwegian Directorate for Education and Training, 2007a).

The Knowledge Promotion is the latest reform in primary and secondary education in Norway, and took effect from August 2006. In the *Quality Framework* formulated in connection with this reform, democracy and diversity are important concepts:

> A clear foundation in values and a broad understanding of culture are fundamental for an inclusive social community and for a community of learning where diversity is acknowledged and respected. Such a learning environment gives room for cooperation, dialogue and negotiations. The students participate in democratic processes and can thus develop a democratic mind, and understanding of active and engaged participation in a diverse society (Ministry of Education and Research, 2006, p.2).

This underlines that Norway is a diverse society, and that giving equal access to knowledge and education within schools through recognition of differences within the school community is crucial, as is the development and practice of a democratic spirit. Also, the White Paper *Culture for Learning*, presented to the Norwegian Parliament in 2004, emphasised that schools need competent and visible school leaders who have positive attitudes to change so as to enable schools to develop into learning organisations.

The Norwegian Government maintains a commitment to the welfare state, but during the 1990s certain aspects changed or disappeared. However, case studies of recent educational reforms have demonstrated that the tradition of striving for equity through centralized welfare state governance is changing in Norway as well as throughout Scandinavia toward a school policy based on choice, deregulation, evaluation and managerialism (Johannesson, Lindblad & Simola, 2002). Both non-social-democratic governments as well as social democratic governments have formulated and elaborated deregulation and managerialism, and the differences between parties have disappeared to a considerable extent. But politicians do not see themselves as tearing down the welfare state. On the contrary, they argue that they are making what is good better.

The policy seems to be moving towards what Giddens (1998) has called the "Third Way," a combination of neo-liberal market reforms and neo-conservative government regulation. This is the case whether the government is a coalition between right wing parties or formed by representatives from social democratic parties. This international trend that favours the reduction of the state and its public sector services presents a radical challenge to all Scandinavian countries that have been known for the value they place on equality. In educational policy discussions, schools are increasingly perceived as the unit of measurement, clearly implying new expectations of public reporting.

Accountability has become a popular concept in this regard. The meaning of the term is, however, more elusive and may be difficult to put into practice. In the English language, it is possible to lexically distinguish between *accountability* and *responsibility*, although accountability to some extent has replaced responsibility, and public trust is to be secured by specifying performance compliance. While accountability is located in hierarchical practices of bureaucracy, responsibility concerns the obligations teachers and school leaders, as part of a profession, have to each other, answering questions about what has happened within one's area of responsibility and providing a reliable story of practice, i.e. what has happened and why it has taken place (cf. Møller, 2007b).

Part of this change is related to the movement towards decentralization which has focused questions around the professional ability of teachers. The diffuse borderline between political and professional responsibility seems to represent a major problem. Conservatives see opportunities for potential abuse in school-level control, particularly if teachers are able to exert greater control in the process of school governance. If school-based management is to be introduced, they suggest that lay control must be assured. From the left it is argued that deregulation, choice and local control will ultimately favour those with greater personal and family resources. Greater inequality will result, with the best getting better and a widening of the gap between rich and poor. At the same time, blame will be decentralized. Central agencies will no longer carry the political burden of confronting those who accuse them of ineffectiveness and inefficiency.

Thus, decentralization of the educational system, irrespective of motives, puts in focus the balance between political and professional power over education (Lundgren, 1990).

The Local Government Act of 1992 paved the way for a substantial degree of self-governance on the part of the municipalities and county authorities. This also applies to provisions that regulate the role and responsibility of principals. At the same time, working within a formal leadership team has become an institutionalized practice in most Norwegian schools. So, although Norway has a national common framework, common law and common national strategies for primary and secondary education and training, school owners at municipality and county level – in addition to private school owners – are responsible for how this is managed and carried out within each school. Norwegian education is thus characterised by diversity and large variations in how local authorities choose to decide priorities and run their schools (Norwegian Directorate for Education and Training, 2007a).

In a modern society it is reasonable that stakeholders require information about curricular processes and educational results to be reported. It raises a number of questions, such as the following: How do teachers and school leadership carry out the socially mandated policy decisions? Are teachers working efficiently and appropriately with students, and is school leadership in control of optimal resource allocation and staff support? Are students learning what they should in our schools? How do teachers and leadership accept the responsibility they have for student attainment outcomes? Although such questions are not new, the multifaceted manifestations of accountability requirements exemplify increased top-down control. During the 80s both politicians and top administrators aired doubts about the extent to which teachers are making claims on behalf of their clients, as against claims on behalf of their own interests as a group. This may explain why external evaluation of education at various levels has become a focus in recent years. Education policy was no longer to be based on widespread trust in the professional competence of educators; instead their performance should be controlled and judged according to criteria established outside the profession. The new understanding of accountability includes making student results the unit for evaluating teachers' instructional practice, as well as establishing the individual school as the unit of institutional achievement.

With the implementation of a national evaluation system in 2005 the issues of accountability were put on the agenda in a different way compared to the past. National tests (in Reading, Mathematics, English) were implemented for the first time in 2005, but researchers conducting the evaluation concluded that the quality of the tests needed improvement (Kjærnsli et al., 2003). The Ministry of Education and Research decided to postpone the tests for a year and new tests will be available by September 2007. The issue of testing is quite controversial and highly debated among students, teachers and researchers.

Even though neo-liberalism has been gaining ground for some time, partly as a result of new globalization, and particularly during the first years of the new millennium, social democratic progressivism is still recognizable in Norwegian educational policy. In September 2005 a Red-Green alliance came to power after the parliamentary elections, and this has strengthened social democratic progressivism's presence in the school debate. Also, it is possible to distinguish a Nordic model of society which is based on cooperation and compromise, with a special balance between the state, the market and civil society. It emerges as a composite of two prevalent European models; the Anglo-Saxon model's emphasis on economic liberalism and competition, and the Continental model's emphasis on a large public sector, social welfare and security (Telhaug et al., 2006).

THEORETICAL AND METHODOLOGICAL PERSPECTIVES

Perspectives on leadership and learning

Both leadership and learning contain contested notions. Although educational leadership is situated in the field of education, much of the leadership discourse in education has been influenced by management discourses in other fields. As such, there are tensions and contradictions connected to the way school leadership is being conceptualized (Møller, 2007a). In this paper a distributed perspective is applied as a lens for thinking about leadership and refers to 'activities tied to the core work of the organization that are designed by organizational members to influence the motivation, knowledge, affect of practices of other organizational members' (Spillane 2006, p.11). The core work in a school is about student learning, and the critical issue is *how* leadership is distributed, not whether it is distributed. Tools and routines are an integral element that constitutes leadership practice. Also, leadership and learning are understood as mutually embedded; a frame which pictures both leading and learning as activities and, as such, offers an open invitation to lead, and to learn as the task or the circumstance demand (MacBeath et al., 2005).

In this way school leadership can be understood as a network of relationships among people, structures and cultures, not just as a role-based function assigned to one person, and it includes a socio-cultural perspective on learning (Wenger, 1999). But leadership is also about power, and school principals are vested with formal powers that include compulsion and reward, economic and structural sanctions. The power of the principal has its source outside the school because it is delegated by the State (Hatcher, 2005).

DISCOURSES OF ACCOUNTABILITY

Accountability means having to answer for one's actions, and particularly the results of those actions. The discourses of accountability are often a mixture of several forms of accountability (Elmore, 2006, Sirotnik, 2005). Sinclair's (1995) refinement of different forms of accountability offers a lens through which we may more closely examine manifestations of accountability. A distinction between five forms of accountability can be made. It encompasses political, public, managerial, professional and personal.

Political and public accountability means being responsible to the mandate and function of that particular organisation in society, and being responsible towards the local community of which one is a part. *Managerial accountability* refers to a person's position in a hierarchy and responsibility to superiors concerning tasks that are delegated. The point is that schools as collective entities are accountable to higher levels of the educational system. It focuses mainly on monitoring inputs and outputs. There is also a *professional accountability*, where a person's commitment to a community of professionals makes him/her perceive a duty to adhere to the standards of the profession. This is about teaching as a moral endeavour. Codes of ethics have for instance become a familiar part of the rhetoric of professional control of the work in schools, even though the influence of these codes is uncertain. Professional accountability implies that teachers acquire and apply the knowledge and skills needed for successful practice. In addition, it involves the norms of putting the needs of the students at the centre of their work, collaborating and sharing of knowledge, and a commitment to the improvement of practice. Finally, the category - *personal accountability* implies the values that are sacred to a person. fidelity to personal conscience, respect for human dignity and acting in a manner that accepts responsibility for affecting the lives of others. This kind of accountability is regarded as particularly powerful and binding but stressful if personal values are in conflict with other kinds of accountability. However, personal standards of good teaching are to a great extent implicit.

When people talk about holding schools accountable for results, the dominating discourse tends to take the form of *managerial accountability,* and neglects a shift in focus in accountability policies during the last decades; from a focus on providing educational inputs and processes, to a focus on measurable outcomes. It means that schools are held accountable for improvement in student performance outcomes, and is based on a view that schools will do better if they are given clear information about their performance on national tests. Test scores are used as evidence of how well the system is performing at an aggregate level. However, this shift in focus brings with it a risk of ignoring some of the most critical purposes of public schooling, for example preparation for participation in a democratic society or processes that creates and sustain social justice, which is not easily or cheaply measured (Sirotnik, 2005).

METHODOLOGICAL APPROACHES

The analysis draws upon and compares findings from two studies. The first is based on findings from the International Successful School Leadership Project which includes a case study on successful school leadership in twelve schools (Møller et al., 2005) and a survey, conducted in 2005, among school principals (Møller et al., 2006). The case study had a multi-site case study approach, and methods included a common interview protocol and procedure[3]. In addition to lengthy conversations with the principal and the leadership team at each school, groups of teachers, students, and parents were interviewed to capture multiple perspectives on the school and the school's leadership. All interviews were transcribed. Field notes from observations of classroom instruction, the principal's activities, leadership teams meetings, and staff meetings were also included as part of the investigation. The questionnaire was distributed to a statistically randomly selected part of Norwegian school principals, based on criteria such as type and size of schools, size of municipalities, geographical dispersion including urban, suburban and rural schools.

The second is an action research project which aimed at exploring leadership for learning (Møller, 2007c). This study included a number of different approaches to data collection. The baseline data gathering was carried out as planned during the fall 2002, and the initial school portrait was derived from the following sources of evidence - a baseline survey of teachers, students and school leaders which aimed at ascertaining key insights (as well as facts) about the leadership, learning and development context of each school; interviews which included information that school leaders and teaching staff themselves viewed as important in presenting as full a picture as possible of their institution. As critical friends we helped the participants to document and synthesize the school portraits. The written accounts worked as a tool for reflection on practice. In addition, as critical friends, we were invited to observe leadership practice at the local school. A centerpiece of our collaboration with the schools was mutual reflection on actions. Usually the schools decided a week ahead what would be the focus for our critical reflections. The principals at all the three schools engaged in the study wanted to be observed for a couple of hours on a 'normal' workday to get feedback on how they were spending their time and whether they gave priority to the same tasks as they said that they wanted to. They also wanted to be observed in meetings with the staff to get a critical eye on their actions and performance related to their vision of a learning organization and how they as leaders should act. Most teachers wanted help closely connected to their teaching. After each school visit, we wrote a detailed account of what we had observed, and this account was sent back to school with a final section focusing on questions for reflection we had come to after writing up our experiences at the school. The purpose was both to keep track on the school's development and to stimulate further reflections. At the same time these field notes had status as data for our analysis related to the research questions (see Frost and Swaffield in this volume).

For the purpose of this article, the focus is on an analysis of how school leaders from these two studies framed living with accountability and mandated change. The excerpts cited in this article are exemplars that represent a number of cases from the total body of data.

FINDINGS

Findings based on the ISSPP study

A common element in the Norwegian case studies was that students' learning appeared to be the focal point for the schools' philosophy and practice. This orientation was expressed through the overarching intentions of the school, the grouping of students, evaluation procedures, and the organization of curriculum units. Both principals and teachers stated that the main goal was to assist individual students in acquiring knowledge and skills, to develop their potential and strengthen their self confidence. This was realised through the continuous work of creating supportive learning environments. Both school leaders and teachers at these schools underscored the importance of the social learning environment in order to reach these goals requiring building communities of professionals with a focus on their own learning (Møller et al., 2005, 2007a). The following excerpt is from an interview with a group of teachers:

> We do our best to provide good teaching, and we collaborate to build a stimulating learning environment where students could flourish and develop as persons and citizens. The students must get the feeling that they learn something that is important for their future life. [...] The school must be a safe environment, and we need to balance high expectations and personalized learning. [...] A successful school is characterized by structure and humanity; everyone is contributing, and everyone is taken seriously, and everyone is met with respect. Structure and visible leadership help this to happen. (Focus-interview with teachers, Upper Secondary School, medium size, author's translation).

Some of the students at this school argued that the student cohort, the students' attitudes, and their willingness to collaborate were the key factors in successful learning, because motivated students influenced the teachers in a positive way. 'I think successful learning is first and foremost dependent on the students themselves. If students decide not to collaborate with the teachers and give a damn in creating a positive, safe, and inspiring school climate, the teachers are in great trouble', one of the students said. At the same time, he emphasized,

> ... a successful school has active students, and how does the student become an active learner? It is indeed important that the leadership team and the teachers motivate and encourage learning, and it is crucial that the leadership team supports the teachers to do a good job. (Focus-interview with students. Upper Secondary School, medium size, author's translation).

In our data there were many accounts that speak to school leaders and teachers' strong emotional commitment to their profession. For instance, in their stories they underscored again and again that the main aim was to provide good learning opportunities so that students could become good citizens in the future, and they were very concerned about the students' well-being. To grow up in a society that focuses increasingly on individualism brought new challenges. Many students had significant problems at home, and the school had a potential to make a difference particularly for these students. A quote from one of our schools may serve as an example of how a majority of teachers and school leaders described successful schools.

> To me, a successful school is able to motivate students, and to provide a safe and sound learning environment. It is important to create this foundation for learning. The school should not be evaluated based on marks or test scores only, because it will create a misleading picture. The most important aim is to develop active citizens, to develop a

collaborative attitude, tolerance and creativity, and that is not easily measured by tests in basic subjects.

Fulfilling such a mission was a continuous team effort, and both the leaders and the teachers believed they could make a difference in their students' lives. This was the mandate they felt responsible for. As such, both political and public accountability was part of their professional and personal ethos. But they had to deal with living in a society that had become more dominated by New Public Management and managerial accountability.

The Norwegian schools which participated in this project may serve as examples of how professional accountability had become established locally. At most schools the leaders and the teachers had worked for years with systemic school based evaluation for the benefit of school development. Such evaluation is a way of being accountable, as they saw it. They were able to provide documentation of the work they were doing to the outside world, but first and foremost they gave priority to school based evaluation in order to develop their practice. Teachers volunteered to take part in evaluation teams, and they reported the results to their superiors. These teachers, in cooperation with the students and the leadership team demonstrated how both external and internal evaluation could be used as a tool for school improvement, and consequently, how professional accountability could be combined with managerial accountability (Møller, 2007b). At the same time, it is important to be aware that the schools that participated in this project were part of a rather exclusive group of lighthouse schools. They had applied for this recognition and were selected from a much larger number of participants. By being chosen they gained public recognition as a good school.

In contrast to the findings based on cases studies in these successful schools, a preliminary report of the PISA+ study[4] claimed that even though schools had managed to create safe and secure environments enabling everyone to cope with failure and respond positively to challenges, many of the observed teachers did not demonstrate a strong focus on learning, nor did they provide systematic feedback to their students. There appeared to be a lack of tools and strategies to enhance thinking about learning and the practice of teaching (Klette & Lie, 2006). Hence, we may assume there is a great variation between Norwegian schools and classrooms in ways of framing and living with accountability.

The findings based on the national survey reveal a picture of mainly very responsible school leaders[5]. 67.4 % of the principals said that they were held accountable to stakeholders to a high or very high degree for ensuring teaching standards were met, and 87.2 % responded that to a very high degree or to a high degree were held accountable for being ethically responsive to the students' needs. However, in a survey it is likely that school principals will present answers which fit within an acceptable range of the story of headship as a Norwegian school. The principals' responsibility for school practice and, in the end, student achievement, is strongly emphasized in the policy documents. It is expected that the principal is accountable for planning, implementing and evaluating school practice. In addition, results from international surveys such as PISA, TIMSS and PIRLS have led to discussions about student achievement in Norway, as in other countries. According to the Norwegian principals' responses on the survey, 76 % said that they were held accountable to school authorities for the level of student achievement, for monitoring school outcomes and for ensuring that the teaching standards were met.

A focus on the school as a basic unit of accountability and reporting of student achievement is however problematic. Patterns of accountability should be reciprocal (Sirotnik, 2005) and include information about the performance of the officials above the level of the school in providing the resources, conditions and opportunities that learning requires. A report about these issues in a Norwegian context has recently been published, and the conclusion about the system for following up at municipal level was alarming (Norwegian Directorate for Education and Training, 2007b). More than 70 % of the municipalities (which are defined as "school owners" within the Norwegian context) lacked a systematic approach to accountability while delegation of responsibility for tasks was unclear. Communication between state officials at municipal level on the one hand and schools on the other were often poor, and there were varying perceptions about approaches to the self evaluation. At the level of rhetoric, a managerial approach to accountability, closely connected to a New Public Management approach, was in place. This report about the role of the municipalities provides a different picture of accountability in practice, and explains why most Norwegian principals don't experience accountability as a problem in the absence of high-stake testing. Perhaps, managerial accountability may be described as an 'anticipated future'.

However, in general, 92 % of the Norwegian principals reported that their job in general had become more demanding in the last couple of years. The findings demonstrate a significant correlation between "tensions between loyalty to the expectations of employers versus the priorities made at school" and the principals' age. Principals over 55 years old experienced this dilemma more than younger principals. The same is the case for tensions "between loyalty to employers and the need to take part in the public discourse about schooling". Moreover, there is a variation in responses from principals located in different municipalities. This may be related to the fact that some municipalities are characterized by stronger top-down governance compared to others.

FINDINGS BASED ON THE "LEADERSHIP FOR LEARNING" STUDY

School leaders and teachers at the three Norwegian schools which had committed themselves to participate in the action research project, all aimed at improving their practice. They valued a shared sense of accountability in which a systematic approach to self-evaluation was embedded at classroom and school level, and they wanted to foster a dialogue about the nature of the educational experience the school was offering. They welcomed the external support their critical friends could provide. According to all three principals the participation in this project has resulted in a stronger focus on teacher leadership, on learning and professional accountability compared to before. But the manifestation of their leadership practice was quite diverse. The principal at school A can be characterized as a strong, innovative and charismatic leader with a clear vision for the school's development, constantly working to build consensus among the staff about long-term as well as short-term goals. The principals at School B and C first and foremost listen to and try to follow up the initiatives coming from the teachers, a strategy which has been part of the established culture for years. At the same time the stories told by these principals, reveal a close connection between the school culture, the understanding of leadership, the personal context of the individual, and the scope of actions for both principals and teachers (Møller, 2007c).

One of our intentions as critical friend has been to reconstruct and reflect on incidents in practice in relation to intentions and purposes, and thereby develop our common understanding of practice, constructing and reconstructing our theories of practice. An underlying assumption is that being a teacher or a school leader represents a reservoir of practical knowledge that is seldom discussed in an explicit way. Habits, routines and traditions as to the correct way of solving problems and doing the work is developed over time. Reflection on action is a way of articulating this taken-for-granted practical consciousness in order to examine if the work is for the benefit of students. The next step then is to clarify actions to improve practice.

The example below is taken from a report written by a critical friend who observed classroom activities at school B. In advance the leadership team and the teachers asked to observe Science teachers in their collaboration with students in beginning a new project about geological forces that act on the surface of the earth. The aim was to discuss the teacher's leadership for learning in a subject such as Science. The example covers observation of a lesson where one teacher was responsible for a group of 25 students.

The Science teacher allowed all the students to schedule their own time during the project work. Only beginning and end times were set by the teacher. In other words students were given a lot of space to choose their own way of working with the topic, and to decide what would be the end product of their work. In this way they had a lot of control over time and operation. The groups of students were set up at random, and no clear instructions about standards for evaluation were provided in advance. As observers to this first day of working with the topic, we noted how some students took advantage of the high level of control they were given. For instance a couple of boys did not focus on the topic at all and left all the work for other group members. Many students queued up for internet search, but without a very clear question to start with. We could hardly say this was an example of a clear focus on learning. Only a few groups of students actually worked in line with the teacher's intentions. The teacher was fully occupied providing the materials the students were asking for, and helping them with technical issues.

By the end of the day we met with all the teachers participating in the project and one member from the leadership team, the assistant principal. We discussed our observations, starting with the teachers' own views. They were quite satisfied because there was a lot of activity going on and students seemed motivated. When we shared our observations with them and asked questions like; what kind of learning do you think was going on? What kind of results or end products do you have in mind in choosing project method for this particular topic? What are advantages and disadvantages of setting up groups of students at random? What are required by the teachers when students are working in projects? There were tendencies to apologise for not having enough time for planning, the school day was so busy, disciplining the students was sometimes difficult and so on. We tried to stay clear of giving answers, and used questions as a way of scaffolding the teachers in their efforts to build accounts of what had happened. The assistant principal asked if the leadership team could play the role as a critical friend similar to the external researchers. The teachers were hesitant in their answers. They were not sure it would be a good idea, and the school leader chose not to negotiate further. It seemed as if she had accepted the teachers' right to say "no thank you". The next day we wrote a summary both of our observations and of the dialogue we had had after the observations and sent it to the teachers and leadership team. We also attached an article based on classroom research, which we hoped could stimulate their discussion. Afterwards we as "critical friends" wondered if the conversation ended up by being only critical. For sure, our feedback based on our observation had demonstrated no clear focus on learning. Did the teachers frame this as constructive feedback? Would the teachers change their practice in the future? How would and could a change be negotiated?

However, when we visited the school three months later, a lot of things had happened. After they received the summary of our visit, the leadership team came together with the teachers involved in order to discuss our questions more in detail. They had decided to organize project work in a much more focused way. They had read and discussed an article we sent them after our visit in order to stimulate their thinking about leadership for learning. They had put up a plan for how they could monitor their work in a more systematic way and how they could share experiences. As a matter of fact, as critical friends we were quite impressed by the way they had taken on the critique in a positive way and used it as a basis for development.

This example from our field-notes only gives glimpses of the job as a teacher, but other field notes show a similar picture. In their espoused theories of successful practice both school leaders and teachers say that they have a strong focus on learning. In reality they are strongly action-oriented and seem to be constantly responding to the needs of the moment. In the last example, it seemed that as critical friends we had managed to contribute, through our questions, to another way of framing the experiences. A *motivation* to change the actions emerged, even though we can't take for granted that the teacher involved is better *able* to deal with similar challenges in the future.

The example can be related to the substance of control and curriculum dilemmas (Berlak & Berlak, 1981). On the one hand, schools are expected to pass on to students generally accepted knowledge. On the other hand, schools are expected to encourage students' independent and critical thinking. This means that sometimes teachers must allow students to exercise control over their own behaviour. The teacher's resolution to the control and curriculum dilemmas were not managed differently for different students, or more correctly, she did not reflect on the dilemmas. She took for granted that by choosing their own way of working students would choose an adequate approach for them to learn the substance of the topic. In the dialogue it became clear that the teacher had not planned for a differentiated approach to the topic based on her knowledge of the students as individuals, partly because of the busyness and constraints she experienced during the school day. As it turned out in this case, the conversation resulted in positive changes. The leadership team and the teachers decided to collaborate in order to gain a clearer focus on learning and to establish a culture that facilitated learning among students, teachers and within the leadership team. It raised the question "In what ways is the leadership team creating conditions favourable to learning for teachers as well as students?" Shared leadership responsibility followed from making explicit the connections between leadership and learning.

CONCLUSION

Dominant approaches to school governance in Norway include a combination of New Public Management and an emphasis on school self evaluation. As demonstrated above, there is a great variation across Norwegian schools and classrooms in respect of framing and living with accountability and mandated change. Even though the municipal governance of schools in Norway sits within a New Public Management discourse, with a focus on managerial accountability, practice at school level appears to be of a different kind. Most schools seem so far to have the "option" of paying little attention to managerial accountability and in fact do not run any risk with this approach. Managerial accountability has more a status of "anticipated future" than a mandated present, but to some degree school principals seem struggle with the tensions of managerial demands from the outside and their own standards as professional educational leaders. Coping with the lack of time for reflection is something they all report and share in common.

Is professional accountability the answer to school improvement? The struggle between political and professional power over education includes a power struggle in society as to who should set the standards in teaching. From a political perspective, there are other social groups wishing to define educational quality, but, as yet, they have had little bearing upon the practice in schools. Intensified administration, in the form of external regulation and managerial accountability, might solve some problems, but new problems will undoubtedly appear. In the long term, there is the risk that teachers' enthusiasm and commitment will be lost - a far greater problem for schools. It has still to be shown that managerial accountability alone produces better schools. Education cannot be developed mechanistically with administrative decrees and regulations. At the same time, findings from different studies within a Norwegian context indicate that there is a need for a stronger focus on learning in many schools. It seems that a combination of a top-down and a bottom-up approach is necessary to move the schools forward.

In addition, the public has a right to know how well our schools are educating future citizens. But at the same time, those who shape accountability systems for schooling must themselves be held accountable for doing it in a responsible way. It is crucial to operate on two fronts simultaneously. Improving education for children in schools is hard work, and it is crucial that policy makers and school officials invest the necessary resources where they are needed most and provide professional development so that teachers can do a good job. The present accountability policy will not increase school performance without a substantial investment in human capital aimed at developing the practice of school improvement in a diverse population of school leaders and teachers (Elmore, 2006).

The way schools respond to accountability is likely to be dependent on their capacity as professionals, involving themselves in internal evaluation of practice. This requires collaborating and sharing of knowledge, and a commitment to the improvement of practice. Findings based on working with schools in the "Leadership for Learning" project demonstrates that change is seldom a smooth and continuous process. There are stages or periods where new problems often surface and teachers and leaders feel "stuck" and unable to find a way though. According to the principals, participating in an action research project, with the support of external critical friends, helped schools, to sustain a stronger focus on learning as well as increasing their confidence to address political, public and professional accountability.

NOTES

[1] The structure of the Norwegian school system is 10 years of compulsory primary and lower secondary education and three years of optional upper secondary education. School starts at age six and 90 % of the students stay in school until at least age eighteen. Norway's educational system is predominantly public. The private sector serves only 2 % of students in compulsory school, and about 4 % in upper secondary.

[2] This reference to Christianity in the Education Act is heavily debated.

[3] The selection of schools was based on maximum variation according to factors like school size, school structure, rural/urban, and gender. In addition the schools were recognized as successful by their superiors.

[4] The "PISA +" study is a research project aiming to pursue problematic PISA findings in the Norwegian context. It includes observational and interview designs to create a deeper understanding of classroom processes and students' learning strategies. 18 teachers/classrooms are selected for observation, 6 each of mathematics, science and mother tongue teachers at grade 10 in lower secondary schools. For more information, see http://www.pfi.uio.no/forskning/forskningsprosjekter/pisa+/english/index.html

[5] As a part of the International Successful School Principalship Project (ISSPP), a survey among a stratified and randomized selection of Norwegian principals was conducted in 2005. One intention was to compare findings from the case studies with answers from a national representative sample of principals.

REFERENCES

Berlak, A., & Berlak, H. (1981). *Dilemmas of schooling. Teaching and Social Change*. New York: Methuen & Co.

Elmore, R. (2006). *Leadership as the practice of improvement*. Paper presented at the International conference on Perspectives on leadership for Systemic Improvement, London 6th July.

Giddens, A. (1998). *The third way: The renewal of social democracy*. Cambridge: Polity Press.

Hatcher, R. (2005). The distribution of leadership and power in Schools. *British Journal of Sociology of Education*, 26(2), 253–67.

Johannesson, I. A., Lindblad, S., & Simola, H. (2002). An inevitable progress? Educational restructuring in Finland, Iceland and Sweden at the turn of the millennium. *Scandinavian Journal of Educational Research*, 46(3), 325–340.

Kjærnsli, M., Lie, S., Olsen, R.V., Roe, A., & Turmo A. (2003). Rett spor eller ville veier?: Norske elevers prestasjoner i matematikk, naturfag og lesing i PISA 2003. Oslo: Universitetsforlaget.

Klette, K., & Lie, S. (2006). Sentral funn. Foreløpige resultater fra PISA+ prosjektet. (Preliminary Findings from the PISA+ project). Det utdanningsvitenskapelige fakultet: Universitetet i Oslo.

Lundgren, U. (1990). Educational policy-making, decentralisation and evaluation. In M. Granheim, M. Kogan, & U. Lundgren (Ed.), *Evaluation as policymaking: Introducing evaluation into a national decentralised educational system*. London: Jessica Kingsley Publishers.

MacBeath, J., Frost, D., Sutherland, G., Swaffield, S., & Waterhouse, S. (2005, October). *A Model for Leadership for Learning Practice*. Paper presented at the Conference of "Sharing, Shaping and Sustaining Leadership for Learning, Athens".

Ministry of Education and Research. (2006). *The Knowledge Promotion 2006*. Retrieved from http://udir.no/templates/udir/TM_Artikkel.aspx?id=2376

Møller, J. (2007a). Educational leadership and the new language of learning. *International Journal of Leadership in Education*, 9, 31–48.

Møller, J. (2007b). *School leadership and accountability – moving beyond standardization of practice*. An invited presentation in a plenary panel at the 20th World ICSEI congress, Portoroz, Slovenija, 3rd – 6th January.

Møller, J. (2007c). *Learning to share leadership in Norwegian schools*. Paper presented at the 20th World ICSEI congress, Portoroz, Slovenija, 3rd – 6th January.

Møller, J., Eggen, A., Fuglestad, O. L., Langfeldt, G., Presthus, A. M., Skrøvset, S., Stjernstrøm, E.. & Vedøy, G. (2005). Successful school leadership - the Norwegian case. *Journal of Educational Administration*, 43(6), 584–594.

Møller, J., Sivesind, K., Skedsmo, G., & Aas, M. (2006). *Skolelederundersøkelsen 2005*. Om arbeidsforhold, evalueringspraksis og ledelse i skolen. Acta Didactica, nr. 1.

Norwegian Directorate for Education and Training (2007a). Improving school leadership. country background report for Norway. OECD, January. Retrieved from http://www.utdanningsdirektoratet.no/templates/udir/TM_Artikkel.aspx?id=2552

Norwegian Directorate for Education and Training (2007b). *Rapport fra felles nasjonalt tilsyn på opplæringsområdet 2006*. Retreived from http://udir.no/upload/Rapporter/RapportFellesNasjonaltTilsyn2006.pdf

Sinclair, A. (1995). The chameleon of accountability: Forms and discourses. *Accounting, Organizations and Society*, 20(2/3), 219–237.

Sirotnik, K. A. (2005). Holding accountability accountable: What ought to matter in public education. New York, London: Teachers College Press.

Spillane, J. P. (2006). *Distributed leadership*. San Francisco: Jossey-Bass, A Wiley Imprint.

Telhaug, A.O., Mediås, O. A., & Aasen, P. (2006). The Nordic Model in education: Educaiton as part of the political system in the last 50 years. *Scandinavian Journal of Educational Research, 50*(3), 245–283.

Wenger, E. (1999). *Communities of practice: Learning, meaning, and identity.* New York: Cambridge University Press.

AFFILIATIONS

Jorunn Møller
University of Oslo
Norway

JIM O'BRIEN AND JANET DRAPER

CHAPTER 15

Leadership for Learning or Learning for Leadership? The Role of Teacher Induction and Early Professional Development in England and Scotland

INTRODUCTION

As the recruitment and retention 'crisis' begins to manifest itself in both England and Scotland, what steps can be taken to fill the gap? As headteachers retire over the course of the next few years, with a consequent loss of knowledge and expertise, there is a heightened sense of urgency to ensure the succession. The question it raises is one of how, and how quickly and effectively leadership can be learned. The Fast Track to leadership in England is discussed as one approach to accelerate the professional learning process but the implementation of the programme highlights the difficulties in moving from the role of leader in the classroom to the leader of one's peers in whole school improvement.

CONTEXT

The United Kingdom's educational systems are becoming increasingly diverse since the devolution *referenda* of the late 1990s. The re-emergence of the Scottish Parliament and the establishment of the Welsh Assembly have resulted in educational policies, while broadly similar to England, increasingly reflecting more specific visions and priorities within these jurisdictions. This is particularly the case with Scotland as it has always had its own distinctive educational system.

At present within the UK, as in other developed education systems, there is concern about the retention of teachers. The demographics of the profession mean that while a range of experienced staff will be retiring in the next few years with a consequent loss of knowledge and expertise, many new staff will be entering teaching. Therefore, teacher induction policy and practice become critical in ensuring an adequate supply of teachers who are committed and appropriately supported. OECD (2002: 169) indicates "Teacher policy needs to ensure that teachers work in an environment which facilitates success". International research studies of induction policy and practice suggest that there are real variations in teacher experiences (Bubb, Earley, & Totterdell; 2005). For many, there is a greater likelihood of initial difficulties rather than early success and this is an unwelcome situation especially given the now established link between early success and teacher retention (Johnson and Birkeland, 2003).

Another demographic consequence is the loss to teaching of many experienced school leaders. The importance of leadership for effective schools is widely acknowledged in the research literature and by policy makers, while the demands on headteachers have become increasingly complex and demanding. In the UK, the emphasis for some time has been on preparing and supporting headteachers (O'Brien and Torrance, 2005). Of late, such emphasis has been strengthened by expressions of concern (particularly in Canada, New Zealand, Australia, USA and the UK) about the downturn in applications for headship and of the potential of a crisis in the supply and retention of headteachers or principals (Draper and McMichael, 2003; Gronn and Rawlings-Sanaei, 2003; Thompson et al, 2003; Rhodes and Brundrett, 2005, MacBeath, 2006). There is also anecdotal evidence of the declining quality of those who do apply. The issue is complex and differentiated, depending on the economic and social circumstances of individuals and of specific schools. For example, in some systems there may be shortages in rural schools but not in urban conurbations. There is now recognition of concepts such as 'distributed leadership' and its potential (Hartle and Thomas, 2003), but while shared leadership is attractive, it may be difficult to overcome the barriers that exist especially associated with notions of accountability and the allied key role expected of headteachers.

Nevertheless, the issue of a 'crisis' in headteacher recruitment makes for compelling newspaper headlines, policy and political chatter. Several reasons exist to support, if not fuel, the notion of a crisis in school leadership. There is clearly a demographic issue that might have been predicted some time ago. Many existing school leaders will retire in the next five years. For example, in Scotland at present 84% of secondary headteachers are aged over 50 and some 170 will be replaced; over the same period in the primary sector, a third of schools (700+) will require new headteachers (HMIE, 2007). In certain systems, for example Australia, research indicates signs of reluctance by senior school staff to engage with the notion of becoming a principal (Cranston, 2007). Secondly, expectations and policies designed to make schools and teachers more accountable are now deep-rooted and increasingly demanding in many education systems.

Educational leaders are expected to develop learning communities, build the professional capacity of teachers, take advice from parents, engage in collaborative and consultative discussion making, resolve conflicts, engage in educative instructional leadership, and attend respectfully, immediately, and appropriately to the needs and requests of families with diverse cultural, ethnic, and socioeconomic backgrounds. Increasingly, educational leaders are faced with tremendous pressure to demonstrate that every child for whom they are responsible is achieving success. (Shields, 2004, p. 109)

To what extent are the educational systems in the UK supporting new teachers in their initial efforts to come to terms with their new found positions and responsibilities? Equally, how are support and development structures preparing these new professional entrants for early leadership roles in both classroom and the wider school professional context to support more effective and imaginative student learning? What, if any steps exist to identify and nurture leadership potential at such a critical stage in a teacher's professional development?

POLICY AND PRACTICE IN INDUCTION FOR BEGINNING TEACHERS: THE UK EXPERIENCE

From the research on induction (Lacey, 1977; Draper, Fraser and Taylor, 1997; Tickle, 2000a; 2000b) we may conclude that a broad understanding of induction is required which encompasses all the following elements of induction:

- socialisation
- organisational familiarisation and sensitisation, including key policies and priorities
- appropriately and individually focussed developmental support
- the identification of scope for contribution.

Certainly new staff need to be socially integrated into the work group or professional community. They need help to adjust to their new environment and responsibilities, to 'learn the ropes', and they have professional development needs that need to be met including needs associated with their long term development as potential school leaders while not forgetting that as new teachers they have a leadership role in promoting effective learning within classrooms and in collaborating with colleagues to enhance student achievement.

The Scottish Experience

The General Teaching Council Scotland (GTCS) was established in 1965. Council, as the professional body, exists to self-regulate and to determine fitness to teach in Scottish schools. Teachers in Scotland's publicly funded schools require to be registered with GTCS and probation was essentially instituted as an opportunity to demonstrate capability, as GTCS is responsible for administering entry to the profession through the provisional registration of beginning teachers. Until 2002, these 'probationers', on satisfactory completion of a two-year period of probation, were afforded full membership of the profession. A minority of teachers failed the probationary experience and the reasons for this highlighted significant variations, difficulties and inconsistencies of practice in the probationer experience including intermittent temporary work opportunities, lack of support and advice and associated professional development opportunities. Most new teachers fulfilled probation requirements with little complication, but some failed to complete their probation for a number of reasons:

- when or where work was scarce it was difficult for some to accrue the required number of days of teaching;
- some had little support and made little progress;
- some were not suited to full time work as a teacher although as students they might have performed well in supportive circumstances;
- some failed to meet unusually high standards;
- some were given classes other experienced teachers had found impossible.
- support, advice, assistance and opportunities for development varied.

A three year national study of probationers (SOP) (Draper, Fraser, Smith and Taylor, 1991) revealed difficulties and inconsistencies in practice concerning the recruitment and employment of new teachers, and also in their induction, support and assessment. Information about school policies and procedures was poorly communicated, if at all to new staff; feedback on teaching ability was rare, many probationers had few or no opportunities to observe other teachers teaching and many were unsure of the adequacy or otherwise of their own teaching until they witnessed the reports written about them at the end of each probationary year. Clearly there were major fault lines in such diverse experience. Around the same time the concept of staff development was beginning to be accepted and probation began to be viewed as an opportunity for development, rather than just for proving competence as a teacher. However lack of information on the practice and development of probationers meant that support, when offered, was often not targeted at current or future needs.

The SOP project suggested that not only did new teachers need support but those in supportive roles needed support themselves in order to carry out their task effectively.

While materials were produced to support new teachers with issues that had been identified by the research as serially problematical for beginners (including class management and organisation, time management, identifying and meeting special needs) responses were not uniform. A booklet for schools on assessing probationers was published by the GTC supported by videos and other materials. Such materials stressed probation as a time for development as well as of assessment, and assessment itself was presented as a mechanism for identifying professional development needs.

A further study (Draper, Fraser and Taylor, 1997) later examined the employment and support experiences of beginning teachers and found signs of improvement in the experience of some, but also established that only half of new teachers had the expected (and desirable) experience of stable employment in one single school, so enabling meaningful identification of needs and targeted support. Many probationers were obliged to change school more than once, and a small but significant group struggled through their probationary period, making up the required 380 days in numerous schools with supply teaching (sometimes for just half a day at a time). The most extreme example recorded was of one teacher who worked in 52 schools with over 120 separate periods of employment, such a profile offering little hope for carefully assessed teaching and targeted support. These teachers had plenty of practice in developing survival skills with new classes but little opportunity to work in the longer term, or in depth, with either pupils or colleagues. Opportunities to demonstrate a range of aptitudes, other than perhaps resilience, were scarce. When it came to their assessment there was little evidence as to their professional practice in any one school and it was clearly difficult to be robust in judgements and assessments in relation to that practice, given struggles to complete the time requirements.

The late 1990s were characterised by teacher industrial unrest in Scotland about workload and the pace of development and serial educational initiatives. The McCrone inquiry was set up to explore the situation (pay and conditions) of teachers, and the subsequent report (SEED, 2001) with the agreement which followed (SEED 2002) brought significant changes to teachers' work, including the incorporation of continuing professional development as part of the job of every teacher in Scotland, as an entitlement and an obligation. Probation came under strong scrutiny and the McCrone report condemned the approach to probation as 'scandalous' and entirely inadequate in relation to beginning a professional career. A series of changes were agreed which radically altered the experiences of new teachers in Scotland and a new standard for probationers was agreed. (GTCS, 2002)

The New Induction Scheme in Scotland

For school session 2002-03, probation was reduced to one year but a full-time teaching post for that period was guaranteed for all those qualifying as teachers in Scotland (from within the European Union). Those entering the profession from university-based Initial Teacher Education have a reduced workload involving 70% teaching and 30% of their time being spent on supported activities, preparation/assessment and professional development. Regular observations and feedback were introduced and each new appointee is allocated an experienced teacher as a mentor or 'supporter' as they are known locally to provide guaranteed support. Subsequently, not all successful probationers have been afforded full-time permanent jobs because manpower forecasting and planning remain an inexact science and at best an educated guess; in addition, politically inspired initiatives, designed to reduce class sizes and consequently employment increase opportunities for probationers, have yet to mature. As noted above, satisfying the requirements of the standard for full registration (SFR), part of a development of a set of standards in Scotland and a career-long framework, involving standards for expert teachers and headteachers, for continuing professional development (Forde et al., 2006; Christie and O'Brien, 2005; Purdon, 2003), would be the target which all new teachers would have to achieve by the end of their induction year.

The new arrangements were introduced in August 2002 and several studies have explored their impact (O'Brien and Christie, 2005; McNally, 2006). Structurally much has been achieved (Robson and Pearson, 2004) and substantial resources have been invested in the initiative but gaps remain. For example, there is little evidence of a consensus around a professional development curriculum for probationers. The emphases relate strongly to classroom issues such as behaviour management and this is consistent with the expressed concerns of new teachers in the research literature. A deficiency identified in our own research (Christie, Draper and O'Brien, 2003) into the first year of the Scottish scheme was lack of liaison between employing authorities and Universities with regard to the content of ITE programmes, leading to many probationers experiencing Authority-based CPD as the reiteration of input which conscientious ITE students would have already thoroughly assimilated. This points to a clear need for better liaison between these 'partners' as well as a research-led debate on what constitutes a useful programme of CPD for the first year of teaching. In this way the first year of CPD can be constructed to form both the logical next step for probationers and the foundation of a lifetime of learning, and might be designed to incorporate leadership elements in an explicit manner. There are many similarities between approaches to induction in England but a major difference lies in the concern expressed there about early leadership development as an important facet of beginner teacher support.

Induction and the 'Fast Track' scheme in England

Changes to induction policy and practice have not been confined to Scotland. Teacher induction in England has had a chequered history (Tickle, 2000b) full of false starts and new dawns, promising much but with the fickleness of politics driving policy in various ways. In 1999, in England, a statutory induction process for Newly Qualified Teachers (NQTs) through the Teacher Training Agency [TTA] (TTA, 1999; Tickle, 2000a) was re-introduced. The 1991 abolition of the probationary year was overturned by the *Teaching and Higher Education Act 1998*. The Act provided for the introduction of *Induction Standards*, combined with requirements to monitor the performance of new teachers, administer associated assessment procedures and the possible de-registration of individuals at the end of their first year. As in Scotland, the NQTs must work towards meeting the Induction Standards - a series of competence statements first issued in 1999, with the addition in 2001 of a requirement to pass the national numeracy test for teacher training candidates (TTA, 2001), while slightly modified Standards were issued in 2003 (TTA, 2003a). As in Scotland, the English Induction Standards are one of a series of guidelines that made up a suite of documents covering Qualified Teacher Status, special needs specialists and coordinators, subject leaders, and headteachers.

Structurally similar approaches in England are evident but with less generous time allocations for support and professional development; mentoring is strong and there have been planned approaches to its introduction with a range of preparation programmes for mentors unlike in Scotland where supporters were allocated with little formal training initially relying on goodwill and experience to create successful experiences. The most recent research on induction in England (Bubb, Earley and Totterdell, 2005; Bubb and Earley, 2006), while confirming that the new arrangements and regulations are an improvement on the previous situation, suggests gaps between policy and practice, between rhetoric and reality. While the

English induction scheme may be seen to embody similar intentions to other modernised schemes of induction, and to rely heavily on a directive coaching style associated with mentoring, recent evidence signals significant problems in implementing the policy. Bubb and Earley identify significant gaps in implementation especially in relation to teachers receiving their entitlement of time 'out of class' and support for their development. They highlight the complexities associated with effective induction and report clear contraventions of the regulations. They attribute failure to fully implement the regulations to a number of sources. These include ignorance (and more rarely deliberate flouting) of the regulations, poor management and leadership in schools and inadequate monitoring by local education authorities. The consequences of under-resourcing are tracked and they identify problems at policy, school and individual teacher levels. The ways in which experiences fall short of intention are described as 'educational vandalism' and they delineate the inevitable results as unrealised teaching potential, the loss of good teachers and diminished student learning.

In a context beset, as many mature education systems are, by problems arising from the age structure of the profession and especially of insufficient staff seeking to be senior leaders in schools, a series of strategies and pilot initiatives have been implemented. These seek to address a combination of acknowledged difficulties, in particular concern over school leadership roles being perceived as unattractive and where the path to senior posts is long (when the average teaching career is shortening). In England, such difficulties themselves could not be ignored, headships were not being filled and re-advertising of vacancies became common, especially in those areas of the country where teacher supply was also particularly problematical. The scale and immediacy of the difficulties led to a swift move to action in England to improve the likelihood of application for leadership roles. Less consideration than might have been useful was perhaps given to a full analysis of the problems requiring to be addressed, especially with regard to the design of senior roles in schools, which might have offered longer-term solutions.

One such initiative in England has been the Fast Track programme. Its aim was to identify potential future leaders and support their development so as to enable them to take up senior leadership roles successfully. In the beginning suitable candidates could enter the programme at any career stage including in Initial Teacher Training at PGCE level. It was designed not to make candidates an extra good teacher or to speed up the process of achieving Qualified Teacher Status (QTS) but as a means of supporting those considering leadership roles in classroom teaching and wider school management. Fast Track was thus designed to offer a quicker route to posts with leadership responsibility by giving additional support and professional development opportunities for leadership and management in schools. Its design reflects a set of leadership and management competences.

The National College for School Leadership (NCSL) website (http://www.ncsl.org.uk/programmes/fasttrack/index.cfm) describes the current version of the Fast Track Teaching initiative "as an accelerated leadership development programme for teachers in the early years of their careers". The approach provides a highly personalised programme of coaching, mentoring and development activities to support teachers in developing the skills required to take on a senior leadership role in education such as assistant head, deputy head or advanced skills teacher (AST). There is a challenging selection process and once accepted such teachers are expected "to achieve challenging objectives, to maintain excellent performance and to realise their potential in the shortest possible time". Candidates are expected to be in senior leadership roles within their fourth year on the programme.

Fast Track began as a two-pronged initiative for both experienced teachers and for teachers in initial training: to develop those with potential and ambition for leadership who were already in the profession and to attract into teaching those who saw management and leadership as part of their career plans. While Fast Track now only operates for experienced teachers, some consideration of the route that was concurrent with initial teacher education enables several points to be raised.

The Fast Track PGCE-related initiative involved selected Higher Education Institutions offering an additional Fast Track programme with their PGCE programme for selected trainees. Application for and selection onto Fast Track involved a process organised by DfES that included psychometric tests and a residential assessment centre and interviews. The selection process into Fast Track was distinct from, and additional to, selection for PGCE. The fast track competencies comprised the criteria for entry to Fast Track and all teachers, both experienced and beginning, went through the same selection process. Fast Track trainees were expected to show qualities which included initiative and enthusiasm and good organisational and social skills.

Fast Track PGCE related programmes varied from place to place, for example the University of Cambridge approach is discussed by Warwick and Swaffield (2006). The Exeter University Fast Track programme had four main strands: action planning for the first (PGCE) year based on detailed competence-related feedback from the selection process, a seminar series on leadership and management with current practitioners (advanced skills teachers, headteachers and so on) discussing their work; an action research project which supported professional development in and out of school, and a focus on the use of ICT to enhance learning and teaching. During school placements opportunities were to be offered to familiarise trainees with leadership management roles and opportunities in the school. For example, this might involve observing senior management meetings, engaging with ongoing whole school or department initiatives in schools. Fast Track trainees also attended regional and national Fast Track events supported by government. As incentives, Fast Track PGCE trainees were supported with additional funding and ICT resources during their PGCE year and received an addition to salary for their first five years on the programme. Once professionally qualified, PGCE Fast Track teachers were expected to hold a post in a challenging school and to secure a promoted post within five years. To help with this, career advice and additional fast track support were offered throughout these early years in post.

As noted, Fast Track was not about being an extra good teacher, a 'superteacher', nor about becoming a teacher more quickly, but misconceptions such as these dogged the initiative from the beginning. Its actual focus was, and is, in its current incarnation about additional support for those who are aiming for leadership roles in schools. Of course all teacher roles have an element of leading in them, but some roles have more than others and the Fast Track programme offers support to enable teachers to become familiar with, and to take on, those more management related leadership roles. Nevertheless, Fast Track trainees encountered misunderstandings and indeed in some cases actual hostility to the whole idea. There were concerns that Fast Track teachers who had come through the PGCE plus Fast Track route were being given special treatment before they had proved themselves as teachers, that their competence as teachers was being assumed, that their management and leadership skills were being seen as more important than the core teaching role, that they were destined for elite status without having proved their strengths at 'the chalk face'. Similar concerns are evident in other professions and roles where accelerated promotion is available, as in the police for example.

Teachers remain in the programme which is now run under the NCSL banner and the focus is now on support for career development rather than financial incentives. The Fast Track programme gives potential future leaders opportunities to develop a management orientation and relevant skills alongside developing as a classroom teacher. The concept of Fast Track initially challenged the idea of maturing into leadership only after the role of teacher had been adequately played, and it brought into teaching a group with a clear commitment to working in management roles in schools.

DISCUSSION

Professional development which supports leadership knowledge, skills, attributes and dispositions at an early career stage for teachers is quickly becoming necessary if the perceived shortages of school leaders is to be overcome. In the induction schemes within the UK, much of what was seen as inadequate has been overtaken, at least to the extent that new arrangements have been introduced, although there remain concerns about equity, variations of experience and consistency of application. Teaching posts are slowly being found for all new teachers and it is predicted this situation will improve dramatically as departures from the profession reach their demographic peak. Initial orientation to key policies and procedures, self-evaluation and feedback and the collection of evidence of competence against the Induction Standards are all part of the induction process. These represent real progress in terms of developing a more satisfactory induction for beginning teachers. However, there have also been concerns. Experience remains varied with, for example, some settings being more supportive than others, some new teachers adjusting more easily to their time out of class, together with variations in number and style of observations. There is also a concern that the Standards and the induction process as a whole have become somewhat instrumental and bureaucratic, with a focus on checking or 'ticking off' performance against the standard and completing the required paperwork rather than offering scope for individual need and development, creativity and innovation. Guaranteed support is clearly welcome and teachers are being socialised into the profession rapidly.

However, clearly concerns about the nature, scope and focus of related professional development and the types of experiences proffered may be voiced. In England there is an overt recognition through Fast Track arrangements that early preparation and support for potential and for early identification of school leaders is important. This is not the case in Scotland where there appears to be more concern about settling into the teacher classroom role and acquiring and demonstrating a range of competences. Indeed in Scotland, the Chartered Teacher initiative by government decree, only allows teachers with 5 or more years of experience to participate in professional development opportunities designed to encourage them to evidence their competence as 'expert' teachers. Is this now tenable? While recruitment and retention of new teachers through induction support is clearly important, the identification of potential school leaders at an early stage would appear necessary too, if systemic failure in subsequently recruiting head teachers or principals is to be avoided. In Scotland a framework for leadership development (O'Brien and Torrance, 2005) has been adopted but there are only limited signs of provision of different types of experience to new teachers such as experience in project management. Work is ongoing, however, and several government-funded experiments are focusing on leadership development for aspirant school leaders using coaching techniques, but these still have to report formally and claims of efficacy evidenced. Another research project (O'Brien, Torrance and van der Kuyl, 2006), still at an early stage, seeks to identify from the literature, and empirically from groups of new teachers, a range of indicators of leadership potential with a view to working with teacher employers to validate a series of early indicators of leadership potential. The intention beyond identifying such indicators is to consider how policy and practice in early professional development might be determined to provide appropriate structures and support to recognise and nourish early leadership. Teachers exercise leadership when they lead and facilitate classroom learning and much of that is transferable to wider contexts within schools when learning about leadership and management. In the Foreword of a recent HMIe report on Leadership and Learning, the Senior Chief Inspector writes:

> Developing leadership is not just about honing the skills of those in the most senior positions, important though that undoubtedly is. It is also about releasing the energies of every member of staff and every learner and about giving each of them a sense that their contributions are valued.
>
> The development of such a culture is important in its own right and as a response to the pressing requirement to build leadership capacity and to develop the leaders of tomorrow.
>
> A desire to take responsibility and to accept accountability is part of good leadership. Ultimate accountability rests with the person at the head of the formal structure but all members of staff must be committed to and feel accountable for their own development and performance. Such commitment lies at the heart of professionalism.
>
> It is essential that we build a leadership culture in Scottish education which encourages initiative, tackles difficult problems directly and is genuinely aspirational.

The concern is that at present, structures and policy may serve to narrow expectations of both new teachers and their supporters and assessors, defining effective teaching and scaffolding a model for professional development which is constrained rather than open-ended and involving necessary leadership themes and experiences.

REFERENCES

Bubb, S., & Earley, P. (2006). Induction Rites and Wrongs. *Journal of In-service Education, 32*(1), 5–12.

Bubb, S., Earley, P., & Totterdell, M. (2005). Accountability and responsibility: 'rogue' school leaders and the induction of new teachers in England. *Oxford Review of Education, 31*(2), 255–272.

Christie, F., Draper, J., & O'Brien, J. (2003). *A study of the induction scheme for beginning secondary teachers in Scotland*, Edinburgh: University of Edinburgh, Centre for Educational Leadership.

Christie, F., & O'Brien, J. (2005). A Continuing Professional Development Framework for Scottish Teachers: steps, stages, continuity or connections? In A. Alexandrou, K. Field & H. Mitchell (eds.) *The Continuing Professional Development of Educators: emerging European issues* (pp. 93–110). Oxford: Symposium.

Cranston, N. C. (2007). Through the eyes of potential aspirants: another view of the principalship. *School Leadership & Management, 27*(2), 109–128.

Department for Education and Employment (DfEE) (1999). *The Induction Period for Newly Qualified Teachers*. Circular 5/99. London: DfEE.

Draper, J. Fraser, H. Smith, D., & Taylor, W. (1991). *A Study of Probationers*. Edinburgh: Moray House Institute.

Draper, J. Fraser, H., & Taylor, W. (1997). Teachers at Work: Early Experiences of Professional Development *British Journal of In-service Education, 23*(2), 283–295.

Draper, J. Fraser, H., & Taylor, W. (1998). Teachers' Careers; accident or design? *Teacher Development, 2*(3), 373–384.

Draper, J., & McMichael, P. (2003). The Rocky Road to Headship. *The Australian Journal of Education, 47*,(2), 185–196.

Draper, J. O'Brien, J., & Christie, F. (2004). First Impressions: the new teacher induction arrangements in Scotland. *Journal of In-service Education, 30*(2), 201–223.

Forde, C., McMahon, M., McPhee, A., and Patrick, F. (2006) *Professional development, reflection and enquiry*. London: Routledge.

General Teaching Council for Scotland (2002). *The Standard for Full Registration*. Edinburgh: GTCS.

Gronn, P., & Rawlings-Sanaei, F. (2004). Principal recruitment and leadership disengagement. *Australian Journal of Education, 47*,(2), 172–184.

Harris, A. (2007) The current crisis in leadership: Threat or opportunity? *School Leadership & Management, 27*(2), 105–107.

HMIE (2007). *Leadership for learning: The challenges of leading in a time of change*. Edinburgh: HMIE.

Huberman, M. (1997). Professional careers and professional development. In T.R. Guskey & M. Huberman (Eds.), *Professional Development in Education* (pp. 193–224). New York: Teacher College Press.

Johnson, S. M., & Birkeland, S. E. (2003). Pursuing a 'sense of success': new teachers explain their career decisions. *American Educational Research Journal, 40*(3), 581–617.

Lacey, C. (1977). *The Socialisation of Teachers*. London: Methuen.

MacBeath, J. (2006). The Talent Enigma, *International Journal of Leadership in Education*, 9.(3)

McNally, J. (2006). From informal learning to identity formation: a conceptual journey in early teacher development. *Scottish Educational Review, 37*, 79–90.

O'Brien, J., & Christie, F. (2005). Characteristics of Support for Beginning Teachers: evidence from the new induction scheme in Scotland. *Mentoring and Tutoring, 13*(2), 191–205.

O'Brien, J., & Torrance, D. (2005). Professional Learning for School Principals: Developments in Scotland, *Education Research and Perspectives, 32*(2), 165–181.

O'Brien, J., Torrance, D., & van der Kuyl, T. (2006). Early indicators of leadership potential. Paper presented at ICSEI, Fort Lauderdale, Florida.

OECD (2002). *Attracting, developing and retaining effective teachers: country questionnaire*. (UK) London: DfES.

Purdon, A. (2003). A national framework of CPD: continuing professional development or continuing policy dominance? *Journal of Education Policy, 18*(4), 423–437.

Rhodes, C. P., & Brundrett, M. (2005). Leadership succession in schools: a cause for concern, *Management in Education, 19*(5), 15–18.

Robson, D., & Pearson, M. (2004). *The Standard for Full Registration: Evaluation of Current Practice in the Teacher Induction Scheme in Scotland.* Paper presented at British Educational Research Association Annual Conference, University of Manchester, 16-18 September.

Shields, C. (2004). Dialogic leadership for social justice: overcoming pathologies of silence. *Educational Administration Quarterly, 40*(1), 109–132.

Thomson, P., Blackmore, J., Sachs, J., & Tregenza, K. (2003). High stakes principalship – sleepless nights, heart attacks and sudden death accountabilities: reading media representations of the United States principal shortage. *Australian Journal of Education, 47*,(2), 118–132.

Tickle, L. (2000a). Teacher probation resurrected: England 1999-2000, *Journal of Education Policy, 15*(6), 701–713.

Tickle, L. (2000b). *Teacher Induction: The Way Ahead.* Buckingham: Open University Press.

Warwick, P., & Swaffield, S. (2006). Articulating and connecting frameworks of reflective leadership: perspectives from 'fast track' trainee teachers. *Reflective Practice, 7*(2), 247–263.

AFFILIATIONS

Jim O'Brien
University of Edinburgh
UK

Janet Draper
University of Exeter
UK

IBRAHIM AHMAD BAJUNID

CHAPTER 16

Leadership for Learning in Malaysia: Understanding the Problems and Possibilities

IN THE BEGINNING

Five decades ago educational priorities in Malaysia were adult education and the provision of universal primary education. The emphasis was on basic literacies, the 3 R's, while adult education was designed to encourage participation in the new democracy including the right to vote, to make choices and make a mark on the electoral ballot. The national goal was the two- pronged goals of national unity and eradication of poverty. Circumstances and phase of development determined the opportunities for schooling or lack of it by geographical area, family status and individual motivation. In rural areas in particular, participation rates were low, multigrade classes were common and there were untrained teachers in all schools. There were many school drop-outs, absenteeism was high, especially during *padi* the cropping season when students had to help parents till the land or go out to sea fishing or do other jobs merely to ensure subsistence and survival.

The success of political mobilization for progress and development raised aspirations of communities, families and individuals and created an increased demand for more schooling. With more schooling and higher aspirations, there came with it higher expectation of what education could do for social mobility and the transformation of the socio-economic status of families. Unprecedented educational development was the tenor of the stand taken by the first Prime Minister - that national development should focus on *Books, not Bullets."* (Tengku Abdul Rahman, 1980). This led to the focus on educational development rather than military development. This political stance was the first evidence of enlightened political leadership supportive of leadership for learning (Oakley & Krug, 1991).

Primary schools were built in almost every village throughout the country and secondary schools were built in urban and suburban areas. During the early years of quantitative expansion of education, with emphasis on universal primary education for six years, secondary education also became mass education while tertiary education continued to be highly elitist. Students were retained at particular grades if they did not meet the standards set by the school. The Malaysian Secondary School Entrance Examination, taken after six years of primary schools, determined whether students could carry on to the secondary levels for the next three years. The Lower Certificate Examinations after three years of secondary schools determined whether students could continue for the next two years to take the Overseas Cambridge School Certificate at Ordinary Level (OSC). There were strict requirements for OSC eligibility. In order to go on to the Sixth Form, students had to sit for the Sixth Form Entrance Examinations. After two years in the Sixth Forms (lower and upper Six) students sat for the Cambridge Higher School Certificate Examinations and had to achieve their Principal Level Passes in order to be eligible to join the University of Malaya.

For over five decades, the nation, through its teachers, had provided each generation with successively greater opportunity to acquire post secondary and higher education. The children of ordinary people, sons and daughters of farmers, fishermen, mechanics, taxi drivers, clerks, blue collar workers and others had opportunities to pursue higher education and families began to enjoy socio-economic mobility through progressively enhanced educational achievements (Education International, 1998; Harper, 2001; Khoo, 2001).

CHANGING STATUS AND PRESTIGE OF TEACHERS: PAST, PRESENT AND FUTURE

Before independence, teachers were the politically active groups who agitated for self-rule. The Sultan Idris Training College (SITC) founded in 1922 (now, the Education University) was the hub of nationalism. The annals of SITC provide ample instances of leadership for learning and leadership by teachers beyond the field of education, specifically in the community and in politics (Awang Had Salleh, 1979). After independence, teachers continued to be the grassroots leaders of political parties, especially the ruling political parties. When university graduates joined the public services and the private sector the nation witnessed the emergence of the professional class. Private sector entrepreneurs created a new leadership cadre, especially in the corporate sector and in multinational corporations. As the political arena expanded and mass media operations expanded with it, the media began to promote politicians and media people as leaders with a particular kind of focus on learning. The attrition of the status and prestige of the teaching profession went hand in hand with this and the status of teachers remained low.

In the wake of development and the knowledge explosion, the majority of teachers tended to be left behind in career and economic opportunities because they had failed to raise their status academically by acquiring university degrees. This was, in part, because they were not given study leave to continue higher education, and, partly because teachers were unduly complacent and did not see any need for further studies. This situation continued until 1997 when the policy decision was that all secondary school teachers should be graduate teachers and eventually that all teachers would be university graduates (Kementerian Pendidikan Malaysia 2001; Government of Malaysia, 2003, 2006).

In the education sector, graduates who work in the educational bureaucracy, as well as secondary school principals, came to be recognised as educational leaders. The knowledge base of these educational leaders and the spokespersons for the profession in specialised fields was typically in the academic field of educational administration and leadership. Leadership was initially defined as administrative leadership. However, in all national training programmes for school principals, one significant component was instructional leadership. In addition, all principals were expected to teach at least five periods a week.

In planning for the career development for the teaching/education profession, three pathways for development were recognized: first, as educational leaders in schools or in the district, state or federal education offices; second, as specialists in the Professional Divisions or Departments, such as curriculum, examinations, teacher education, educational technology, school inspection; and, third, for the majority, as classroom teachers. The recognition of over two thousand Master Teachers (from 1995 to 2007) was the first step in recognizing leadership for learning. This recognition, however does not go far enough because no strategic advantage was created, and there was no mobilization of a critical mass of experts, nor creation of leadership teams to engage in professional conversations, capture best practices or identify failures. There was no impetus or capacity to generate and disseminate deep professional knowledge, and drive the profession to the next threshold so as to improve the quality of student learning in every classroom, in every subject and in every teaching-learning event. There was no incentive to make schools places for the joy of learning and acquisition of relevant knowledge (Caldwell & Hayward, 1998; Bakri, 2003).

RECLAIMING LEADERSHIP OF THE NOBLE PROFESSION

In the Malaysian context, the focus of educational leadership is policy leadership, not practice leadership, which, for Hoyle (1974, 1982) is characterised by confident professionalism. In an educational system where the majority of teachers have not acquired a first degree and where teachers are regarded by the civil service bureaucrat as "support staff" equal to nurses, teaching does not meet the criteria of a "profession". Within the teaching community itself, however, with its Professional Code and structured training there is the continuing move to promote itself as a true profession.

While historically in the Asian-Malaysian context, teachers had always been respected in society, the growth of the middle class and new cadre of highly salaried jobs actually served to reduce and diminish the status of teachers. Within the notion of profession, there is the argument that the medical professional is a technical profession where the doctor uses expertise to help patients one at a time. Educational leaders, on the other hand, work through other people and are considered "more of leaders who influence" than leaders who use specific technical leadership. Master teachers, however, who are expert in diagnostic and formative assessment and can provide intervention measures to ensure mastery of content or skills, are actually comparable to the members of the medical profession as they display technical expertise (Thomson, 1992).

At the school level, typically those regarded as leaders are the principals. These educational leaders are expected to understand structural, human resources, political and symbolic frames (see Bolman and Deal, 1985) in order to function well as leaders. Also, these leaders are expected to exhibit qualities of civic and politically savvy leadership, managerial leadership and instructional leadership. Teachers who are defined as leaders, then, are so regarded by virtue of their skills in classroom management, their political leadership is organizational politics, including student and staff politics, as well as in relations with parents. The real test is in respect of their instructional leadership which qualifies them as "true professionals". This is translated as an ability to attend to every client one at a time, recognising symptoms, signs, conducting diagnosis and ensuring health and well being in learning. The civic leadership expected of every teacher is the reaffirmation of the dignity of the noble profession and caring for the environment, raising the quality of life, elimination of diseases, promotion of rights, maintenance of high culture, habits of discipline and so on.

The success of teacher leadership in practice is, nonetheless, measured by public examination results demonstrating tangible, if limited, evidence of the academic attainments of their students. The educational system has not yet developed instruments for the assessment of personality, aptitude, nor is it yet able to grapple with more complex notions such as multiple intelligences. Teachers have not provided the leadership either to develop such instruments nor to advocate for better and broader assessment measures.

While there are standards and leadership, these seem to be more driven by the system and the structured sets of procedures and processes rather than the powerful exercise of the "soft skills" of leadership for learning.

QUALITY CONTROL CIRCLES AND LEADERSHIP FOR LEARNING CIRCLES

In the education system, quality imperatives were assured by the Public Examinations System which adopted the Cambridge Examinations System Quality Protocols as well as the protocols of other public examination bodies. The Malaysian School Certificate, Ordinary and Higher Advanced Levels are recognized internationally for admission into appropriate university programmes. The National Inspectorate of Schools has its own responsibilities for quality assurance, nationally. Other agencies such as the Textbook Bureau/Division have their own rules, regulations procedures and criteria for quality standards for textbooks. In all these "Quality Systems," as individuals or in teams, teachers contribute significantly as resource experts and as knowledge leaders but they do not initiate programmes. These programmes follow system-based manuals which lay down procedures and functions and are not teacher led. Even after fifty years of independence, there are really very few professional activities which are teacher initiated, although almost all activities pertaining to educational development require the central involvement and thoughtful contributions of teachers.

One of the most important domains of educational development is the quality journey domain. The education sector has its own quality assurance tradition, consistent and compatible with the integrity of educational processes exemplified by the Examinations Syndicate and the Textbook Division. However, the teaching service is part of the public service system and therefore, the initiatives and overarching principles and agenda of the public service system also apply to the teaching service (Ahmad Sarji, 1994), acting as a constraining force on teacher initiative and innovation or unleashing creative teaching initiative.

School leaders in Malaysia have, for the past decade, seen themselves as on a quality journey, engaging in conversations around the Good School Movement, the Quality School Movement, The School Improvement Movement, and the School Effectiveness Movement (Cheng, 1996a, 1996b). The educational perspective with its own criteria and indicators was enhanced (some regard it as displaced) by the quality movement agenda and the passion for excellence in the public services and business sector (Peters & Austin, 1989). In the 1980's the school system was exposed to the Quality Control Circle Movement in Education. This was the period when throughout the country in many schools, there were Quality Control Circles (QCC) and school staff, academic and non-academic, engaged in structured, management supported workplace conversations for problem solving and school improvement. Those who were involved in QCCs became familiarised with QCC problem solving tools.

There were state and national and even international competitions which supported the QCC movement. Although QCC was management supported, it was led by QCC teams, most of whom were teachers. The teacher led QCC initiatives focused on the whole range of school problems and challenges although not specifically on learning. The ultimate aim of most of the QCC sessions was, nonetheless, to ensure effective school management which in turn was expected to ensure effective learning. Ideas of quality assurance, quality control, zero defect, and culture of excellence were in vogue but had to find educationally compatible applied definitions, practices and meanings. At the time when the QCC Movement was well into nation-wide implementation, the school effectiveness movement was also promoted among school administrators. In the midst of these initiatives emerged The Total Quality Movement, taking the form of a national drive with organizations rushing to acquire ISO certification (Bajunid, 1982).

The National Institute of Educational Management and Leadership (Institut Aminuddin Baki-IAB, 1999) itself became one of the earliest educational training organizations in the country to acquire ISO certification. IAB then guided the first primary and secondary schools in the country to acquire ISO certification. This was followed by the IAB guiding polytechnics, universities and other training organizations embarking on their quality journey to achieve ISO. It was, however, argued by educators from the beginning that ISO was not appropriate for the education sector which had its own quality determinants. It was also argued that the ISO was too cumbersome for teachers and took too much of their time away from class, and was also too expensive by virtue of fees needed to maintain certification. While itself going for the ISO certification, the IAB began to develop its own quality instrument incorporating school improvement and school effectiveness principles. This initiative was then taken over by the National Inspectorate of Schools which used its already existing quality frameworks, instruments and standards to incorporate the latest Quality Measures and Principles in its newly redeveloped Educational High Quality Standards (EHQS).

In a very hierarchical educational bureaucracy, to all good intents and purposes, leadership for learning is the province of key personnel from the Professional Divisions of the Ministry of Education, mobilizing teachers top down. These typically take the form of one-off seminars and workshops which are "implementation" driven rather than characterised by a continuing conversation discourse aimed at further in-depth understanding of educational phenomena. There is ample evidence of fragmented, one-off leadership activity or attempted leadership activity by administrators in the educational bureaucracy, as well as by teachers in classrooms and schools but the idea of leadership as being for learning is simply assumed to exist. It is taken for granted but does not really happen except for the one off professional meetings in workshops, seminars or conferences and for the fortunate few nominated and sponsored to attend such meetings. There is no continuous dialogue, no protocol and procedure of examination of practice, no recording of best practices, no examination or exploration of implicit principles and theories behind effective teaching-learning practices. Today the few selected school principals recognized as Super Principals are given recognition by engaging them in mentoring other principals throughout the country. However, not all the 2,000 Master Teachers who have been promoted and play peer leading roles are challenged to exercise leadership with a focus on promoting, supporting, critiquing and sharing learning. There is no strategic value-added approach nor an explicit value system which would allow teachers to benefit from the collective wisdom of their colleagues. If the profession is to sustain its credibility, there will have to be more tangible and embedded demonstrations of teacher leadership in promoting professional and student learning (Hoyle & John, 1994).

KNOWLEDGE EVOLUTION AND THE CHALLENGES OF LEADERSHIP FOR LEARNING.

Perhaps the most important challenge of leadership for learning is equipping learners to acquire thinking and self evaluation tools, empowering them to reclaim their right to the workings of their own mind (Fraser, 1995; Ratey, 2002). A student engrossed in a large library or on the web can be so distracted by the diverse materials and so overwhelmed that (s)he loses the capacity to make sense of fragments of voluminous information. This reclamation of the intellect must be a conscious purpose which is ongoing, appraising information and framing knowledge in new and intelligible ways (Langer, 1989; Gardner, 1999; Freiberg, 1999).

The paradigm change which came about in the wake of the Multimedia Super Corridor Initiative in Malaysia and the Smart School flagship, saw the Ministry of Education formulating Information Communications Technology (ICT) policies so as to ensure that all schools had computer laboratories and could use PCs effectively as teaching tools. Investments were made in upgrading the technology infrastructure, spending hundreds of millions on tabletop computers. Broadband and wireless were introduced and laptops and palmtops have become affordable and are now being widely used by students, at schools, in homes, in cyber cafés, especially by students from socio-economically advantaged families (Multimedia Development Corporation, 2005; Bajunid, 2001; Tiffin & Rajasingham, 1995). In fact, such advantaged students have moved on to use Mobile Learning as a way of life. Meanwhile, many families who are less privileged carry the technological baggage of the recent past, unaware that the future just happened (Hargrove, 2001; Lewis, 2002). Due to the of the pace of technological changes, many members in societies are left behind, while others hurriedly jump to the next new generation of technologies so that technologies come to be used in overlapping transitional stages (Connors, 1997; Moschella, 1997; Buderi, 2000).

In the context of information and knowledge divides, reinforced by cultural, socio-economic, and linguistic divisions, the classroom teacher has to be sensitive to, and able to master such changes. It is a lot to ask but when there is no awareness, no professional will, no immediate support or mobilisation opportunities to improve the quality of learning, opportunities are lost for advancing the profession itself (Bajunid, 1995). For generations, teachers learned in the Socratic tradition which emphasized the art of asking questions, in the Prophetic tradition of emphasizing self knowledge, in the community tradition of learning by doing, and in the story telling tradition by listening. Many of the best educational ideas exist in these milieux but have not been "codified' or packaged, legitimized and marketed as "learning products". One such simple idea is that of "the learning organization". The concept had to find moorings in the corporate sector and civil service before returning home to the education sector.

Another related idea with relevance for the Malaysian context is that of teachers as "reflective practitioners", consciously and continuously examining their own craft/work. It took scholars like Chris Argyris (1993), Donald Schon (1983), and Peter Senge (1992) to develop the idea before its was applied in organizations and revived in an educational context. Yet the paradox remains, that while schools are learning organizations for students, schools are not learning organizations for professional peers, and not maximally exploited for teacher learning. This is partly because the tools of observation, thinking, and writing, recording and researching have not been appropriately packaged and legitimized and considered as essential element of the curriculum for teachers. There is a close alliance here with the concept of lifelong learning which has indigenous roots in Malaysia but was displaced by modern schooling. Reintroduced by UNESCO in 1971, it had to wait for another three decades to gain respectability and influence (Faure 1972; Delors 1996; Longworth & Davies, 1996; Field, 2001) but it is yet another approach to the reclamation of the mind, the best of longstanding tradition and a helpful in reframing the management of cumulative and non cumulative knowledge considered worthwhile (Bajunid, 2000).

THE KNOWLEDGE CAPITAL FOR LEADERSHIP FOR LEARNING

The potential for change as well as for inertia is massive. The reservoir of expertise developed, and yet to be developed, is enormous. Out of a teaching force of approximately 400,000, in the formal education system there are approximately 10,000 teachers not serving in schools. About 2,000 serve in Departments and Divisions of the Ministry of Education, 1,000 serve in State Education Department, 1000 in District Education Offices, 500 in Teacher Activity Centres, 3,000 in Polytechnics, and 27,900 in Teacher Training Colleges. Non-educators in the Education Ministry number approximately 70,000. There are approximately 180,000 Graduates Teachers and 220,000 non-graduate teachers. There are 8000 primary schools, 1,800 secondary schools, 27 teachers colleges, 34 polytechnics, and 57 universities. In every school there are two assistant principals and a principal. There is a full time counsellor in every one of the 1800 secondary schools. On paper, except for counsellors and those who work in administrative posts at the education system level, numbering 10,000, all teaching professionals, by definition, have responsibility as leaders of learning.

To this considerable intellectual and social capital may be added 80,000 lecturers in public and private universities and several thousand trainers and consultants. There are approximately 400 doctoral and several thousand Masters Degree holders in fields of knowledge related to education. There are also something like 200,000 first-degree holders in various school subjects, including the Bachelor of Education Degrees. Of the hundreds of doctoral dissertations and the thousands of master level research exercises there are few indeed focused on pedagogies or classroom practices. There are to date, no substantial research findings on school teaching-learning and pedagogies which constitute a significant reservoir of indigenous educational knowledge (*Report on Seminar on Strengthening Educational Research in Developing Countries*, 1991).

The Southeast Asia Ministers of Education Organizations (SEAMEO) which has fifteen organizations, are treasure houses of knowledge corpus on culture, the sciences and mathematics, and educational management and innovations (Rajendra, 2001) but not used because of difficulties of access, costs, mechanism of membership, professional habits of teachers and lack of mastery of the international language used in these Centers. There is as yet, no strategic use of the 'treasure within' (MacBeath, 2002), of cultural resources on the one hand and manpower resources on the other. This is, in part, because there has not been the appropriate knowledge management to create the linking, triggering, tipping point of ideas sufficient to inspire and transform society (Davis and Davidson, 1991; Toffler, 1974; Gibson, 1998; Bajunid, 2003). There is no critical mass of leaders of learning to translate the transformative potential into practice.

The policy-making community is represented by the top echelons of the education service with a few teachers invited as representatives (ad hoc not full-time). Typically, the policy making community policy-making does not involve teachers but does involve university lecturers, teacher unions and professional association leaders, but may involve only exceptional teachers who have unique strengths and have been recognized as such. In sum, in the centralized, highly bureaucratic, hierarchical education system, teachers do not play a significant role in the broader aspects of education policy making.

The policy-making community operating across sectors with the bureaucratic support of the government and other committed stakeholders has the capacity to mobilize expertise and the machinery to engage constituencies and move various educational agenda forward, including in Parliament and pass laws. However, communities of practice are limited in resources and lack the professional leverage and organisational infrastructures which are able to genuinely mobilize the profession. There are, for instance, over 22 professional associations related to education which are registered under the Registrar of Societies but most of these are poorly financed, with voluntary leadership and small membership. Typically, decision-making by teachers is limited by financial constraints. If teachers are members of one or two teachers' trade unions or any other professional associations, they cannot afford to be members of other associations, especially weak ones.

PREPARATION FOR THE PLANNED FUTURE

Leadership for learning must ultimately be for the betterment of students which in turn means the achievements of the trivium goals of education: character development; transmission of what is considered worthwhile; and education for employment and re-employment. While the chief domain in which these three goals are played out is the traditional classroom, this domain is now expanding to be the borderless classroom with e-learning and other means of knowledge acquisition. It is self-evident that in the these new and emerging contexts for learning the competencies of classroom management have to be redefined, expanded and adapted to new ways of learning and new strategic approaches to leading learning.

The contexts of learning may include the following: extra- or co-curricular activities, clubs, uniformed units, residential experiences, field trips, religious and cultural festivities, holiday camps, study and supported learning, breaks and lunch times, playing fields, buses to school, all of which may encompass initiatives such as learning musical instruments, going to concerts or plays, designing and building a model, attending a philosophy session, writing poems, drawing, swimming, caring for the aged, the sick and the disadvantaged. With carefully planned learning experiences each of these contexts can broaden and deepen the quality of learning.

In the Malaysian context the third purpose of education, that is, education for employment, has much to do with decision-making by leading figures outside the education sector. In an age of uncertainty, national leaders envision futures and set out blueprints for dealing with both planned and unplanned change. This is in recognition of the fact that while some traditional jobs which existed will continue into the future, new jobs will constantly be emerging and reshaping the profile of skills needed. Leadership for learning should demonstrate the capacity to link the nature and quality of learning to the evolving competencies, mindsets, attitudes and relationships required in the newly emerging work places (Fullan, 1991; Fahey & Randall, 1998). Leadership for learning recognises the need to enrich classroom and school learning so as to prepare young people for the knowledge society and to make sense of the challenges posed by a new and unfamiliar social and economic context. The next generation of Malaysians will need above all to master "the ability to create access and use knowledge that is becoming the fundamental determinant of global competitiveness."

REALITIES BEYOND CLASSROOMS AND SCHOOLS

In a centralized educational system, waiting for the lock step development of the new formal curriculum, courses of studies, syllabuses, resource materials, may be a wait too long (a curriculum cycle may take up to 6-12 years) and a whole generation of students will leave school without the benefits of the enlightened leadership of the teachers.

For fifty years and with Eight Malaysia Development Plans and thousands of projects, Malaysia has moved forward in progression and development. With critical hindsight the nation's intellectual leaders have contributed to the 9th Malaysia Plan within which is embedded the National Mission with Five thrusts as follows:

- 1st Thrust: To raise the Malaysian economy up the value chain.
- 2nd Thrust. To raise national knowledge and innovation capacity and to foster the development of "first class mentality."

- 3rd To address the recurring socio-economic gaps and imbalances in constructive and productive ways.
- 4th To raise the level and sustainability of the Quality of Life.
- 5th To strengthen institutional capacity building and implementation capacity.

(Government of Malaysia, 2006).

The Blueprint or Master Plan for Educational Development in Malaysia 2006 promises to build a Malaysian nation, to develop human capital, to make national schools attractive, to narrow educational divides, and to raise the prestige and status of the Teaching Profession. The Education Blueprint calls for educational leadership to contribute effectively and efficiently to ensure that the development of the Human Capital Agenda is achieved, encompassing social capital, knowledge capital, intellectual capital, cultural capital, even religious capital and professional capital (Despres & Chauvel, 2000; Frappaolo, 2002; Fuller, 2002). When these are articulated the questions raised for educational practice at every level are: How are all these various challenges met by teachers within every subject, across the curriculum, through the wider experience of school life, day by day for over 21,000 school days or 15,000 hours of schooling? Embedded in this is the accountability issue – how do school repay the investment made in them by parents and by the wider society?

Ministerial and academic documents provide a wealth of ideas, drawing on national and international sources but the translation and interpretation of these ideas on the ground is the task which falls to school leaders. School leaders responsible for the learning of students and staff alike cannot remain impervious to the importance of social well-being, economic resilience and the political stability of the nation. They have a key role to play in the drive for national unity and integration, the economic competitiveness of the nation, knowledge creation and innovation. They need to have a voice in addressing recurring social problems and imbalances in the quality of life. They have something important to contribute to the move from the feudalistic, colonialistic and bureaucratic mindsets to positive forward looking mindsets and knowledge building communities (Mahathir, 1991; Bajunid 2002).

LEADERSHIP FOR LEARNING WITHIN CLASSROOMS AND SCHOOLS: OPPORTUNITIES FOR EXCELLENCE

Under existing laws of the nation, teachers cannot create new syllabuses or curriculum. However, professional leadership implies a capacity to enhance the existing curriculum, to enrich its content and to develop pedagogic processes which prepare students both for a known present and an uncertain future.

The knowledge revolution is as relevant to educational practice, as to other fields if not more so. It requires discriminating judgement to sift one's way through the plethora of emerging theories and proposed solutions to longstanding problems – maximized learning, accelerated learning, mastery learning, super learning, quantum learning, transformative learning, thinking skills, multiple intelligences and much else besides. It is a test of professionalism to know how best to draw from the diversity of approaches, as well as preserving the more traditional Socratic approach.

It is through ongoing professional conversations that teachers can explore together how to develop strategies most suited to their students, their subject of study and their students' prior learning. It is that ongoing professional discourse which creates and sustains the learning organization. For teachers, as for their students, the demands of a changing world imply some unlearning and some relearning, how to integrate and synthesize, how to question, how to understand what lies behind the question, learning how to generate solutions and solve problems and innovate creatively. (Freire, 1970; Goodman, 1973; Hallak, 1990; DePorter & Hernacki, 1992).

CONCLUSION

The potential of leadership for learning in Malaysia is enormous. It means embarking on a journey in which there is a map and compass, and milestones which mark both the distance travelled and the goal ahead. It is not, however a simple linear path, but one that faces setbacks and diversions as mistakes are made and directions re-established.

The journey is one in which alliances and networks are formed and people come to share a common language register, developing a maturing body of professional knowledge, establishing linkages within and among communities of practice and with the policy making community. The challenge for schools, for school leaders and teachers in Malaysia is to embrace a lively research culture, one which permeates thinking and practice at all levels and tunes into teachers', students and parents' voices and is able to learn from multiple perspectives. Such linkages need to extend beyond national borders to global partnerships. These are the essential nurturants of a lively leading profession, promoting the growth of dynamic leadership which puts learning at its heart.

NOTES

This paper is written based on the background of the exciting discourses initiated by the Cambridge Leadership for Learning Network. In the centralized Malaysian context there is strong leadership for learning but it is led by people in the system taking leadership initiatives. When those who lead move to some other positions or retire, usually the initiatives wither and die. Teacher led initiates are best seen in the leadership of voluntary professional associations. There are great opportunities to foster teacher led leadership for learning initiatives in order to set in motion professional transformations and new thresholds of quality learning.

REFERENCES

Ahmad Sarji, A. H. (1994). *Perkhidmatan awam Malaysia: Satu peralihan paradigma* [The Malaysian public service: A paradigmatic change]. Kuala Lumpur: Percetakan Nasional Malaysia.

Ambigapathy, P., & Chakravarthy, G. (Eds.). (2003). *New literacies, new practices and new times*. Serdang: Universiti Putra Malaysia Press.

Argyris, C. (1993). Knowledge for action: A guide to overcoming barriers to organization change. San Francisco: Jossey Bass.

Awang Had Salleh. (1979). *Malay secular education and teacher training in British Malaya*. Kuala Lumpur: Dewan Bahasa dan Pustaka.

Bajunid, I. A. (1982). *Establishing quality control circles in education: Initiating and facilitating excellence in schools*. Paper Presented at the Conference for District Education Officers. Universiti Sains Malaysia, Penang. Institut Aminuddin Baki.

Bajunid, I. A. (1995). Assessment of accountability systems in Malaysian education. *International Journal of Educational Research, 23*(6), 531–544.

Bajunid, I. A. (2000). Rethinking the work of teachers and school leaders in an age of change. In C. Day et al. (Eds.), *The life and work of teachers: International perspectives in changing times* (pp. 175–194). London: Falmer Press.

Bajunid, I. A. (2001). The transformation of Malaysian society through technological advantage: ICT and education in Malaysia. *Journal of Southeast Asian Education, 2*(1), 104–146.

Bajunid, I. A. (2002). Changing Mindsets: Lifelong learning for all. In Integrated approaches to lifelong learning paper presented at the ASEM International Conference on lifelong learning, Kuala Lumpar, Asia-Europe Institute.

Bajunid, I. A. (2003, September 25-26). *Internationally transferable lessons for educational and national development*. Paper presented to the Ministry of Science and Technology, Buenos Aires, Argentina.

Bakri, M. M. (2003). *An education system worthy of Malaysia*. Petaling Jaya: Strategic Information Research Development (SIRD).

Bolman, L. G. and Deal, E. T. (1997). *Reframing organizations: Artistry, Choice and Leadership*, 2nd Revised Edition, San Francisco: Jossey-Bass.

Bruner, J. (1996). *The culture of education*. Cambridge, MA: Harvard University Press.

Buderi, R. (2000). *Engines of tomorrow*. New York: Simon & Schuster.

Caldwell, B. J., & Hayward, D. K. (1998). *The future of schools*. London: Falmer Press.

Cheng, Y. C. (1996a). *The pursuit of school effectiveness*. Hong Kong: Hong Kong Institute of Educational Research.

Cheng, Y. C. (1996b). School effectiveness and school-based management. London: Falmer Press.

Connors, M. (1997). *The race to the intelligent state*. Oxford: Capstone Publishing.

Davis, S., & Davidson, B. (1991). *2020 vision*. New York: Simon & Schuster.

Delors, J. (1996). The treasure within: Report to UNESCO of the International Commission on Education for the Twenty-First Century. Paris: UNESCO.

DePorter, B., & Hernacki, M. (1992). *Quantum learning: Unleashing the genius in you*. New York: Dell Publishing.

Despres, C., & Chauvel, D. (Eds.). (2000). *Knowledge horizons.* Boston: Butterworth Heinemann.
Education International. (1998). *Education is a human right.* Brussels: E.I Publications.
Fahey, L., & Randall, R. M. (Eds.). (1998). *Learning from the future.* New York: John Wiley & Sons.
Faure, E. (1972). *Learning to be.* Paris: UNESCO.
Field, J. (2001). Lifelong education. *International Journal of Lifelong Education, 20*(1/2), 3–15.
Florida, R. (2002). *The rise of the creative class.* New York: Basic Books.
Frappaolo, C. (2002). *Knowledge management.* Oxford: Capstone Publishing.
Fraser, S. (Ed.). (1995). *The bell curve wars.* New York: Basicbooks.
Freiberg, H. J. (Ed.). (1999). *Perceiving, behaving, becoming: Lessons learned.* Alexandria, VA: Association for Supervision and Curriculum Development (ASCD).
Freire, P. (1970). *Pedagogy of the oppressed.* Harmondsworth: Penguin Books.
Fullan, M. G. (1991). *The new meaning of educational change* (2nd ed.). London: Cassell Educational.
Fuller, S. (2002). *Knowledge management foundations.* Boston: Butterworth-Heinemann.
Gardner, H. (1999). *Intelligence reframed.* New York: Basic Books.
Gibson, R. (Ed.). (1998). *Rethinking the future.* London: Nicholas Brealey.
Goodman, P. (1973). *Compulsory miseducation.* Harmondsworth: Penguin Books.
Government of Malaysia. (2003). *Education development plan 2001-2010.* Malaysia, Kuala Lumpur: Ministry of Education.
Government of Malaysia. (2006). *The 9th Malaysia plan 2006-2010.* Malaysia, Putrajaya: Author.
Hallak, J. (1990). *Investing in the future.* UNESCO/ Pergamon Press.
Hargrove, R. (2001). *E-leader.* Cambridge, MA: Perseus Publishing.
Harper, T. N. (2001). *The end of empire and the making of Malaya.* Cambridge: Cambridge University Press.
Hoyle, E. (1974) Professionality, professionalism and control in teaching. London Education Review, 3(2).
Hoyle, E. (1982). The professionalization of teachers: A paradox. *British Journal of Educational Studies, XXX*(2).
Hoyle, E., & John, P. (1994). *Teaching: Professional knowledge and professional practice.* London. Cassell Education.
Institut Aminuddin Baki (IAB). (1999). *Lessons from Educational Leaders* [Ikhtibar Pemimpin Pendidikan]. Genting Highlands: Ministry of Education.
Kementerian Pendidikan Malaysia. (2001). *Pembangunan pendidikan 2001-2010.* Kuala Lumpur: Author.
Khoo K. K. (2001). *Malay society: Transformation and democratisation.* Kelana Jaya: Pelanduk Publications.
Langer, E. J. (1989). *Mindfulness.* Reading, MA: Addison-Wesley Publishing.
Lewis, M. (2002). *The future just happened.* New York: W.W. Norton.
Longworth, N., & Davies, W. K. (1996). *Lifelong learning.* London: Kogan Page.
MacBeath J. (2002, January 3-6). *Leadership for learning: The Cambridge network.* Paper presented at the 15th International Congress for School Effectiveness and Improvements (ICSEI), Copenhagen.
Mahathir, M. (1991). *Malaysia: The way forward.* Kuala Lumpur: Malaysian Business Council.
Mapes, J. (2003). Quantum leap thinking: An owner's guide to the mind. Naperville, ILL: Sourcebooks.
Multimedia Development Corporation. (2005). *The smart school roadmap 2005-2020: An educational Odyssey* (A consultative paper on the expansion of the smart School Initiative to all schools in Malaysia). Cyberjaya: Multimedia Super Corridor.
Moschella, D. C. (1997). *Waves of power.* New York: American Management Association.
Nonaka, I., & Takeuchi, H. (1995). *The knowledge-creating company.* New York: Oxford University Press.
Oakley, E., & Krug, D. (1991). *Enlightened leadership.* New York: Fireside Book.
Palmer, P. J. (1998). *The courage to teach.* San Francisco: Jossey-Bass Publishers.
Perkins, D. N. (1981). *The mind's best work.* Cambridge, MA: Harvard University Press.

Peters, T., & Austin, N. (1989). *A passion for excellence: The leadership difference.* New York. Warner Books.
Phenix, P. H. (1964). *Realms of meaning.* Maidenhead. Mcgraw-Hill.
Rajendran, N. (2001). The teaching of high order thinking skills in Malaysia. *Journal of Southeast Asian Education,* 2(1), 42–65.
Ratey, J. J. (2002). *A user's guide to the brain.* New York: Vintage Books.
Report on Seminar on Strengthening Educational Research in Developing Countries. (1991). Stockholm: UNESCO & Institute of International Education (IIE).
Ritchhart, R. (2002). *Intellectual character.* San Francisco: Jossey-Bass.
Rusk, R. R. (1965). *The doctrines of the great educators* (3rd ed.). New York: St. Martin's Press.
Schon, D. (1983). The reflective practitioner: How professionals think in action. New York. Basic Books.
Senge, P. (1992). The fifth discipline: The art and practice of the learning organization. New York. Random House.
Tengku Abdul Rahman. (1980). *Looking back.* Kuala Lumpur: Star Publications.
Tiffin, J., & Rajasingham, L. (1995). *In search of the virtual class.* London: Routledge.
Toffler, A. (Ed.). (1974). *Learning for tomorrow.* New York: Vintage Books.
Ulich, R. (Ed.) (1971). *Three thousand years of educational wisdom* (2nd ed.). Cambridge, MA: Harvard University Press.

AFFILIATIONS

Ibrahim Ahmad Bajunid
Universiti Tun Abdul Razak
Malaysia

HUI-LING PAN

CHAPTER 17

School Leadership for Organizational Learning and Empowerment: The Taiwan Perspective

INTRODUCTION

In this new century, school leaders in different parts of the world are facing various challenges from educational reforms. Decentralization of central authority towards school-site level in decision-making has drastically changed the educational environment in which school management has become much more demanding. The role and responsibility of school leadership have also changed accordingly. Over the last few years school leaders in Taiwan have witnessed the impacts of decentralization on their schools and on their efforts to enhance teaching and learning.

This chapter explores how school principals in Taiwan cope with the wave of decentralization in school management, in particular, how the practice of school leadership has cultural implications and how school leadership influences organizational learning in Taiwan schools.

DECENTRALIZATING REFORM

The education system in Taiwan has gone through great changes in the last decade, echoing the strong demands for developments in the local community as well as educational reforms in a global context. In reviewing educational reforms in most western societies in the past twentieth century, the pursuit of efficiency was found to be a significant theme for the first half of the century (Short & Greer, 1997). Although progressive education was fashionable in the 1950s, students' academic performance was still deemed as the main target in school education. Various movements of curriculum reform and innovation in mathematics, science and humanities emerged in the 1960s and 1970s. In general, centralization and top-down strategies were the feature of these reforms. However, most of these large-scale reforms ended up as failures due to a failure to recognise teachers' need for participation and support.

Since 1980s, another wave of school restructuring movements began to call for systemic reform in education. Different from previous reforms that were fragmentary whether on curriculum, teaching or teacher quality, this wave characterized itself by its comprehensive and holistic nature (Hargreaves, Lieberman, Fullan, & Hopkins, 1998). Changes in school governance in response to decentralization was one of major features of this new wave of school reforms. School-based management, teacher empowerment, parental choice and voice became key elements in school restructuring in Taiwan as in other parts of the world (Murphy, 1993; Pan, 2002). Power relationships and the roles of principals, teachers and parents also underwent change, as, several acts were promulgated to restructure staff relationships. These included the Teacher Act, the revised Compulsory Education Act and Education Basic Act. Part of the authority in decision making was decentralized from central to local governments and from local governments to schools. However, decentralization operates in a bureaucratic manner in which the traditional ideology still prevails, so that decentralization does not in fact imply less control. School-based management treats power as an individual commodity to be shifted around by the school district board or central office to the school site. In a society such as Taiwan in which power is concentrated within conventional hierarchies, "sharing power" is something of a misnomer as school principals are reluctant to give up administrative power, while for teachers there is an equal reluctance to exceed the boundaries of their traditional role. So, in Taiwan schools, cultural beliefs and traditions continue to play a vital role in the conduct of teaching and learning.

CHANGING ROLES OF SCHOOL LEADERS

In 1980s, school principals tended to be seen as instructional leaders. They were expected to define school missions and goals, manage school activities, supervise teaching and learning, promote educational quality, coordinate the school curriculum and monitor students' learning progress and outcomes. In particular, they were expected to promote an academic climate, nurturing orderly and meaningful learning (Marsh, 2000; Murphy, 1990).

While instructional leadership continues to be promoted within the policy environment, the role of school principals in Taiwan has changed dramatically in the last decades. School leadership aimed at promoting teacher autonomy and involvement has been given greater emphasis in the current educational environment. How to empower teachers and lead their schools for educational change presents a new challenge to school principals.

As leaders for learning in schools, principals in Taiwan have to be able to fulfil the following functions (Chapman, 1993; Short & Greer, 1997):

- building an environment supportive of school members to work through difficult issues and dilemmas;
- enabling teachers to engage in shared decision making;
- developing the capacity for sustaining learning and school renewal;
- creating a collaborative, caring and trusting community in school;
- relating new and visionary ideas in education to the organizational tools and apparatus able to realize them;
- continuously striving to reconcile value-laden issues.

In this new and complex environment what can Taiwanese principals do to create a collaborative learning culture in their schools, involve staff in decision making, promote teacher professional growth and generate a mechanism of school self renewal? Addressing this question has led to a new emphasis on transformational leadership (Leithwood, Jantzi & Steinbach, 1999), moral leadership (Sergiovanni, 1992) and empowering leadership (Blasé & Anderson, 1995).

CULTURE AND SCHOOL LEADERSHIP

Inquiries into school leadership in Taiwan tend not to embrace a cultural perspective. As Walker and Dimmock (2002) lamented, the field lags behind other disciplines in exploring the influence of societal culture on leadership. There are, however, studies which may be drawn on, focusing on cultural influences, for example Cheng and Wong (1996), Hallinger and Kantamara (2000), Dimmock and Walker (2002) and Lam (2002). These studies have offered analytical frameworks, providing insights into cultural interpretations of school leadership.

After studying more than 11,700 IBM employees from 66 countries, Hofstede (1991) suggested four dimensions that could be used to analyse cultural variations in organizational behaviours. Based on the Hofstede' dimensions (1991), Walker and Dimmock (2002) proposed a six-dimension framework to describe and explain the cultural aspects of school leadership. These dimensions were labelled as power-distributed/power-connected, group-oriented/self-oriented, consideration/aggression, proactivism/fatalism, generative/replicative and limited relationship/holistic relationship. For Cheng and Wong (1996), views of East Asian culture commonly accepted in the contemporary literature could be summarised in three categories: the individual-community relationship, the ability-effort dichotomy and the holistic and idealistic tendency.

With reference to educational change in Thailand, Hallinger and Kantamara (2000) used Hofstede's cultural map with empirical support for the following propositions:

- In a society of high power distance, people exhibit a high level of deference to those of senior status. Reinforcing the belief that individuals in positions of authority should take decisions.
- The collectivist culture in Thailand puts the group is first, then the individual. Staff then identify their role in change through their referential social groups.
- The tendency to avoid uncertainty makes Thai people see change as disruptive making them more likely to seek stability.
- The feminine dimension in Thai culture manifests itself in the fostering of a harmonious atmosphere and strong spirit of community.

What Hallinger and Kantamara (2000) found was consistent with the characteristics of the group-oriented Asian societies while Walker and Dimmock (2002) reported that the role of school principals in Asia tended to emphasize harmony in their schools, enforcing commonly accepted standard approaches to governance, organization, curriculum and instruction. Moreover, they contended that in societies where power is associated with extrinsic factors, leadership tends to be from the "top".

All the above frameworks and findings may offer the lens for understanding school leadership for organizational learning and empowerment in Taiwanese culture.

Investigating ways in which school leadership plays out may be conceptualised at three levels - macro, meso and micro levels. At the macro level, studies focus on how school leadership is related to the social development and to changes in society. At the meso level, studies may investigate how school leadership deals with the interface issues between schools and the local communities including key stakeholders and other social organizations. At the micro level, studies may explore how school leaders as individuals develop and perform in their schools (Maxcy, 1991). It is no surprise that issues at the macro level (decentralization reform) tend to be related to leadership issues at the meso and micro levels. In order to investigate the characteristics of school leadership for promoting organizational learning and teacher empowerment across these levels in Taiwan, the author conducted several studies including Pan and Wang (2000), Wang and Pan (2000), Lam, Wei, Pan and Chan (2002), Lam, Chan, Pan and Wei (2003), and Pan (2002, 2004, 2005, 2007).

SCHOOL LEADERSHIP FOR ORGANIZATIONAL LEARNING

In the context of school restructuring in Taiwan, schools at the centre of change have to learn and adapt to the fast changing environment if they are to survive. Organizational learning has become a buzz word in Taiwan's literature. In order to develop their schools as learning organizations principals need to provide moral support to staff, build a common vision and communicate this as a guide for the school's day-to-day operation (Wei, 2002). Establishing partnerships with universities also provides valued support in promoting organizational learning.

Although the literature of organizational learning suggests strategies and actions which may inform principals' work, different contexts and school characteristics impact in different ways on the development of organizational learning. This was a key finding of an empirical study of Lam, Chan, Pan and Wei (2003). During the transition of educational reform towards decentralization, they employed a two-by-two typology to study staff's perceptions of organizational learning plotting "process" (OLP) against "outcomes" (OLO). Composite standard scores were then categorised into "high" and "low" along the two dimensions, so generating the following typologies: low OLP and low OLO (LpLo), low OLP and high OLO (LpHo), high OLP and low OLO (HpLo), as well as high OLP and high OLO (HpHo).

Investigating 51 elementary and 37 secondary schools, the study identified a bipolar pattern of schools in the process of developing organizational learning. Approximately half of the schools (N=39) fell into Type 1 (LpLo) and about 31 schools were in Type 4 (HpHo). Fewer schools were in Type 2 (LpHo, N=11) and Type 3 (HpLo, N=7) respectively (See Table 1). It suggests that despite decentralization a large proportion of schools sampled (39) appeared to be little affected. 31 schools that were deemed to be successful in becoming "learning organizations" both in terms of process and outcomes. 18 schools, in a stage of change, displayed a hybrid type of experience – either high in outcomes and low in process or vice versa (Lam, Chan, Pan & Wei, 2003).

Table 1: Typologies of Organizational Learning

Organizational Learning Process	Organizational Learning Outcomes	
	Low	High
Low	Type 1 (39)	Type 2 (11)
High	Type 3 (7)	Type 4 (31)

Several factors may help to explain the developmental variations among these schools in the process of decentralization, including factors such as inadequate funding, lack of transformational leadership, and size of schools. Among them, transformational leadership was found to be of particular significance. School leaders performed quite differently in the four categories of schools, tending to reflect how school leadership was conceptualised and how it related to the development stage of the school in moving towards organizational learning.

Below the threshold of awareness stage. In Type 1, schools were marked by the status quo during the reform process. There were few major changes in schools and without any evidence of a transition to organizational learning. Hierarchical division of labour remained central to the school's operation. For the most part, authority was in the hands of the principals who were in charge of decision making, while teachers confined their roles in the classroom to instruction. In the process of rapid transition to decentralization, principals appeared to be overwhelmed and unable to keep pace with reform. The safe strategy was, therefore, "waiting to see." A typical response was *"What should be decentralized and what needs to be under central control remains unclear. I will wait for while before I invite all staff to establish new rules of the game."*

Germination stage. In Type 2, schools seemed to be aware of the notion of organizational learning but as yet there was no collective learning among staff Principals worked hard to achieve tangible outcomes while shouldering most of the tasks which they might have delegated to their staff. Re-tailoring curriculum, re-focusing instructional objectives, and producing and publicizing the policy and administrative documents were major tasks of school management. Principals in Type 2 continued to carry the main burden of change. As some principals expressed it:

> When I find that the school culture has not adapted well to the reform, I will take charge. This is the responsibility of a leader.

> Decentralization has created excessive work for my staff. I am trying to shoulder as much as I can myself.

These principals tended to adopt a paternal role, assuming responsibility on behalf of their staff. Structural factors such as funding and school size were the conditions which offered support to principals who were willing to try out new ideas and approaches.

In both Types 1 and 2, principals were not yet ready to adopt new strategies tailored to the new challenges. The tendency to avoid uncertainty and stay with the status quo reflected the traditional mentality of school leaders in the face of decentralised educational reform. Only occasional examples of collective professional learning were in evidence in schools of these two Types.

Transformation stage. Type 3 schools started to embed collective professional learning through exchanging views of teaching and learning and participating in drafting school policies. However, the sudden shift from the vertical top-down decision making mode to the horizontal collegial consultative process required time to accommodate to. When principals were willing to change their decision-making mode, staff were able to embark on the journey towards shared, organizational, learning. In the words of two principals:

> For my staff to recognize that school reforms are a collective responsibility, I try to emphasize the roles of my staff as a group and de-emphasize my own leadership role.

> To encourage more of my staff to take part in decision making, I provide unlimited moral support and even incentive grants to consolidate a team spirit.

Principals at this stage were different from Types 1 and 2. They believed that staff needed to change their roles and behavioural patterns if school restructuring were to achieve its desired purposes. The major role of principals was to support teacher growth. However, since teachers themselves felt compelled to respond first and foremost to government-imposed initiatives, internally driven change process took time to happen.

Embedding stage. In Type 4 schools, collective learning was an integral feature of professional life during the transitional decentralization process. Staff took time to discuss key issues together and the processes in which they engaged were often productive. Two internal school factors, flexible working arrangements and transformational leadership, were most conducive to moving schools from Type 3 to Type 4. Fox example, two school principals said:

> We've routinely utilized our Wednesday staff development day to share new insights about teaching and to engage in self-reflection in order to reap the greatest benefit from team learning.

> To develop consensus about the need for reform, I try to ensure that financial resources are maximally utilized so that no staff feel that their welfare is being sacrificed. This helps to eliminate their fear of uncertainty.

Schools at this stage were maturing in their embrace of organizational learning. Common goals and team commitment to those goals were acknowledged while leaving space for variation in strategies adopted by school members. In a society, in which emphasis was put on social relations, school leaders were expected to show concern for the welfare of their staff, reflecting of something endemic to a Taiwanese culture.

SCHOOL LEADERSHIP FOR TEACHER EMPOWERMENT

Shared governance in school has been a significant feature of educational reforms over the last decade. Teachers Associations in schools gained their legal status from the Teachers Act passed in 1995. However, evidence of teacher empowerment is equivocal. Studies have shown that in schools with teacher associations there is in fact a lower perception of empowerment among teachers than with their counterparts in schools without teacher associations (Pan, 2002; Pan & Wang, 2000; Wang & Pan, 2000). One of possible explanations may be that in the early stage of Teacher Associations, teachers are learning about participatory decision making, expecting more power than is realistic.

Several years after decentralization reform, Pan (2007) conducted another survey using national samples of approximately 1,300 elementary and secondary school teachers in order to examine how they perceived empowerment. The study revealed that the overall average of teachers' scores was 4.53 on a 6-point scale of empowerment. Scores for elementary and secondary teachers were similar - 4.54 and 4.52 respectively. Among the five dimensions of the scale, self-efficacy was ranked the highest (4.77), followed by professional growth (4.74), autonomy (4.60), professional status (4.51), while professional impact was given the lowest score (4.04).

Wilson and Coolican's (1996) concepts of teacher empowerment provide further insights into the empowerment issue, exploring what they term extrinsic and intrinsic power. The exercise of extrinsic power is aimed at improving teachers' professional status. So teachers may gain the information needed to perform their job and to participate in decision-making as exemplified by site-based management, for example. Intrinsic power refers to teachers' personal attitudes rather than positional power or the ability to control others. A teacher with intrinsic power is confident when demonstrating his or her skills and evidenced in self-determination, ability to make decisions, and sense of self efficacy. He or she believes that the real source of authority comes from within. The results of Pan's (2007) study illustrated the scope and potential that exists for Taiwan schools to move progressively toward an empowering community where teachers may have opportunities for shared governance and professional growth combining both extrinsic and intrinsic power.

In order to explore how school leadership is related to teacher empowerment, strategies employed by the principals were also an aspect of Pan's study (2007). Interview data were collected from eight schools, selected as the high and low empowered schools according to their scores on the teacher empowerment scale. It was found that principals of higher empowered schools used more strategies to promote shared governance, goal setting, job enrichment, and information sharing. The distinguishing characteristics of principals of the higher empowered schools from those of the lower empowered schools included the following:

Principals:
- solicited opinions from different school sectors to inform decision-making
- delegated his/her power by assigning the right person to the right tasks
- built school visions together with staff;
- planned short-, mid- and long-term school plans together with staff;
- enhanced the morale of staff by helping to remove obstacles to change

Quantitative findings were supported by qualitative data. Qualitative data offered a more sophisticated picture of ways in which principals led their schools. Among the eight selected schools for interview, four were lower empowered schools. Among the four principals in these four schools, two still retained their authoritative mindset. Although they were aware of the concept of power sharing with staff, they still dominated decision-making practices in their schools. Two of the principals in the lower empowered schools were in their second term in a larger school in which the strategies they had employed in their former, smaller, schools did not transfer easily to the new setting. They precipitated changes too fast with the result that teachers were disempowered rather than empowered. Although these two principals shared some features of their colleagues in higher empowered school, their leadership skills were not as proficient as their counterparts in the higher empowered schools.

SHAPING HARMONIOUS SCHOOL ATMOSPHERE

In interviews with principals, creating a harmonious atmosphere was frequently mentioned as the priority task for school leaders in Taiwan. In an oriental culture, the need to foster community spirit and a pleasant environment without conflicts are a feature of the wider culture as well as among school staff in particular. As Hallinger and Kantamara (2000) and

Walker and Dimmock (2002) observed in Asia, ensuring harmony among staff is of central concern for school principals.

Besides, in a group-oriented society such as Taiwan, losing face is considered to be a serious issue. People care about their "face", so that respecting others and taking care to avoid others losing face is essential to interpersonal relationships. In the lower empowered schools, the negative perceptions from teachers may be attributed in part to the feeling that they were not respected by their principals, with the accompanying perception that they were not cared for. In the higher empowered schools, principals used various ways to express their caring for their subordinates. This was manifested in the principals' behaviours, such as perceiving and picking up on other people's needs and giving assistance. Even writing birthday cards was considered as a sign of caring. As some teachers said in interviews:

> She (the principal) is very considerate. She always notices how teachers are doing. If a teacher is not faring well, she will approach him/her. She's empathetic.

> He writes birthday cards to staff. In the past, if he had time, he wrote in calligraphy. His calligraphy is pretty. He may not always be able to give the card in person to every teacher since we have more than 100 classes. This is a big school. However, I did receive a card from him once.

ACTING AS A MODEL

In Chinese "Analect", it is said that excellence in the emperor may be compared to the wind; and in the people, to the grass. When the grass is stirred by the wind, it must bend (The Analect, 13: 19; quoted in Ware, 1977, p. 120). Since the leader exerts great influence on the followers, the virtue of the leader is highly regarded. Sergiovanni's (1992) contention that a higher level of leadership is to be found in the professional and moral domains resonates with Chinese intellectual traditions (Wong, 1998) where a moral standing on the part of the leader enjoys strong grounding.

Principals in higher empowered schools usually demanded of themselves that they set an example through their own conduct. They arrived at schools early in the morning, greeting students at the school gate. They rolled up their sleeves, working with staff to implement school policies. Having principals as such role models encouraged teachers to face the challenges. A teacher described her principal as follows:

He himself is a model. He did the thing first. Of course, he has the capacity to do it. He needs to have the capacity to carry out the policy.

STEERING SCHOOLS WITH VISIONS AND GOALS

Setting clear vision and goals is a key element in studies of transformational leadership (Leithwood et al., 1999). In Taiwan, after the Grade 1 to Grade 9 New Curriculum was implemented in 2002, schools were required to develop their own visions. Both "bottom-up", "top down and bottom-up integrated" approaches were used to develop school visions, and communicated through meetings, the internet and booklets to stakeholders. In order to make one's vision clear to all the stakeholders, a principal in the study said: *"I would like to inform parents in my school district that our school has a new principal, so I wrote articles, a kind of "soft article," to let people know what I think."* Creative ideas for publicizing school visions were also evident. One principal said that they made bookmarks containing school visions, distributed to each member of the school.

However, having visions without specific goals does not mean that those visions would necessarily materialize in practice. In the higher empowered schools, there were clear goals providing a guidance which teachers worked toward. For example, in one school with seriously falling roles, how to attract district students back was a great challenge for the principal. A target for student recruitment was set, and communicated as a shared goal for all school participants. Then, different approaches were used to pursue and achieve the goal, for example exploring how to make the school more attractive to students, how to communicate effectively with parents and community. In contrast, a principal in one of lower empowered schools had few ideas as to how to address impending stagnancy. His failure to share concerns and generate ideas together with his staff simply exacerbated conflicts between the teachers and the principal.

HAVING TEACHERS' VOICES HEARD

Taiwan society is moving towards greater democratic participation. As decentralization gathers pace, how to tune into teachers' voices and listen to their concerns and ideas for improvement assumes a higher priority for school principals. There are several ways in which teachers' voices may be heard. Sometimes principals walk around the campus to find out what the teachers need setting aside time to chat privately with teachers. School meetings are more formal occasions for staff to exchange opinions. Such events were, however, less evident in the lower empowered schools where teachers typically complained that the time given to meetings did not allow for adequate discussion. Administrative briefing occupied most of the time and meetings were more a ritual symbol of democratic participation rather than a forum for open discussion. As one staff member said:

> In meetings, there is not much discussion time. Most of the time is given to administrators' briefing. But, I feel that a lot of things need to be discussed. Meeting time is too short.

A step towards authentic expression of teachers' voice is to involve them in school decision making. As traditionally, teachers regard classroom teaching as their essential business, how to prompt them to step out of their classroom and become involved in school affairs, especially relating to curriculum decisions, is a matter of considerable concern to school leaders. Blasé and Blasé (1994) defined "teacher empowerment" as "decision participation, authority over issues concerning professional life both at the classroom level and at the school level, and opportunities to acquire knowledge necessary to warrant such authority" (p. 8). Reconceptualizing power relationship is the pre-eminent challenge for Taiwanese principals and is at the heart of in this new wave of education reforms in Taiwan. However, "power with" is a construct invented in the Western context. In a society of high power distance such as Taiwan, decision makers are by definition those in the positions of authority. Engaging in democratic participation will take time both for principals and teachers to adjust to such a major paradigm shift in school culture. The challenge is as much for principals as for their staff as it is still common for principals to dominate decision-making, loathe to relinquish power. Nonetheless these are principals who have been able to make a smooth transition from autocracy to democracy, for example through committees which allow genuine teacher participation in making decision-making on school affairs. As one school principal commented:

> I am not like the older generation, who thought the power is theirs. I tend to believe that the power belongs to the whole school community. Power is realised in delegating authority to teachers.

> I am in the process of releasing power and creating room for public discourse. Public discourse is an important mechanism for teacher decision-making.

SCHOOL LEADERSHIP FOR ORGANIZATIONAL LEARNING AND EMPOWERMENT

PROMOTING TEACHERS FOR PROFESSIONAL GROWTH

Opportunities for reflections allow teachers to break from habitual ways of recognizing and dealing with situations (MacKinnon & Erickson, 1992), to critically review their existing frame of thinking. Principals in the studies asked teachers to reflect on their routine teaching through questions, such as *"what kind of educational philosophy you have? What kind of instructional theory you used in your teaching? What kind of teaching activities you designed? And what kind of teaching methods you used?"*.

This reflective and questioning process is an integral part of building a professional community as characterised by Louis and Kruse (1995). These American researchers identified five dimensions of a professional community as reflective dialogue, deprivatization of practice, focus on student learning, collaboration, and shared values. The principals in my studies created teams of teachers in learning areas of "Language," "Math," "Social Studies," "Science and Technology," "Health and Physical Education," and "Arts and Humanities" to create forums for professional dialogue. Formal time was created school wide for teachers to meet and talk. An agenda for discussions was set up before each meeting. In order to promote the quality of dialogue reading materials were sent out to teachers periodically, and the products of curriculum development were posted on the internet for knowledge sharing.

Creating such opportunities for professional discourse is what constitutes transformational leadership. It starts with a response to teachers' concern, builds their self-esteem individually and collectively. The principals in our high empowerment schools set the stage for teachers to exercise leadership for learning. In turn this earned them recognition from parents, the community and within their own professional circles. Greater transparency and open sharing of experiences with a wider constituency of stakeholders served both to enhance motivation for teachers as well as enhancing the status of the profession.

CONCLUSION

In this century, school leaders in Taiwan shoulder greater responsibility in response to the call for educational accountability. It is clear that the quality of principals' leadership in Taiwan schools leads to differential school progression in terms of organizational learning and teacher empowerment. This chapter has argued that the societal culture acts as a filter, mediating the implementation of policy on decentrelization in schools. In an oriental society such as Taiwan, when the traditional culture encounters the Western pattern of educational change, assimilation and accommodation emerge and express themselves in tensions at the school-site level where resolution is determined by the quality of transformational leadership. The case of Taiwan provides a unique perspective for understanding school leadership for learning and teacher empowerment in Asia, especially in those areas where the heritage of Confucius remains a powerful force.

REFERENCES

Blasé, J., & Anderson, G. L. (1995). *The Micropolitics of Educational Leadership: From Control to Empowerment*. New York: Cassell.

Blasé, J., & Blasé, J. R. (1994). *Empowering Teachers: What Successful Principals Do*, Thousand Oaks, CA: Corwin Press.

Chapman, J. (1993). Leadership, school-based decision making and school effectiveness. In C. Dimmock (Ed.), *School-based management and school effectiveness* (pp. 201–218). New York: Routledge.

Cheng, K. M., & Wong, K. C. (1996). School effectiveness in East Asia: Concepts, origins and implications. *Journal of Educational Administration, 34*(5), 32–49.

Dimmock, C., & Walker, A. (2002). Connecting school leadership with teaching, learning and parenting in diverse cultural contexts: Western and Asian perspectives. In K. Leithwood & P. Hallinger (Eds.), *Second international handbook of educational leadership and administration* (pp. 395–426). London, UK: Kluwer Academic.

Hofstede, G. (1991). *Cultures and organizations: Software of the mind*. New York: McGraw-Hill.

Hallinger, P., & Kantamara, P. (2000). Educational change in Thailand: Opening a window onto leadership as a cultural process. *School Leadership & Management, 20*(2), 189–205.

Hargreaves, A., Lieberman, A., Fullan, M., & Hopkins, D. (1998). Introduction. In A. Hargreaves, A. Lieberman, M. Fullan, & D. Hopkins (Eds.), *International Handbook of Educational Change* (pp. 1–7). London: Kluwer Academic.

Lam, Y. L. J. (2002). Defining the effects of transformational leadership on organizational learning: A cross-cultural comparison. *School Leadership & Management, 22*(4), 439–452.

Lam, Y. L. J., Chan, C. M. M., Pan, H. L. W., & Wei, H. C. P. (2003). Differential developments of Taiwanese schools in organizational learning: Exploration of critical factors. *The International Journal of Educational Management, 17*(6), 262–271.

Lam, Y. L. J., Wei. H. C. P., Pan, H. L. W., & Chan, C. M. M. (2002). In search of basic sources that propel organizational learning under recent Taiwanese school reforms. *The International Journal of Educational Management, 16*(5), 216–228.

Leithwood, K., Jantzi, D., & Steinback, R. (1999). *Changing Leadership for Changing Times*. Philadelphia: Open University Press.

Louis, K. S., & Kruse, S. D. (1995). *Professionalism and Community: Perspectives on Reforming Urban Schools*. Thousand Oaks, CA: Corwin.

MacKinnon, A., & Erickson, G. (1992). The roles of reflective practice and foundational disciplines in teacher education. In T. Russell & H. Munby (Eds.), *Teachers and teaching from classroom to reflection* (pp. 192–210). London: Falmer Press.

Marsh, D. D. (2000). Educational leadership for the twenty-first century: Integrating three essential perspectives. In M. Fullan (Ed.), *The Jossey-Bass reader on educational leadership* (pp. 126–145). San Francisco: Jossey-Bass.

Maxcy, S. (1991). *Educational Leadership: A Critical Pragmatic Perspective*. New York: Bergin & Garvey.

Murphy, J. (1990). Principal instructional leadership. *Advances in Educational Administration: Changing Perspective on the School*, I, 163–200.

Murphy, J. (1993). Restructuring: In search of a movement. In J. Murphy & P. Hallinger (Eds.), *Restructuring schooling: Learning from ongoing efforts* (pp. 1–31). Newbury Park, CA: Corwin Press.

Pan, H. L. (2002). Retrospects and prospects: What do we learn from school change? In H. L. Pan (Ed.), *School innovation: Theory and practice* (pp. 443–473). Taipei: Xue Fu.

Pan, H. L. (2004). *Educational leadership in school innovation.* Technical report funded by the National Science Council. National Taiwan Normal University, Taipei, Taiwan.

Pan, H. L. (2005, January). Leadership for school improvement. Paper presented at the Hawaii International Conference on Education, Hawaii, USA.

Pan, H. L. (2007). *Reconceptualizing power discourses of school leadership in a changing era.* Technical report funded by the National Science Council. National Taiwan Normal University, Taipei, Taiwan.

Pan, H. L., & Wang, L. Y. (2000). Crisis or turning point: The influence of Teacher Association on school management. Paper presented at the Conference on the Theory and Practice of School-based Management, Hwalien Teachers College, Hwalien, Taiwan.

Sergiovanni, T. J. (1992). *Moral leadership: Getting to the heart of school improvement.* San Francisco: Jossey-Bass.

Short, P. M., & Greer, J. T. (1997). *Leadership in empowered schools: Themes from innovative efforts.* Upper Saddle River, NJ: Prentice-Hall.

Walker, A., & Dimmock, C. (2002). Moving school leadership beyond its narrow boundaries: Developing a cross-cultural approach. In K. Leithwood & P. Hallinger (Eds.), *Second international handbook of educational leadership and administration* (pp. 167–202). London, UK: Kluwer Academic.

Wang, L.Y., & Pan, H. L. (2000, December). A survey study on the empowerment of school participants and the cause analysis in junior-high schools and elementary schools: Teacher Association as a focus. Paper presented at the Conference of the Vision and Planning of Educational Development in the New Era, National Taiwan Normal University, Taipei, Taiwan.

Ware, J. R. (Trans.). (1977). *The sayings of Confucius.* Taipei: Confucius Publishing.

Wei, H. C. (2002). Constructing a learning school: An action research. In H. L. Pan (Ed.), *School Innovation: Theory and practice* (pp. 363–401). Taipei: Xue Fu.

Wilson, S. M., & Coolican, M. J. (1996). How high and low self-empowered teachers work with colleagues and school principals. *Journal of Education Thought, 30*(2), 99–117.

Wong, K. C. (1998). Culture and moral leadership in education. *Peabody of Journal of Education, 73*(2), 106–125.

AFFILIATIONS

Hui-Ling Pan
National Taiwan Normal University
Taiwan

ALLAN WALKER AND PAULA KWAN YU-KWONG

CHAPTER 18

School Leader Development in Hong Kong: Status, Challenge and Adjustment[1]

This chapter discusses the recent history and current state of school leader development in the Hong Kong Special Administrative Region. Given the extent of the area involved, a fully comprehensive account cannot be provided in a single chapter. Our aims are therefore to outline the recent history of school leader development in Hong Kong, sketch a picture of the current 'state of play' in the area and suggest a number of issues which the system and/or leader development programme providers may consider as they move forward. In short, the purpose of the chapter is to provide a basic understanding of leader development in Hong Kong over the last 15 or so years and then comment on its possible future development.

The chapter is divided into five main sections. The first section provides a brief description of the Hong Kong context in general, an introduction to how education is structured and a summary of the recent education reform environment. This section is important as these multiple contexts frame leader development policy, programmes and processes. The second section recounts Leader Development Programmes (LDPs) in Hong Kong before the year 2000. This is widely recognised as the year that the Government became more intimately involved in leader development and laid the groundwork for a soon-to-be-formalised certification policy. The third section looks at leader development from 2000 to the present. This period witnessed almost frenetic activity in the area, including the implementation, for the first time, of a guiding conceptual framework, mandatory principal certification and differentiation of levels of leadership. The fourth section relates to this activity outlining some of the evaluations conducted on parts of the new policy. Although it is still early days for some elements of the new leader development framework, initial programme evaluations, though somewhat unsophisticated, suggest positive movement. The fifth section summarises the current state of leader development in Hong Kong and makes some recommendations for taking it forward. These include the need for further embedding networked learning, deeper evaluation of the

J. MacBeath and Y.C. Cheng (eds.), Leadership for Learning: International Perspectives, 305–325.
© *2008 Sense Publishers. All rights reserved.*

impact of leader development in schools and student learning, and shifting emphasis from structures to learning processes.

CONTEXT OF LEADER DEVELOPMENT

Societal and systemic context

Hong Kong is located at the south-eastern tip of China, has a population of about 6.8 million and covers a total area of only 1,103 km^2. Approximately 98 per cent of the population is ethnic Chinese (Hong Kong Special Administrative Region [HKSAR] Government, 2005a). Hong Kong became a Special Administrative Region (SAR) of the People's Republic of China on 1 July 1997, after 150 years of British rule. Under Hong Kong's constitutional document, the Basic Law, the existing economic, legal and social systems will be maintained for 50 years. The SAR enjoys a high degree of autonomy except in the areas of defence and foreign affairs (HKSAR Government, 2005b). Chinese (Cantonese) and English are the official languages.

The Education and Manpower Bureau (EMB)[2] formulates and reviews education policy, secures funding from the Government's overall budget and oversees the effective implementation of educational programmes (HKSAR Government, 2005c). The Secretary for Education and Manpower heads the EMB. Education consumes the largest share of public expenditure, accounting for about one-fifth of total recurrent public expenditure (HKSAR Government, 2005b).

Hong Kong provides nine years of free and universal basic education. All students between the ages of 6 and 15 are entitled to a school place at no cost. Students enter primary school at around 6 years of age, receive a six-year primary education and attend secondary school for three years. All Secondary 3 students studying in publicly funded schools who have the ability and desire to progress are provided with subsidized Secondary 4 places or other training opportunities. On completion of Secondary 5, students sit two public examinations for entrance to sixth form and tertiary institutes/universities, respectively. Of the relevant age group, approximately 48 per cent are enrolled in post-secondary education. The structure of secondary schools will soon undergo massive change - schools are currently preparing for this. Kindergarten education is offered to children in the 3-5 age group in private kindergartens run by voluntary organizations or private bodies.

There are four main types of schools: *Government schools,* which are wholly operated by the Government; *aided schools,* which are also fully funded by the Government but run by voluntary bodies; *private schools,* which are international schools that depend largely on parental contributions in the form of tuition fees and/or debentures as the major source of financial support; and *direct subsidy schools*, which are allowed to collect tuition fees from students in addition to receiving financial subsidies from the Government. In the 2004/05 school year, there were 759 primary schools and 519 secondary schools (as well as 66 special schools), with a student and teacher population of over 920,000 and 52,000, respectively (HKSAR, 2005b). The majority of schools in Hong Kong are aided schools, operating under the aegis of School Sponsoring Bodies (SSBs) which, in turn, manage their schools through a School Management Committee (SMC) within the school-based management framework. Starting from the 2004/05 school year, schools were encouraged to establish Incorporated Management Committees (IMCs), ostensibly to replace SMCs in order to allow teachers and parents to participate more directly and fully in school decision making (EMB, 2004b). According to the findings of the Programme for International Student Assessment (PISA) in 2003 (Hong Kong Programme for International Student Achievement [HKPISA], 2005), Hong Kong 15-year-old students performed well and were ranked among the top 10 countries/regions in all four of the assessment domains (ranked first in mathematics, second in problem solving, third in science and tenth in reading).

THE EDUCATIONAL REFORM CONTEXT[3]

While our purpose here is not to provide a comprehensive picture of education reforms in Hong Kong, some understanding of the reform context is necessary to locate leadership development. Cheng (2000) describes education reforms in Hong Kong as arriving in two overlapping waves, roughly separated by the release of the Education Commission Report No.7 (ECR7) in 1997. The first wave, pre-1997, can be characterised as a top-down approach to reform, with an emphasis on increasing resource input. Post-1997 reforms targeted a school-based, bottom-up approach. Hong Kong now appears to be on the cusp of a new, more hybrid wave which uses a combination of the top-down and bottom-up approaches. One example of this is school-based management and school self-evaluation.

From 1984 to 1997, literally hundreds of policy recommendations were proposed by the Education Commission (EC), the pre-eminent education policy advisory body in Hong Kong (Cheng, 2003; Lo, 1997). Viewed together, the resultant policies covered a broad range of issues, including the medium of instruction, teacher education, the private school sector, special education, assessment and selection mechanisms, curriculum development, teaching and learning conditions, school management and school inspection (Cheng, 2000, 2003). Although all impacted school leadership, perhaps the most influential was the School Management Initiative (SMI), which represented the Education Department's first attempt to target the school as the unit of change (EMB & ED, 1991). The SMI provided a school-based management framework with clearer roles for principals, greater participation in decision making, more systematic planning and evaluation of school activities, and more flexibility in using resources (Dimmock & Walker, 1998).

Following the change of sovereignty in 1997, the new SAR Government confirmed its dedication to education reform. In comparison with earlier reform efforts, the emphasis shifted to a very different theory of action for driving educational improvement. First, the reforms focused much more deliberately on schools as the unit of change, concerned primarily with improving internal school conditions and the quality of student learning. Second, they recognized the uniqueness of individual schools and differing needs and problems with improvement strategies based largely on the diagnosis of the needs within specific school-based contexts. Third, they involved melded organisational (school organization and culture) and classroom interventions (related to teaching and learning) to effect change in schools. Policies also promoted networking and the sharing of effective practice (Li, 2004; Chiu & Chung, 2003).

Other reforms included major changes in approaches to learning and teaching and to a deeply entrenched examination system (Education Commission, 2000, 2000a). In order to make more room for the ideals incorporating new learning, reforms also moved to fundamentally change the academic structure, admission system at different levels, and assessment mechanisms (especially public examinations) (EMB, 2005c). This package of reforms, particularly the more progressive approach to curriculum, pedagogy and assessment (Curriculum Development Council [CDC], 2001), poses a significant challenge to school leaders.

A related line of reform sought to improve school governance and management (Advisory Committee on School-based Management [ACSBM], 2000), school accountability (EMB, 2003a, 2003b), and the professional development of teachers and principals (ED 2002; Advisory Committee on Teacher Education and Qualifications [ACTEQ], 2003). In 2003 Quality Assurance carried out by a body of inspectors was replaced by school self-evaluation and external review (SSE and ESR) together with a five year longitudinal evaluation of its impact on schools (MacBeath and Clark,

2005, MacBeath, 2007). These reform 'lines' are drastically altering the work lives of school practitioners and place increasing demands on school leaders to improve their own and their school's performance.

SCHOOL LEADER DEVELOPMENT IN HONG KONG: A RECENT HISTORY

As certification of school leaders in Hong Kong is controlled by the Government, not by tertiary institutions, it is not necessary to gain an academic qualification, such as a Masters Degree, in order to become a principal or gain promotion. There are three school leadership centres based in three tertiary institutions offering leadership development programmes while a fourth university also offers development programmes in their Department of Educational Studies. These institutions compete with each other for Government funding to run and develop programmes which has often meant, at least to some degree, that offerings had little or no relationship with each other.

In the decades prior to 2000, leadership preparation and development in Hong Kong followed an incoherent and fragmented path (Walker & Dimmock, 2006). New principals were required to attend a basic 9-day (primary principals) or 10-day (secondary principals) course focusing on administrative matters only. Induction programmes aimed to equip newly appointed principals with the basic knowledge and skills needed for leading and managing schools. Other opportunities for potential, newly-appointed and serving principals were diffuse and organised on an *ad hoc* basis by the Education Department (ED),[3] different SSBs, higher education providers and their associated specialised centres, and some professional associations (Walker, 2004). Preparation was linked only loosely to major education reform initiatives and rarely touched 'real' leadership life in schools. The focus of preparation and 'upgrading' courses was determined by the formal system (at its various levels), by the preferences and/or expertise of local academics or their visiting colleagues from overseas. In terms of methodology, the few centrally supported programmes for education leaders pre-2000 were overwhelmingly classroom based, tendered out to universities, rarely involving practising leaders in more than 'legitimising roles' and, with few exceptions, were largely detached from school life (Walker & Dimmock, 2005). From 1992 onward, additional resources were committed to help schools implement the School Management Initiative (SMI). The ED commissioned local tertiary institutions to run a 30-hour training programme for school supervisors, principals and assistant principals. From June 1998, the ED also organised district-based workshops and seminars to provide similar training for principals of non-SMI schools (Task Group on

Training and Development of School Heads, 1999; Walker & Dimmock, 2006).

In 1999, the Chief Executive announced in his annual policy address that from 2000-2001, all newly appointed principals would need to complete certain requirements prior to appointment (HKSAR Government, 1999). This edict prompted a rush of programme and policy activity in leadership development.

Consultation for improved professional development in 1999: Prompted by the EMB's growing reform agenda, particularly related to reforming governance structures, and increased demands within the education community, in June 1999, the ED established a Task Group to look into the training and development of school heads. Its produced a draft programme and framework "to equip and develop school principals with the necessary knowledge, skills and attributes to become competent leaders to take schools into the new millennium" (Cheng, 2000, p. 68). The paper also proposed that:

(a) with effect from the 2000/01 school year, newly appointed principals should be required to complete certain parts of designated training prior to taking up office;
(b) by 2004/05, all newly appointed principals should have obtained a certificate of principalship prior to appointment; and
(c) all serving principals must obtain the certificate by September 2007 (Task Group on Training and Development of School Heads, 1999).

Even though the general philosophy of their consultation document was applauded, principal interest groups expressed reservations about certain recommendations, including the institution of a 'uniform' programme for all principals (and potential principals) and the requirement that serving principals obtain a 'certificate of principalship'. In reaction to these concerns, consultation and subsequent action appeared to go 'underground' for over a year, only to resurface in a somewhat different form in early 2002, when a second consultation document was released and finally adopted as formal policy. The development and implementation of the programme for newly appointed principals was the Government's first priority and important as it was developed and instituted while the overall framework was being debated. It oversaw the construction of the first set of local principalship standards and introduced a very different programme from those which came before. As such, it can be seen as the testing ground for later broader-based LDPs and methodologies.

School Leader Development after 2000

LDP for newly appointed principals: The LDP was introduced for newly appointed principals (NAPs) in 2000/01. The formal two year programme included four components underpinned by the locally developed set of 'qualities' (standards) organised as clustered sets of values, knowledge, skills and attributes, *the six core areas of school leadership*: Strategic Direction and Policy Environment; Teaching, Learning and Curriculum; Leader and Teacher Growth and Development; Staff and Resource Management; Quality Assurance and Management; and External Communication and Connection (Education Department, 2002).

Figure 1: Newly Appointed Principals Programme 2000

Year	Part	Purpose
1st	1. Needs Assessment for Principals in Hong Kong (NAFPhk)	For newly appointed principals to achieve a self-understanding of their professional development needs
	2. Induction Programme	For a familiarization with common issues faced by principals
	3. School Leadership Development (SLD) Programme comprising 3-day residential workshops (based on the NAFPhk group profile)	For the development of leadership skills
2nd	4. Extended Programme (based on the NAFPhk group profile)	For providing a theoretical foundation of the principal's work and for development of action learning skills

NAPs were required to complete the designated programme (See Figure 1) in their first two years of principalship. This was generally positively evaluated (see Walker & Dimmock, various years; Walker, various years; Wong, 2005; Cheung & Walker, 2006). and formed the foundation of the comprehensive leader development framework *Continuing Professional Development for School Excellence* (Education Department, 2002a [see Figure 2]). This reduced the strict requirements for serving principals suggested in earlier consultative documents, but presented a more coherent framework for overall development. The new policy constituted a substantial shift from the *status quo* by delineating levels of leadership development, introducing mandatory requirements and a time-regulated structure (including certification). It demanded that (at least) aspiring principals pay for certification, adopting a set of 'local' leadership beliefs and standards, encouraging school leaders to take responsibility for their own and their colleagues' learning, and aimed to significantly elevate the value of formal, non-university accredited development programmes. In short, the policy attempted to effect change through both cultural and structural pathways. The beliefs and major requirements are summarised in Figure 2. (Education Department, 2002a).

Figure 2: Continuing Professional Development Framework for School Principals 2002 (Education Department, 2002b)

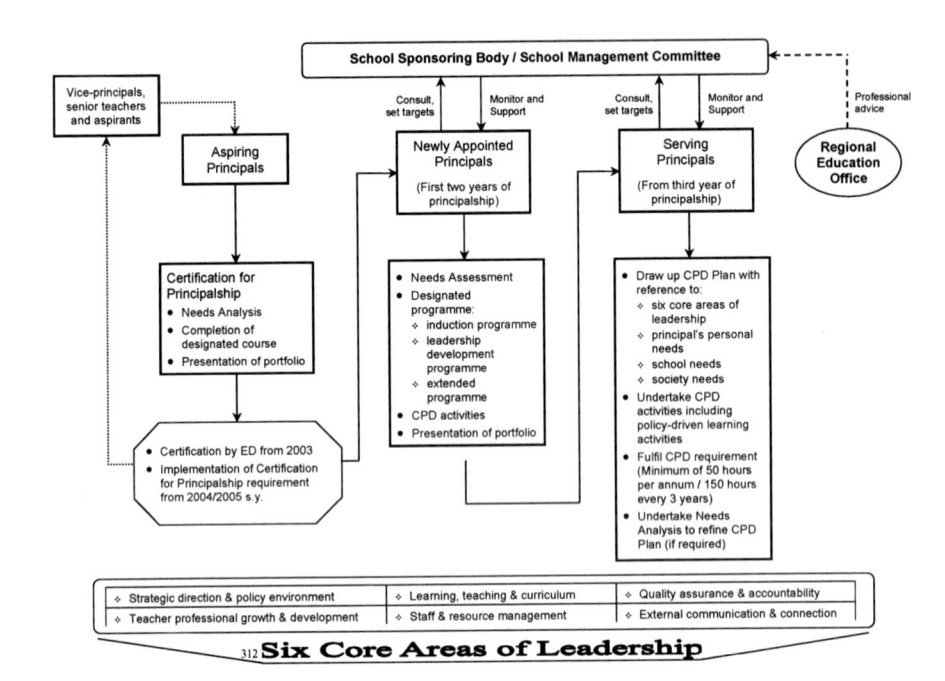

```
                    ┌──────────────────────────────────────────────┐
                    │ School Sponsoring Body / School Management Committee │◄─ ─ ─ ─
                    └──────────────────────────────────────────────┘         │
                          ▲         ▲           ▲         ▲                   │
    Vice-principals,   Consult,  Monitor and  Consult,  Monitor and     Professional
    senior teachers    set targets  Support   set targets  Support         advice
    and aspirants
         │
    ┌──────────┐      ┌──────────────┐      ┌──────────────┐         ┌──────────┐
    │ Aspiring │      │Newly Appointed│     │   Serving    │         │ Regional │
    │Principals│      │  Principals  │      │  Principals  │         │Education │
    └──────────┘      │(First two years of│ │(From third year of│    │  Office  │
                      │ principalship) │    │ principalship) │        └──────────┘
                      └──────────────┘      └──────────────┘
```

- Certification for Principalship
  - Needs Analysis
  - Completion of designated course
  - Presentation of portfolio

- Needs Assessment
- Designated programme:
  ◊ induction programme
  ◊ leadership development programme
  ◊ extended programme
- CPD activities
- Presentation of portfolio

- Draw up CPD Plan with reference to:
  ◊ six core areas of leadership
  ◊ principal's personal needs
  ◊ school needs
  ◊ society needs
- Undertake CPD activities including policy-driven learning activities
- Fulfil CPD requirement (Minimum of 50 hours per annum / 150 hours every 3 years)
- Undertake Needs Analysis to refine CPD Plan (if required)

- Certification by ED from 2003
- Implementation of Certification for Principalship requirement from 2004/2005 s.y.

| ◊ Strategic direction & policy environment | ◊ Learning, teaching & curriculum | ◊ Quality assurance & accountability |
| ◊ Teacher professional growth & development | ◊ Staff & resource management | ◊ External communication & connection |

Six Core Areas of Leadership

(a) Principals are responsible for their own professional growth.
(b) Principals have a mandate to be professionally up-to-date and to provide a role model for their own teaching staff in terms of CPD.
(c) CPD enhances principals' professionalism and leadership for the benefit of students and student learning.
(d) CPD builds on principals' individual strengths and is by nature developmental.
(e) CPD opportunities need to be varied to reflect the needs of aspiring, newly appointed and experienced principals and be open to individual selection.
(f) CPD embraces collegial input and support from the education sector as well as other professional sectors.

Running alongside, if somewhat disconnected from, formal Government-sponsored or tendered programmes, are initiatives developed by a variety of other organisations. For example, a 2002 ED survey found that from 1999 to 2002, 17 SSBs organised their own professional development programmes for principals. There has also been movement lately in leader development in international schools. For example, the English School Foundation has recently initiated a year long programme aimed at improving the capacity of its middle level leaders. The programme, 'Leading Upstream' (Walker & Quong, 2006), is based on an action learning approach and built around cross-school, small leader learning communities.

EARLY EVALUATIONS OF PRINCIPAL LDPS

Most of the evaluations to date have focused on the NAP programme, given that it began almost three years before other components. However, initial evaluations of the Preparation for Principalship course are beginning to appear (see EMB, 2004a; Hickman, 2004; Walker, 2005; Walker and Kwong, 2005). An insightful study by Wong (2005) investigated the impact of leadership training on new female principals in middle/secondary schools, reporting that "it seems that all Hong Kong respondents found the NAP programme useful in providing them with a support system, which included a databank of information and a professional network with other principals, both new and experienced. By knowing that they were not alone, sharing experiences and practices, the respondents felt more confident and were able to look at their roles with a wider perspective..." And "...both the NAPs from Hong Kong [and England] found that the NAP training was essential and had been useful in enhancing their confidence and in providing some kind of emotional support, though they vary in telling exactly what the impact was" (p. 15). Her findings generally found support in studies conducted by scholars from various tertiary institutions (Wong, 2004; Wong, 2005a, 2005b).

PROSPECT: STATUS, CHALLENGES AND POSSIBLE ADJUSTMENT

Leader development in Hong Kong is in many ways at a crossroads. While quite remarkable progress has been made over the last five to seven years the challenge now is to keep this momentum and, at the same time, gear the emphasis of the programmes and processes more toward leadership learning (Walker & Dimmock, 2006). Although school leader development has progressed substantially in Hong Kong since about 2000, there is a widening recognition that it needs to take on a more organic form.

The issues discussed in the following section are grouped under the categories of framework, policy and expansion; flexibility and contextual/ cultural sensitivity; professional involvement, control and regulation; evaluation, feedback and linkage; networks and communities of practice; and mechanisms, content and learning gateways. Although presented under separate sub-headings, careful reading of the issues shows plainly that they are closely interrelated. For example, policy adjustment will influence the extent of leader control of their own learning, which will in turn affect relevant learning methodologies and design, and so on. We do not presume to cover all related issues, but attempt to address some of the more salient of these.

FRAMEWORK, POLICY AND EXPANSION

Status: Central policy has successfully established a framework to formalise and guide leader development, or at least that relevant to preparing future principals and keeping serving principals 'on the move'. Over the same period, the EMB has generally shown a willingness to shift and change this policy and specific components in line with demands and has supported a degree of experimentation with new ideas.

Challenges: At least two further challenges directly target central policy makers. The first is whether policy makers may revert to a stance which preserves the *status quo* and therefore stifle continuing change and experimentation. This may result from over-adherence to bureaucratic norms and procedures (an unwillingness to 'take a chance'), overreaction to pressures from powerful higher education providers, or an over-concentration on easily measurable outcomes. Policy to date has clearly targeted the principalship, and while this is obviously a key starting point, if effective future principals are to be nurtured, development interventions need to target other levels of school leadership.

Adjustment: Policy makers may take a future- and improvement-oriented stance to leader learning which encourages developers and providers to actively seek new and more effective programmes, structures and methods within a flexible centralised framework. While the framework is very important, it should empower change rather than restrict it. Policy makers may also heighten acknowledgment of the importance of building leader capacity throughout the school both as a way of improving the current effectiveness of schools and so as to nurture the next generation of senior leaders. To date most resources and energy have been devoted to aspiring and new principals. So far, little thought has been given to the leadership competencies necessary for leaders other than principals. When considering this framework it should be noted that some mid-level leaders do not aspire to a principalship whereas others do (Kwan & Walker, in press). It is important that the CPD of both these groups be addressed.

FLEXIBILITY AND CONTEXTUAL/CULTURAL SENSITIVITY

Status: There is movement, be it rather slow, toward grounding leader learning in the local context in at least two ways. The first is by locating more components of leadership development programmes themselves within the workplace. This is happening through action learning, context-based forums and shadowing exercises. The second is through the realisation that development programmes need to be based on a localised curriculum, both in terms of knowledge and culturally-sensitive approaches to learning and leading. However, with some exceptions, most programmes continue to be based on a standardised package of provider- and system-sanctioned knowledge.

Challenges: Although promising, initiatives which attempt to promote flexibility and localise content and process face a series of challenges. First, the majority of formal knowledge and programme methodology draw heavily on Western theory and research (Walker & Dimmock, 2004). Although this is obviously informative in an internationalising world, it is often unsuitable for local leaders in terms of both foundational values and pedagogy. Second, although leaders have responded well to shifting, or at least basing, some programme components in their schools, an entrenched belief that professional development only happens in university classrooms and flows from 'experts' endures. Third, the need for centralised regulation and control, as well as the number of leaders involved, perhaps understandably results in the development of static, uniform packages by university providers. This may militate against innovation and flexibility in terms of addressing emergent or individual needs and new reforms.

Adjustment: Programmes need to work with and not against the culture and context within which leaders work. This means encouraging flexibility in terms of content, process and methodology, and implies that programmes should consider their intended impact not only on the school but also the system and the differentiated expectations which may stem from the need to balance these. It is important for programmes to note that learning how to do a job does not occur in a professional or organisational vacuum. As such, principals, as well as system leaders, university teachers and policy makers must recognise how social change impacts the socialization and learning of principals.

A clear message is that learning should be grounded within the reality of schools and school improvement. This does not mean that all learning should happen 'in' schools, although an increasing proportion may well be in principals' own and other schools, but that the intent and design of programmes is purposefully related to what leaders do to make a difference. As such, programmes may incorporate 'real' problem- or story-based foci, opportunities for acknowledging diverse views, increasing personal awareness and individual or cooperative action learning. While there is obviously an ongoing need for the meaningful infusion of theoretical frameworks and knowledge, and inspirational motivation from 'outside', if principals do not see learning as impacting meaningfully on what they do in schools, it is missing the mark. This is true of learning needed in values and culture building areas as well as for meeting accountability requirements.

PROFESSIONAL INVOLVEMENT, CONTROL AND REGULATION

Status: Over the last five or so years, more leaders have been involved in mentoring-type roles in LDPs. In fact, central requirements now mandate that experienced practitioners be included when bidding for programmes. Principals have been involved as instructors, portfolio assessors, mentors and coaches, and feature on Government working groups and advisory bodies and have taken some part in both the structuring and assessment of a number of leader development initiatives. This can be seen as granting practitioners a form of professional control and regulation.

Challenges: Whereas the quantitative expansion of principals is encouraging, when examined more deeply, the quality or depth of involvement remains questionable. In too many cases their involvement is used as a legitimising device rather than for programme improvement. At a pragmatic level, principals have little time to commit to programmes and many appear content to restrict their involvement to the symbolic. Whereas time constraints are a very real issue, this may indicate a lack of understanding of the link between work and learning (Bredeson, 2003), inadequate resource provision and/or an absence of the history or tradition of meaningful involvement with their own learning.

In terms of professional control and regulation, while principals are involved peripherally in programmes and not given any real control, they are unlikely to seek more. While accreditation is governed by others, principals may see either little need or hope for self regulation. A problem here appears to be that bureaucratic control and regulation of formal requirements are not seen as relating directly to learning and improvement by either officials or many leaders themselves. In other words, accreditation and other forms of regulation are seen as something that is done to leaders, rather than for or with leaders, and discrete from actually making learning meaningful.

Adjustment: A clear message to all involved in leadership development in Hong Kong is that both values and structures must shift in unison. To increase the meaningful involvement of principals, policy makers and providers can endeavour to increase the scope and quality of involvement. This means that as well as involving principals in mentoring, coaching, advising and instructing, they can be involved in design, content and oversight of professional learning. Although time will still need to be protected, more complete involvement may well lead to greater commitment, which in turn will flow on to, for example, more effective mentoring and more relevant programmes. In short, the involvement of good practitioners helps programmes to retain a focus on reality, something often missing in higher education institutions and Government offices. However, 'intense' involvement should still be in partnership with academics and system officials and consciously structured to be forward-looking rather than simply reproductive. It is also important that principals or others involved are themselves adequately trained, recognised as effective leaders with a defined role and, importantly, with a firm code of ethics.

Leader development remains largely in the hands of universities and central policy makers. At present, there is no over-arching professional body designed to ensure the quality of programmes offered, to ensure coherence or, more importantly, to ensure that the leaders themselves are heard. It may well be time that Hong Kong establishes some type of representative overseeing/governing structure – such as a principals' institute – to take this role. This is presently difficult because of the diffusion of school governance structures and professional organisations, a lack of sufficient resources and, perhaps most tellingly, a lack of the wherewithal to get it started.

EVALUATION, FEEDBACK AND LINKAGE

Status: LDPs have long been evaluated by providers and by the EMB. For example, all providers must formally evaluate their programmes, normally once during the programme and then again when it concludes, and submit these to the EMB. Feedback, if it comes, is referred back to providers (directly and/or indirectly) and built into subsequent tender documents. The framework discussed earlier in the chapter aims to provide a form of coherence.

Challenges: The policy framework provides significantly more coherence and feedback in terms of guidance, structures and content than anything that has come before – this is to be applauded. However, in many instances the coherence exists at a formal level only and does not necessarily carry through at an intellectual or practical level. Whereas coherence should not equate to strict uniformity, it is necessary to ensure that all essential areas are covered and that duplication is minimised.

Recent evaluations can largely be classified as programme evaluation (or even policy fulfilment mechanisms) rather than programme-impact evaluation. In other words, they use 'tick-the-box' participant feedback to gauge programme effectiveness in terms of whether they 'liked' the programme or 'found it useful', but rarely in terms of whether it made a difference to practice in the schools. If LDPs do not make a difference to improving the exercise of leadership and do not have as their ultimate goal improved student learning, their purpose is questionable.

Adjustment: There is an obvious need for empirical studies that investigate the impact of programmes on what principals do – including their level of skills, knowledge, and also their values and attitudes, and how these influence what happens in school. It is particularly important to investigate the impact of programmes on student learning. Formative, summative and longitudinal evaluations within and across programmes that explore knowledge transfer are needed. In addition, studies into programme efficacy should link to broader system reforms and change. As well as impact studies and programme evaluations, participants themselves should be encouraged to look deeply into what the programmes have done for them on a personal learning level and within their professional roles.

Achieving coherence is a difficult task in that authorities must tread a fine line when building and adjusting frameworks. This line runs uncertainly between being overly-prescriptive on the one hand, and on the other, allowing so much latitude that programmes become little more than a disjoined mess. Coherence may be achieved through establishing a professional overseeing body, more logical distribution of programmes and, as noted above, evaluating impact and then feeding back outcomes through values structures, the formal framework and content realignment.

NETWORKS AND COMMUNITIES OF PRACTICE

Status: The governance of Hong Kong education is a jumbled affair, brimming with numerous formal and informal agencies, networks and interest groups. This is plainly reflected in the school leadership community, where the majority of such affiliations focus narrowly, either politically or educationally. Few have ongoing leadership learning as an explicit goal. A small number of recent programmes (Walker & Quong, 2006, 2007) have worked purposefully to build and nurture communities of practice (learning) - these are slowly starting to take root.

Challenges: Bringing together leadership communities of practice is difficult within the present structure but, paradoxically, this makes it more important that they be nurtured. Given the diffuse nature of schools, if principals from different school groupings do not mix and share learning, both good and bad practice may endure in unconnected pockets. The formation of communities is again constrained by time and other resource constraints and also by a lack of confidence among principals that they can actually add to each other's learning beyond just 'how to do it' hints. One challenge is how to get principals (and providers) to see the value in worthwhile networked learning, how to help them structure networks which target learning, and how to have this recognised professionally and systemically as valuable. Hidden within this challenge is the high power distance and inter-school competitiveness which prevails throughout the system. This can interfere with open sharing and establishing equity within networks.

Adjustment: Arguments throughout this chapter have affirmed that learning is more likely to result if school leaders are members of learning and support networks. Although most principals are members of various networks, it is important that these be shaped or expanded to incorporate a stronger emphasis on learning and the conditions which make learning more likely to happen. This can be achieved, for example, through purposefully constructed learning sets (linked by interest or a structured task), group-oriented mentoring and user-friendly electronic venues for staying connected. Networks can develop at a number of levels, from neighbourhood to international, from educative to industrial, from principal colleagues to other leaders and educators. However, it is pointless to try and structure all networks; programmes can also encourage informal, self-driven networks within and beyond educational and hierarchical divides. This is the real key; the major adjustment needed in Hong Kong is to work with principals so that they value learning together. The place of the system and of providers in this is to supply structures and support mechanisms which minimise demands on principals to carry-out programme-related, organisational and clerical tasks, and to provide stimulus and facilitation to help them maintain momentum.

MECHANISMS, CONTENT AND LEARNING GATEWAYS

Status: The last five or so years have witnessed the opening of additional gateways to leadership learning and a revamp of the content included in the various LDPs. For example, content has moved beyond skills-based induction courses toward more challenging and sophisticated content. Frameworks have been built around locally developed flexible standards and some programmes have experimented with purposefully developing different approaches to learning and development. The majority of programmes, however, remain structured around formal face-to-face didactic instruction.

Challenges: The challenge here is to open up both what comprises the programmes - content and mechanisms - and how it is worked through with leaders. It is about identifying and providing access to multiple learning gateways and developing culturally appropriate mechanisms and contextually relevant content which allows leaders at different stages of development to access opportunities in line with their needs. Much of this depends on leaders engaging more in deeper learning, difficult to do within their already crowded work lives.

Adjustment: Ongoing adjustments can be considered in terms of reflection, flexibility, methodology and design. Opportunities for individual and group reflection are important for school leaders to make sense of and apply learning in their schools. Complex, contextualised learning takes time and involves intricate thought processes. Individual reflection (or 'self talk') can be encouraged through, for example, programme-structured or freer flowing written journals or reports. Reflection through social interaction within and outside the school is also important. As noted above, learning networks of various forms and sizes (within and across schools and levels) to house and stimulate reflective discussions may be tried – this is also useful for building trusting professional relationships. Variously shaped reflective forums allow opportunities for different levels of professional learning and encourage life-long learning.

Leaders not only need to take more responsibility for their own and colleagues' learning but also for how and when learning takes place. School leaders are busy people, with many demands on their time. In line with grounding learning more deeply within school contexts and away from simplistic classroom-based approaches, programmes should build in 'flexibility within structure', which asks leaders to determine more of the pace, form, level of involvement, timing and even focus of their learning. While this needs to be adequately supported and stimulated by providers, for learning to be worthwhile, leaders need to share control of their development.

Given that potential and practicing principals learn in different ways, they may require multiple opportunities and ways to learn. Such avenues call for multiple delivery modes (for example, electronic forums, problem-based learning, cooperative 'in the job' learning across schools or focused learning sets) which allow for differing learning purposes and styles. The content available through different gateways also needs to remain in a fluid state in order for programmes to cover the necessary 'basics' as well as variable situations. Gateways to learning can include strong personal and ethical components and draw on learning both in and outside schools and indeed education. Constructing multiple learning gateways also encourages life-long learning.

Although leadership learning programmes need to employ multiple learning opportunities, encourage greater participant control and focus on immediate learning contexts, this should not be taken to imply that the search for better practice should be a loose, flighty process – learning must still have form and guidance. In short, learning happens best if it uses grounded methods, is underpinned by 'learning conditions' and follows a purposeful design. Again, such a design may be built around the principle of 'flexibility within structure'. Designs should have clear purpose (related to school improvement for student learning), link to socialisation experiences, include internal and external quality assurance, and fit within cultural expectations and settings. Given a shift from pure content-driven to process-driven programmes, more useful cross-fertilisation internationally may be possible.

The issues discussed above cover only some of the challenges to school leader development in Hong Kong. Other issues, such as clarifying linkages between individual programmes and formal university degrees, also need to be addressed. Although this is beginning to happen, the major education providers have been slow to formally accredit professional development programmes within their degree structures. As a result, some school leaders face the prospect of working on involved professional development programmes at the same time as they work on an academic degree, even when both may be run by the same institution. All parties involved need to work toward a solution that contributes to greater coherence, reduces duplication and improves quality.

CONCLUSION

A caveat running through the chapter is that the programmes and framework discussed are outside formal university degrees, which play no role in leader accreditation. This may differentiate Hong Kong from some other contexts, such as the US. This chapter attempted to highlight the important elements of the school leadership development landscape in Hong Kong, mainly over the last fifteen years. There is little doubt that targeted central policy initiatives have begun to successfully address the thinly-spread and largely incoherent approach to leadership development that typified Hong Kong throughout the 1990s. Within a relatively short time, the reforms have embedded forward-looking structures, frameworks and programmes into the psyche and plans of future and serving school leaders. The reform policies set requirements to guide leadership preparation outside of academic qualifications and in doing so has started to shift beliefs about different forms of leadership learning. However, much still needs to be done. The way forward is to simultaneously consolidate the established framework and policy mandates and, within this, encourage the more flexible and imaginative structures needed to entrench worthwhile, student-focused leadership development in the professional community.

NOTES

[1] This project is supported by the Research Grants Council of Hong Kong through an Earmarked Grant (CUHK4619/05H). Parts of this paper are taken from Walker and Kwong (2006) and Walker and Dimmock (2006).
[2] The new Education and Manpower Bureau (EMB) was formed by the merger of the old Bureau and the Education Department (ED) on 1 January 2003.
[3] For further information on the Hong Kong reform context see Cheng (2003 & 2005), Mok and Welch (2002), Morris and Stott (2003), and Walker (2003).

REFERENCES

Advisory Committee on School-based Management. (2000). Transforming schools into dynamic and accountable professional learning communities – School-based management consultation document. Hong Kong: Printing Department.
Advisory Committee on Teacher Education and Qualifications (ACTEQ). (2003). Towards a learning profession – The teacher competencies framework (TCF) and the continuing professional development (CPD) of teachers. Hong Kong: Printing Department.
Bredeson, P. (2003). Designs for learning: A new architecture for professional development in schools. Thousand Oaks, CA: Corwin Press.

Cheng, K. M. (2002). The quest for quality education: The Quality Assurance Movement in Hong Kong. In J. K. H. Mok & D. K. K. Chan (Eds.), *Globalization and education: The quest for quality education in Hong Kong* (pp. 41–65). Hong Kong: Hong Kong University Press.

Cheng, Y. C. (2000). The characteristics of Hong Kong school principals' leadership: the influence of societal culture. *Asia Pacific Journal of Education, 20*(2), 68–86.

Cheng, Y. C. (2003). Trends in educational reform in the Asia-Pacific region. In J. P. Keeves & R. Watanabe (Eds.), *International handbook of educational research in the Asia-Pacific region* (pp. 3–16). Netherlands: Kluwer.

Cheng, Y. C. (2005). Globalization and educational reforms in Hong Kong: Paradigm shift. In J. Zaida, K. Freeman, M. Geo-JaJa, S. Majhanovich, V. Rust, & R. Zajda (Eds.), *The international handbook on globalization and education policy research* (pp. 165–187). Dordrecht, The Netherlands: Springer.

Cheung, M. B., & Walker, A. (2006). Inner worlds and outer limits: The formation of beginning school principals in Hong Kong. *Journal of Educational Administration, 44*(4), 389–407.

Chiu, C. S., & Chung, Y. P. (2003). *The quality school project: Final report*. Hong Kong: Faculty of Education, The Chinese University of Hong Kong.

Curriculum Development Council. (2001). *Learning to learn: The way forward in curriculum development*. Hong Kong: Curriculum Development Council.

Department of Educational Administration and Policy, The Chinese University of Hong Kong. (2004). Preparation for principalship course (Cycle 2 to Cycle 4). Unpublished report, Hong Kong: The Chinese University of Hong Kong

Dimmock, C. (2000). *Designing the learning-centred school: A cross-cultural perspective*. London, New York: Falmer Press.

Dimmock, C., & Walker, A. (1998). Transforming Hong Kong's schools: Trends and emerging issues. *Journal of Educational Administration, 36*(5), 476–491.

Education Commission. (2000). Learning for life, Learning through life: Reform proposals for the Education System in Hong Kong. Hong Kong: Printing Department.

Education Commission. (2000a). Reform proposals for the education system in Hong Kong (September 2000). Hong Kong: Printing Department.

Education Department. (2002, February & September). Continuing professional development for school excellence consultation paper on continuing development of principals. Hong Kong, Education Department, Hong Kong Government.

Education Department. (2002a). Continuing professional development for school excellence – Consultation paper on continuing professional development of principals. Hong Kong: Printing Department.

Education Department. (2002b). Administration Circular No. 31/2002 – Principals' continuing professional development. Hong Kong: Education Department.

Education and Manpower Bureau. (2003a). Enhancing school development and accountability through school self-evaluation and external school review (Education and Manpower Bureau Circular No. 23/2003). Hong Kong: Education and Manpower Bureau, HKSAR.

Education and Manpower Bureau. (2003b). Enhancing school development and accountability through school self-evaluation and external school review: The use and reporting of key performance measures (Education and Manpower Bureau Circular No. 269/2003). Hong Kong: Education and Manpower Bureau, HKSAR.

Education and Manpower Bureau. (2004a). Report of the panel for the review of the designated programme for newly appointed principals. Unpublished report, Hong Kong, Education and Manpower Bureau, HKSAR.

Education and Manpower Bureau. (2004b). Committed parents, quality schools. Hong Kong: Printing Department.

Education and Manpower Bureau. (2005a). Key statistics on kindergarten, primary, secondary and special Education, Figures and Statistics, Retrieved on 28 February 2007, from http://www.emb.gov.hk/index.aspx?nodeID=92&langno=1

Education and Manpower Bureau. (2005c). The new academic structure for senior secondary education and higher education - First stage consultation report (Executive summary), Retrieved on 28 February 2007, from http://www.emb.gov.hk/FileManager/EN/Content_4745/exe_sum.pdf

Education and Manpower Branch, & Education Department. (1991). The school management initiative: Setting the framework for quality in Hong Kong schools. Hong Kong: Government Printer.

Hickman, R. (2004). Quality assurance report on needs assessment for principals in Hong Kong workshops for Aspiring Principals. Unpublished report, England: University of Cambridge.

HKSAR Government. (1999). *Policy objectives*. Hong Kong: Printing Department.

HKSAR Government. (2005a). Hong Kong: The facts (education). HKSAR: Information Services Department.

HKSAR Government. (2005b). Hong Kong in Brief, Retrieved on 28 February, 2007, from http://www.info.gov.hk/yearbook/2004/en/index.htm

HKSAR Government. (2005c). Hong Kong 2004, Retrieved on 28 February, 2007, from http://www.info.gov.hk/yearbook/2004/en/index.htm

Kwan, P., & Walker, A. (in press). Vice-principalship in Hong Kong: Aspirations, competencies and satisfaction. Manuscript submitted for publication.

Kwong, S. C. I. (2005). Perception of beginning principals on the usefulness of the 'Blue Skies' programme. Unpublished paper. Hong Kong: Hong Kong Centre for the Development of Educational Leadership, The Chinese University of Hong Kong.

Li, Y. Y. (2004). Issues encountered by programme facilitators during comprehensive school reform: The first year of the Quality Schools Project in Hong Kong. *Educational Research Journal, 19*(1), 93–120.

Lo, L. N. K. (1997). Policy change and educational development in Hong Kong. *American Asian Review, 15*(4), 325–370.

Mok, J. K. H., & Welch, A. R. (2002). Economic rationalism, managerialism and structural reform in education. In J. K. H. Mok & D. K. K. Chan (Eds.), *Globalization and education: The quest for quality education in Hong Kong* (pp. 23–40). Hong Kong: Hong Kong University Press.

Morris, P., & Scott, I. (2003). Educational reform and policy implementation in Hong Kong. *Journal of Education Policy, 18*(1), 71–84.

Programme for International Student Assessment Hong Kong Centre (HKPISA). (2005). The second HKPISA report (PISA 2003). Hong Kong: The Chinese University of Hong Kong

Task Group on the Training and Development of School Heads. (1999). Leadership training programme for principals consultation paper. Hong Kong: Education Department, Hong Kong Government.

Walker A. (2003). School leadership and management. In J. Keeves & R. Watanabe (Eds.), *The handbook of educational research in the Asia-Pacific region* (pp. 973–986). Kluwer Press: Netherlands.

Walker, A. (2004) Constitution and culture: Exploring the deep leadership structures of Hong Kong schools. Discourse: Studies in the Cultural Politics of Education, 25(1), 75-94.

Walker, A. (2005). Report on the 5th cycle of Needs Analysis for Aspiring Principals. Unpublished report, Hong Kong: Hong Kong Centre for the Development of Educational Leadership.

Walker, A. (2007). Leading authentically at the crossroads of culture and context. *Journal of Educational Change, 8*(3), 257–273.

Walker, A. (various years). The developmental assessment of newly-appointed principals in Hong Kong – Final reports, 2003 & 2004. Hong Kong: Hong Kong Centre for the Development of Educational Leadership.

Walker, A., & Dimmock, C. (2004). The international role of the NCSL: Tourist, Colporteur or Confrere? *Educational Management Administration and Leadership, 32*(3), 236–287.

Walker, A., & Dimmock, C. (2005). Developing leadership in context. In M. Coles & G. Southworth (Eds.), *Developing leadership: Creating the schools of tomorrow* (pp. 88–64). Milton Keyes: Open University Press.

Walker, A., & Dimmock, C. (2006). Preparing leaders, preparing learners: the Hong Kong experience. *School Leadership and Management, 26*(2), 125–147.

Walker, A., & Dimmock, C. (various years). Needs assessment for (newly-appointed) principals in Hong Kong (NAFPhk) – final reports 2000, 2001, 2002. Hong Kong, Hong Kong Centre for the Development of Educational Leadership.

Walker, A., & Kwong, K. S. C. (2006, June). *School management training - Country report*: Hong Kong Special Administrative Region, People's Republic of China. Oslo, Norway: University of Oslo.

Walker, A., & Quong, T. (2005). *Blue skies: A professional learning programme (package) for beginning principals in Hong Kong*. Hong Kong: Hong Kong Centre for the Development of Educational Leadership.

Walker, A., & Quong, T. (2005). Gateways to international leadership learning: Beyond best practice. *Educational Research and Perspectives, 32*(2), 97–121.

Walker, A., & Quong, T. (2006). *Leading Upstream: A learning programme (package) for front-line leaders in international schools*. Hong Kong: Hong Kong Centre for the Development of Educational Leadership.

Walker, A., & Quong, T. (2007). Blue Line: A professional learning programme (package) for serving principals. Hong Kong: Hong Kong Centre for the Development of Educational Leadership.

Walker, A., Dimmock, C., Chan, A., Chan, W. K., Cheung, M. B., & Wong, Y. H. (2002). *Key qualities of the principalship in Hong Kong*. Hong Kong: Hong Kong Centre for the Development of Educational Leadership.

Wong, K. C. (2005a). Report on the school leadership development and extended programme for newly appointed principals (secondary and special Schools). Unpublished Report, Hong Kong: The University of Hong Kong.

Wong, K. C. (2005b). Report on the school leadership development and extended programme for newly appointed principals (primary schools). Unpublished Report, Hong Kong: The University of Hong Kong.

Wong, P. M. (2004). The professional development of school principals: Insights from evaluating a programme in Hong Kong. *School Leadership & Management, 24*(2), 139–162.

Wong, S. L. (2005). *Impact of leadership training on newly-appointed female principals in middle/secondary schools in England and Hong Kong*. Nottingham: National College for School Leadership.

AFFILIATIONS

Allan Walker and Paula Kwan Yu-Kwong
The Chinese University of Hong Kong
Hong Kong

JOHN MACBEATH

CHAPTER 19

Leadership for Learning: Concluding Thoughts

Connecting leadership and learning is the primary challenge which confronts schools, advisers and critical friends, inspection systems and governments in all of the countries whose stories are told in these 18 chapters. What we learn from these accounts is that those connections are by no means self evident or unproblematic. 'Challenge' is by nature unsettling, pushing people out of their comfort zone, requiring a reframing of received wisdom and a revisiting of deeply institutionalised practices with regard to both learning and leadership. Resistance is the natural bedfellow of change and is overcome not by exhortation and pressure but by removing barriers and creating the space for professional reinvigoration. The challenge of making the connections is not only for individual leaders operating from the apex of the organisational pyramid but for everyone with a capacity to learn and an inherent capacity to lead.

There are two possible starting points for understanding how leadership and learning are connected. We can start from what we know about leadership and work towards learning, or we can start from what we know about learning and work from there to grasp the implications for leadership. In this final chapter we have opted for the latter approach.

Through these pages we gain deeper insights into the nature of learning. There is a broad measure of agreement among these authors that to see learning solely as the business of children and young people is to miss the point. Learning is also the essential business of teachers, senior leaders, schools as organisations and 'the system' itself. The evidence is powerful and convincing - the quality of student learning is dependent on the learning that goes on around them. Students fall too easily into bad habits if their teachers do the same and if the learning environment is not one that invites them to explore, experiment, take risks and share insights into the process and progress of their learning.

The message from Lieberman and Friedrich in the U.S. and Brotto and Barzano in Italy is that, just like their students, teachers too need opportunities to explore, share insights and begin to lead in new directions. It is a risky business because it may be a step too far out of prescribed role. For students who expect omniscience it may convey an unsettling sense of vulnerability while for teacher colleagues it may be resented as a presumptuous exceeding of conferred status or institutional remit. The challenge is, as Portin and colleagues write, is both complex and multi-layered:

As Bajunid writes in the Malaysian context (chapter 16), 'the paradox remains, that while schools are learning organizations for students, schools are not learning organizations for professional peers, and are not maximally utilized for professional development. This is partly because the tools of observation, thinking, and writing, recording and researching have not been appropriately packaged and legitimized and considered as the essential curriculum for teacher learning'.

A SENSE OF AGENCY

The 'essential curriculum' for teacher learning is to grasp the potential of 'agency', a recurring theme running through these chapters. 'Put simply, human agency is about the capacity for intentional action and the knowingness that enables us to monitor our own actions. It is what singles us out from other animals' write Frost and Swaffield in chapter 6. 'Agency' is a deeply human impulse, to act, to make a difference, to refuse to settle for the status quo. But it is all too often inhibited by institutional conventions, hierarchies of authority, low and inappropriate expectations, mistrust and a host of constraining factors which Peter Senge describes as 'organisational learning disabilities', the most potent of which is 'I am my position'. This is disabling because it allows, or promotes, refuge in status, thereby denying one's own sense of agency and that of others. So, just as teachers are held in their place by their status as classroom teacher, as willing follower, students adopt their ascribed role as dutiful recipients of information 'delivered' by their teachers.

In organisations with clearly demarcated authority and bounded roles students' agency expresses itself in many forms. The restless drive to act, to make a difference, may express itself in confrontation or provocation, in anti-social activity, aggressive competition or simply in defiant withdrawal. These responses may manifest themselves in the classroom and attract a variety of labels, all of which serve to close, rather than open, portals to learning. The less visible exercise of agency occurs in the 'underlife' of schools, spaces where students create their own codes of behaviour and valued knowledge. All of these ways of behaving, widely open to misinterpretation, derive from the same impulse - the need to do something, to make a mark, not to settle for immediate reality but to search for novelty, to set up and resolve tension.

The more astute our observation of these behaviours is the more we understand about the nature of 'behaviour settings'. When we turn our attention to the setting rather than the individual behaviour we can begin to grasp the difference between learning 'in the wild' and learning in captivity as David Perkins put it. The metaphor suggests parallels between the repetitive behaviour of the caged lion and the ritualised performance of students and teachers unable to escape from the tightly enclosed boundaries of their relationship. The explanation for the apparent lack of agency to learn or to lead lies primarily in the nature of the environment. Yet, unlike the tiger's cage, organisational environments are not immovable objects within which behaviour is simply contained because, as Giddens has argued, human agency is a reserve (too often untapped) of bottom-up power able to recreate social and physical structures.

It is this tension between structure and agency that is one of the keys to opening the connecting doors between leadership and learning. When teachers, students, managers, governors, support staff and parents are alive to this there is a liberating sense of conjoint power to recreate the school as a learning and 'leaderful' community. When schools are not alive to their incipient agency the everyday discourse among staff is, by default, shaped by policy pressures, constrained by the demands of organisational convenience, and slowly and insidiously absorbed by students into the intellectual and emotional bloodstream. Learning comes to be seen as what happens in classrooms as the result of teaching and leadership is seen as the province of those who make the big decisions about the future. All too easily, learning as a vibrant shared activity, ceases to be the main consideration. All too easily the potential to lead learning is left to others.

Learning-led schools do not see themselves as places for passing on knowledge to children. They see themselves as communities of learners. They are places in which student learning is inseparable from professional learning and the culture is one in which learning flows across boundaries of role and status. The professional learning environment sets the stage for the student learning environment, a stage set generously. It gives a central role to social learning and takes cognisance of the crucial importance of the social composition of the school. It casts one of the primary purposes of learning as lived learning, from and with others - a social system in miniature. The title of Peter Senge's book *Schools that Learn* shifts the focus of our attention from the student as learner to the school as learner. The search for knowledge is embedded in the structures and cultures of the school, growing virtually on a daily basis, so it may be said one never steps into the same school or classroom twice.

The school is never the same from day to day when the culture is one of organic growth. Children no longer come into the school to be taught but come into the school to learn, to build on prior knowledge and dismantle inert ideas. In a learning school the same holds true for teachers. The communal staffroom, no longer a site for exchanging war stories, becomes a place for a vibrant learning exchange in which teachers from different grade levels or departments work side by side, exploring ideas, sowing the seeds of more formal planning.

As we discover through these pages, learning thrives in an environment which impels it, just as leadership comes immediately to the surface in a situation which demands it. So, from our focus on learning – individual, professional and organisational – the agenda for leadership gains a new clarity. In chapter 2 Y.C. Cheng characterises leadership as 'multi-level', so described because a) it attends to every level, or sphere, of the school's activity and b) it is embedded in every level, or sphere of the school's activity. 'Within this model school leadership itself is also a process of action learning, in which a leader or a group of leaders draw on the wisdom and the knowledge-in-action of their colleagues'. This is close to what Peter Gronn (2007) terms 'hybrid leadership', allowing for leadership to be manifest *both* as individualized and as distributed, both in shared activity and individual agency, both as led from within and from the 'top'.

We are offered in this volume many examples of how leadership, individual and distributed, creates and sustains the environmental conditions for shared learning and shared leadership. Peer lesson observation, collaborative lesson planning and lesson study are all powerful ways of framing and stimulating dialogue. Lesson study, in which a group of staff watch, comment on, and replay a lesson provides the occasion for theory building and transfer of practice. In China and Japan and where the idea originated, parents may also be invited in, as many as twenty at a time if a classroom, or hall, is large enough to accommodate such a number. The principle is to make learning and teaching visible not as simply a demonstration lesson but as an opportunity for critique and improvement.

There is always a danger, however, that these good ideas are incremental and do not flow naturally from a fundamental recasting of leadership and accountability. Such recasting will typically fall to 'the principal' (a word imbued with singular power) to promote a sense of internal accountability, one which rests on mutual trust and a strong sense of collegiality. The principal or senior leadership team may be the prime mover but it may arise more collegially in schools where leadership is already widely distributed.

Internal accountability contrasts with external accountability because it precedes a sense of duty or compliance to external demands. Internal accountability describes the conditions in a school that shape its own responses to pressure that originates in policies outside the organization. The level or degree of internal accountability is measured by the degree of convergence among what individuals say they are responsible for (responsibility), what people say the organization is responsible for (expectations), and the internal norms and processes by which people literally account for their work (accountability structures), Elmore (2003:17).

Without a strong sense of internal accountability, schools and teachers will always be subject to external pressures and remain reactive to externally driven change. When there is shared understanding of the difference between what they can and can't do they are more able to counteract the local, national and international forces at work. When there is a sense of agency allied to internal accountability teachers feel empowered enough to push continuously at the boundaries of the possible. So change forces arise from the inside, from a deeply rooted commitment to what is important and of lasting value.

CONTEXT MATTERS

Yet, there is a need to pause, to reflect on one of the major lessons that these eighteen chapters have to teach – the power of history, culture, context and politics. If we do not grasp the deep meaning and impact of these elemental forces good ideas will remain as simply aspirational. One of nettles to be grasped is the loose-tight nature of policy and practice within systems, that is, the constraining or facilitating structures at national/state level in relation and how they parallel structures at school level. So, for example, we may rightly expect a different kind of policy/practice relationship in countries such as Australia, Canada and the U.S. where it is states or provinces who set the stage for decision-making latitude at school level, compared to the more direct relationship between schools and national government as in England, Hong Kong, Taiwan or Singapore. Much of this, but not all, is explained by geographical scale and administrative reach, but also by the nature of governance.

To take England as an example, its approach to policy and practice been characterised as tight-loose. That is, governments determine school provision, the structure of the national curriculum, form and frequency of testing, public reporting of school results, inspection, the use of data for comparative purposes between and within schools, all tightly prescribed from the centre. However, something in the region of 90 per cent of government funding goes to schools that 'enjoy' considerable latitude to interpret and enact policy within their own context. They are in a sense let 'loose', although many headteachers and staff do not necessarily see it that way.

There are close parallels with Hong Kong which shares many similar features in terms of school structuring, and restructuring, centrally determined curriculum and testing, and school review with schools exercising some 'loose' latitude within the parameters set. Comparative performance of schools and review/inspection reports are, however, not made public. Like their English counterparts, nonetheless, Hong Kong teachers tend to see themselves as driven by government policy with very little wiggle room for their own initiative while government tries hard to persuade them that their capacity for leading learning is much greater than they think.

England and Hong Kong provide a sharp contrast with the United States in which the policy/practice relationship has been described as loose-loose (Stevens, 2007). This is, in part, because of the huge diversity that exists nationally and lack of tight connections between the state, the school district and schools. This tri-level mix of policy is set within a fourth overarching level - federal bi-partisan policy which holds a number of ring-fenced 'Title' funds, plus a government policy of No Child Left Behind which is powerful and punitive on underperforming districts and schools. Multi-level leadership thus presents a highly complex equation as it may be powerful or weak at state level or district level and may (or may not) constrain what happens at school level. In contrast to those systems which devolve their budgets to school level and cut out the 'middle man' (such a local authorities in England or communes in Norway) district leadership in the U.S. may play a strong interventionist role in relocating staff, particularly senior leaders, with a broader overview of what individuals schools need or deserve. So leadership for learning may lie less at the school than at district level or be a more complex function of both.

Understanding something of how multi-level leadership impacts on schools and classrooms helps to make sense of the possibilities that exist for multi-level learning. In the *Carpe Vitam* project referred to by Jorunn Moller (chapter 14) and Frost and Swaffield (chapter 6), the international research team borrowed and adapted the 'wedding cake' model from colleagues at the University of Washington. The reconstituted wedding cake is composed of four tiers - student learning, professional learning, organisational learning and system learning. Each tier is connected by the vertical struts so that there is a close iterative relationship as learning flows up and down the four inter-connected layers. Organisational and system 'abilities' (as contrasted with Senge's *dis*abilities) therefore can have a highly significant impact on professional and student learning and provide the optimum degree of looseness for their agency to be exercised. One of the main messages of this book is that student and professional learning and leadership are not simply reliant on the space they are afforded by the top tiers but that their activity and initiative can feed upwards to reshape organisational and system thinking.

THE PISA EFFECT

The complexity underlying the wedding cake metaphor is most powerfully illustrated in OECD's PISA reports which appear every few years to excite policy makers and provide headlines for news editors. Country league tables are pored over and comfort taken from the fact that countries that perform well in one area may perform relatively poorly in another. What captures the headlines are the countries whose students top the table in terms of measured performance on PISA tests. These simple data do, however, conceal more than they reveal and successive reports provide a rich source for trying to untangle and shed some light on the four layers of the wedding cake. It requires a close reading to find correlational or explanatory factors, for example, for Finland's continuing position at the head of the table on student performance while the U.K. and the United States have slipped down the rankings since previous studies. One of the most intriguing of histograms shows the U.K. topping the table on the use of performance data for holding schools accountable, while Finland occupies the bottom position. A telling paragraph compares what might be characterised as a contrast between internal and external accountability purposes.

There remain diverging views on how results from evaluation and assessment can and should be used. Some see these primarily as a tool to reveal best practices and identify shared problems in order to encourage teachers and schools to improve and develop more supportive and productive learning environments. Others extend their purposes to support contestability of public services or market-mechanisms in the allocation of resources e.g. by making comparative results of schools publicly available to facilitate parent choice (OECD Executive summary, p. 41).

This aptly describes the tensions facing many of the schools portrayed in this volume. In a policy climate which is pushing schools in every country towards a more market orientated managerial system. However, the sharing of problems, the encouragement of teachers 'to improve and develop more supportive and productive learning environments' is the primary challenge and the common way forward in all country contexts. It is the first and foremost connection between leading and learning. For all.

REFERENCES

Elmore, R. (2005). *Agency, reciprocity, and accountability in democratic education.* Boston, Mass: Consortium for Policy Research in Education.
Giddens, A. (1984). *The constitution of society.* Cambridge: Polity Press.
OECD Pisa. (2006). *Science competencies for tomorrow's world.* Paris: OECD.
Senge, P. (1994). *The fifth discipline: The art and science of the learning organisation.* New York: Doubleday.
Stevens, C. (2007). *Unpublished respondent contribution at the Policy Symposium on School Inspection*, University of California at Davis, 11th December.

CONTRIBUTORS

John MacBeath OBE is Chair of Educational Leadership at the Faculty of Education at the University of Cambridge and Director of Leadership for Learning: the Cambridge Network. His research and consultancy brings together work with schools and with policy makers in Britain as well as internationally. He has worked in a consultancy capacity with the OECD, UNESCO and the European Commission and currently advises policy makers in Hong Kong on school self evaluation and inspection. For a decade he has worked closely with the National Union of Teachers and since 2002 has conducted four studies for the NUT with his Cambridge colleague Maurice Galton. He is currently President of the International Congress and School Improvement

Yin-Cheong Cheng is the President of the Asia-Pacific Educational Research Association and also the Head of the Asia-Pacific Centre for Education Leadership and School Quality of the Hong Kong Institute of Education. Professor Cheng has published 18 academic books and nearly 200 book chapters and academic journal articles internationally in the area of educational management, reform, leadership and paradigm shift. Some of his publications have been translated into Chinese, Hebrew, Korean, Spanish, Czech, Thai and Persian languages. He has also been invited to give nearly 60 keynote/plenary presentations by national and international organizations in different parts of the world.

Ann Lieberman is an emeritus professor from Teachers College, Columbia University. She is now a Senior Scholar at The Carnegie Foundation for the Advancement of Teaching Her recent books include: *Inside the National Writing Project: Connecting Network Learning and Classroom Teaching* with Diane Wood and *Teacher Leadership* with Lynne Miller published by Jossey-Bass. Her unique contribution has been that she has been able to go between school and university - embracing the dualities that plague our field - theory/practice; process/content; intellectual/social-emotional learning; policy/practice - helping to build a more comprehensive understanding of teachers and schools and what it will take to involve them in deepening their work. To do this she has fashioned a way to be both a scholar and an activist, a practitioner and a theoretician.

Linda Friedrich is a Senior Research Associate at the National Writing Project in Berkeley, CA. Her research interests include teacher research, teacher leadership and professional development, professional learning communities, and the diffusion of knowledge. Prior to joining the National Writing Project in 2002, she served as director of research at the Coalition of Essential Schools. She earned her Ph.D. in Administration and Policy Analysis at Stanford University's School of Education.

Page Hayton Lee is a College Counselor at Loyola Academy in Wilmette, Illinois. Prior to joining the Loyola Academy faculty, she earned her Master's degree in Human Development and Social Policy at Northwestern University's School of Education and Social Policy. Working with Professor James P. Spillane, she focused her research on social network theory and its application to school leadership and reform implementation.

James P. Spillane is the Spencer T. and Ann W. Olin Chair in Learning and Organizational Change at Northwestern University where he is a Professor of Human Development and Social Policy, Learning Sciences, and Management and Organizations and a Faculty Fellow at the Institute for Policy Research. He is a senior research fellow with the Consortium for Policy Research in Education (CPRE). With funding from the National Science Foundation, Spencer Foundation, and Institute for Education Sciences, Spillane's work explores the policy implementation process at the state, school district, school, and classroom levels, and school leadership and management. He is author of *Standards Deviation: How Local Schools Miss-Understand Policy* (Harvard University Press, 2004), *Distributed Leadership* (Jossey-Bass, 2006), *Distributed Leadership in Practice* (Teachers College Record, 2007), and numerous journal articles and book chapters.

Neil Dempster is a Professor in Education at Griffith University and former Dean of its Faculty of Education. His research interests are in school governance and leadership, school improvement and the role that professional development plays in leadership, policy implementation, learning and organisational change. Neil is an Honorary Fellow of the Australian Council for Educational Leaders, a Fellow of the Australian College of Educators and its National President.

David Frost is a member of the Leading Learning for School Improvement team at the University of Cambridge Faculty of Education. He is the co-ordinator of the HertsCam Network and editor of the journal Teacher Leadership. His research and writing focuses on teacher leadership, organisational capacity and school improvement.

CONTRIBUTORS

Sue Swaffield is a member of the Leading Learning for School Improvement group at the University of Cambridge Faculty of Education, and one of the founders of 'Leadership for Learning: the Cambridge Network'. She researches and teaches in the fields of educational leadership, school improvement and assessment, and has particular interests in leadership for learning, critical friendship and assessment for learning. Sue's work at the University of Cambridge builds on her previous experience as a teacher and adviser.

Larry Sackney is Professor Emeritus from the University of Saskatchewan. His research interests include learning communities, knowledge management, school improvement, leadership, and systemic reform. He is a Past President of the International Congress on School Effectiveness and Improvement. His most recent publication is a chapter in a book entitled *Intelligent Leadership* He has been awarded the University of Saskatchewan Distinguished Research Supervisor Award and the Canadian Association for the Study of Educational Administration Distinguished Service Award.

Coral Mitchell is a Professor in the Faculty of Education, Brock University, St Catharines, Ontario. Her areas of research are the development of extended learning communities in schools and the educational role of school principals. She co-authored *Profound Improvement* with Larry Sackney and is currently working on a new book with him *Building Learning Communities that Endure*.

Oduro holds a PhD (CANTAB) degree from the University Of Cambridge, United Kingdom. He currently lectures at the Institute for Educational Planning & Administration (IEPA), University of Cape Coast, Ghana. His research interests lay in the cultural and gender dimensions of educational leadership, and strategies for enhancing quality teaching and learning in disadvantaged schools. Prior to his lectureship appointment at the IEPA, Dr Oduro worked with the Leadership *for* Learning-Cambridge Network, Faculty of Education, University of Cambridge as a Post-Doctoral Research Associate. He is a Fellow of the Cambridge Commonwealth Trust, the All Saints' Educational Trust, UK, and the Association for Commonwealth Universities.

Bill Mulford is an internationally recognised educator with a deep interest and extensive research and publication record in the areas of educational leadership, educational change and school effectiveness and improvement.

CONTRIBUTORS

His most recent book is Leadership for organisational learning and student outcomes and he is editor for the Leadership and Management Section of the highly respected International Encyclopaedia of Education. A former teacher, school principal, Assistant Director of Education, Faculty Dean, and Past President and Fellow of national and international professional associations, Bill has high legitimacy within the profession. He continues as adviser to numerous state and national Departments of Education and international organisations such as OECD and UNESCO. His awards include the Australian Council for Educational Leadership Gold Medal - for academic attainment, successful practice and an outstanding record of contributing to the field.

Daming Feng is Associate Professor of the East China Normal University and Research Fellow at the National Institute of Reform and Development for Basic Education. His academic interests include school effectiveness and improvement in disadvantaged schools, cultures in different educational leadership contexts.

Bradley S. Portin is Associate Professor of Educational Leadership and Policy Studies and Director of International Partnerships at the University of Washington, College of Education. Dr. Portin's research and publications over the last decade have examined current principal roles and how roles are changing to meet new imperatives, effective preparation for school leadership, leadership for school improvement, and international policy trends in educational reform. His publications include the co-edited book *Self-Reflective Renewal in Schools* (2003), *Making Sense of Leading Schools: A Study of the Principalship* (2003), and *Redefining Roles, Responsibilities, and Authority of School Leaders* (2006).

Margaret Plecki is Associate Professor of Educational Leadership and Policy Studies at the University of Washington, Seattle. She received her Ph.D. from the University of California, Berkeley. Her teaching and research activities focus on school finance, teacher quality, educational leadership, and education policy. Dr. Plecki has served as President of the American Education Finance Association.

Michael S. Knapp, Professor of Educational Leadership & Policy Studies and Director of the Center for the Study of Teaching & Policy at the University of Washington, focuses on educational policymaking, school reform, leadership development, and policy research methods, with emphasis on how policy and leadership connect to classroom and school improvement. His studies often concern the education of disenfranchised populations, mathematics and science education, and professional learning. Dr. Knapp has written extensively about his research, including eight books, among them, *School Districts and Instructional Renewal* (2002), *Self-Reflective Renewal in Schools* (2003), and *Connecting Leadership with Learning* (2006).

Michael A. Copland is Associate Professor of Educational Leadership and Policy Studies in the College of Education at the University of Washington, and has extensive experience with the preparation and professional development at school and district level. His research interests include issues related to the preparation and professional development of school and district leaders, learning-focused leadership in school and district reform, central office transformation, transformation of comprehensive high schools, and distributed leadership in the context of whole school reform. Dr. Copland's recent publications include the book *Connecting Leadership with Learning*, as well as pieces in *Phi Delta Kappan*, *Journal of School Leadership*, *Educational Evaluation and Policy Analysis*, and *Educational Administration Quarterly*.

Oon-Seng Tan, PhD FSEDA(UK), is Head of Psychological Studies at the National Institute of Education, Nanyang Technological University. He is Editor-in-Chief of the journal *Educational Research for Policy and Practice*. Prof. Tan is the immediate past President of the Educational Research Association of Singapore and President-elect of the Asia-Pacific Educational Research Association. He is also the Vice-President (Asia and Pacific Rim) of the International Association for Cognitive Education and Psychology. He was previously Director of the Temasek Centre for Problem-based Learning where he won an Innovator Award (The Enterprise Challenge) from the Prime Minister's of Singapore.

Francesca Brotto is a school head, experienced teacher educator and consultant seconded as adviser to the Director General of the International Relations Department at the Italian Ministry of Education in Rome. Her main interests lie in language teaching and learning, school self-evaluation and leadership, and strategies to enhance the European dimension of education at school, also relating these topics to professional development issues. She has run an 8-country international project with Prof. John MacBeath and is a member of expert groups advising the European Commission and the Council of Europe.

CONTRIBUTORS

Giovanna Barzanò is an inspector of the Ministry of Education in Italy, working for the Directorate General of Lombardy. She has a broad experience in international cooperation and for over ten years was the Italian representative for network C in the OECD INES project (Indicators of Education Systems). She has coordinated and participated in several EU-Socrates projects on educational leadership, school self-evaluation and citizenship. Since 1998 she has been the scientific coordinator of the STRESA self-evaluation project, involving some 30 schools in the Lombardy region.

Francesca Brotto is a school head, experienced teacher educator and consultant seconded as adviser to the Director General of the International Relations Department at the Italian Ministry of Education in Rome. Her main interests lie in language teaching and learning, school self-evaluation and leadership, and strategies to enhance the European dimension of education at school, also relating these topics to professional development issues. She has run an 8-country international project with Professor John MacBeath, organising the translation of Sefl Evaluation in European Schools into eight languages. and is a member of expert groups advising the European Commission and the Council of Europe.

Jorunn Møller is Professor at the Department of Teacher Education and School Development, University of Oslo. She currently holds a position as Professor II at the University of Tromsø. Her professional interests are in the areas of educational administration and leadership, supervision, action research, and school evaluation. She is presently involved in research on educational leadership and policy change.

Jim O' Brien is currently Dean and Head of School in The Moray House School of Education, The University of Edinburgh, and Director of the Centre for Educational Leadership (CEL). His development work and research interests lie mainly in the field of teacher continuing professional development including induction, school improvement and school leadership. He is co-editor of the *Education Policy and Practice Series* (Dunedin Academic Press: Edinburgh), an elected Board member of the International Congress on School Effectiveness and Improvement (ICSEI), the current President of the International Professional Development Association (IPDA) and an Associate Editor of the *Journal of In-Service Education*.

CONTRIBUTORS

Janet Draper is currently Professor and Associate Head in the Department of Education Studies at Hong Kong Baptist University following her tenure at Moray House Institute of Education in Scotland and from 2004 the School of Education and Lifelong Learning at the University of Exeter. .Her research interests are teacher development and teachers' work and careers, including the induction of staff at all stages of their careers, school leadership and work life balance. In 2003 she co-edited *School Leadership* with Jim O'Brien and Daniel Murphy (Int Specialized Services).

Ahmad Bajunid Ibrahim is Director of the Regional Center for Educational Planning- (UNESCO-RCEP), Al Sharjah, United Arab Emirates and was formerly Professor of Management, Leadership and Policy Studies at University Tun Abdul Razak (UNITAR) and former Director of Institut Aminuddin Baki [IAB] - The National Institute of Educational Management and Leadership. He is Fellow of the Council of Education Administration in Commonwealth Countries, Distinguished Fellow, Institute of Strategic and International Studies (ISIS) Malaysia, Fellow Emeritus IAB, Fellow of the National Research Institute on Youth and Senior Fellow of the Malaysian Social Institute. He has written over four hundred articles and academic papers on educational subjects and the author –editor of several books.

Hui-Ling Pan is Professor and Director of the Graduate Institute of Educational Policy and Administration, National Taiwan Normal University. Previously she was the Director of the Center for Educational Research. She has been the board director of a number of associations. Her research areas include school effectiveness and improvement, educational research and evaluation, and gender issues.

Allan Walker is Professor of Educational Administration and Policy and Chair of the Department of Educational Administration and Policy at The Chinese University of Hong Kong. His research interests include the influence of culture on school leadership, leadership learning and development and leadership values and ethics. Allan runs a number of innovative leader learning programs and is Associate Director of the Hong Kong Centre for the Development of Educational Leadership. For details of Allan's work, please visit the Educational Leadership Development Net at http://www3.fed.cuhk.edu.hk/ELDevNet.

CONTRIBUTORS

Paula Kwan is a Professional Consultant in the Department of Educational Administration and Policy at The Chinese University of Hong Kong. Paula is trained in the field of Management and is particularly interested in investigating the application of management theories and practices in educational contexts. Her most recent research projects include work lives and job satisfaction of vice principals, principal recruitment and selection, and organizational culture. She has published in both educational and business journals. In addition to teaching, she has been involved in a number of management consultancy projects contracted by Hong Kong SAR Government and a number of private sector organizations.

INDEX

A
Accountability, 2, 3, 14, 18, 19, 21, 65, 66, 109, 115, 116, 123, 130–133, 156, 158, 166, 186, 189, 193, 226, 229, 230, 241, 243, 244, 246, 248, 250–252, 255, 256, 260, 270, 284, 301, 308, 312, 316, 330, 331, 333
  inquiry based, 2, 133
  internal, 3, 116, 330, 331, 333
  managerial, 246, 250, 251, 255
Activity theory, 117, 202n, 308
Agency, 110, 116–118, 155, 192, 196, 199, 200, 224, 225, 228, 243, 277, 319, 328–331, 333
Agential, 117
Assessment for learning, 127, 132

B
Bottom up, 9, 111, 115, 117, 255, 299, 307, 329
Bureaucracy, 2, 243, 275, 278, 279

C
Capacity building, 129, 190, 202n, 284
Change, 1, 2, 4, 7, 8, 17, 18, 28, 29, 33, 43, 46, 49, 52–61, 83, 87, 95, 110, 114, 123, 128, 143, 145, 146, 156, 158–160, 164, 165, 167, 176, 180, 183, 190, 206, 207, 210, 211, 213, 215–220, 226, 232, 242, 243, 248, 254–256, 263–265, 279–281, 283, 289, 290, 292–295, 297, 301, 306, 308, 312, 314–316, 318, 327, 331
Coaching, 11, 192, 196, 213, 266, 267, 270, 317
Collaboration, 3, 6, 9, 26, 57, 73, 74, 102, 103, 111, 114, 126, 155, 162, 164, 179, 180, 215, 216, 218, 219, 230, 248, 252, 301
Comfort zone, 2, 59, 327
Communities of practice, 5, 42, 49, 66, 117, 282, 285, 314, 319
Competencies, 10, 11, 15, 129, 160, 173, 206, 210, 212, 213, 237, 244, 262, 265, 267, 269, 282, 283, 315
Competition, xi, 21, 22, 30, 31, 53, 60, 88, 160, 178, 225, 245, 278, 328
Competitive, 11, 18, 20, 21, 34, 81, 225
Conflict, 29, 31, 32, 49, 89, 134, 156, 157, 159, 233, 246, 261, 297, 299
Conjoint agency/power, 117, 329
Constructivist, 68, 126, 212
Control, 1, 5, 24, 66, 81, 93, 117, 130, 149, 154, 187, 198, 227, 241, 243, 244, 246, 253, 254, 277, 278, 290, 294, 296, 314–317, 321
Critical friend, 103, 105, 113, 247, 248, 252, 253, 254, 256, 327
Cultural, 1, 3, 4, 7, 8, 12, 13, 15, 17, 22–24, 26, 28, 32, 33, 62n, 105, 114, 115, 121, 137, 141, 155, 162, 189, 227, 242, 261, 280, 281, 283, 284, 290–292, 312, 314, 315, 320, 321
Cultural conditioning
  learning, 149–150
  organizational, 29, 242
  school, 9, 16, 47, 57, 59, 112, 129, 130, 177, 252, 294, 300
Culture, 3–10, 13, 16, 26, 41, 44, 47, 49, 50, 52, 55–57, 59, 61, 67, 101, 103, 111, 112, 115, 120, 125, 129, 130, 157, 159, 160, 162–164, 166, 177, 200, 206, 215, 218, 219, 224, 225, 238, 242, 245, 252, 255, 270, 276, 278, 281, 285, 291, 292, 294, 297, 300, 301, 308, 316, 329–331
Curriculum, 10, 11, 17–22, 24, 27, 44, 45, 55, 56, 58, 65, 73, 75, 81, 109, 114, 128, 153, 155–157, 181, 182, 202n, 205, 208, 209, 211–215, 217, 218, 248, 254, 264, 275, 280, 283, 284, 289, 290, 292, 294, 299–301, 308, 311, 312, 315, 328, 331, 332

D
Decision making, 15, 31, 82, 90, 94, 96, 98, 126, 128, 130, 161–164, 212, 223, 227, 282, 283, 289–291, 294–297, 300, 307, 308, 331
Development planning, 162
Dialogue, 2, 6, 7, 9, 59, 62n, 66, 73, 75, 77, 103, 104, 106, 107, 109, 110, 112, 113, 116, 126, 142, 159, 180, 189, 238, 242, 252, 254, 279, 301, 330

INDEX

Discourse, 102, 105, 106, 108, 110, 132, 133, 237, 241, 245, 246, 251, 279, 285, 300, 301, 329
Diversity, xii, 29, 31, 32, 69, 104, 153, 242, 244, 285, 332

E
Economy, 11, 184, 205, 206, 216, 283
Equality, 243
Equity, 88, 161, 162, 167, 192, 242, 269, 319
Ethnic/ethnicity, 242, 261, 306

F
Federal (policies), 14, 193, 332

G
Gender, 53, 55, 58, 59, 138, 149, 151, 154, 160, 242, 256n, 337
Globalization, 11, 15, 22, 23, 25, 35, 245
Government, 7, 81, 86, 87, 89, 109, 123, 132–134, 138, 143, 145, 147, 156, 158–161, 173, 175, 177, 184–186, 202n, 218, 242–244, 268–270, 275, 282, 284, 290, 295, 305–310, 313, 316, 317, 327, 331, 332

H
Hierarchy, 13, 246
Hofstede, G., 4, 32, 291, 292
Human capital, 256, 284

I
Indicators, 270, 277
Inquiry, 11, 42, 112, 120, 125, 127, 133, 190, 199, 200, 212, 213, 215, 263
co-inquiry, 103, 104
Inspection/school inspection, 275, 308, 327, 331, 332
Intellectual capital, 284

L
Leadership as
dispersed, 163, 194
distributed, 7, 41, 69, 101, 112, 114, 117, 126, 156, 162, 167, 191, 198, 223, 224, 226, 227, 242, 245, 247, 260, 291, 299, 330
heroic, ix, 2
hybrid, 133, 293, 307, 330

political, 7, 14, 21–23, 28, 31, 32, 54, 55, 59, 82, 115, 116, 256
transformational, 123, 127, 159, 160, 226, 227, 291, 294, 295, 299, 301, 302
visionary, 113, 156, 160, 291
Leadership capacity, 129, 151, 192, 196, 197, 199, 270
Learning
conditions for, 8, 308, 321
context of, 192, 270, 282, 283, 321
deep, 9, 111, 206, 320
independent, 210, 212
lifelong, 22, 25, 205–207, 209, 210, 215, 228, 280
life wide, 207, 213
problem based, 208, 211, 214–216, 218
self directed, 11, 32, 210, 213
for transfer, 207
Learning community, 5, 6, 42, 51, 56, 110, 121, 124–126, 129, 131, 155, 163
Learning culture, 5, 9, 26, 160, 291
Learning ethos, 233, 237
Learning organisation, xi, 164, 242, 332
Learning school, xi, 10, 25, 26, 123, 127, 132, 147, 330
Learning to learn/learning how to learn, 25, 180, 186, 206, 207, 210
Legislation, 7, 223, 225, 227

M
Managerialism, 1, 81, 101, 243
Managerialist, 81
Manpower, 24, 28, 206, 217, 264, 282, 306, 322
Market, xi, 18, 20, 21, 34, 102, 162, 227, 243, 245, 333
Marketing, 81
Mentor, mentoring, 15, 51, 97, 98, 115, 185, 192, 195, 196, 198, 201, 264–267, 279, 316, 317, 319
Modelling, 5, 10, 126, 154, 155, 208, 228, 230
Monitoring, 4, 14, 20, 21, 34, 95, 127, 132, 133, 145, 147, 165, 166, 218, 238, 246, 251, 266

N
Narrative, xii, 15, 228, 231, 232

344

O

OECD, 33, 81, 154, 231, 259, 333
Organisational capacity, 104, 166
Organisational learning, 163, 164, 328, 332

P

Paradox, 1, 114, 224, 226, 231, 280, 319, 328
Pedagogy, 6, 9, 12, 112, 126, 163, 164, 181–183, 211–213, 308, 315
Performativity, 10, 101
Policy maker, xii, 10, 22, 150, 174, 185, 205, 207, 216, 256, 314–317, 333
Policy making, 23, 282, 285
Portraiture, 104, 236, 247
Power distance, 4, 292, 300, 319
Pressure, xi, 4, 9, 81, 110, 115, 116, 123, 133, 148, 156, 261, 314, 327, 329, 331
Problem solving, 11, 182, 207, 209, 212–215, 278, 307
Professional development, 3, 6, 9, 16, 32, 42, 46, 48, 54, 61, 62n, 74, 81, 82, 90–94, 106, 110, 125, 127–130, 161, 163, 164, 179, 184, 185, 192, 195, 198, 223–227, 229, 235–237, 256, 259, 261–265, 267–270, 308, 310–313, 315, 321, 328

Q

Quality assurance, 21, 145, 277, 278, 308, 311, 312, 321

R

Reflection, 3, 4, 9, 10, 15, 22, 62n, 85, 98, 104, 105, 107, 112, 125, 127, 128, 164, 165, 202n, 216, 235, 238, 247, 248, 252, 255, 295, 301, 320
Reflective practitioner, 210, 280
Reframing, 108, 202n, 281, 327
Risk, 1, 8, 54, 55, 130, 140, 163, 164, 177, 180–183, 185–187, 206, 230, 238, 247, 255, 327

S

School district, 41, 44, 69, 125, 132, 192–194, 196, 201, 202n, 290, 299, 332
School effectiveness, 19–21, 28–34, 101, 102, 118, 123, 146, 202n, 277, 278
School improvement, 31, 50, 70, 101, 103, 113, 123, 126, 132, 145, 147, 149, 229, 232, 250, 255, 256, 259, 277, 278, 316, 321
Self evaluation, 229, 232, 233, 251, 252, 255, 279, 307
Shared leadership, 89, 90, 114, 115, 255, 260, 330
Social capital, 154, 155, 165, 231, 281, 284
Strategic planning, 92, 216
Struggle, 4, 12, 29, 31, 32, 42, 76, 83, 224, 255, 263

T

Targets, 6, 17, 25, 28, 30, 66, 102, 129, 132, 133, 181, 197, 199, 237, 264, 289, 299, 308, 312, 314, 319
Top down, 7, 47, 72, 116, 156, 162, 186, 215, 238, 244, 252, 255, 278, 289, 295, 299, 307
Teacher leadership, 41, 43, 46, 48, 54, 59, 65, 252, 276, 279
Team building, 238n
Transformation, xi, 22, 110, 165, 273, 286n, 295

V

Values intro, x, 4, 5, 9, 10, 13, 15–18, 20, 25–28, 41, 44, 60, 73, 74, 84, 87, 89–95, 102–103, 106, 107, 110, 123, 138, 140, 145, 146, 149, 162, 184, 193, 202, 213, 214, 217, 265, 274, 278–281
Vision, 11, 22, 29, 33, 48, 49, 51, 52, 54, 58, 102, 107, 110, 114, 158–160, 165, 167, 173, 177, 180, 187, 206, 248, 252, 259, 293, 297, 299